Album—On and Around Urs Fischer, Yves Netzhammer, Ugo Rondinone, and Christine Streuli, Participating at the 52nd Venice Biennale 2007

Album—On and Around Urs Fischer, Yves Netzhammer, Ugo Rondinone, and Christine Streuli, Participating at the 52nd Venice Biennale 2007

Edited by
Daniel Kurjaković

Designed by
Aude Lehmann
and Lex Trüb

Published by
the Swiss Federal Office
of Culture, Berne
and JRP|Ringier, Zurich

PREFACE

Switzerland has no regularly recurring exhibitions of international contemporary art. For this reason, since 1920, the Venice Biennale has represented a crucial site of artistic representation for Switzerland. In 1988, the Swiss pavilion in the Giardini was supplemented with a second exhibition site in the Baroque church of San Stae on the Canale Grande, further underscoring the central importance of the Biennale for Switzerland.

The history of Switzerland's presence at the Biennale shows a complex relationship between the state and art as well as an often highly conflictual relationship between the politically-based allocation of resources and the ambitions of an artistic elite. Even if numerous institutions in Switzerland promote artistic production and present artistic work, and the country can boast a very dense network of stipends and grants, purchasing possibilities, studios at home and abroad, and favorable conditions for art dealing, national representation of Swiss art does not come easy.

In retrospect, Switzerland's participation at the Biennale shows how difficult it has been to satisfy both the interests of Swiss artists as well as the demands for international attention. In the past 85 years, the attempt has constantly been made to find compromises between the expectations of the Biennale, the international art world, the individual language regions of Switzerland and the natural preferences of the members of the Federal Art Commission that selects the artists for Venice.

PREFACE

At this year's 52nd Venice Biennale, well aware of the complex and high expectations when it comes to national representation, the Federal Office of Culture once again presents a cross-section of Swiss artistic production. In the pavilion, the work of two young artists, Christine Streuli and Yves Netzhammer, can be seen. While the church of San Stae offers a view into the work of the renowned artists Urs Fischer and Ugo Rondinone.

Urs Staub
Head of the Art and Design Department
Swiss Federal Office of Culture

CONTENTS

12 Editorial Note

14 From Venice to Miami—Notes on Art and Tourism
Tan Wälchli

29 Swiss Myth—The Art World Remix
Marc Spiegler

39 The Silence of the Artists—On the Professionalization of the Artist in Switzerland
Philip Ursprung

45 Turn Up the Volume—A Conversation with
Urs Fischer
Daniel Kurjaković

72 The Critics on Urs Fischer

77 Images—Urs Fischer

89 Art and Shock—The Reversal of Reversed Reality
Klaus Theweleit

107 Journey Through the Country
Katarina Holländer

112 Bodies in Search of Matter—A Portrait of
Yves Netzhammer
Tim Zulauf

130 The Critics on Yves Netzhammer

135 Drawings—Yves Netzhammer

CONTENTS

148 Animality and Humanity—On a Shifting Relationship
Ludger Schwarte
Visual Essay by *Roland Lüthi*

172 Where Do We Go from Here?—Biennials Today and Tomorrow
A Survey with Statements by *Vanessa Beecroft, Ralf Beil, Davide Croff, Ingvild Goetz, Eva González-Sancho, Ulrike Groos, Paul Groot, Marina Gržinić, Jörg Heiser, Claudia Jolles, Kasper König, Elisabeth Lebovici, Michael Lingner, Michael Lüthy, Ken Lum, Oliver Marchart, Rita McBride, Heike Munder, Marie Muracciole, Hans Ulrich Obrist, Sandi Paučić, Stella Rollig, Nicolaus Schafhausen, Christoph Schenker, Katharina Schlieben, Peter J. Schneemann/ Nicola Müllerschön, Marketta Seppälä, Dieter Schwarz, Barbara Steiner, Robert Storr, Birgid Uccia, Gianfranco Verna, Anton Vidokle, Florian Waldvogel, Rein Wolfs and Tirdad Zolghadr*

199 Viewpoints
Friederike Kretzen

205 Pop Emotionality—A Portrait of Ugo Rondinone
Bice Curiger

216 The Critics on Ugo Rondinone

221 Images—Ugo Rondinone

CONTENTS

233 Unexpected Islands of Contemplation—
Thoughts About Time
Gaby Hartel
Visual Essay by *Roland Lüthi*

245 The Throes of Time—On Art and Truth
James Lord

261 Out of the Country
Jörg Kalt

268 A Surplus of Form—On Some of Christine Streuli's
Photographic Vignettes
Roman Kurzmeyer, Fanni Fetzer and
Susann Wintsch

291 The Critics on Christine Streuli

296 Paintings—Christine Streuli

313 Artists
314 Authors
316 Credits
325 Colophon

EDITORIAL NOTE

This book is published on the occasion of the Swiss contribution to the 52nd Venice Biennale 2007 and the exhibitions of the four artists whose work is featured within this frame: Urs Fischer, Yves Netzhammer, Ugo Rondinone and Christine Streuli. It has been clear from the outset that their work is rather unrelated in terms of style, form and ideology, and therefore we have sought to provide space for different modalities and fields of interest. As a result the outcome is marked by both structure and randomness.

This seeming contradiction might also be seen as reflecting the process of putting the publication *Album* together, which in itself has been a lively negotiation with the contingencies of different perspectives and visions of the participants. By way of introduction let us state our intentions: to introduce the four artistic practices and their respective characteristics; to take into account the backdrop of the large scale exhibition in Venice with its implicit questions about national representations and global dynamics in art; and to encompass topics of a more general aesthetic or cultural interest. All along, we tried to keep the project marked by a certain velocity or perhaps better put *esprit*, we took a journalistic rather than academic approach and we sought to preserve a sense of adventure that mirrored our own journey of discovery in the process of making the book.

Even though this diversity has partly come about due to the primary task—as a medium for introducing the artists—we have also wilfully played with the idea of mixing and matching genres. Here specially commissioned texts: reports, essays, conversations, literary texts, and theoretical statements, can be found alongside visual material: visual essays, inserts, exhibition views and illustrations. This heterogeneity of genres and approaches might be viewed as a reflection, not only on the artists and their works, but also on the challenge of art publishing itself. Recent history shows how ways of talking about art have become more stratified and even de-centered (something which the frequent announcements of "crisis" in art criticism attest to). On the one hand, mainstream art publishing has assimilated the respective experiments of the neo-avant-garde of the 1960s and 1970s with its artist books legacy, and on the other, its formats bear witness to genre transfer from publishing in the fields of science, fashion and lifestyle. This historical backdrop is an inspiring factor for us in thinking about the inner workings of *Album*.

Again, diversity has been treated as a natural given with interesting potential, and one hopes that the publication will provide the reader and onlooker with stimulating counterpoints and lead them to interesting insights. Obviously, none of this would have been possible without the talent, commitment and hard work of the various contributors.

Daniel Kurjaković
May 2007

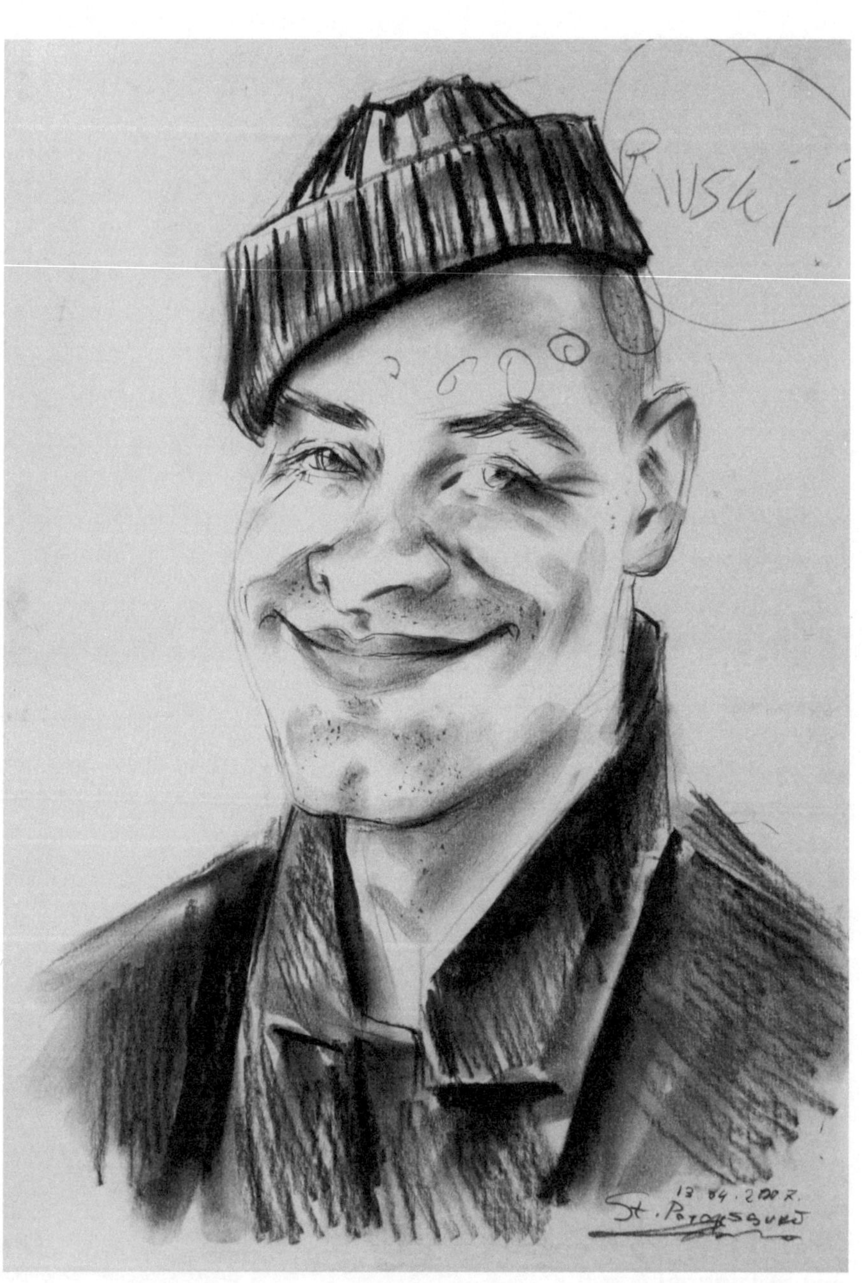

From Venice to Miami—Notes on Art and Tourism

Not all too long ago it would have been impossible to conceive the degree of interpenetration between today's contemporary art world and global tourism. But history does not stand still. What thirty years ago seemed like an insoluble antagonism between the avant-garde and the masses is today symptomatically intertwined in instruments like the virtual travel agency "Grand Tour 2007", where art travel between Venice, Basel, Münster and Kassel is made easy for an international customer base. Second-degree tourism finally completes the neo-avant-garde transformation of art into communication, distribution and sociality. The historical goal is thus fulfilled—just a little differently than intended. The logo "Grand Tour 2007" evokes wide expanses and the pleasant fleeing-flying speed of today's culturati racing across Europe. While the idea is perhaps not so new in terms of cultural history, according to Tan Wälchli, today it exhibits several new undertones. Erik Steinbrecher contributes images from *Rote Socken in St. Petersburg.—dk*

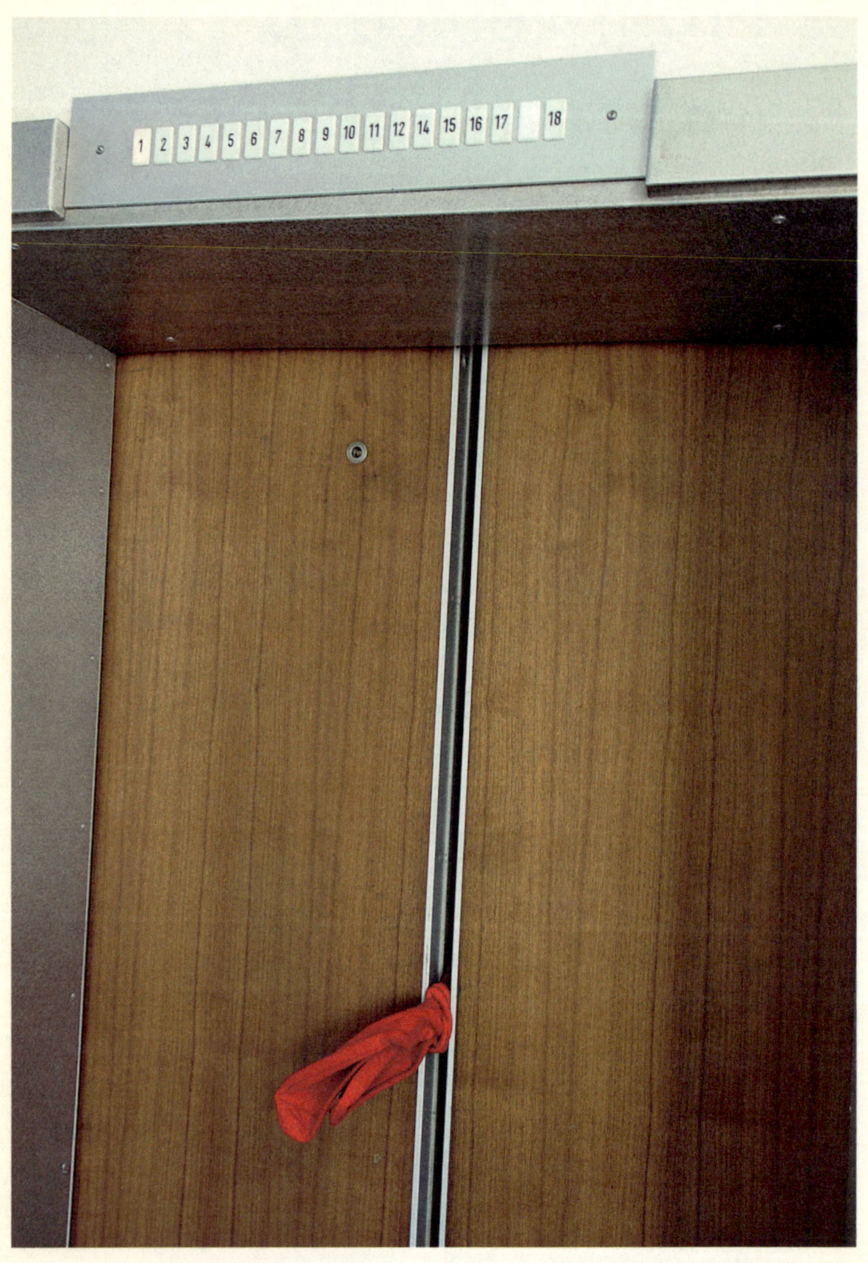
1
2
3
4
5
6
7
8
9
10
11
12
14
15
16
17
18

Openings

The 52nd Esposizione d'Arte Internazionale de La Biennale di Venezia this year launched a Web site entitled "Grand Tour 2007" together with documenta 12, the 38th Art Basel, and Skulptur Projekte Münster 07, which is to function as a virtual travel agency allowing users to individually arrange and book trips to all four shows. The platform takes its idea from a prominent model, "the historical Grand Tour" of the seventeenth to nineteenth centuries, as they explain on their Web site: an "extended journey to the great cultural sites of Europe, in particular of Italy ... which became a settled ritual of the high bourgeoisie." Whatever one may understand as "high bourgeoisie" nowadays, the historical comparison immediately sounds a bit highfalutin. Why should the art audience of the year 2007 go on an "Italian journey" in the style of Goethe? On the other hand, one can hardly fail to notice the close connection that continues to exist between art and tourism. While vacationers make pilgrimages to Florence's *David*, the *Mona Lisa* in Paris, and the Sistine Chapel in Rome, insiders of the art business are professional tourists permanently visiting studios, show openings, and art fairs across the globe. Perhaps it could be instructive, after all, to more closely examine what the cipher "Grand Tour 2007" stands for.

Time Travel

Let us first follow the reference made on the Web site and start with the eighteenth century. What was the audience looking for on the Grand Tour at the time? It was most certainly a journey to the cultural past, to Roman and Greek antiquity. The fine arts, in particular architecture and sculpture, were regarded as expressing this past in the most pronounced way. For Winckelmann, these

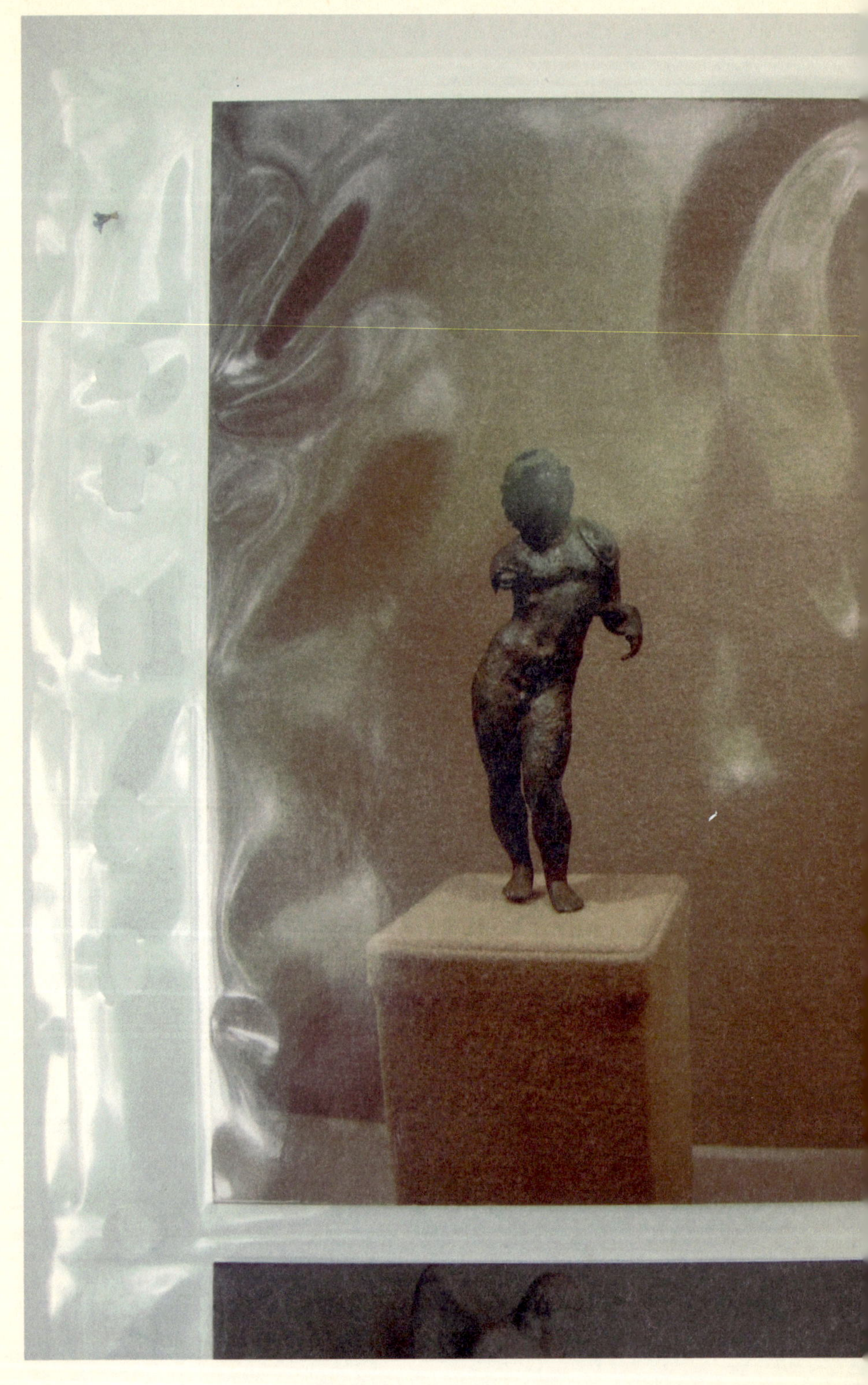

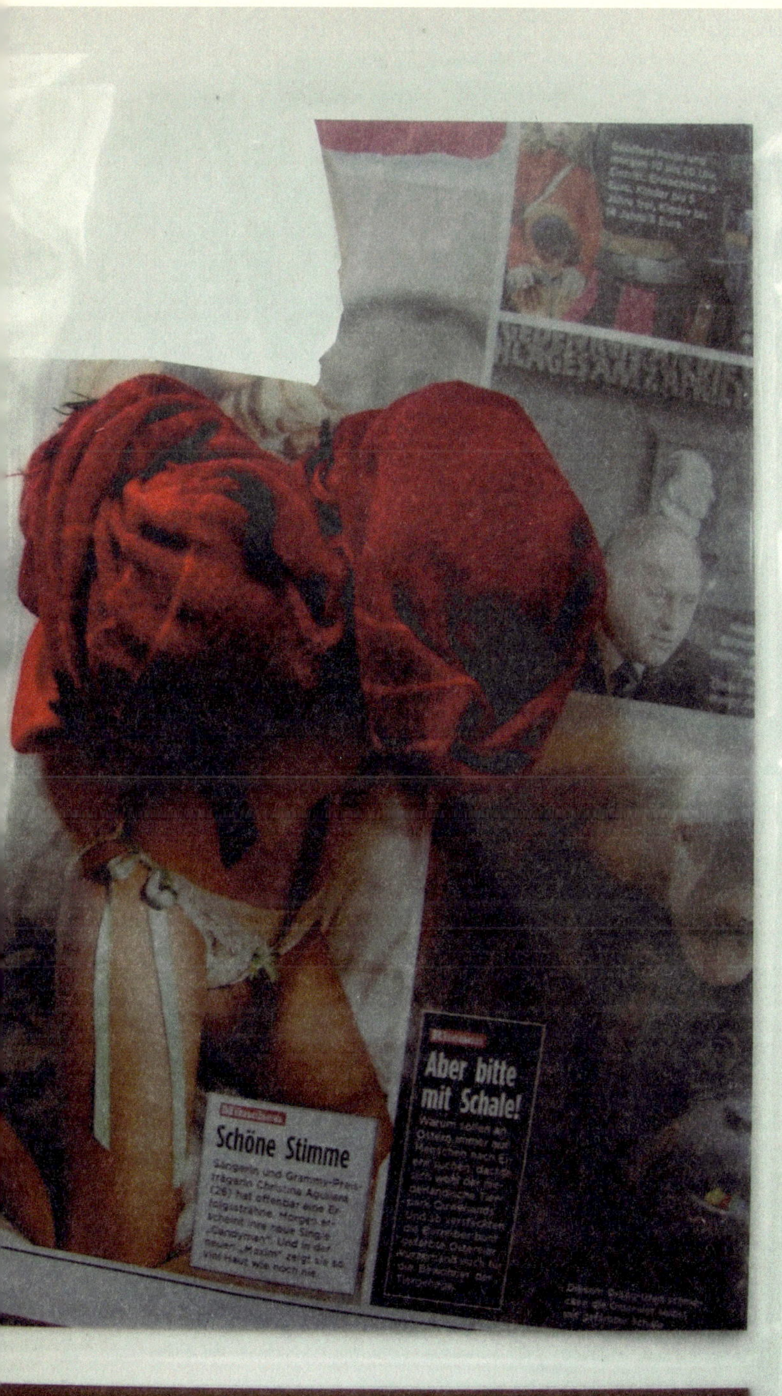
Schöne Stimme
Aber bitte mit Schale!

works represented the ideal, and he declared the understanding and copying of this ideal as the main objective of all education and creativity. Hence, the tour to the south was meant to induce the revival of the ancient ideas at that time.

70 years later, Heinrich Heine assessed the situation differently. In his essay *The Voyage from Munich to Genoa* (1828), he noted that the educational trip by no means served to revive the ideal of classical antiquity; quite to the contrary. It was about assuring oneself that the Old World was in ruins and had been successfully overcome by the modern age. For it was precisely the "whisper of *broken* columns" that fascinated those traveling to Italy. And the foundation for this had been laid by the Teutons, who once attacked the Roman Empire. Since "some tribes could not yet write," the conquerors instead of immortalizing themselves on the walls of buildings—had to "destroy something." And "that sufficed, because these ruins speak more clearly than delicate letters."

The last formulation, where ruins speak "more clearly than letters," is especially remarkable, for Heine precisely captures the original definition of allegory here. The allegory, as Erich Auerbach has taught us, was once a piece broken out of a textual context, possessing a "deeper meaning" than the mere letters and indicating the surmounting of the culture from which it stemmed. And as Erwin Panofsky has shown, in the art of the modern age, particularly since the Renaissance, this allegory became a popular, visual stylistic means, not least to depict the ancient world in new paintings. To conclude our brief visit to the past, this means that the audience of the eighteenth century attempted to educate itself in two ways: on the one hand, by listening to the "whisper" of the "broken" sculptures of classical antiquity, on the other, by delving into the Renaissance works of art, since these had already demonstrated how to make the "ruins speak."

Old Europe

Now returning to the present-day, it seems as if not all too much has changed. Tourists still visit both the "broken columns" of classical antiquity and the allegorical master-pieces of Da Vinci or Michelangelo. And if the objection is made that, in regard to the "Grand Tour 2007," Kassel, Münster, and Basel are not located in Italy, one can easily explicate the inaccuracy in the use of that old term. As pointed out on the Biennale's Web site, the promotion campaign above all targets a non-European audience. Moreover, one is aware that Europe as a whole, from the perspective of the United States or Asia, shrinks to the "Old World," no matter if one happens to be in Germany or Italy.

Woody Allen's comedy *Small Time Crooks* (2000) gives an account of the educational tour from an American point of view. The film narrates the story of the New York proletarian gangster couple Ray and Frenchy Winkler unexpectedly becoming incredibly rich through legal means. So as to adopt the high-society lifestyle, Frenchy (Tracey Ullman) takes private lessons with the art dealer David Perret (Hugh Grant), who assists her in building up an art collection. Upon learning the basics at the Metropolitan Museum, Europe is now on the agenda. For, as Frenchy explains to her husband Ray (Woody Allen), it is the place "to see some sites," namely, "churches, opera houses, ruins." Hence, a four-week tour is planned, and during the first highlight of their "cultural develop-ment," Frenchy sits in the Venetian Jesuit church Santa Maria del Rosario listening to a string quartet. But Ray is

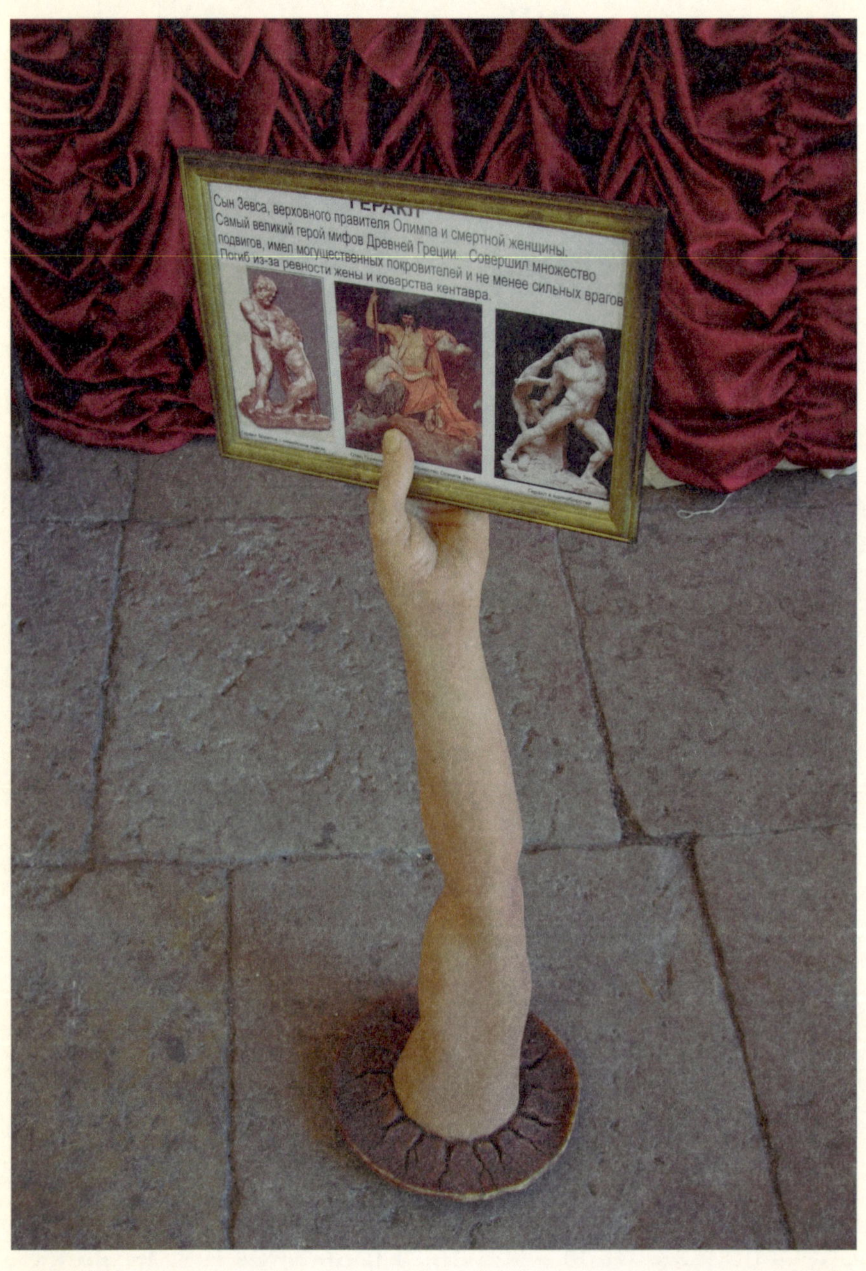
ГЕРАКЛ
Сын Зевса, верховного правителя Олимпа и смертной женщины.
Самый великий герой мифов Древней Греции. Совершил множество
подвигов, имел могущественных покровителей и не менее сильных врагов
Погиб из-за ревности жены и коварства кентавра.

not with her. From the onset, he has been opposed to adapting the standard of life to a standard of education. He is entirely contemptuous of art, deeming it all but absurd "to fly 3000 miles to see ruins." His idea of a successful life is "to go to Florida and swim." He makes repeated attempts to persuade Frenchy to give up the art thing and move with him to the beach. Not to Palm Beach, however, which Frenchy could imagine under certain conditions, because it's too "ritzy" for Ray. No, it has to be Miami: "I wanna be at the dog track every day." Since Frenchy wants none of that, they become increasingly alienated, and the marital row ends with him watching TV and drinking beer, while she sits with David in the Jesuit church. Suddenly her cell phone rings and much to the other listeners' chagrin, she even starts chatting away loudly. It turns out to be an emergency: defrauded of their entire assets by their bookkeepers, the Winklers have to file a petition for bankruptcy. Frenchy flies back home the same day, and she and Ray reconcile. Sitting on the sofa they no longer own, they make plans to sell a Duke of Windsor case she stole from David at her departure and start a new life in Miami.

New Shores

From the church in Venice to Miami Beach! Isn't it incredible that just two years after Allen's film, Art Basel installed the largest art fair of the Americas at a location where Ray Winkler hoped to distance himself as far as possible from the gallery scene? Two lousy years have past, and the opposite of gangsterdom and high society, with which Allen's film plays, appears to have become obsolete.

Must we thus assume that in the United States uneducated parvenus of the likes of Ray are meanwhile interested in art and that the market has adapted to their

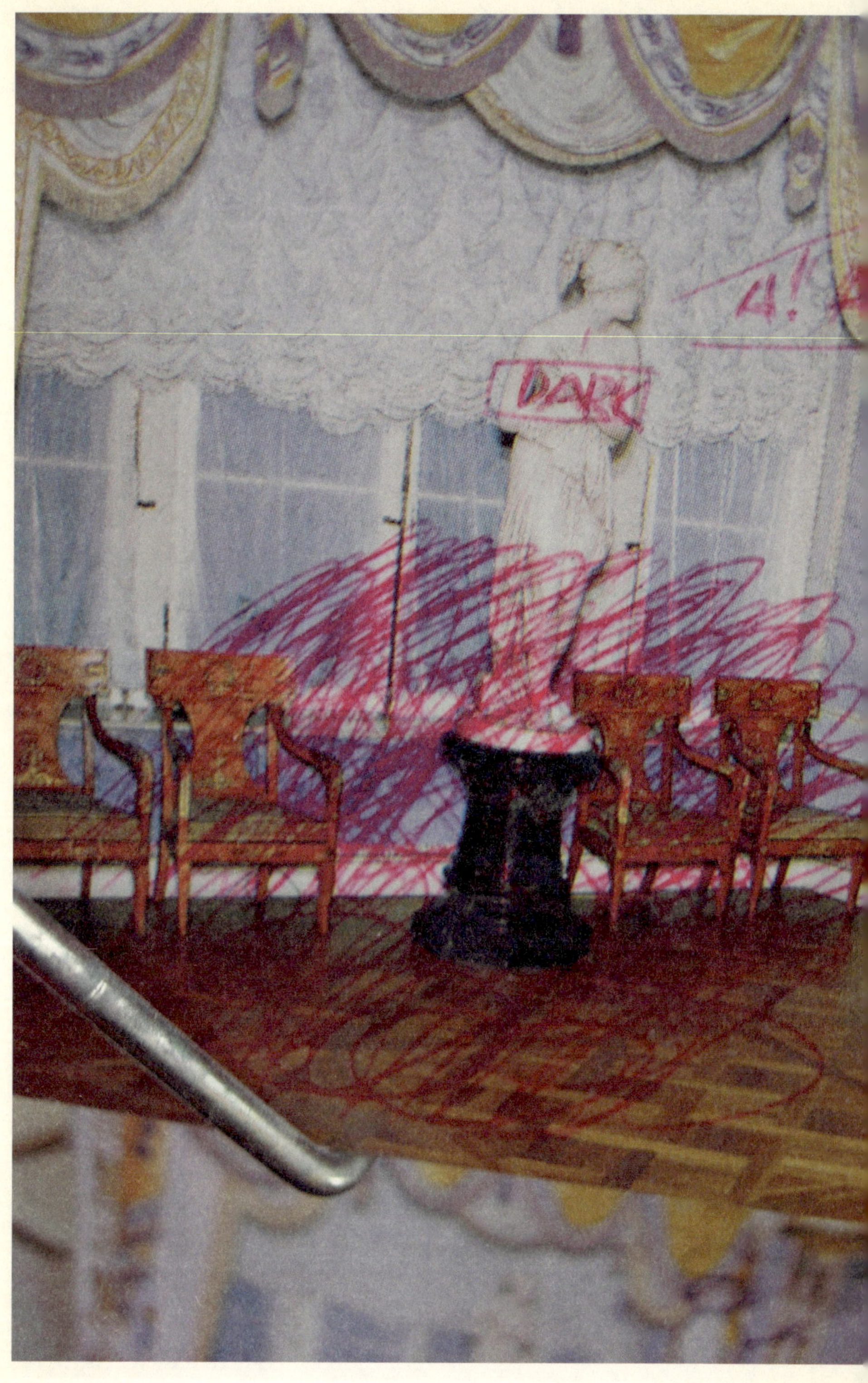
4!
DARK

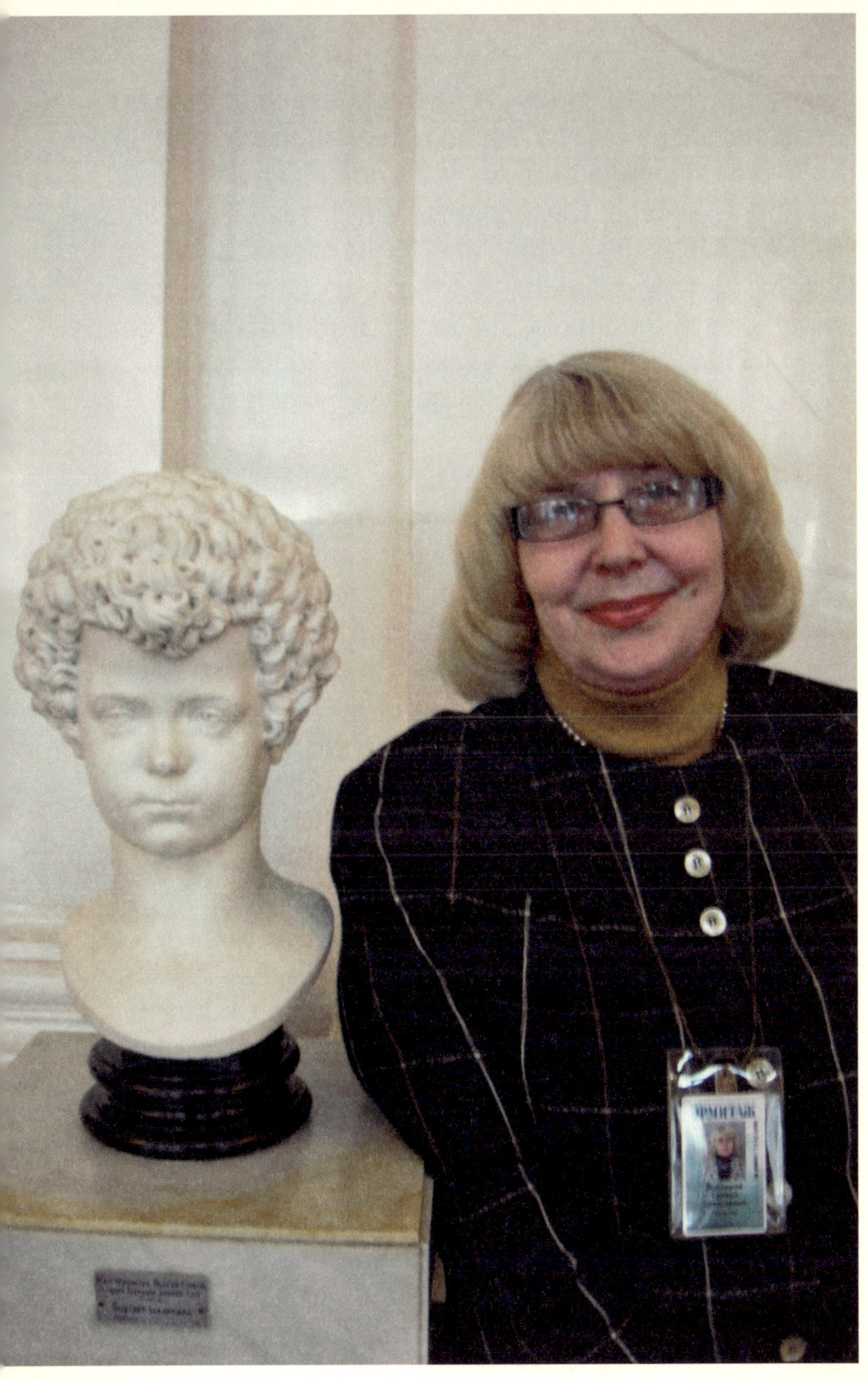

standards? Hardly, since Ray would have found the art parties in Miami Beach just as ritzy. It is much more likely that—the other way around—American high society has adopted one of Ray's arguments: It is not very enticing "to fly 3000 miles to see ruins." Put differently: Miami Beach probably indicates that the American audience no longer deems the ideological superstructure of the "Grand Tour" through Europe necessary to enjoy art. (The mentioned Web site is most likely the desperate attempt to counter this development...)

The example of Miami Beach also demonstrates that, for this reason, the connection between art and tourism is far from outdated. It is now arranged in a new way: Art offers occasions for party vacations at the beach instead of educational tours; and this tendency is not at all restricted to the US. In Venice, for example, one no longer needs to sit reverently in a church, like Frenchy in Allen's film. Be it on the roof terraces of the old city, the beaches of the grand hotels on Lido, a chartered boat, or an island rebuilt as an art pavilion—the outdoor party has replaced "education" as the quintessence of art tourism.

But what does all this entail? Let us conclude with a hypothesis: if journeys to the past appear to have lost their attraction, doesn't this mean that the dissociation from classical antiquity, which was so important for the modern age, has become less relevant? Doesn't it mean that the art audience has finally arrived in the post-modern age? It seems as if it were less and less expected from art today to present allegorical depictions of the past, but instead to enable one to grasp a mystical moment of absolute presence. It's party time! No matter where you are now. Here today, there tomorrow—from Venice to Miami.

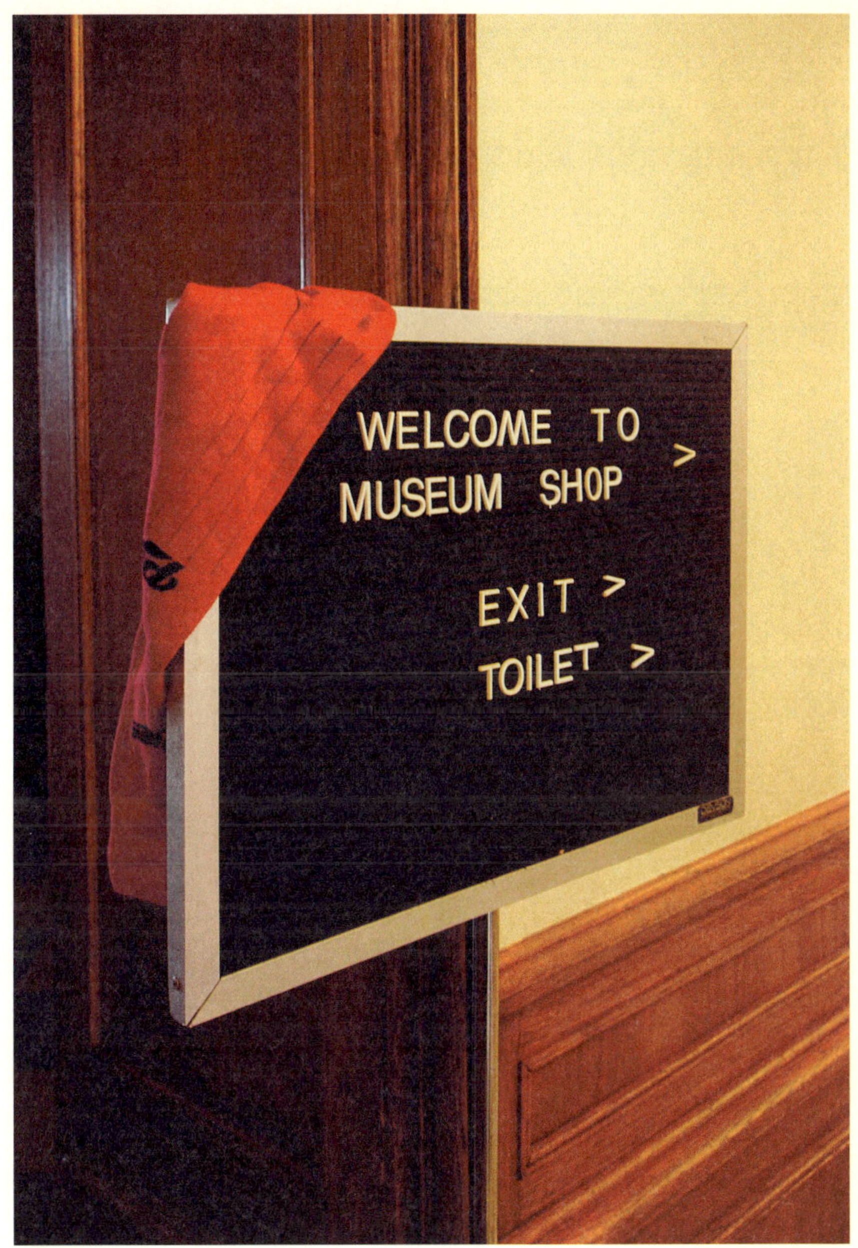
WELCOME TO
MUSEUM SHOP >
EXIT >
TOILET >

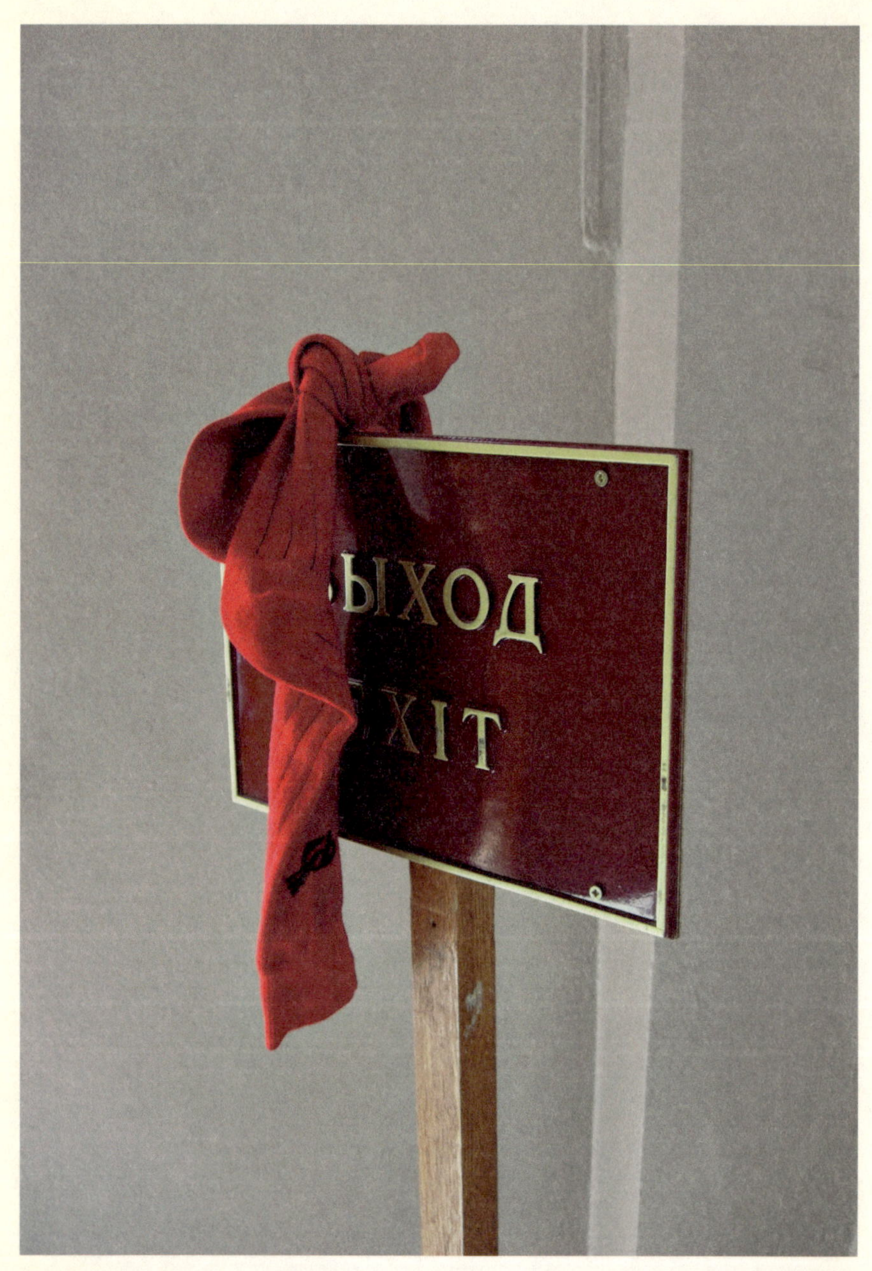
ЫХОД
XIT

29 Marc Spiegler

Swiss Myth—The Art World Remix

Everyone is interested in art. Be this a welcome or worrisome state of affairs: it is undeniable that the experiential mode we call "art" today meets with broad acceptance. How has this come about in recent years? What made it possible? And who works to maintain this? Seen internationally, the work of the artist is increasingly marked by economic and/or institutional relations. In various places, we can see how networks are becoming ever tighter: artists, critics, gallerists, museums, and auction houses are moving closer and closer together. Private persons, companies, and institutions interact with one another to an increasing degree. Links, networks, and processes of exchange seem more dynamic than ever. Using the example of the Swiss art world, Marc Spiegler sketches out the outlines of today's situation, tentatively comparing supposed myth and imagined fact.—*dk*

Any country is constructed of myths—the myths that define a nation to its residents and the myths that define them to foreigners. In that sense societies are like people; you cannot truly judge them before you understand how they judge themselves. When one is newly arrived in a country—as I was to Switzerland in 1999—the first task is to learn the myths. And the second task is to question them.

Sprawling all over the globe, the art world functions as a post-geographic state—complete with its rules for admission, warring parties and occasional insurgencies—and its patriots promulgate equally hyperbolic notions of specialness and complex origin myths.

But what happens when you mix the myths of Swissness and those of the art world? Because the Swiss art world has been my main window into Swiss society, it is also my opportunity to measure myth against reality. And while some myths turned out to be truths (or at least close enough to serve as truths), others shattered under examination, crumbling like a fragile cornice under the weight of an unsteady tourist's foot.

Myth or fact? The Swiss are risk-averse.

Myth. In this regard, there's a deep split between Swiss society and its art world. Because while there can be little doubt the Swiss as a people tend toward caution, the Swiss art world teems with radical innovators. Harald Szeemann, for example, invented an entirely new profession when he left the Kunsthalle Bern and set out to be a free-ranging independent curator. And Basel's Emanuel Hoffmann Foundation created an entirely new sort of institution in 2003 when it opened the Schaulager, a museum-meets-warehouse synthesis precisely adapted to the realities of today's contemporary art (and the people involved with it).

Likewise, the country's collectors have consistently proven among the first worldwide to take the plunge into purchasing art considered too avant-garde, intellectual or otherwise hard-to-sell in other nations. A decade before the whole art world went mad for Chinese contemporary art, for example, Uli Sigg was already building his encyclopedic collection, by traveling all over China (before and during his time as the Swiss ambassador) to discover artists in local scenes unknown even to their compatriots.

Myth or fact? The Swiss are insular.

Myth. In this respect, the Swiss art and finance worlds are similar, involving a constant flow of transnational actors—people whose activity is better defined by the group of people they work with worldwide than by any group or local clique. Walk around any busy street of Geneva or Zurich (but also Berne and Basel) and you're likely to hear a dozen languages spoken per hour.

Once notorious for a distrust of strangers evoking its isolated-mountain-villages heritage, today's Switzerland functions as nexus, a global crossroads, and its art world exemplifies that reality. The most extreme version of that comes every June, of course, during Art Basel, when the banks of the Rhine become the summer palace of the art world. One would be hard-pressed to find anywhere a greater concentration of art world power than the crowd at the Kunsthalle restaurant and its outdoor Campari Bar on the fair's opening nights.

But there's also the period in Zurich late every August, just before the opening of the art season. Because Zurich is the first city to re-open its galleries every summer, gallerist Bob van Orsouw once described these *vernissages* to me as "the art junkies weekend"—the Zurich art scene suddenly finds itself inundated with people from all over Europe, *aficionados* who simply could not wait another week to attend an art opening. For two weeks before the three-night event, the anticipation builds, as the city starts to crawl with artists and curators busily preparing the shows that will open. (Not to mention the collectors planning to buy those shows and journalists who will review them.)

If these were only one-off moments of cosmopolitanism, the Swiss art scene would still be essentially insular. But that's hardly the case. Due to the commercial activities at the galleries, the constant mounting of shows at institutions, and the collectors visiting their artworks (or their bankers, or both), never a week goes by without some out-of-town art world type calling me up for recommendations on what shows to see and where to eat afterwards. Not to mention the unexpected artists, dealers and collectors one stumbles across at openings. (I'll never forget the night I dropped into an opening at the Löwenbräu Areal, casually dressed for early spring weather, and stumbled across half the London art scene, in town to support Rebecca Warren and dressed to the nines. Oops...)

Myth or fact? Switzerland is decentralized.

Myth. When it comes to galleries, at least, the recent past has been a period of dual centralization. Strong contemporary-art galleries such as Francesca Pia, Susanna Kulli and Elisabeth Kaufmann have all moved to Zurich (from Berne, St. Gallen and Basel, respectively). The same holds true for foreign galleries such as Arndt & Partner and Gmurzynska. But within Zurich as well a centralization has taken place, with ever-more activity focused around the Löwenbräu Areal, which boasted three institutions and ten galleries as of this writing (with several more likely to be announced before the reader reads this text).

But also fact. Because when one looks beyond galleries, the power in Switzerland's art scene remains widely spread, from the Fotomuseum Winterthur to the Attitudes off-space in Geneva, not to forget Schaffhausen's Hallen für Neue Kunst. Perhaps this reflects the nature of the art world today—catering to buyers with ever-less time, dealers cannot isolate themselves. But those further from the market can afford to be less convenient.

Myth or fact? Switzerland is essentially harmonious. Fact. In some countries, such as the United States, private interests dominate the art world: collectors and galleries drive the discourse; private philanthropists and corporations underwrite the museums. In other countries, the state plays a massive role—Holland is a marked example, but France is also famously *étatiste*. By comparison, Switzerland's contemporary-art family has no weak siblings, perhaps because there is such a seamless cooperation between the different sectors. Or perhaps there is so much cooperation because all the sectors are operating from such a strong base.

Regardless of the causality, the fact is that Switzerland's art world has strong institutions, both private (e.g. Fondation Beyeler) and publicly supported (e.g. Kunsthaus Zürich), and the galleries enjoy active support from both private collectors and corporations (such as UBS, Credit Suisse and Swiss Re). True, Switzerland's high cost of living makes its biggest cities a hard place to be a struggling artist, a sort of anti-Berlin. But that's partially offset by a complex system of grants and prizes (from many levels of government, but also corporations such as Manor) that allow promising artists years to find a working model for their practice, rather than facing the rapid sink-or-swim survival test common in New York or London.

Even local economic-development agencies have caught on, actively trying to re-brand Swiss cities as potential "creative clusters," and thus attract the knowledge workers that economists trumpet as the key to having a thriving economy today. Art plays a big role in their tactics. Once a freakish hobby of interest only to a small elite, it is now embraced as a key component of any educated person's *culture générale*. Does it benefit the art world to risk being instrumentalized in these "cool city" campaigns? That remains to be seen.

And whether all this seamless harmony is a good thing remains equally debatable. Although it's more than fifty years old, the classic quote from Orson Welles in the *Third Man* still seems to hang like an anvil around Switzerland's neck: "In Italy, for 30 years under the Borgias, they had warfare, terror, murder, bloodshed—they produced Michelangelo, Leonardo da Vinci and the Renaissance. In Switzerland, they had brotherly love, 500 years of democracy and peace, and what did that produce? The cuckoo clock." Granted, that doesn't apply so well to the innovative and avant-garde end of the Swiss art world. But you certainly do hear people muttering that the milieu could benefit from a few proper feuds, or more cultural controversies like the one surrounding the 2005 Thomas Hirschhorn exhibition at the Centre Culturel Suisse in Paris.

Myth or fact? The Swiss are modest.

Fact. In the last half-dozen years, major collectors in cities such as Miami, London and New York have taken to publicizing their holdings by opening their homes to the art world during fairs. Some of them even have online catalogs of their collection, publicly available. But Swiss collectors still continue to play a much more low-key role: Every year, I'm asked by *ArtNews* magazine to update its "Top 200" collectors list, and every year I'm begged through intermediaries not to suggest certain obvious candidates for inclusion.

Likewise, one can hardly imagine the collectors of Basel hosting the hordes of curious visitors that go tromping through Miami's mansions and villas every December to visit its vaunted private collections. Rather, the Swiss tend to wait until they have an honest-to-god museum-worthy collection and then found an institution—the two prime examples being Basel's Fondation Beyeler and Schaulager, easily among the top private exhibition sites in the world. So perhaps it's less about being modest than about Swiss caution, i.e. feeling damn sure that you actually have something to show before inviting people in to see it.

Myth of fact? The Swiss monetize discretion.
Fact. From the New York selling rooms of auction houses (whose catalogs have started to resemble fashion magazines, in their thickness and the lushness of their illustrations) to the artists studios of Beijing (currently overrun by "collectors" intent on buying China's future Pollocks and Rauschenbergs, and then profitably reselling them to China's future Geffens and Rockefellers), to the mushrooming Bethnal Green scene (which has dotted London's East End with galleries run by theoreticians-turned-dealers), the art market has been buoyed by the notion of art as a commodity, as a financial device, as a new "asset class."

One would think that this paradigm should extend to Switzerland, which ranks high among the world's finance capitals. Yet when dealing with the Swiss art world, one rarely has the feeling—so common in New York or London—of having boarded a runaway train populated by opportunists and "lifestyle" promoters. By comparison, the market here seems placid.

That's deceptive. Because (just as in finance, and for many of the same reasons) Switzerland plays an utterly outsized role in the art market. Despite its small population, the country usually ranks fourth worldwide in estimates of its total volume of annual art transactions. But as with the country's private banks, much of the real action in the Swiss art market is essentially invisible, conducted behind closed doors or inside free ports, where major deals often involve the simple transfer of a painting from one storage room to another down the hall.

I once had the opportunity to tour several of a free port's secured chambers in one afternoon—the experience proved mind-blowing. In one room, African antiquities were stacked on jumbled-looking shelves. In the next, Persian carpets, each worth the price of a small house, were piled 20-high atop each other. In the third, the dealer had installed all the Louis XV furniture and antique clocks that he owned, creating a museum-quality exhibition that looked almost like a palatial living room. (Well, a palatial living room without any windows.)

Free ports are paradoxical complexes. On the one hand, they are fortresses, as imposing as a Soviet housing block, built to survive any cataclysm known to man, secured by armed guards and impregnable without proper authorization. The free ports create around them whole industries, including not just the obvious shippers and art handlers, but also the photographers, art assessors, conservators and consultants who work with the clientele. Yet from a taxation standpoint they might as well be floating off the coast of Antigua. That makes the free ports art-market magnets. I have several friends who regularly fly from New York or London, are met at Kloten or Geneva-Cointrin by a car and driver, visit a free port to spend 20 minutes with a single painting in a neon-lit room, then rapidly return from whence they came.

Others spend much longer. The late German collector Gustav Rau, a bush doctor based in Congo, amassed a collection valued between $250 million and $500 million —everything from El Greco to Canaletto to Renoir to Munch—and kept it all at the Embrach free port (close to Zurich). Rau would visit his art for a few interludes every year, full-day sessions spent in the storage racks, examining all the pieces from which his African altruism had exiled him.

There's a second dimension in which Switzerland's art-market power is veiled. The strong markets of the United States and England are visible in their auction rooms, which also attract collectors all over the world—Russia, China, India, South America. By comparison, Switzerland's auctions are sedate, confined principally to Swiss art and the blockbuster diamond sales traditionally centered in Geneva. Yet no other country's collectors export so many works to London and New York's auction rooms. And that flow goes in both directions, even if you'll never see Swiss collectors waving their paddles in auction rooms to triumphantly broadcast their newest acquisition.

By chance and by choice, the Swiss art world has functioned as my portal into Switzerland, my route for parsing its myths. Was it a distorting lens through which to perceive my new homeland? No doubt. Because like every art scene, Switzerland's cultural players are an unrepresentative sample—more unconventional in their thinking and more international in their experiences. But the distortion does not seem so massive. Because just as the notion of Swiss exceptionalism proves year upon year to be ever-more mythical, and just as the art world becomes ever-more enmeshed with the "real" world, the notion that the Swiss art world is exceptional within Switzerland does not stand up to scrutiny. In truth, the Swiss art scene draws more strength from being Swiss than from being un-Swiss. And in any case, there's nothing more Swiss than not wanting to be seen as too Swiss.

The Silence of the Artists—On the Professionalization of the Artist in Switzerland

Our expectations have become more realistic: artists today are no longer figures located at the symbolic boiling point of the social imagination. But have we already arrived in the prosaic world of everyday business, where being an artist has become simply another profession? Self-taught artists, artists with a background in craft, and intellectuals: various models form the historical stock in Switzerland. This is the starting point for Philip Ursprung's observations. The field is unified neither in terms of theory nor of practice. Does any one of these models still dominate today, or have they all been surpassed? What about the current background of the professionalization and institutionalization of artistic training? Even if the implications of all current symptoms are not clear, or at least remain difficult to evaluate, unavoidable transformations are underway that are changing the cultural field.—*dk*

Swiss artists have the reputation of being quiet and apolitical. Unlike their colleagues trained and active in Germany, England, the US, or Scandinavia, they are considered to be artists who, ever since the "Swiss wonder" of the 1990s, have skillfully been able to assert themselves internationally. They are commercially successful and institutionally well-connected, artists who can rely on a solid system of support, but who at the same time keep out of current theoretical debates and avoid commenting on other artists. At best, they speak about the work of other artists sporadically in interviews; but generally, these interviews rarely go beyond anecdotal comments on their own work, and do not seek to leave a mark on the international debate. The state of artistic debate in Switzerland is just like the country's architectural, literary, musical, and historical debates. One keeps to the background, avoids too much prominence, criticizing contemporaries in private conversation or between the lines, but not explicitly or publicly. If one wanted to publish an anthology of texts by artists in Switzerland, analogous to the representative account *Das Kunstschaffen in der Schweiz 1848–2006* published by the Swiss Institute for Art Research in 2006, only a slim volume would result.

A pamphlet like the book *Achtung die Schweiz*, written by Lucius Burckhardt, Max Bill, and Markus Kutter in 1955, would be impossible to imagine today. Why is it that with the exception of Max Bill, Richard Paul Lohse, Gottfried Honegger, Rémy Zaugg, Silvie und Chérif Defraoui, Olivier Mosset, and John M Armleder there are hardly any texts by Swiss artists? Why is there no group of intellectuals, of the rank of a Frisch or a Dürrenmatt, who are eager to debate and willing to speak up? Why is it that there is no *peintre érudit* in this country, no one who beside art production also pursues a theoretical body of work, comparable to Gerhard Richter, François Morellet, Peter Halley, Mike Kelley, Jutta Koether, Mira Schor, John Miller, Andrea Fraser, Thomas Ruff, Olafur Eliasson, Liam Gillick, or many others? And what about those Swiss artists of the middle generation who might be called intellectual in the sense that their work is open to a theoretical discourse and is internationally perceived as being so, artists like Relax, Ingrid Wildi, Christian Philipp Müller, Gianni Motti, Christoph Büchel, Theresa Hubbard, and Alexander Birchler, Sylvie Fleury? Why do they not produce discursive texts worth mentioning?

Historically speaking, the silence of the artists is due to the fact that in contrast to the neighboring countries with their aristocratic traditions, there were never art academies. There is no tradition of central institutions of artist training that establish state norms of quality, face international competition, and hire the artistic elite of their time to teach upcoming artists. With the exception of the Geneva Ecole des Beaux-Arts, the art academies here take a very applied approach, focusing on artistic craftsmanship or the training of drawing teachers. Since the nineteenth century, the best artists have left Switzerland to train in Düsseldorf, Paris, Vienna, Rome, or New York. And the few artists of international status who are active as teachers do their teaching abroad.

Will this change with the current professionalization of artists, the restructuring of the art schools in Zurich, Berne, Basel, and Geneva? How will the political pressure to strengthen research and theory that has been exercised for a number of years affect the coming generation? Will Swiss artists play a more prominent role in theory debates? Will the schools here begin to attract top-notch foreign students? Or will the specifically Swiss style of art—if there is one—begin to change, will an international process of leveling take place? Indeed, will the bureaucratization of research and training lead to a loss of creative originality, so that fewer younger artists dare to reject existing norms and do new things, as is feared by some? Will things go so far that the academy, as was true at the end of the nineteenth century, will become a synonym for the conventional and conservative?

A look at recent art history shows that there is no alternative to the academicization and professionalization of the artist. The American art boom from the late 1950s to the 1970s is inseparable from the intensification of training. The art schools created in the US after the Second World War—most of them closely associated with university art history departments—as well as the regular courses of study offered there formed the foundation for the unparalleled success of American students that took place since that period. The exception of Robert Smithson confirms the rule—the self-taught slowly disappeared from the art world of that time. And the success of art in Germany since the 1970s is inseparably associated with the active academic life of the German art schools. Institutions like Kunstakademie Düsseldorf, Universität der Künste Berlin, Nova Scotia College of Art and Design, Goldsmiths College in London, Glasgow School of Art, and the Whitney Independent Study Program are crystallization points of the art world around which continuous and successful traditions have formed. There's no question that such an institution would be an asset for Switzerland, and that it must remain our goal to improve artistic training.

The lack of an institution on the level of an art academy, just as much as the lack of international biennial or triennial exhibitions, stands in the way of the artists' professionalization here. In the country with the most important art fair in the world, there are still no international biennials. The competition, the public attention, and the exchange that these exhibitions bring with them is lacking—or it takes place elsewhere, and the accompanying critical engagement is suppressed all the easier. Finally, there are few platforms for discursive exchange and debate in art criticism.

The silence of the artists is not just a problem of the artists alone. It affects the art world as a whole. The professionalization of artists cannot be separated from the professionalization of art criticism and teaching art. Not only the artists are silent, but also the critics and curators. They also accept the silent consensus to not publicly express critique, instead discretely implying it. They are also afraid of too much prominence. Ever since Harald Szeemann's 1969 exhibition When Attitudes Become Form at Kunsthalle Bern there has not been an exhibition here with an international impact. And this exhibition, which today, at least in Switzerland, enjoys mythical status, was not a controversial exhibition in the sense that it might have triggered a political debate. And even more importantly, it had no followers. Szeemann left, and the fear of public engagement as well as the loss of sponsorship monies since then have been omnipresent in curators' minds.

In the early years of the art world as it established itself in the 1960s and 1970s, this isolation and networking offered a foundation for artistic vitality. The pose of the self-taught, who develops his art from out of himself and withdraws from debate, worked within a relatively small art world grouped around a few centers. With the rapid expansion of the art world since the 1980s—a cultural field that follows the laws of the globalized economy; that is, concentration of cultural capital, abolition of national laws, a high, equal price level, and reduction to a small portfolio of artist stars—this self-imposed silence becomes a problem. The art scene here risks isolating itself, and falling into the provincial stagnation which it so successfully had overcome in the late 1980s. Of course, in the future the artists, like the mountain farmers, will be able to count on national solidarity on the part of the authorities. Of course, in the future the best artists will be able to assert themselves on the international playing field. But the pressure is increasing. The art world here should not react with defiant retreat, but by laying the tracks so that artists from elsewhere also come here and the battles to be fought are fought on our own turf. The professionalization of the art world, first of all that of training, is a prerequisite for this. There is no way around it.

Turn Up the Volume—A Conversation with Urs Fischer

Urs Fischer's studio is located on the outer limits of Long Island City, in the midst of garages and storage halls. From the outside, nothing betrays anything of the work that takes place inside the well-organized studio, where Fischer works with his assistants on several international exhibitions simultaneously. Leaning against the walls are oversized aluminum panels, printed and painted, that seem to resemble huge portals. The conversations with the artist took place in March this year, during three visits with the artist: in his kitchen (wallpaper with motifs by Franz Kafka, Franz West, and Francis Bacon! Holy Trinity!) and in his two offices. The conversations are not so much about individual works, but revolve around the "zone of risk" (Fischer) in which the artist seeks to change his way of proceeding, examining parameters, and thinking about the ambition behind the work of other artists. Urs Fischer and Eugene Tsaï contribute photographs.—*dk*

DK: I've prepared a few questions. So, first question: what does society expect from the artist?
UF: No idea (*laughing).*
DK: I'd thought as much *(laughs too).*
UF: No really, I don't know. I have the feeling that the people that get the most out of art are those who make it. This is how I see it: I know nothing about music, I don't play an instrument. But seen from the outside, that looks good, that sounds good. Seen from the inside, for people who can do it, it's pretty bad. If you turn it around... The things you know nothing at all about, that's what you find interesting. There's simply a distance, something exotic... But, as an artist that looks quite different.
DK: How different?
UF: I don't know, I see it in a much more structured way, not in terms of subject, well, also in subject terms, but not from the outside. You take a look at someone's overall oeuvre. There are always people that surprise you, but usually, when it comes to art, you know how that was done, what steps... It's just another way of approaching it, how people make things...
DK: What do you mean, "make things"? How people work with the system or with their work?
UF: System? No! It's always just about the work. The system is really irrelevant. You just see that differently. Perhaps there's also a pleasure in that. Sometimes I'm surprised at the way people think about artworks who don't themselves make art.
DK: A gallerist certainly expects something from an artist that is different from what an art critic or the broader audience might expect. I would be interested in what your recent experience has been in such matters.
UF: For me, if you ask me about my experience, it's always about actions, about what's coming up next.

When it comes to what you do, the system doesn't really play a role at all. That sounds more naïve than it actually is. You do your thing, you are part of something, you're not alone. The thing with the system, that comes automatically. You're always reacting to something, handing something on, something that's already there. You're a medium that passes on information. Where the interest comes from, that's a riddle for me too, in part. All artists are flawed in their own special way, you have to be flawed in some special way...

DK: You work consciously with that?

UF: What do you mean, work consciously with it?

DK: I don't know either.

UF: Who says you have to do something consciously?

DK: You could, for example, exploit it, doing something where the person and the work enter a mutually reflecting relation...

UF: For example?

DK: What comes to my mind are Charcot's pictures of hysterics. There, you really ask yourself, what kind of study is that? In that case, it's quite clear how he's flawed. The hysterics are a kind of projection of this study.

UF: Yes, to each his own. I really don't know, but you just carry on, and it's not really so important. There are so many different ways of being flawed. It's not really worth going into any more. But I do think that if you ask yourself what society expects that there will always be people who make art; they have some reason to engage with life in this way. There are surely many reasons, talent of course plays a role, that you can do something well, regardless of what it is. But you've got to have an interest. Most people don't have the interest. Then there are also fantasies about how it would be, if you were like that, or if you did something that way.

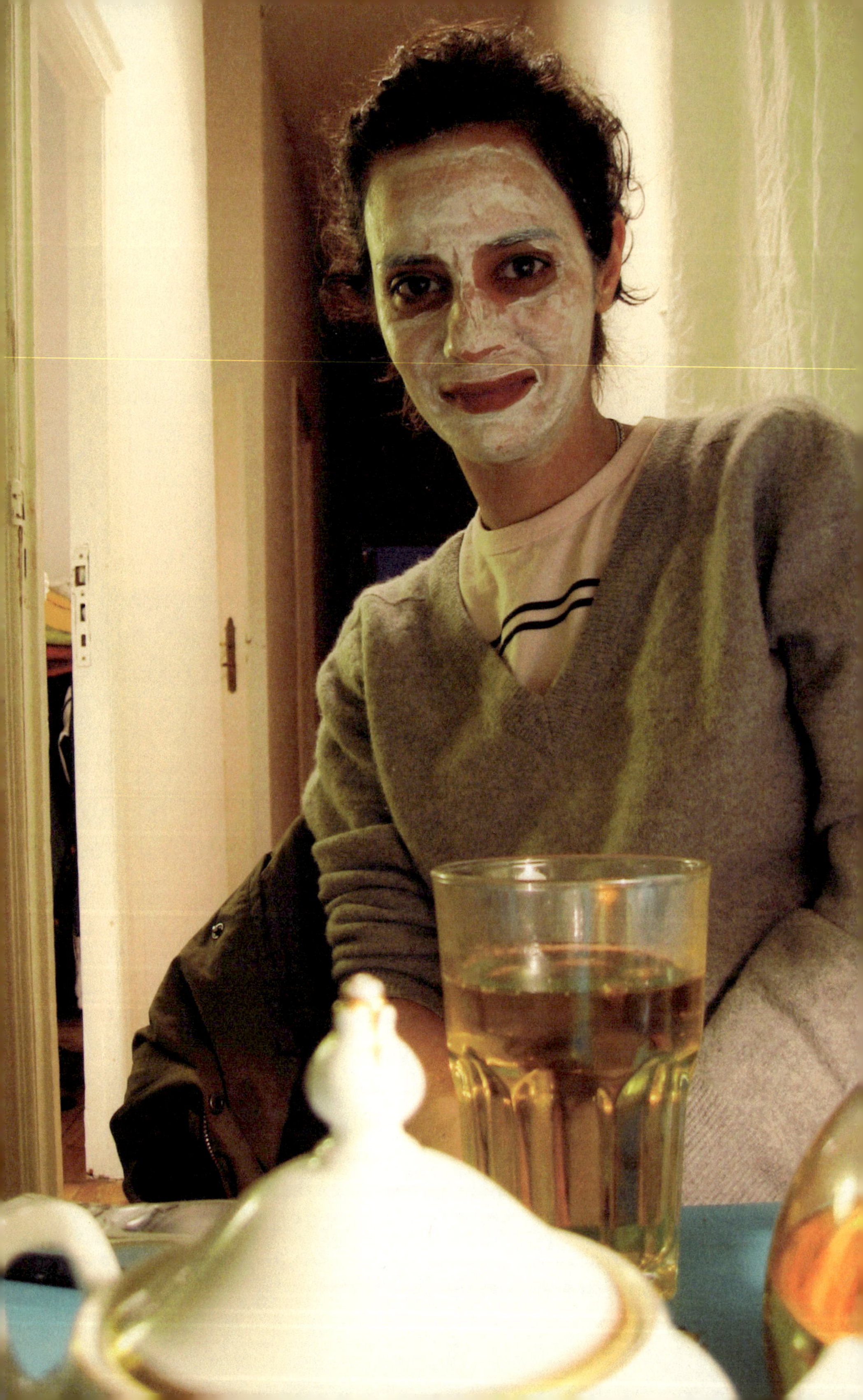

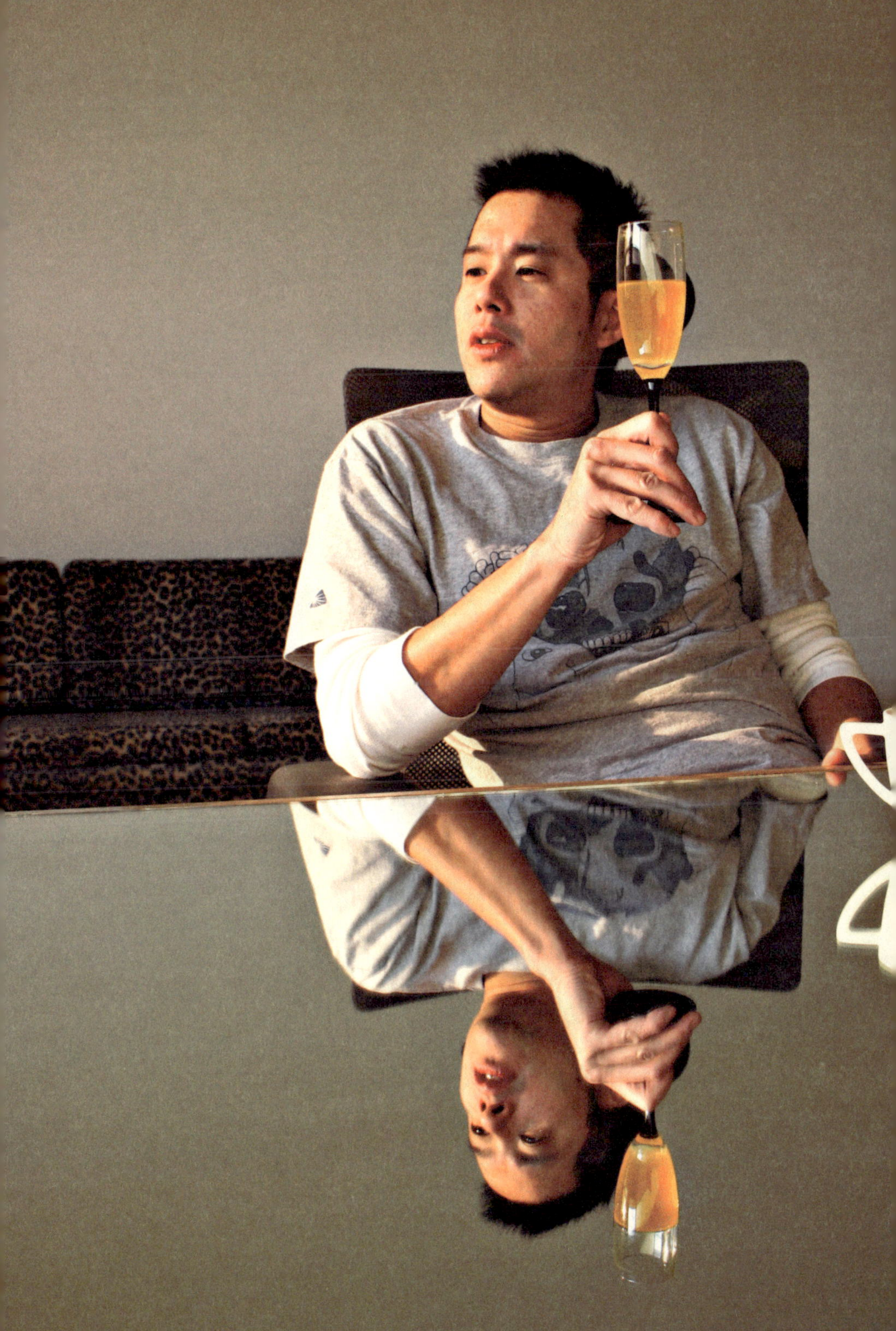

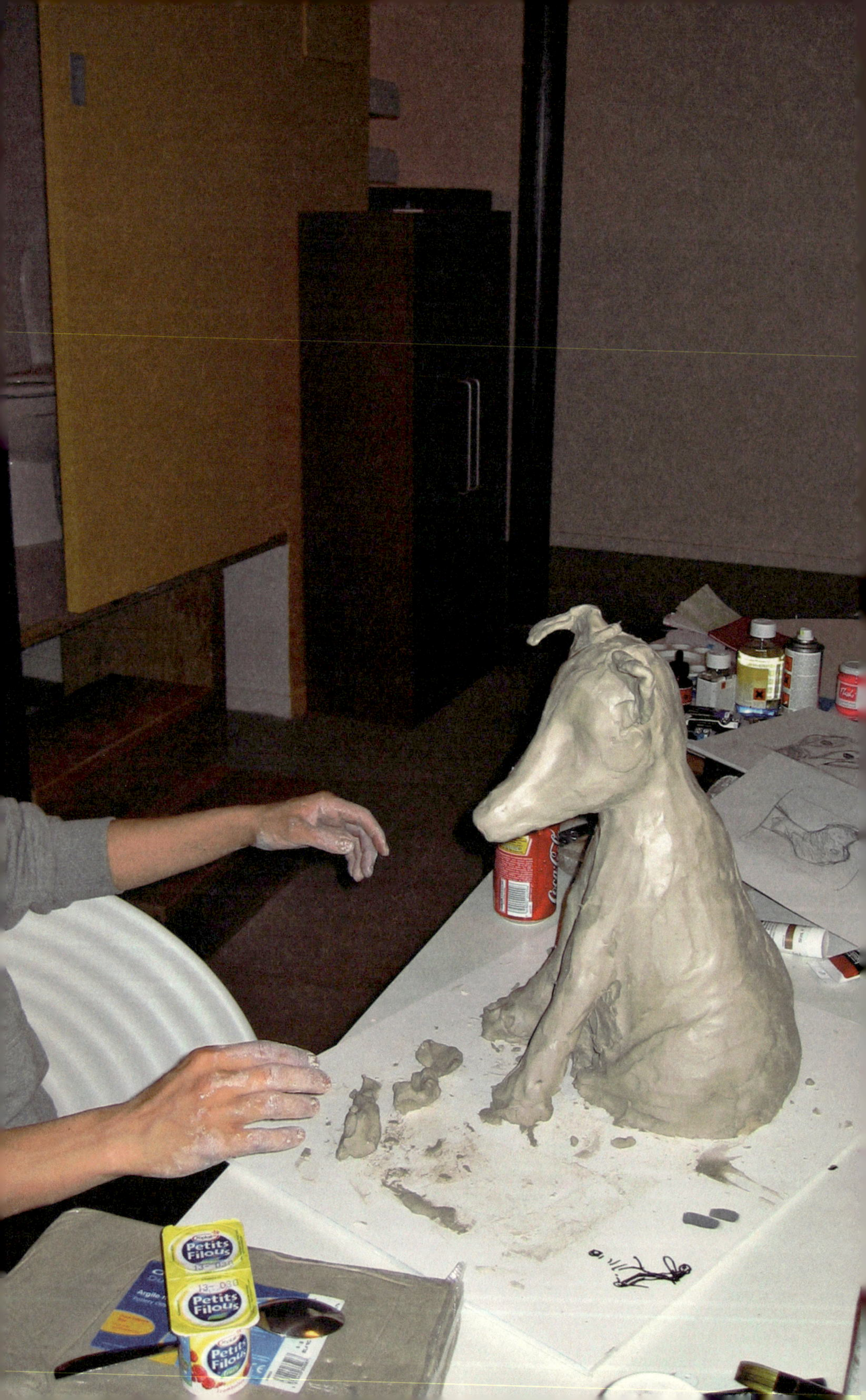
Petits Filous
Petits Filous
Petits Filous

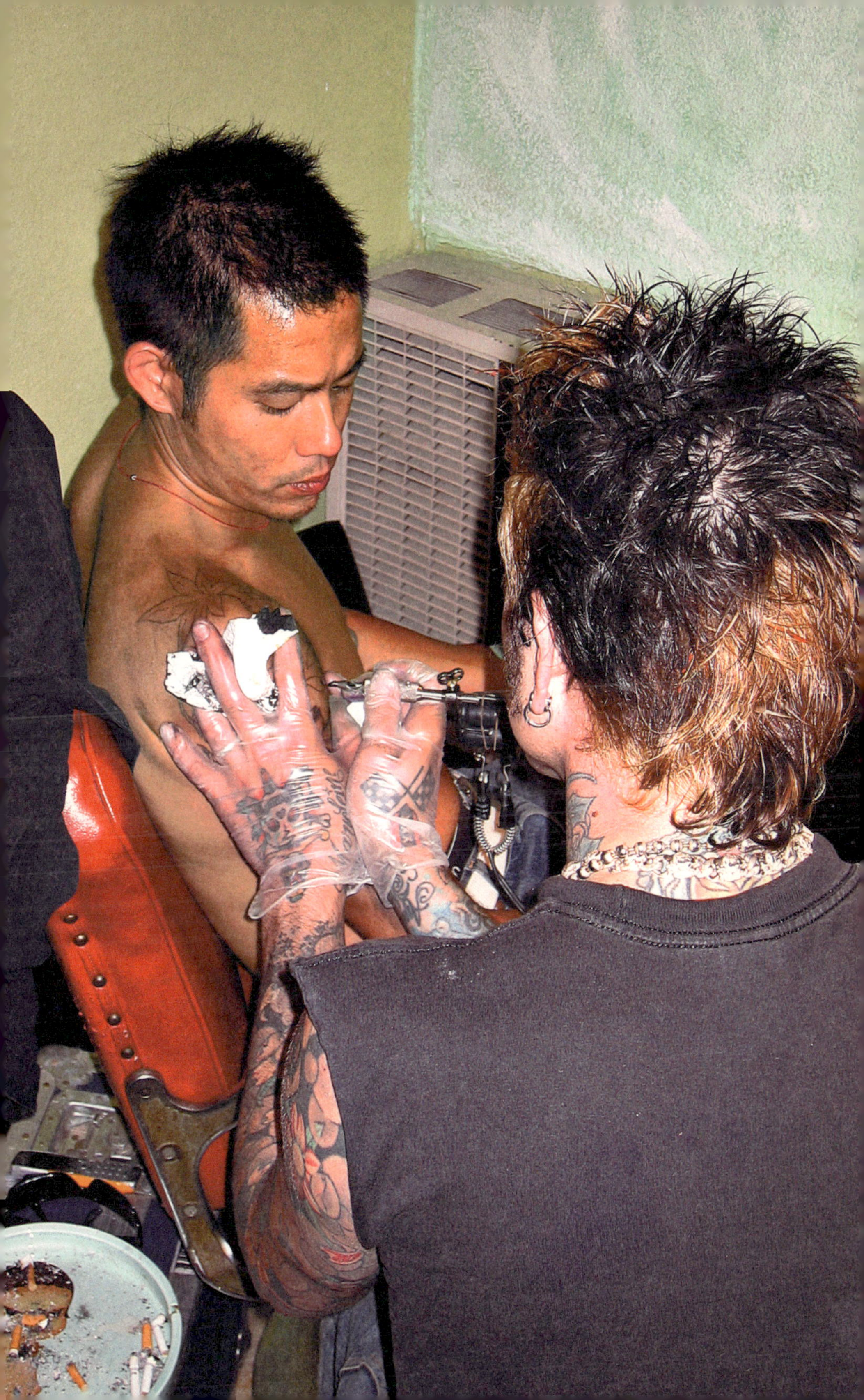

DK: Say something more about this fantasy.
UF: It's simply about certain projections... That's a lot clearer when it comes to someone who sings. Someone who sings, that's kind of cool. It's cool as a fantasy, but I don't know what it's like for someone who sings: I don't sing. Then it's probably also simpler, or more technical. Back to the notion of talent: You can also get devoured by your talent. Like Hans Erni. Talent plays a role. Projections play a role. Ultimately, it's nothing really special: you do what you do. An even better example is the film actor, the Hollywood star. That's just a job that's very technical. Not just, but there are some people that are insanely good, who in certain phases of their lives are just great. Now there are a lot of external circumstances as well: if the face is no longer interesting, between forty and fifty, say, and suddenly it becomes interesting again. But you never know. You don't have much influence on that.
DK: But you do have a certain influence. Isn't art precisely something where many artists work with these elements of projections?
UF: For example?
DK: Bruce Nauman, who did a work with the title *Get out of My Mind, Get out of My Room.* That's already a relatively direct reaction to the audience's expectations.
UF: Maybe that's right, I see it a bit more generously.
DK: OK, tell me how.
UF: Just a bit more generously: it's about who you are, what you are, how you deal with it.
DK: Okay... Last time we also talked about the national context. There's one exhibition, the Biennale, it's a bit loaded with the question of national representation.
UF: I think that's a relic, Venice, this kind of national representation, that's from a time where there were

still world exhibitions where nation-states represented themselves.

DK: I was getting at something else. It seems to mean that you're interested in the nation, Switzerland, in the sense of how one's socialized as an artist, what artist models or myths have their roots in Switzerland as the place you come from. There were the self-taught like Robert Walser, or people like Max Bill who came from the modernist, craftsmanship corner, or the intellectual titans like Max Frisch or Friedrich Dürrenmatt.

UF: Dürrenmatt, Bill, Frisch... that's all fifty years ago. I mean, it's a bit difficult to make a general statement about that.

DK: One possible way of breaking it down would be to say: does artistic intellectuality still play a role in public?

UF: In relation to Switzerland? I guess so. I haven't been there for a while. Maybe I've lost track here. That Switzerland plays a role, that only has to do with questions about my background, where you come from and the like. That only interests me in that way. Basically quite egoistic. Not as an interest in the collective thing. Personally, when it comes to this stuff, its basically about me.

DK: And what do you do with that?

UF: It's more about limiting, and a certain way of looking at things, that is somehow also culturally determined. Suddenly you look at something and ask, why is it that way? Or you find it great that you think it's that way, without thinking I'm French or Swiss, etc. Then there are things like humor that are national, or have to do with your background. You just notice that with friends from here you have a whole different way of talking. You first notice humor when you're in another language, up to a certain degree you can transfer that. Other things you can't even translate. It's just not funny. Then you notice that there are limits, limiting aspects. But that means also that you suddenly discover certain assumptions in what you do, a certain understanding for what is real and what is pretend. The role playing, that is, where we come from, not something you do. Although everybody does it, but they wouldn't declare it openly. Here, that's totally normal, and not hypocritical. It's a kind of honesty. That's what I'm getting at, that's what I mean: then it's less about Switzerland than about my background, my interests, my world, and how it reveals itself. It's not that what I find here's better. It's simply the collision that interests me.

The other is a certain form of sensibility; you have that basically everywhere, regardless of where you are. But you have a sensibility. That's something you can't replace in life, you can bring new things to it, but your origin stays with you somehow. Of course, that all plays a role when you do things as an artist, when you think about things and work. On the one hand, you're limited, but this limitation is also a strength, your limits are precisely where your interest lies, where it produces something, where something happens. Kind of in the zone of risk, something like that.

DK: What about the myths about the *creative act*, according to which art is a form of thinking that has to do with lucidness, or conversely is a site of the orgiastic?

UF: There are some people who live out these myths. It's also the idea of authenticity, the idea that you're somehow an authentic artist. That it's all not the subject of too much reflection, that you just do it.

DK: Or the other way around: that what you're doing is metaphysically charged. That would be the other end of the spectrum.

UF: That's also a role you play. It's not a problem if you

see that it's a game, as long as you don't suddenly start believing it yourself.

DK: That's tricky.

UF: Yeah, it is tricky. (*Both laugh.)*

DK: Sometimes a bit unsettling.

UF: Today, there are a lot more reflections and energy from outside... the more things get reported about, the more energy comes from the outside. The individual person has to deflect this, or be able to turn it off. There are already people who do a work, and the work suddenly gets received in such and such a way. It's suddenly about something that wasn't so clear to the person beforehand. And the funny thing is that what really characterizes the work, falls by the wayside, the unclearness drops away and what remains is just a core that's actually boring. Or not a core, but scaffolding, and that's boring, because it wasn't about the scaffolding. All the studies on life or whatever issues, that comes on its own anyway. It just doesn't interest me.

DK: Or your defense mechanisms are better trained?

UF: It depends on what work you do. It's good that it's relatively unclear what I do.

DK: And you're still able to complicate it?

UF: No, some of it isn't clear to me! There are people who are very rigid. That again you can see in two ways. That it's a mirror of life, or that the rigidity reflects the attempt to keep things together, so that it doesn't all fly away. If there is beauty, for me that's where it is. That, you can't hide. The more you try to control a work, the clearer it becomes that you are someone who wants to control it. And that is something that interests me. It's not about what kind of art is standing about in the galleries at the moment, who is a hotter artist at the moment, and the like. That's really totally irrelevant. Most of the

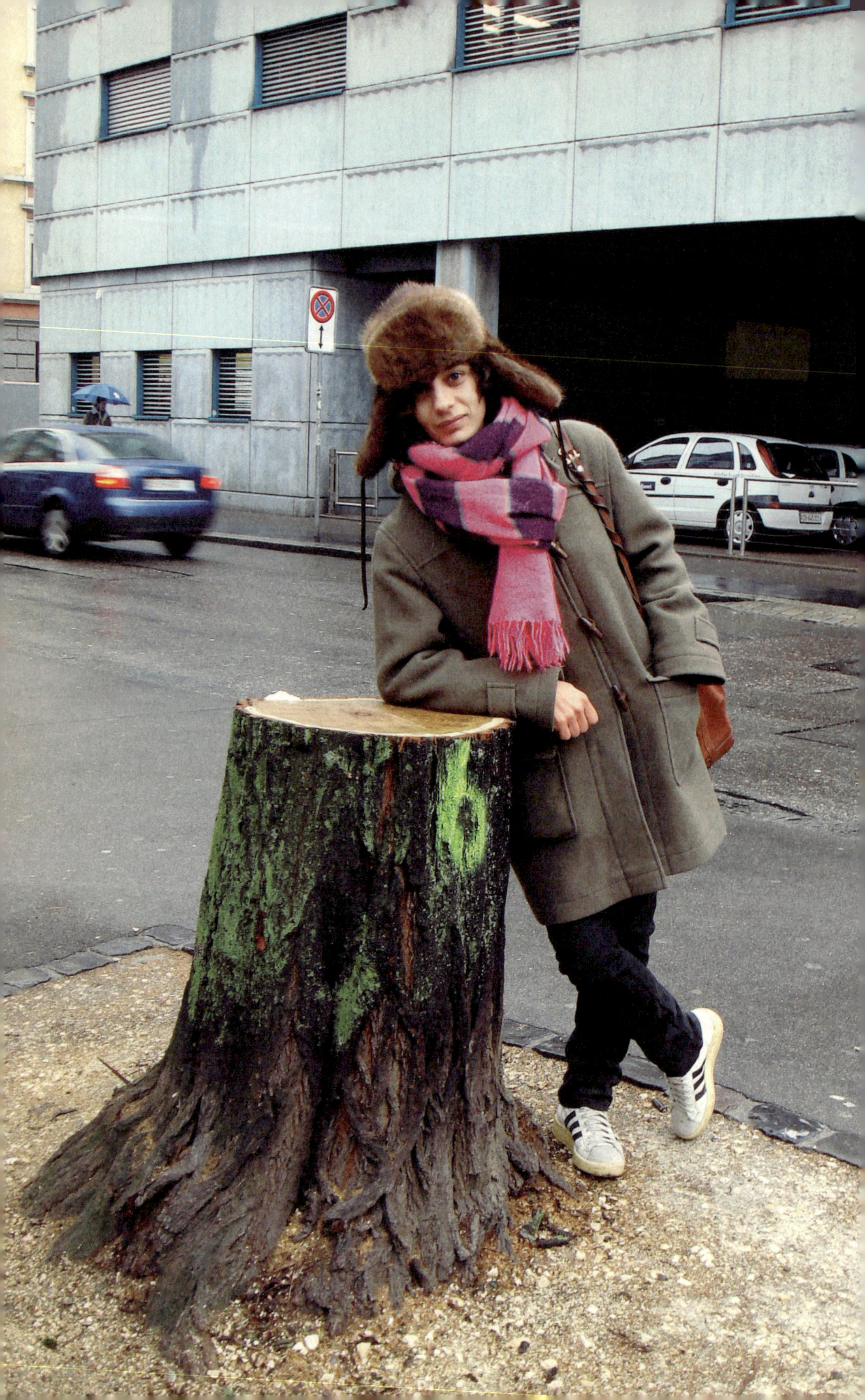

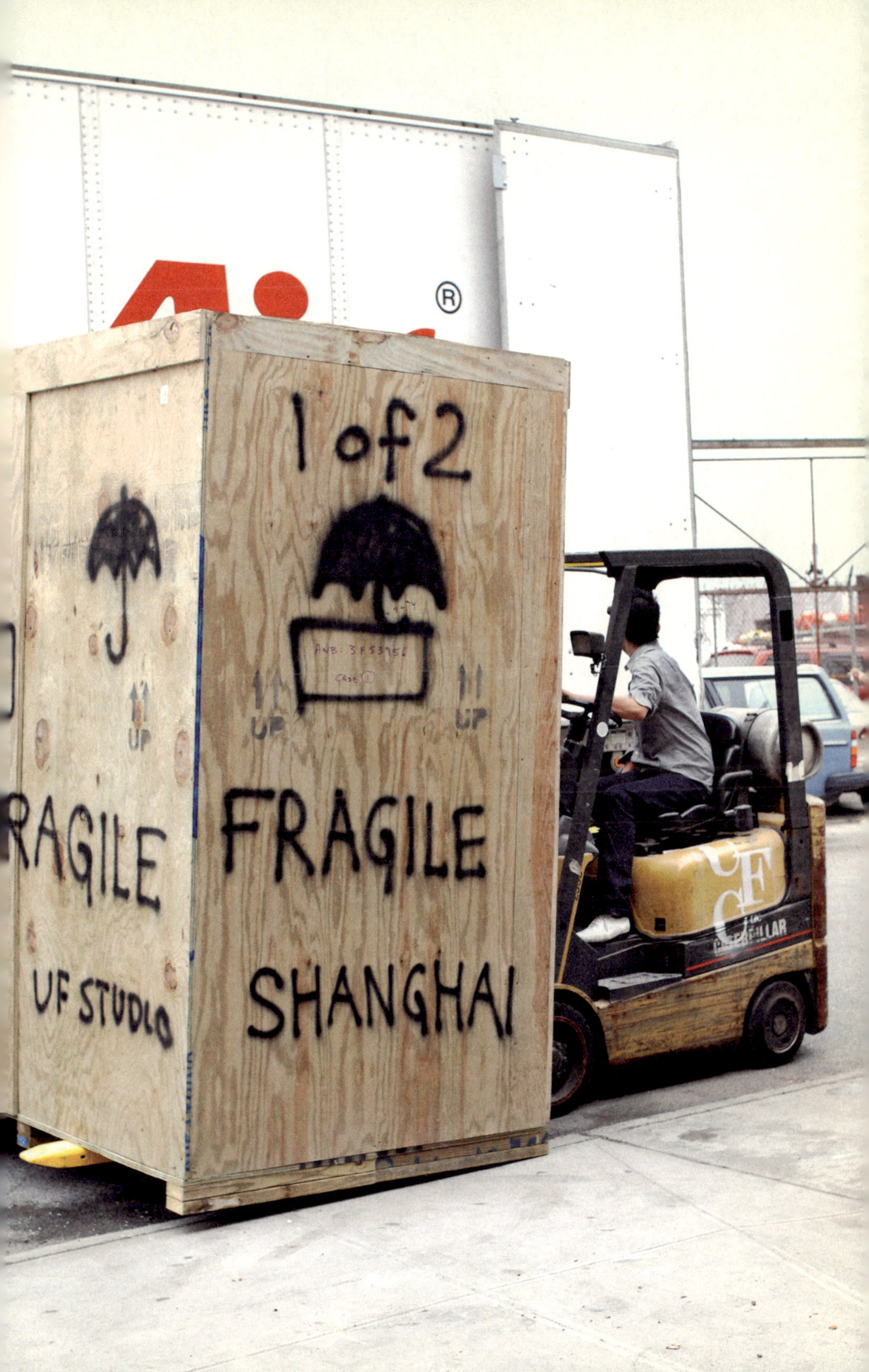
1 of 2
UP
UP
UP
RAGILE
FRAGILE
UF STUDIO
SHANGHAI

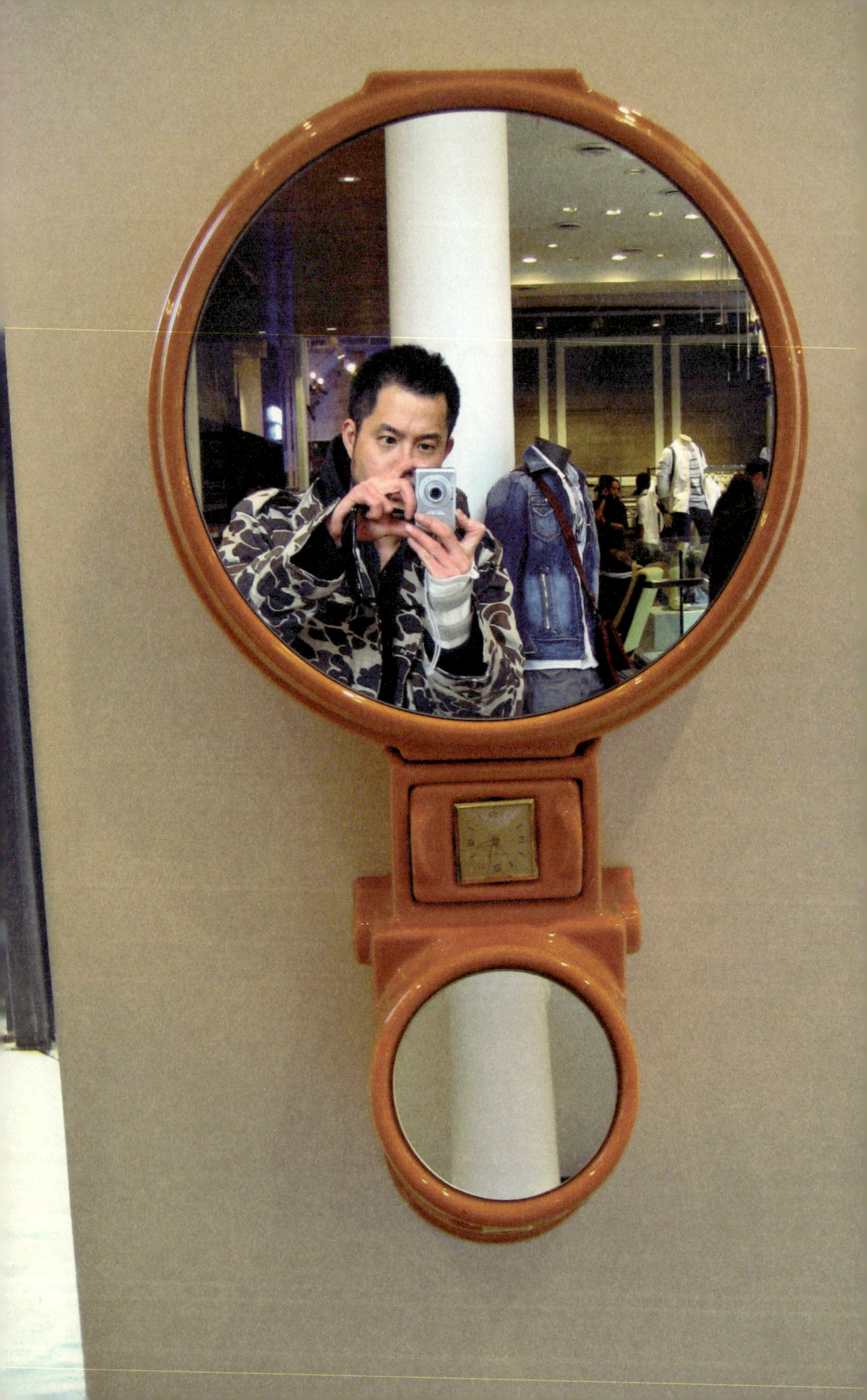

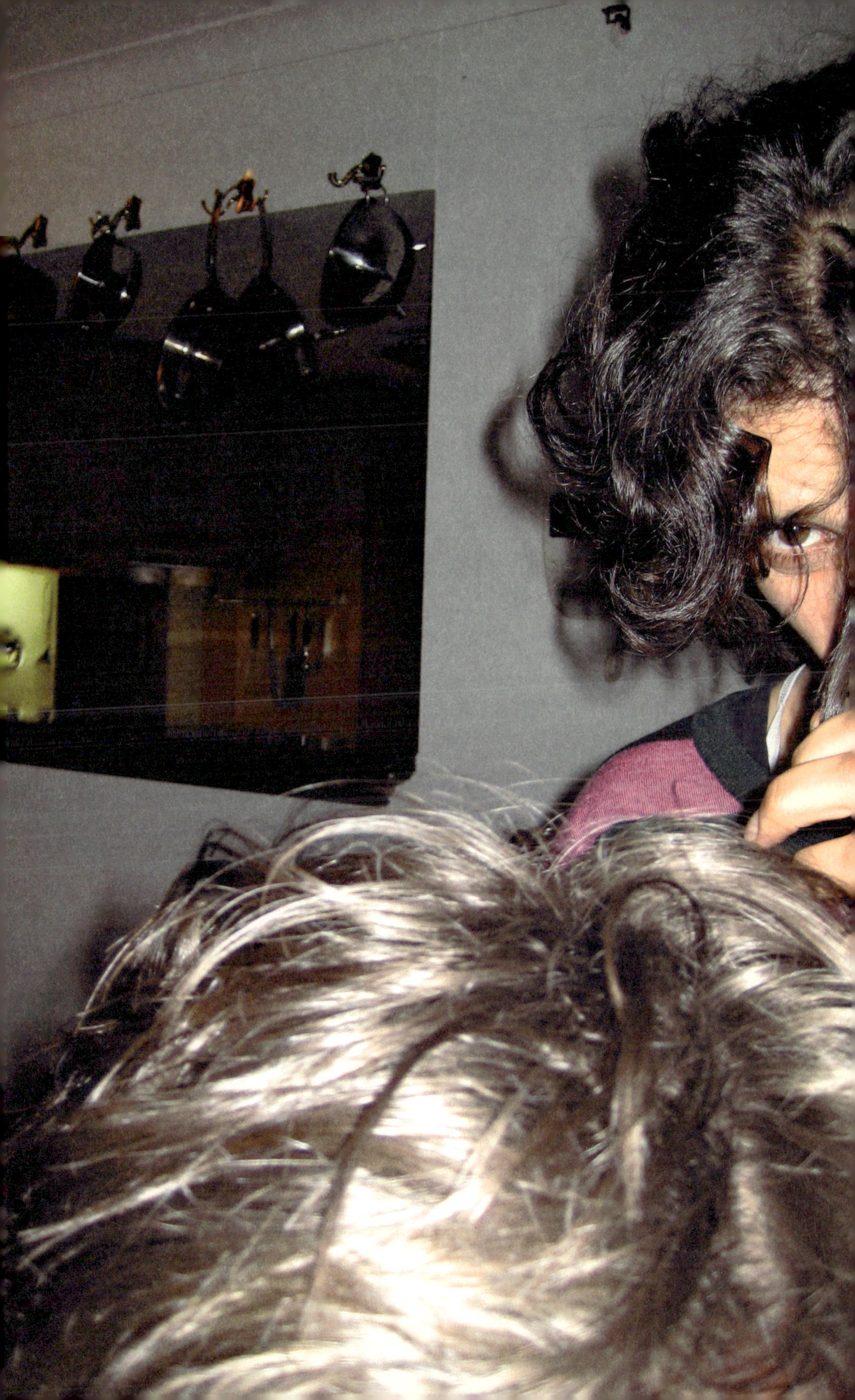

stuff I like is older anyway. Now and then there are a few new things I think are great. Then there are the things that I suddenly rediscover. There's no end to it. The life of an artwork lasts until it falls apart. Later, it can maybe still work as a photograph. Tatlin's tower, for example, can also work as a fantasy based on the photograph. I don't do anything new; I just do what was already there.

DK: But don't you want to contribute something to this society? Surely, you want to manifest yourself in some way, otherwise you just wouldn't do it, right?

UF: But you do that automatically.

DK: Yes, but *how* you do it, that's the decisive thing.

UF: You can't work if you're thinking, "It's about society and responsibility." You'd go mad.

DK. You don't have to take on such an explicit role.

UF: Something that interests me: you see work by somebody who's worked his or her whole life at something, and as an artist, your enemies are the other artists. (*Laughs.)* Then it's not about society at all. What interests me is as much...

DK: ... volume?

UF: Yes, volume, but also extension, where the issue is how much you can stuff into life before you die.

DK: But it's irrelevant whether it's an On Kawara method or a different one.

UF: Yes, that plays no role at all.

DK: Or Marcel Duchamp, who in *Etant Données...* does "nothing" for twenty years.

UF: Sure—but don't fool yourself. Duchamp probably worked more than anybody else. He had a very ascetic attitude. You see, that there's something in there. He did interviews until the end of his life, and still did not explain what he meant with all that stuff. People would even obsessively come up to him with interpretations and present them to him. But he'd just say, "A nice approach, interesting!" And nothing else. That's a total game, but a huge work that he did all his life. Doing "nothing," but he's someone who didn't stop. That's an ingenious work (*lights a cigarette*).

DK: And analogous to lifespan.

UF: It's exactly about that. And that's automatic, as long as you don't completely lose contact with your own interests. The work has a life of its own. You want to get out of it, but you just don't have the grit in a certain moment to do that, or perhaps you don't have the overview. But it's not important, it's more about going somewhere, so that you can do it better for yourself. It's not important what was there first. It's not about a great plan, but something else, its about a movement, in our lives as well, that can take on a total beauty: that all belongs to the game.

DK: Game? In what sense?

UF: That you're doing it! No one's so naïve as to not realize that it can also be a shit work, even if you work on it for an entire lifetime. But regardless. With play, I meant obsession. And play is something that you can expect or anticipate, you have movements in life on every level etc. Last Saturday, I was in a showroom where there were huge Warhol pictures, two Rorschach tests, and then some sculpture. The Warhol stuff's old, the sculpture new. Then you noticed: that's *competition!* You look at it, and think, wow! In part I didn't know what to do with it, but it simply had power.

DK: Where do you see yourself in relationship to this?

UF: I don't see myself in any kind of relation to it. That makes no sense.

DK: Okay, not in relation. Do you find this erotic, does it turn you on?

UF: Yes, that's hot, it generates lust, grit, generosity. It's simply cool.
DK: Do you mean material and size?
UF: No, not necessarily the size. The thing I saw was actually in a small room. Works by Carl André. There were really only a few...
DK: I know vaguely what you mean, but I want to hear more precisely... when you say...
UF: ... that it's hot? (*laughing quietly*)
DK: No, I can easily understand that kind of energy and interest. But you mentioned certain concepts, like *competition.*
UF: Yeah, that's more for me. That kind of thing energizes you. That's what I mean by competition, I don't mean something in the sense of, "I can do that, I do that too, just bigger." Instead, you feel that the "claim" of the artist is so aloof. And that drives you...
DK: ... that it manifests itself.
UF: Yes, that turns you on, your mouth starts watering...
DK: ... that it can exist at all.
UF: Precisely. The Warhol pictures, the Rorschach Tests, full of paint, that has such a power. It's not that some-one worked at it for three years, but really simply the desire to see it.
DK: At the same time, what these artist project are phantasms.
UF: That's also the beautiful thing about it. But it doesn't play out in a brief time frame; it's not just about a single thing, but the entire universe of these people. That interests me; that's when I get a kick.
DK: Do you get a "kick" when you go to the Cy Twombly Gallery in Houston? Or visit a Dan Flavin hall?
UF: Yes, that's fabulous. I believe in the work as a thing. Regardless of how it manifests itself.

DK: Let's return to the issue of criteria for a moment. The fundamental question of how to choose the criteria. Can you take that further?
UF: You can define the criteria beforehand, but it remains an organic process. You imagine something, and then it doesn't turn out that way. That's also the cool thing about it; it retains something important. If you define it, and do it exactly that way, then you industrialize it. That doesn't work. Unless you play exactly with this moment. But ultimately, in my view, the stuff does its own thing. Of course you control it, but you don't really know what it is.
DK: Does doubt come into play here?
UF: Sure, that's normal. (*Plays with a coin.*)
DK: There are elegant forms of doubt.
UF: Elegant?
DK: There are surely very different forms: some more elegant, more tattered, some that can be controlled.
UF: There are those that you know, and that's more like being a coquette with yourself.
DK: That's what I mean by elegant.
UF: And then there is real doubt.
DK: Tell me about it.
UF: It's not really at all about doubt, but about fear. In everything. When you're in doubt, who cares? But with fear that get's blown up, like everything else in life. You could then throw in frustration too.
(*Telephone rings in the background.*)
DK: Frustration, doubt, fear... Just four more then we have the seven virtues of artistic work.
UF: Sure, megalomania. What else is there?
DK: Vanity?
UF: Ambition.
DK: Is that a sin?
UF: I don't think so at all. It's a virtue!

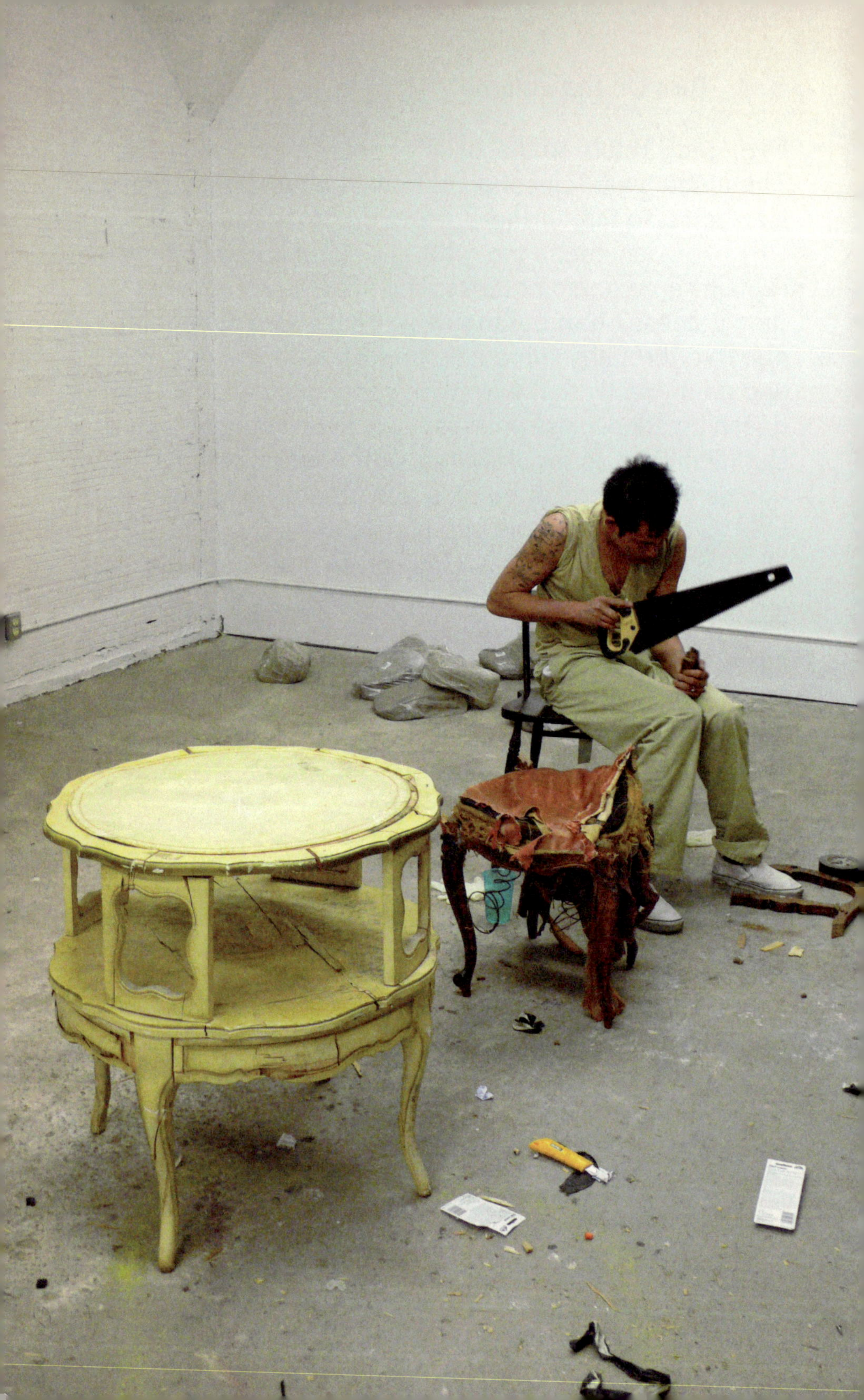

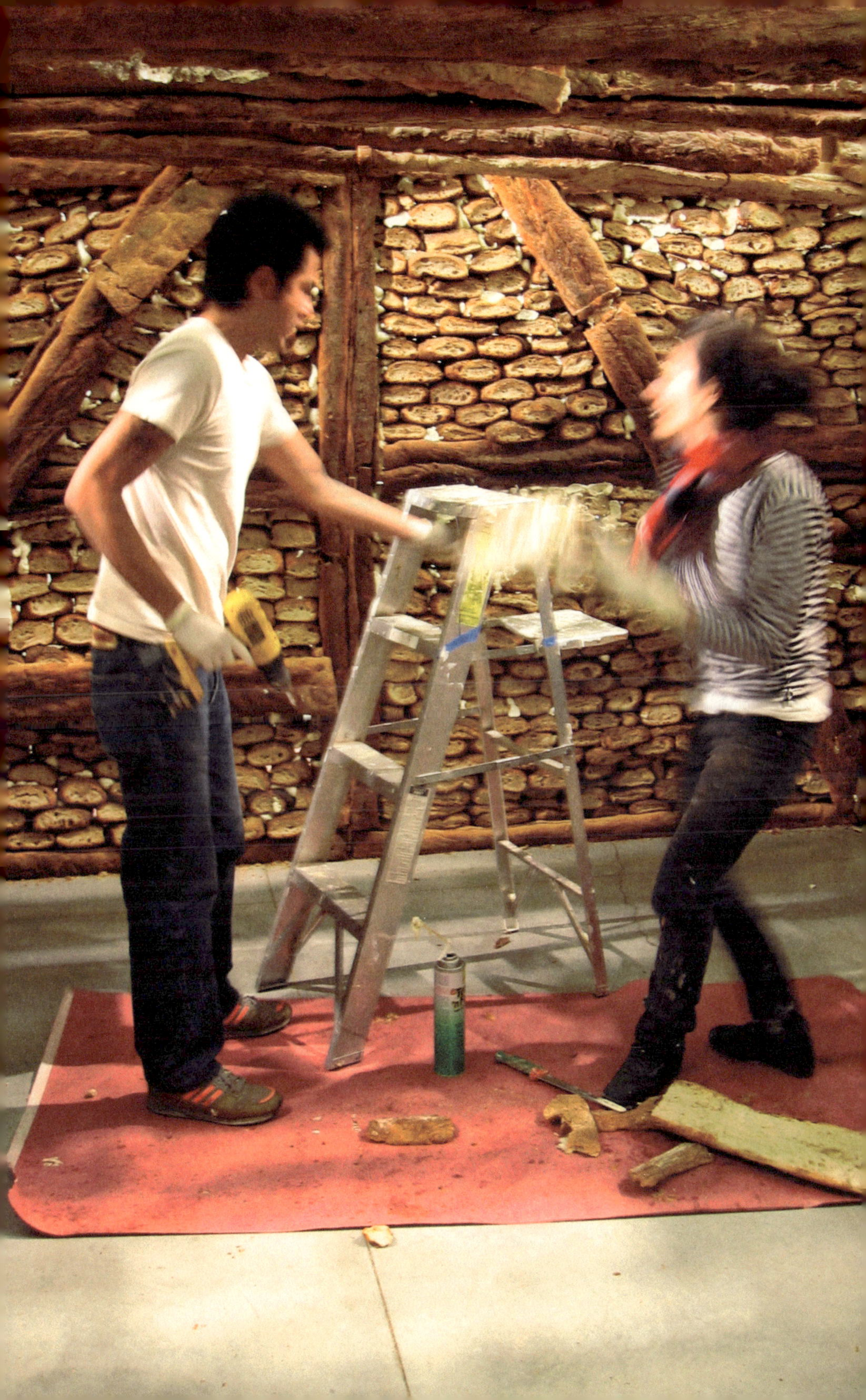

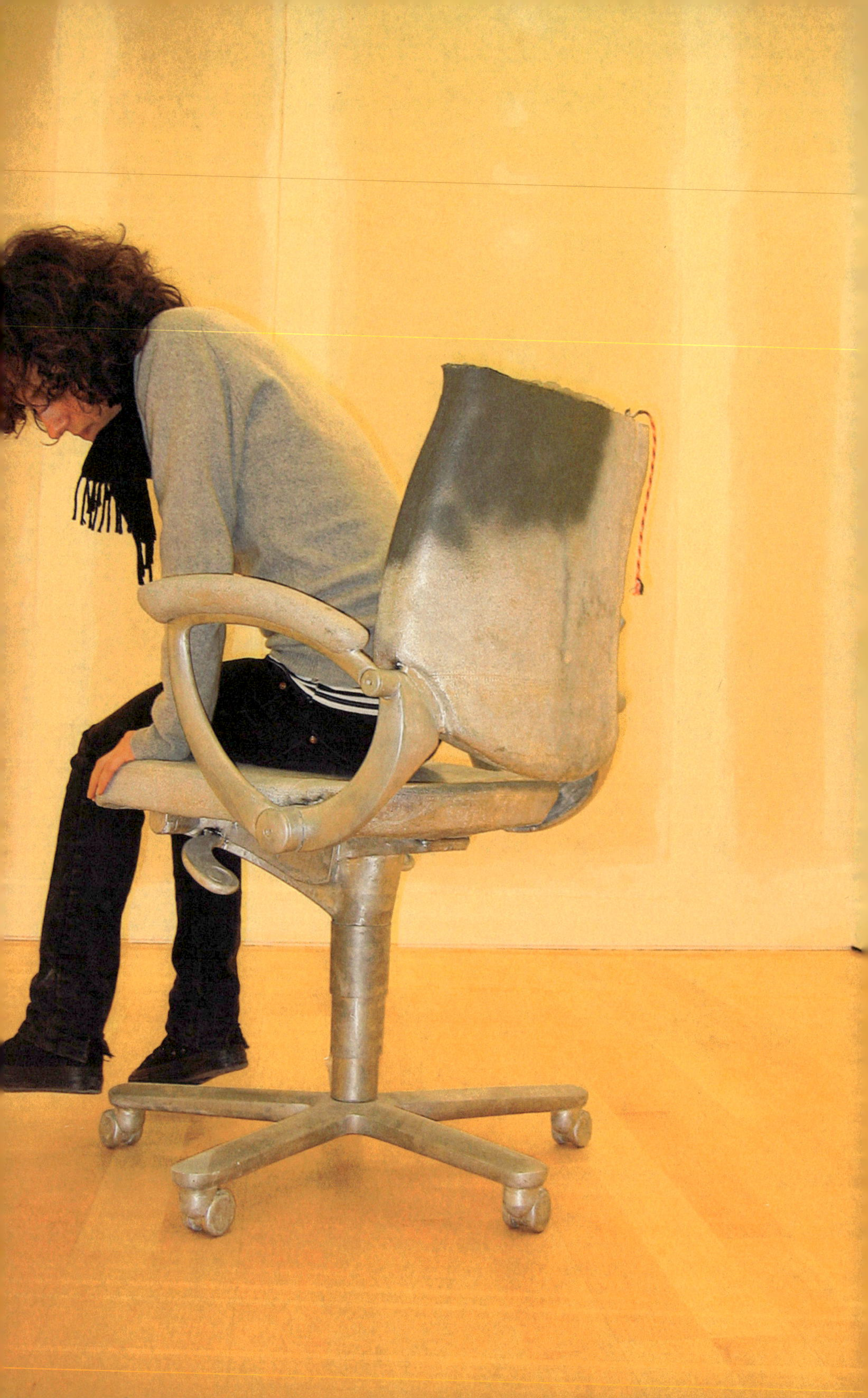

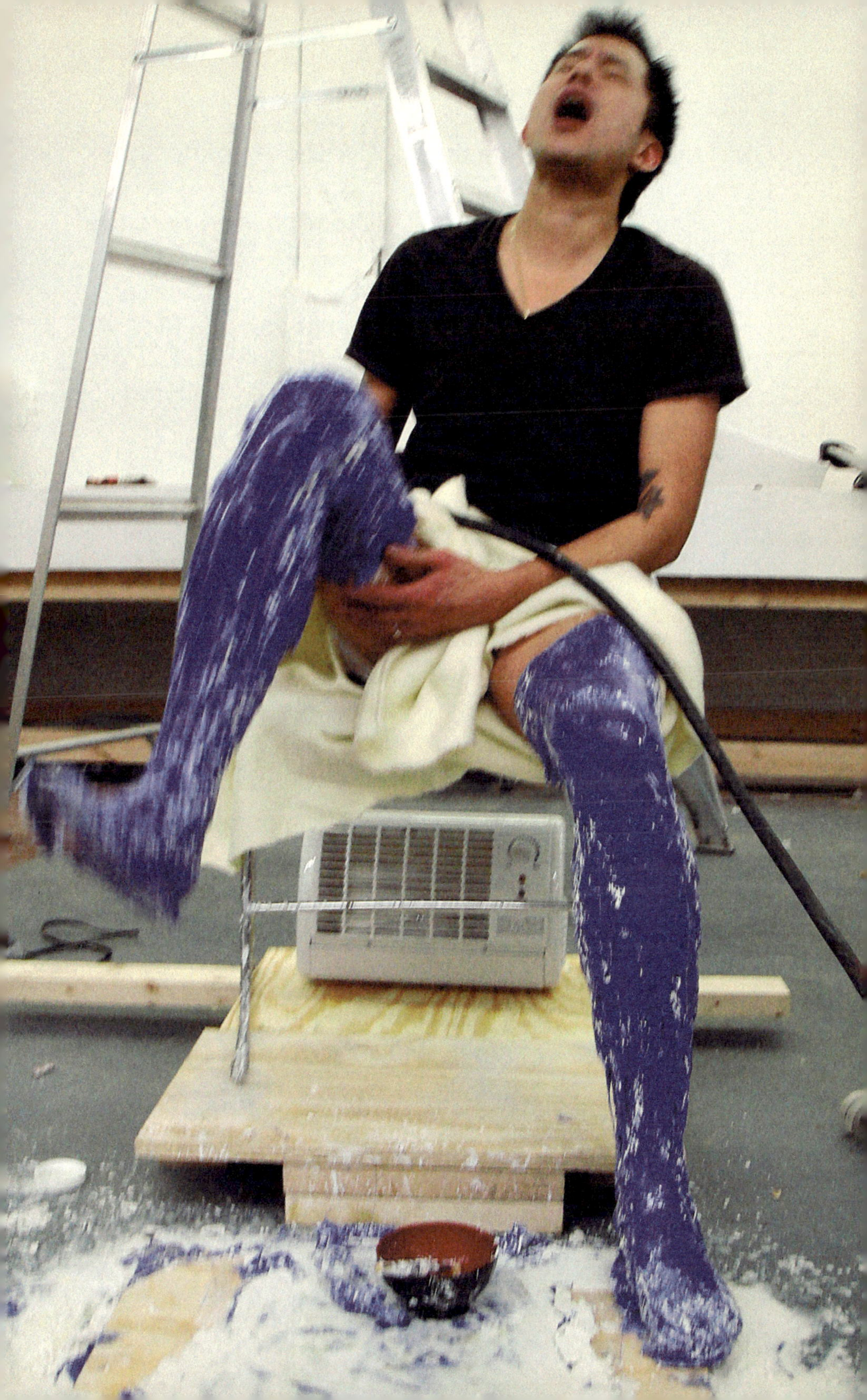

DK: Megalomania: the titanic. We spoke before about Dürrenmatt and Frisch...
UF: They're just figures that you peripherally perceive as a child...
DK: Now we have five virtues.
UF: Doubt's OK. Fear is more something that gets in your way. Fear is the foundation for everything. But you meet with a lot more artists than I do, you'd have to know that better than I.
DK: Is fear the motor?
UF: Fear is life's motor.
DK: Are fears individual, or does everyone have similar fears?
UF: Why are you asking me that? I only know my own, my girlfriend's, and my dog's.
DK: You know your dog's fears too? *(Laughs.)*
UF: Sure.
DK: But you need fear to work?
UF: You can approach it in different ways. You can let it out in a scream.
DK: Like Munch?
UF: Yes, or you can express it like hysteria, you can express it in the situation from which the fear comes, you can deal with it in all sorts of ways. It doesn't have to be the image of fear. You can create fear through a work. The work doesn't play out on just one level, not like in film. Communicating a mood in that way, that doesn't interest me either.
DK: Sure, but you're not interested in it on that level.
UF: I do think it's great if someone can do that. But it doesn't interest me. But for example the size of my works in Venice is important. It has to do with the fact that it's overwhelming. An overwhelming panel that devours the visual field, the field of what you can see, so that it

becomes truly physically present, without a background and foreground, a thing. A portal, that has aggression. Where it's about a confrontation with the work. It's about physical experience for someone standing before it. This level, it's not the scream that you express as an image. Richard Serra, that's material that crushes you or smothers you, like a castle wall.

DK: The images you just evoked are part of the standard iconography of human fear: monument, wall, portal, they're almost all archetypes.

UF: That's something one reacts to. It's about the fact that it's got to be massive for it to work at all, and not be an anecdote of a single moment. It needs a certain brutality, that's what interests me.

DK: Could that move towards catharsis? One is gripped by an experience. Where deeper moments that trigger feelings of fear, horror have a purifying effect.

UF: It's not reality, it's always about translation.

DK: Not even like in the theater?

UF: No. In principle, as far as art goes you have for all social memories your own collection in your head. You can summon that up, but you carry the mood along with you. If you've seen a photograph, where somebody told you something about it, then you engage with it less than with the moment. It's also about the afterward... Something where reality is displaced.

DK: Like a fantasy.

UF: Fantasy as image, sure.

DK: We spoke about what the work can be in the sense of extension, volume. Not the view of the single work, that is to be read or interpreted, but as a component within a movement. Do you think that fear is a compass for directing movement?

UF: No.

DK: Are you troubled by the discrepancy that can emerge between the reception of your work and the inner perspective? If at least from the outside a signature style becomes fixed?
UF: Not really. It's an outside observation. The observation from within is different. Stereotypes, style... that's all garbage. You could take any example, where you've been doing the same thing for twenty years, but really nobody gives a damn any more. Now, work is work. If it is something really important for you, than everything is acceptable. Thinking back is done all the time in different ways. There are certain things... as I did it, I found them crap, five years later I thought they were cool, now I think they're crap again. It's a constant changing relationship to the works. For me, that's strong, an extreme disinterest, I find it horrible to exhibit a work that I did a few years ago, a year ago, six months ago. Horrible. Sometimes you just let it be. With other things, you ask how you did it. Funny decisions.... You have to find a path, to constantly confront what you do. It's interesting when you confront yourself. The longer you do something, the more it forms you, and the less you redig the foundations. It's all predefined. Then there are these breaks in your biography that come from the inside or the outside. You try to renew yourself, but you will always have a residue from your past; mistakes that you don't reflect upon, or don't even notice. They come in part from your origin. I try—and this is condemned to failure—to look at that and be tougher about choosing approaches in the work.
DK: Toughness?
UF: I mean simply reduction. A formal reduction. Art-immanent things: figuration, form, etc. The approach to these questions interests me at the moment. In part it's

sculptures that are just a gesture, that work gesturally. The problem is, how do you materialize such a gesture? I'm interested in leaving things out when it comes to form. Going back to the question of fear, portal, these forms... they are not foundationless or founded upon just art-immanent issues. At issue here, so to speak, is not the word, but the gesture. Michelangelo, who stops in the middle sculpturally, that's also a gesture, that gives the stimulus. It simply gives a certain power to the things that interest me.

DK: Now we've come a long way from the seven virtues of being an artist. Two are still missing.

UF: Two are missing? That's just as it should be.

1996
Claudia Spinelli
Kunst-Bulletin

"The artist, born in Zurich in 1973, is one that stands in the midst of it all. His interest is not in larger contexts or global concepts, but he seems to take a position that takes equally seriously all that he encounters or comes to him and integrates it without valuation or hierarchy in his work. [...] The self-evidence with which Fischer operates with the found, the new, and his own material and the conscious refusal of simplicity are quite impressive. A great deal seems exorbitant, sometimes playful or ironic—and quite believable for precisely that reason. Here an artist has started off without fear."

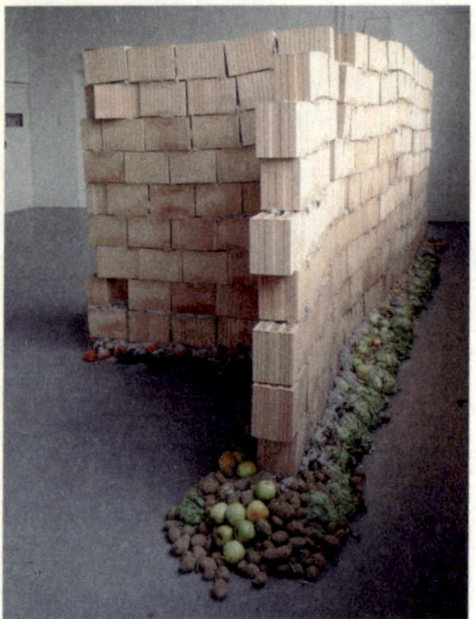

Faules Fundament, 1998

1999
Anna Helwing
Kunst-Bulletin

"An engagement with contemporary art is one thing, the other is a connection to art history. Fischer still holds on to painting and sculpture: within these realms he uses traditional genres and motifs over and over as models. If his drawings are often based on portraits, nudes, or landscapes, in his often installative objects and sculptures, in contrast, we can recognize still-lifes and interiors."

2000
Beatrix Ruf
Time Waste: Radio-Cookie

"Trained as a photographer Urs Fischer works primarily in the classic artistic media of drawing, sculpture, and painting; occasionally he uses photography or also film. He uses all possible ordinary materials as well as materials traditionally associated with art. His works are not characterized by a signature-creating artistic trademark (which would allow him to be categorized easily), but rather by an 'attitude' which expresses itself in a process-related dialogue with the media and the materials (and by which his works can be recognized). This 'attitude' allows him to question the structures and systems, relations, constellations, and operational mechanisms of both art and of the 'world' in a manner that is 'styleless' and permanently in motion. Urs Fischer integrates his creations, which are presented as dense installations and ensembles, into a complex domain of individually and socially relevant fields of experience. The encounters he creates with objects and images are altered in their mood, but are not charged with an aura."

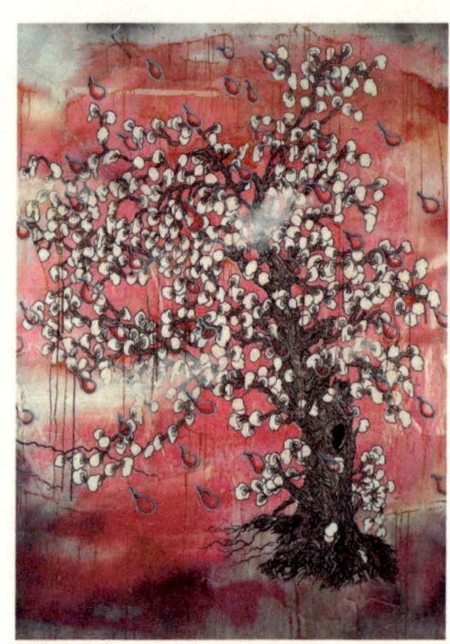

Baum, 2002

2002
Nicolas Siepen
Frankfurter Allgemeine Zeitung

"His installations, which often fill an entire room, no longer show that Urs Fischer originally comes from photography. At the same time, he operates throughout with realist signs, immediately recognizable, but here they have been displaced in their impact. In so doing, the artist uses very different techniques that sometimes move towards the surreal, sometimes becoming dream-like alienations, sometimes expressive."

2002
Kirsty Bell
Frieze

"Fischer's subject matter is random, incidental and handled with the same grab-and-run approach as his materials. The momentum of his production [...] demands a similar agility of reception, the point being not so much narration, form or nostalgia in themselves but rather the elusive and circular process of transformation in which idea confronts material and object confronts idea."

2003
Alison Gingeras
Artforum International

"He is able to produce a complex ecosystem of extremes—beauty and ugliness; process and completion; delicacy and brutality; 'poignant emotion' and wicked humor—all with an uncommon formal and narrative economy. This frugality is not a simple revisiting of *arte povera's* ideologies of shabby materiality, poetic significance, and political gravity; eschewing any dogmatic vision of the world of artmaking, Fisher contrives, adopts, and appropriates the formal and conceptual strategies necessary to flush out the banal, contradictory, and oft overlooked details of life and art."

2004
Daniel Binswanger
Weltwoche

"Fischer is well-known for his lackadaisical-roguish irony, for his intelligent, loose humor, with which he ably forms all sorts of material into massive installations and sculptures, or fans out poetic multiples with fast drawings and fine scribbles."

2004
Brigitte Ulmer
Bolero Men

"Fischer's strategy is basically also subversion. That the establishment embraces rebels has been part of the art business ever since art was released from the power of the church and kings."

2004
Giovanni Carmine/Urs Fischer
Flash Art

"'I admire poets and musicians. They only need limited material qualities to arrive at an expressive form. They can work more directly. That would suit me. I often try to work like that, on the spot, including the surroundings, as if it were 'live'. But it usually degenerates into a time debacle. It seems to be getting worse and worse. One way out would be to make it part of the work, but that doesn't interest me particularly. [...] I use a lot of materials because I'm lazy and short of time. You can make something of them immediately, without having to tie up a huge amount of time or other people. But that doesn't mean they have the material quality I'm looking for.'"

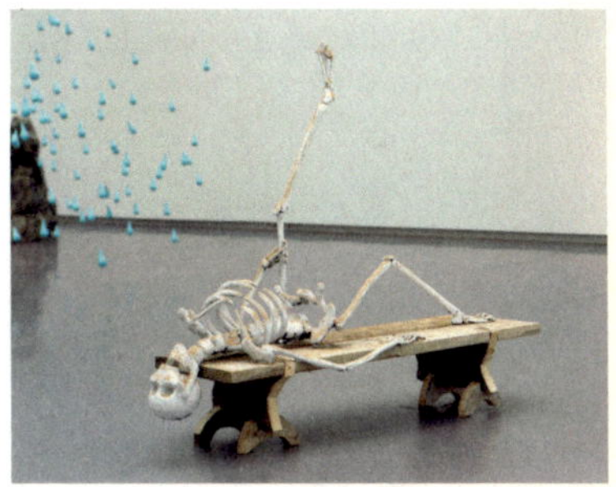

Kuckuck Backwards, 2004

2004
Alison Gingeras
Espace 315

"Urs Fischer's radicality comes from a paradoxically classical source—his on-going engagement with a specific genre of art history. From his earliest works, he has built his practice primarily on a dialogue with the still life, or as it is more appropriately termed in French, *nature morte*. In fact, sculptural vignettes of 'dead nature' are often literally enacted through Fischer's recurring use of real fruits and vegetables, as well as in the arrangement of furniture that recall the backdrops of such genre paintings. Fischer has liberated the still life from a long history of academic painting, giving the moribund genre new vitality in three-dimensional form. These pieces most explicitely illustrate Fischer's interest in transforming that bourgeois genre into a metaphorical vehicle for the exploration of base human condition. These decaying fruits stand in for Fischer's own worldview, one that oscillates between self-indulgent passivity and pragmatic action. The humble poetry of his titles—*Routine: Automatic Melancholy; The Trick is to Keep Breathing; Eternal Soup of the Day*—confirms Fischer's grounding in the most banal aspects of quotidian existence."

2004
Beatrix Ruf
Parkett

"Fischer's works are not only shapes and images but also narratives of encounters with collective agreement on the reality of individual worlds of experience; they therefore also embody the metamorphosis of the known into the uncanny, the weird, and the surreal. However, as shown explicitly by his recurring skeletons, they are also *vanitas* images, which embroil the vulnerability of material forms of appearance in a contemporary and above all demythologizing discourse with our concepts."

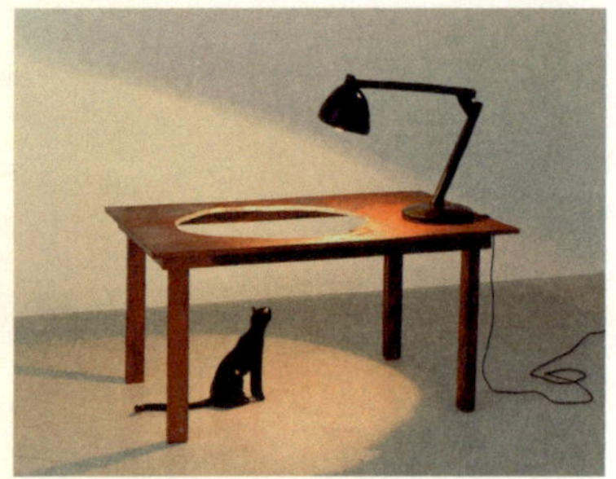

Daylight Pillow, 2004

2004
Jörg Heiser
Kir Royal

"For Urs Fischer, studios are no more and no less than temporary working spaces, rented for a limited period, where material is produced with a view to specific exhibition projects. This bypasses the tired critique of the myth of a romanticized, authentic locus of inspiration, with the studio becoming a constantly available mobile volume of production and waste—right down to plasterboard partition walls that he uses as giant pinboards for specific projects. And he confronts the tired utopia of 'post-studio' production, of elegant withdrawal from the spatio-physical limitations of the studio, with a shifting of backdrops that reveals the latent theatricality of artistic creation via an openly theatrical approach."

2004
Mirjam Varadinis
Kir Royal

"Fischer plays with a wide variety of divergent formal and conceptual strategies, only to instantly jettison the associations that automatically arise. He consciously undermines expectations and extends his process-orientated approach to the simultaneous incorporation of various styles. Whatever the thought that surfaces, it is not characterized by unity but by plurality."

2004
Claudia Spinelli
Weltwoche

"Consumer culture—an echo of Beate Uhse, rock romanticism, and Hollywood—mixes in Fischer's work with high culture—Bruce Nauman, Gordon Matta-Clark, or Claes Oldenburg. With no consideration for hierarchy, value, or lack of value, these visual creations flow from him easily, and apparently innocently."

2004
Stefan Zweifel
Frankfurter Allgemeine Zeitung

"All this trash—ashes and dust, wood and metal splinters, but also quotations from art history—arrange to form a narrative current. The abject, since it became canonic through George Bataille's theory on the 'big toe' and the 'formless' through the studies of Rosalind Krauss or Georges Didi-Huberman, is a directionless undercurrent here and held wondrously together by the signature of one and the same art subject named Urs Fischer. [...] Urs Fischer surfaced as suddenly as the Surtsey Islands off Iceland that Dieter Roth captured for all eternity with transitory materials. Before he was a doorman at the Zurich high-end disco Kaufleuten, now he can open the doors to the museum, in the meantime he stood at Dieter Roth's last Zurich bar. From Roth he not only takes the tendency to use all sorts of materials, adding polyurethane foam, fiberglass, and so much more, but also the almost daily production of visual ideas. For that's precisely what he is: a volcanic island that hopefully will not erode in the foamy surf of the market and sink. The danger is real, but Fischer's resistance seems great. Not least because he moves in a fixed circle of faithful helpers."

2004
Tom Morton
Frieze

"To domesticate something is to defuse its wildness, making it safe, livable-with. Walt Disney famously did this with animals (think of the difference between a mouse scurrying across your kitchen floor and the white-gloved, kid-hugging Mickey), and it's useful to compare the animator's work with the way Fischer, who often riffs on cartoon aesthetics, un-domesticates that which has been domesticated, whether it be bourgeois implements and the social practices they imply, exhausted images from myth, or icons of modern art."

2004
Paul Ardenne
Art Press

"Once again, here classical references (portrait, landscape, still life) are put through the blender in a reading that is as far as could be from the obvious reading (pretend naivety, offbeat quotes, etc.). Clearly, then, coolness, the distancing of pathos and the disappearance of the author are even less on the agenda than ever. The artwork? An analogue to a psychological object. Art? Therapy. The vein this artist mines is at least as expressionist and vitalist as it is critical."

2005
Sue Hubbard
The Independent

"Fischer is a sculptor, one who has taken the Duchampian notion of the ready-made and stood it on its head. For, whereas Duchamp presented a real urinal to a shocked world and called it art, Fischer casts everyday objects, such as a broom or a revolving office chair, in aluminium and paints them so that they look just like the real object—except that they have been rendered impotent, divorced from their function and purpose by being turned into art."

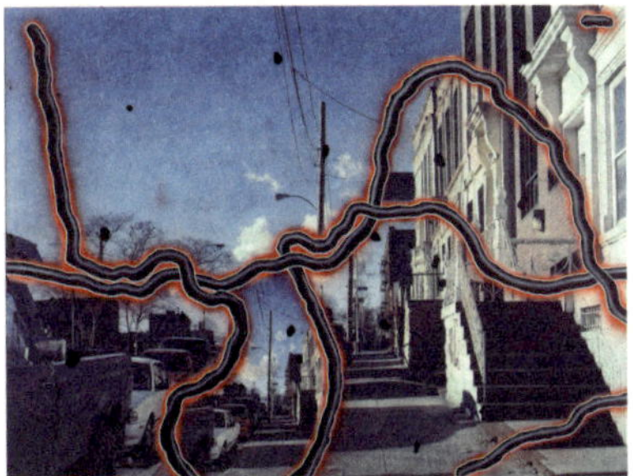

A Novel and It's Novelist, 2005

2005
Roberta Smith
The New York Times

"Set on a large patch of Oriental carpets, 'Bread House,' [...], was definitely startling. It inserted a slightly barbed bit of Old World sentimentality, wholesomeness and craft into the pristine confines of the art gallery; Heidi's grandfather lived here. [...] The perky tribute to tradition has become a half-ruin in a crunchy desert, a monument to ephemeralness and artistic license, and a disruption of business-as-usual in the art world. After all, even though it is made of the stuff of life, 'Bread House,' in the parlance of the 1960's, is also made of money, as in 'dough' or 'bread'."

2005
Nicola Kuhn
Tagesspiegel

"In Urs Fischer, things are turned inside out: nothing is ever the way it should be. What appears at first sophisticated, his multi-layered drawings, his puzzling verse, [...] that overgrows the pictures and sculptures, can seem banal in the very next moment. And the other way around."

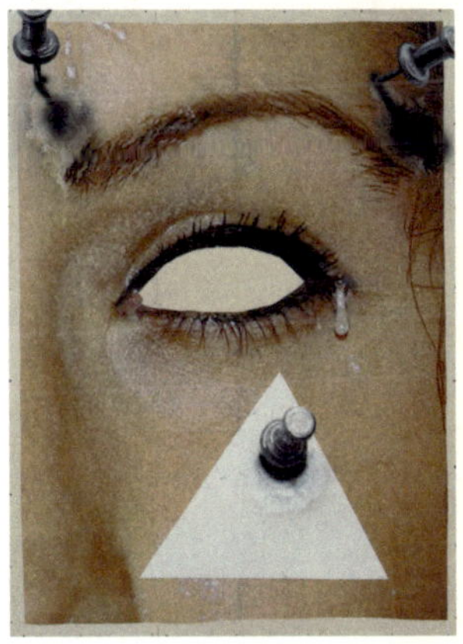

Office Theme/Addiction/ Mhh Camera, 2006

2006
Beatrix Ruf
The Vincent van Gogh Biennial Award

"In Urs Fischer's case, however, the presence of faux-pas of depiction, narratives and the conventional models of artistic expressive possibilities results in a breaking free of the compromises that the history of art and of the visual media as a whole can impose on artistic activity. Urs Fischer is not interested in superficial beautifications, aesthetic ideas or a classical canon of expressive possibilities, which enables him adroitly to prevent artistic control from imposing style and intention as a comparative reading in his objects, sculptures, installations, paintings, drawings and collages. Likewise, he shows that finding meaning in the artwork is a trap for our interpretations; he converts all this into an openness vis-à-vis the objects of his art and to our experiences, most secret imaginations and so-called lives."

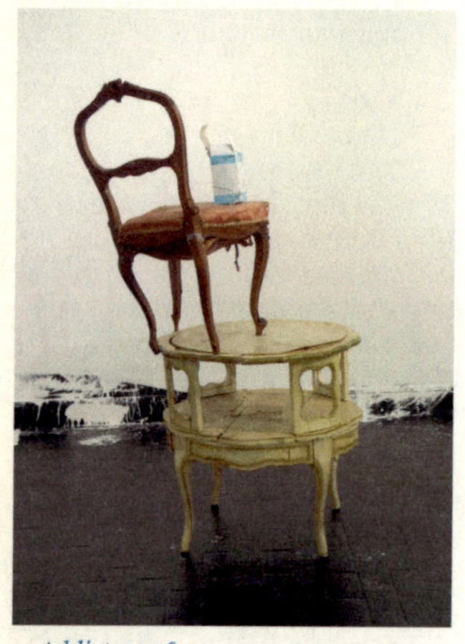

Addict, 2006

2006
Claudia Schmuckli
Mary Poppins

"Allusions to popular myths, fairy tales, and science fiction provide temporary excursions into the parallel worlds of fantasy and magic that Fischer likes to invoke to remind us that any notion of reality is relative and that the extraordinary—the surreal as well as the uncanny—is all around us. Drawing freely from a multiplicity of sources without regard for tradition and hierarchy, his work effortlessly combines elements of high, mainstream, and underground cultures in a convincing demonstration of how irrelevant such categorizations have become. Fischer's work, oscillating between rawness and tenderness, all-too-knowing experience and willful innocence, evokes an existence ruled by extremes that deftly balances humor and tragedy, delicacy and brutality, complexity and banality, to create poignant vignettes of everyday life."

Further reading

Urs Fischer—Time Waste: Radio-Cookie und kaum Zeit, kaum Rat, exhibition catalog, Kunsthaus Glarus, ed. Beatrix Ruf, Zurich: Edition Unikate, 2000.

Urs Fischer—Kir Royal, exhibition catalog, Kunsthaus Zürich, Zurich: JRP | Ringier, 2004.

Urs Fischer—Espace 315, création contemporaine et prospective, livre numéro 2, exhibition catalog, Musée national d'art moderne du Centre Georges Pompidou, Paris, ed. Françoise Bertaux, Paris: Éditions du Centre Pompidou, 2004.

Urs Fischer—Mary Poppins, exhibition catalog, Blaffer Gallery, the Art Museum of the University of Houston, Houston: Blaffer Gallery, 2006.

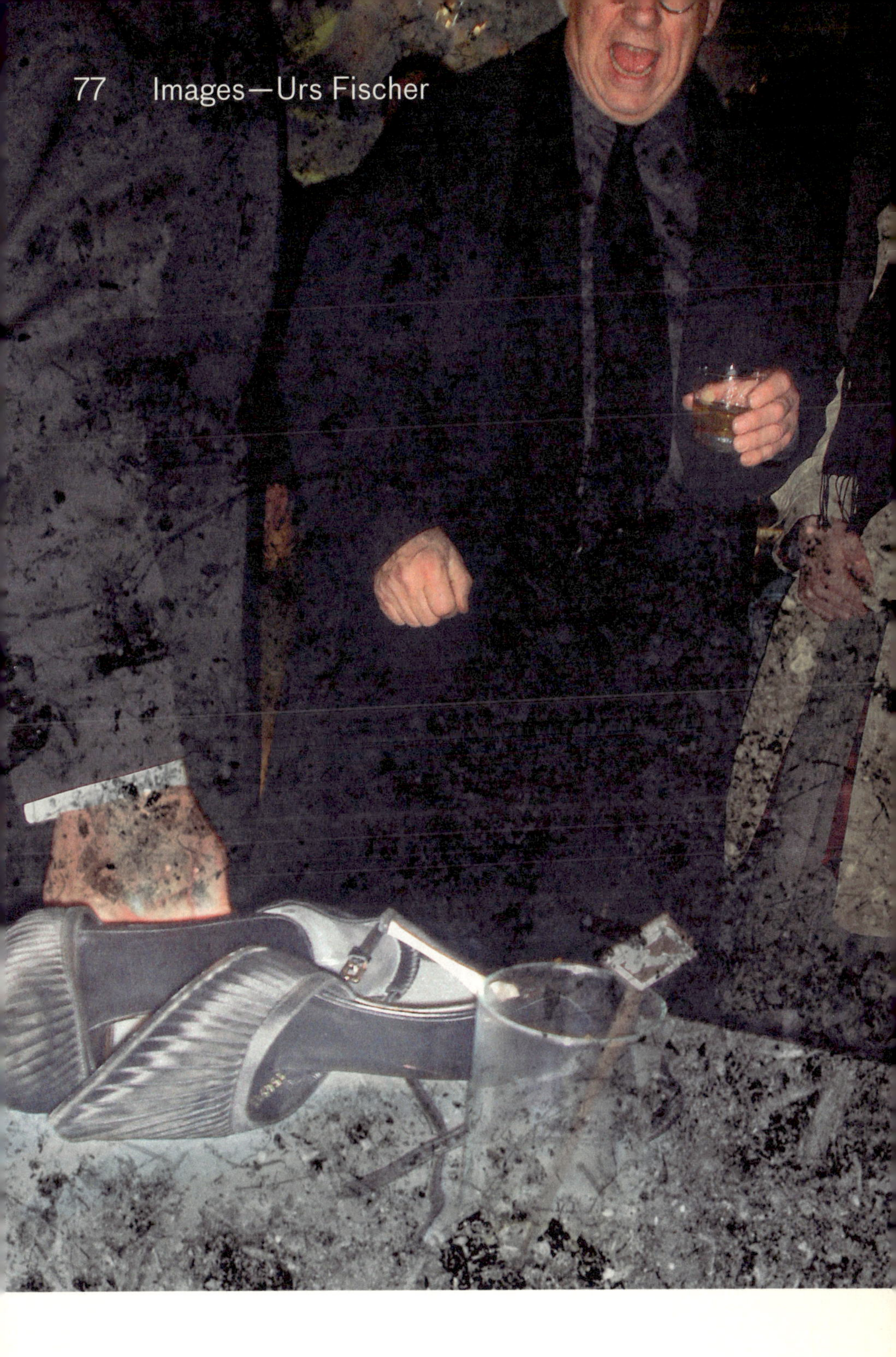

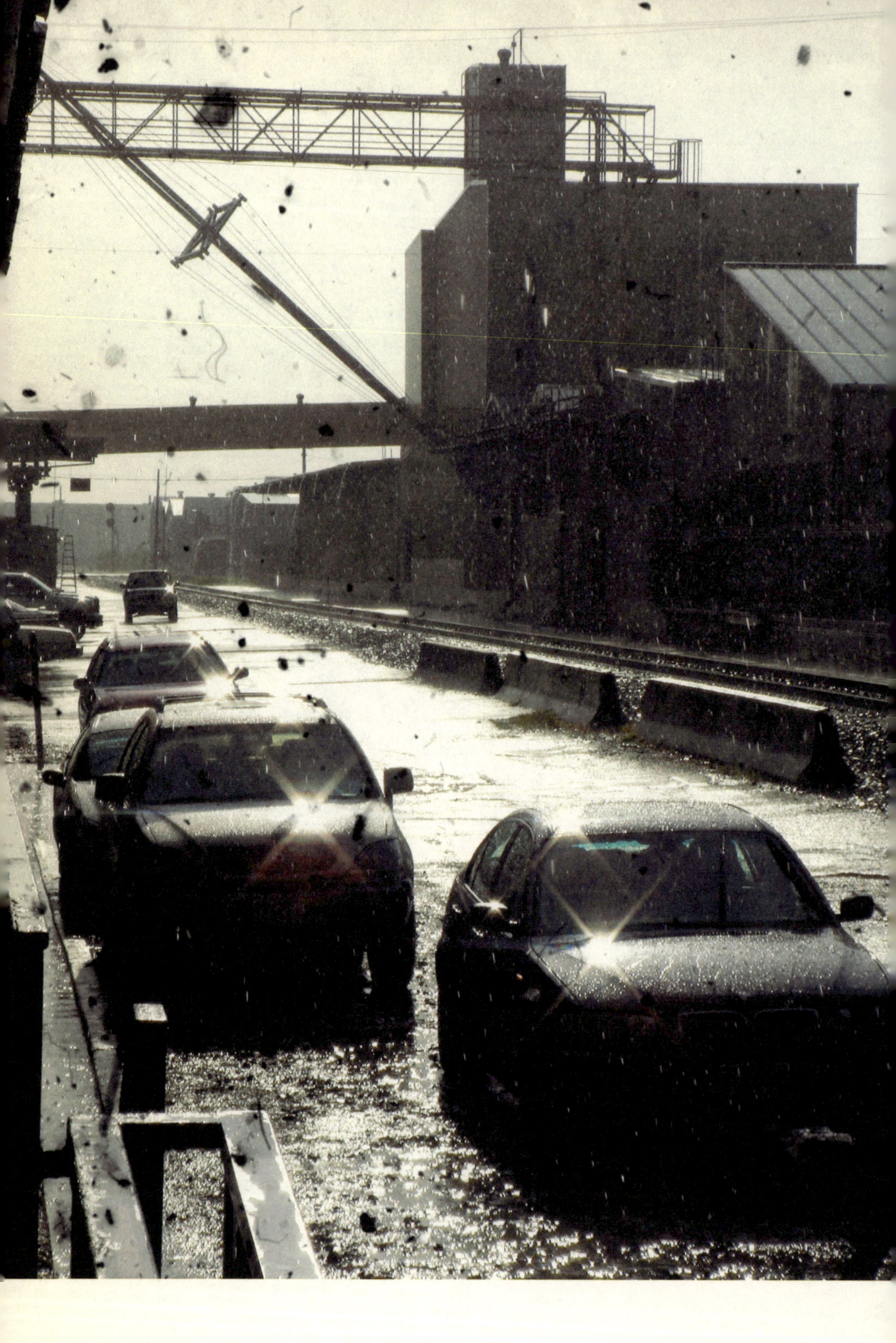

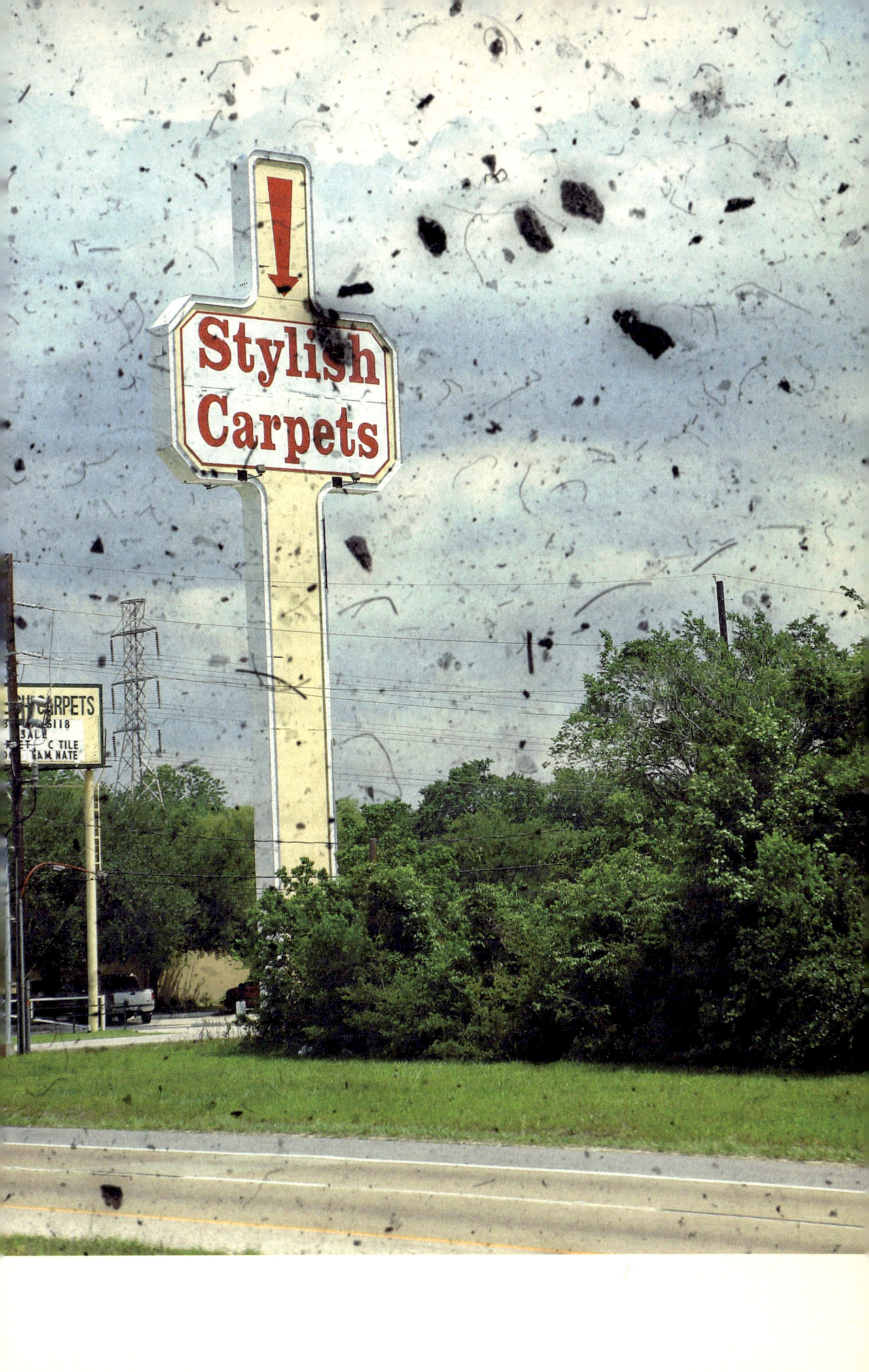
Stylish
Carpets
CARPETS

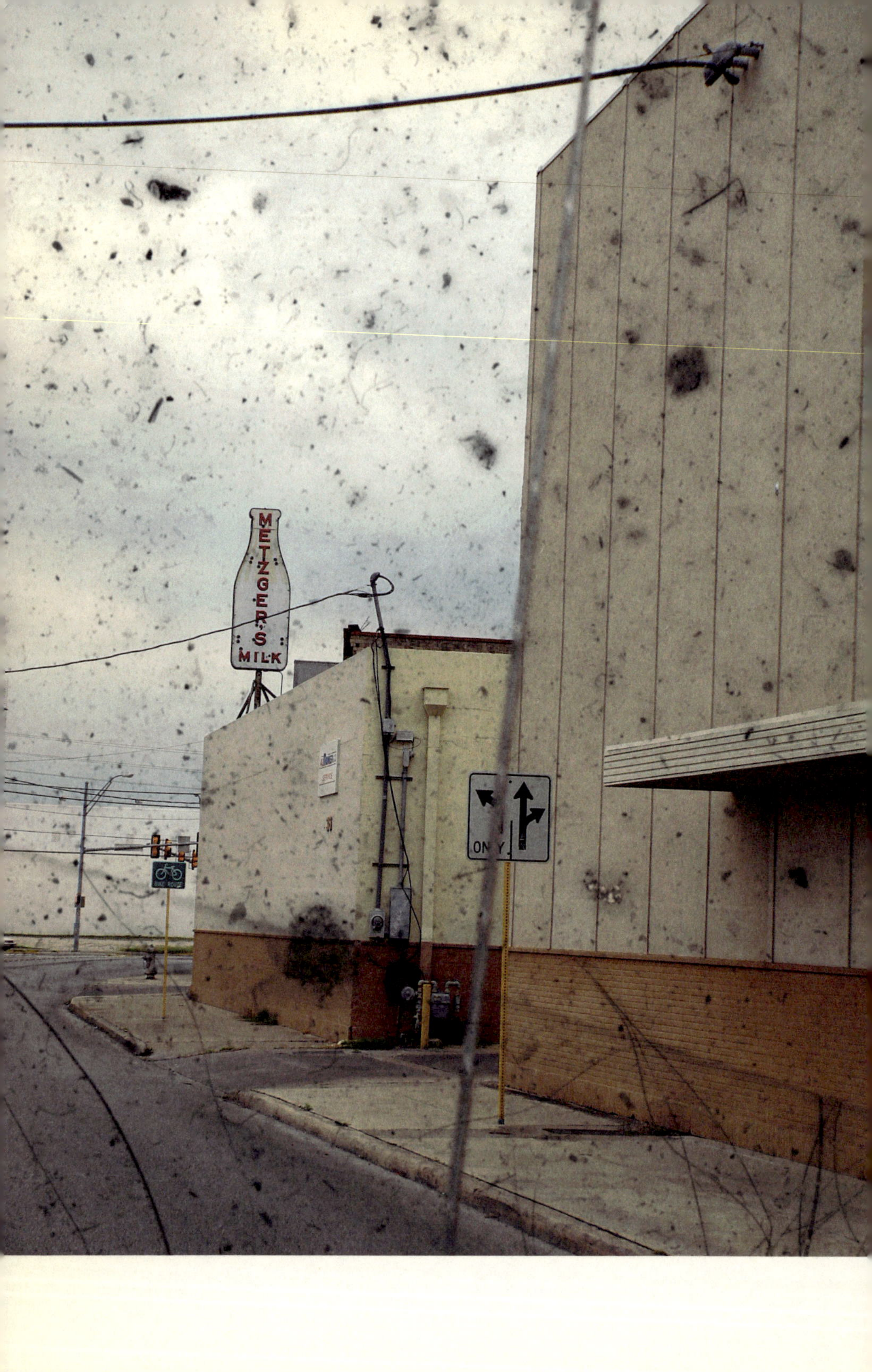
METZGER'S
MILK
ONLY

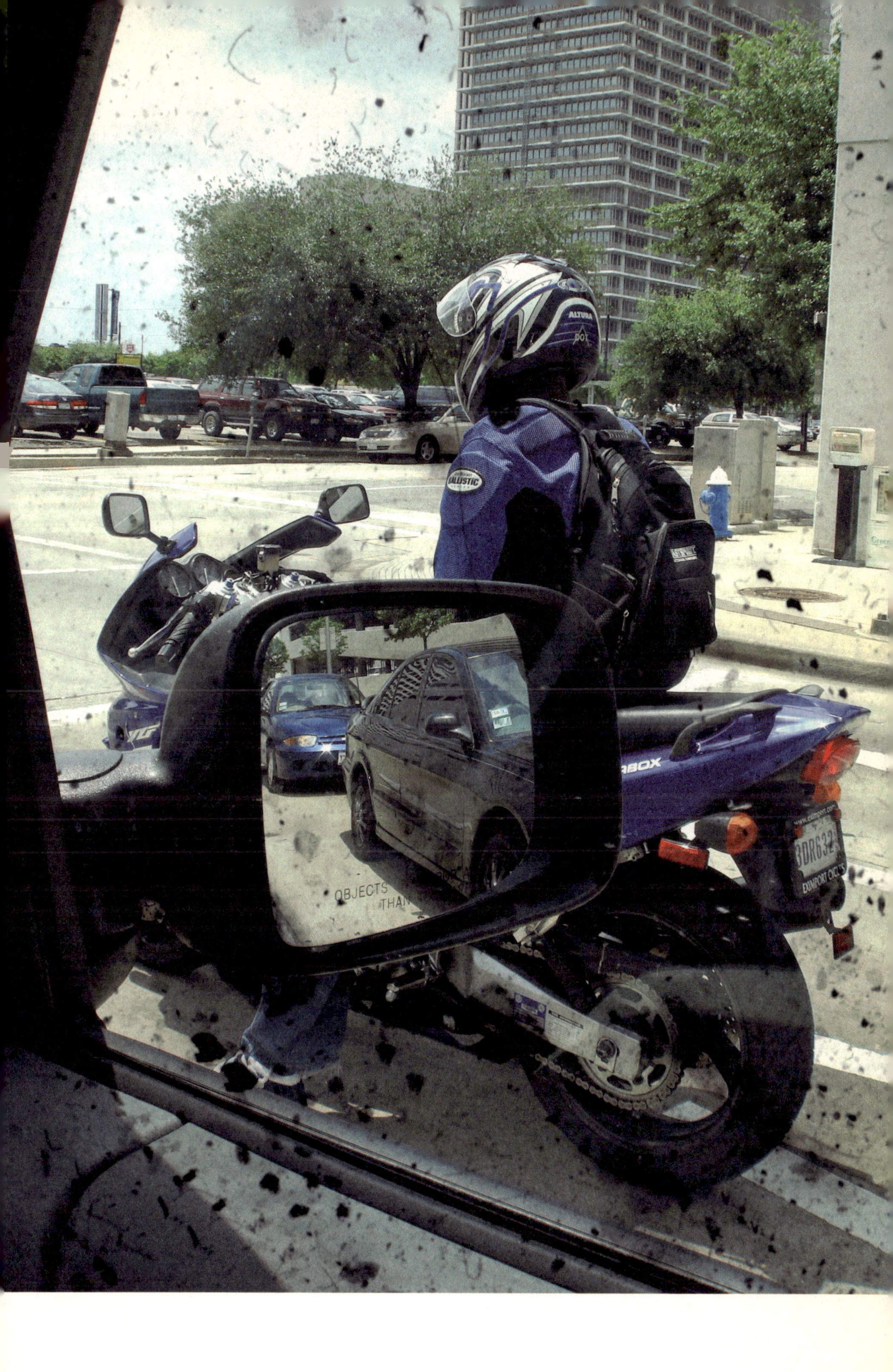
ALTURA
BALLISTIC
OBJECTS
THAN
RBOX

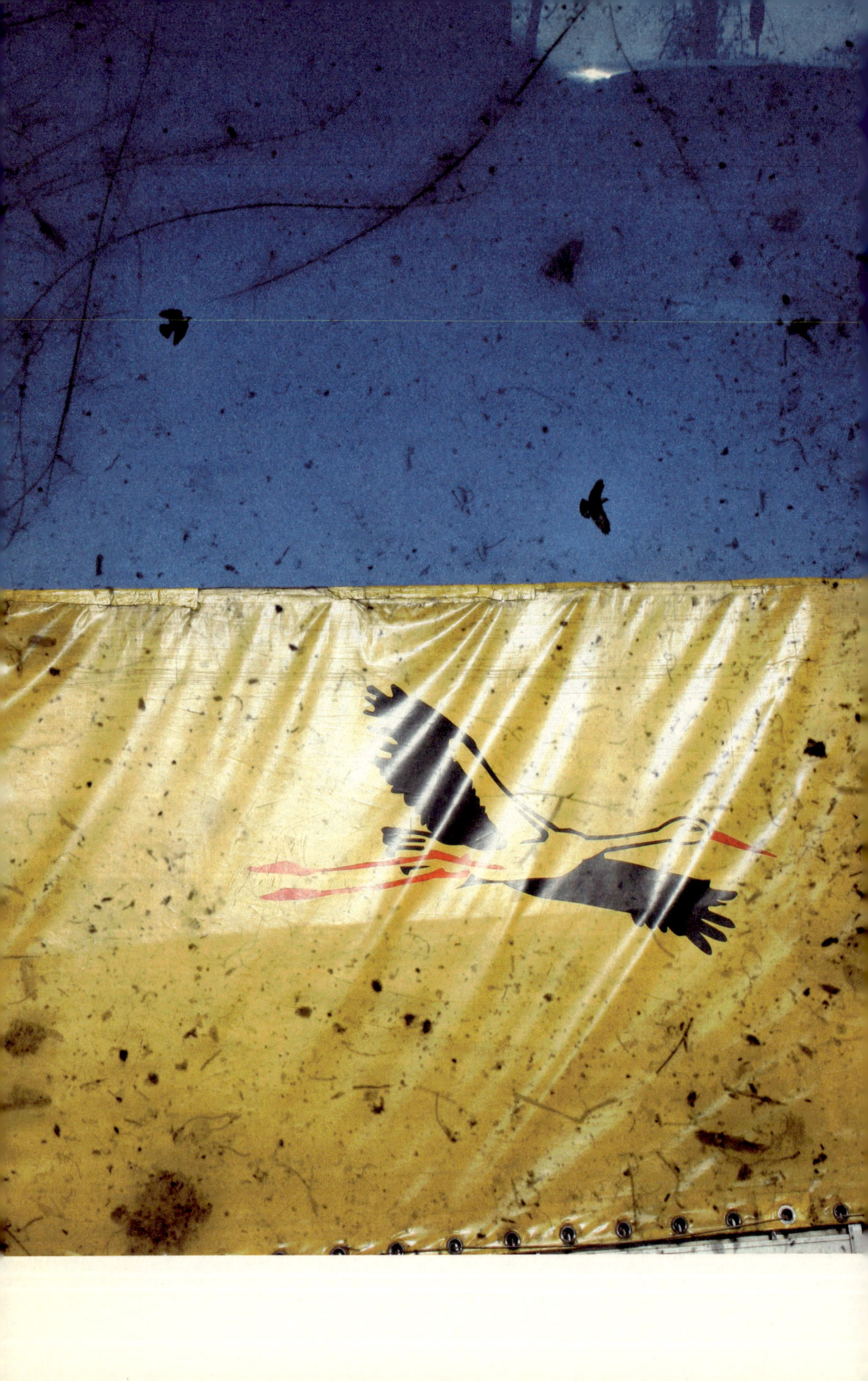

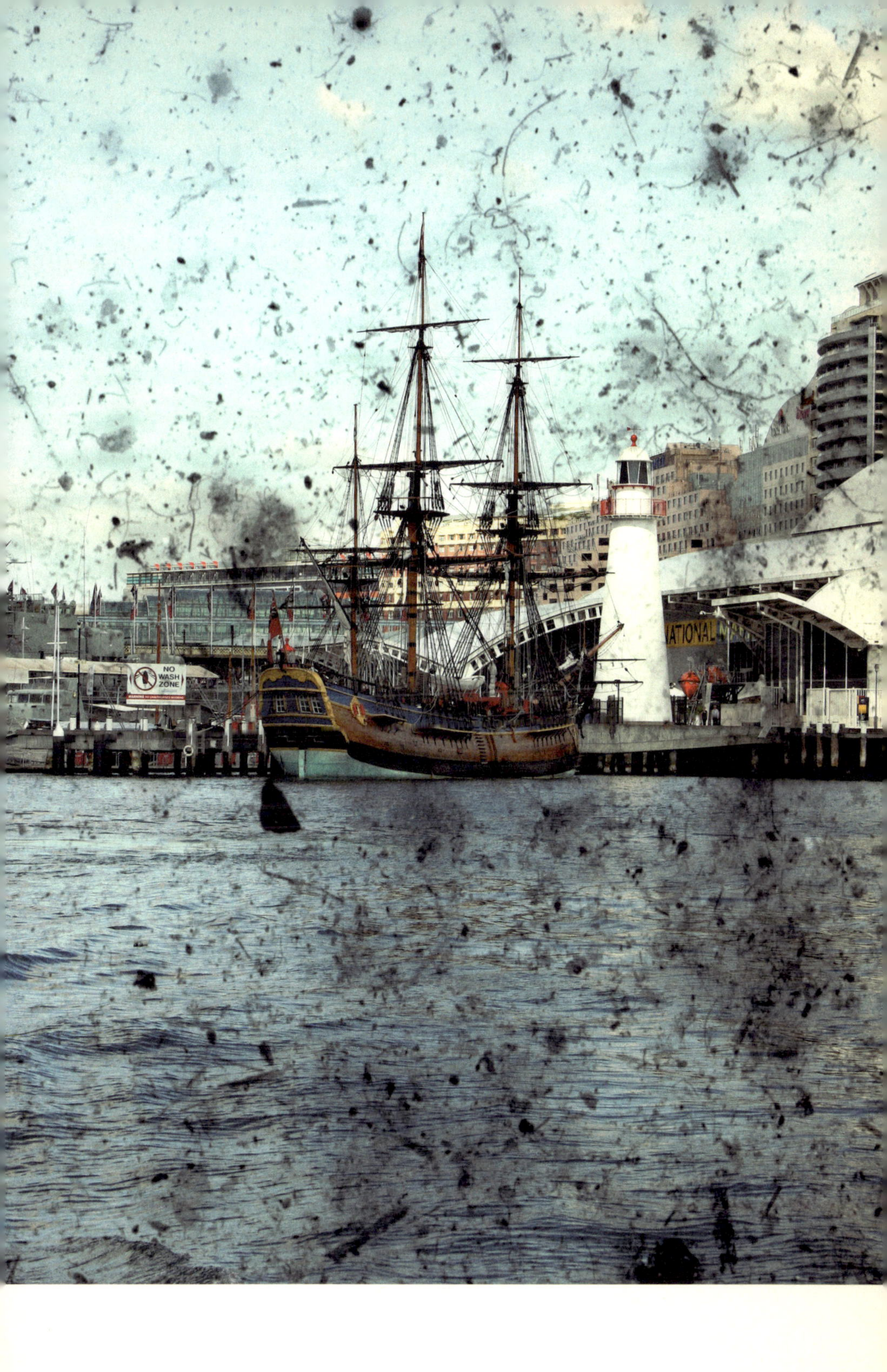
NO
WASH
ZONE
NATIONAL

11FL05

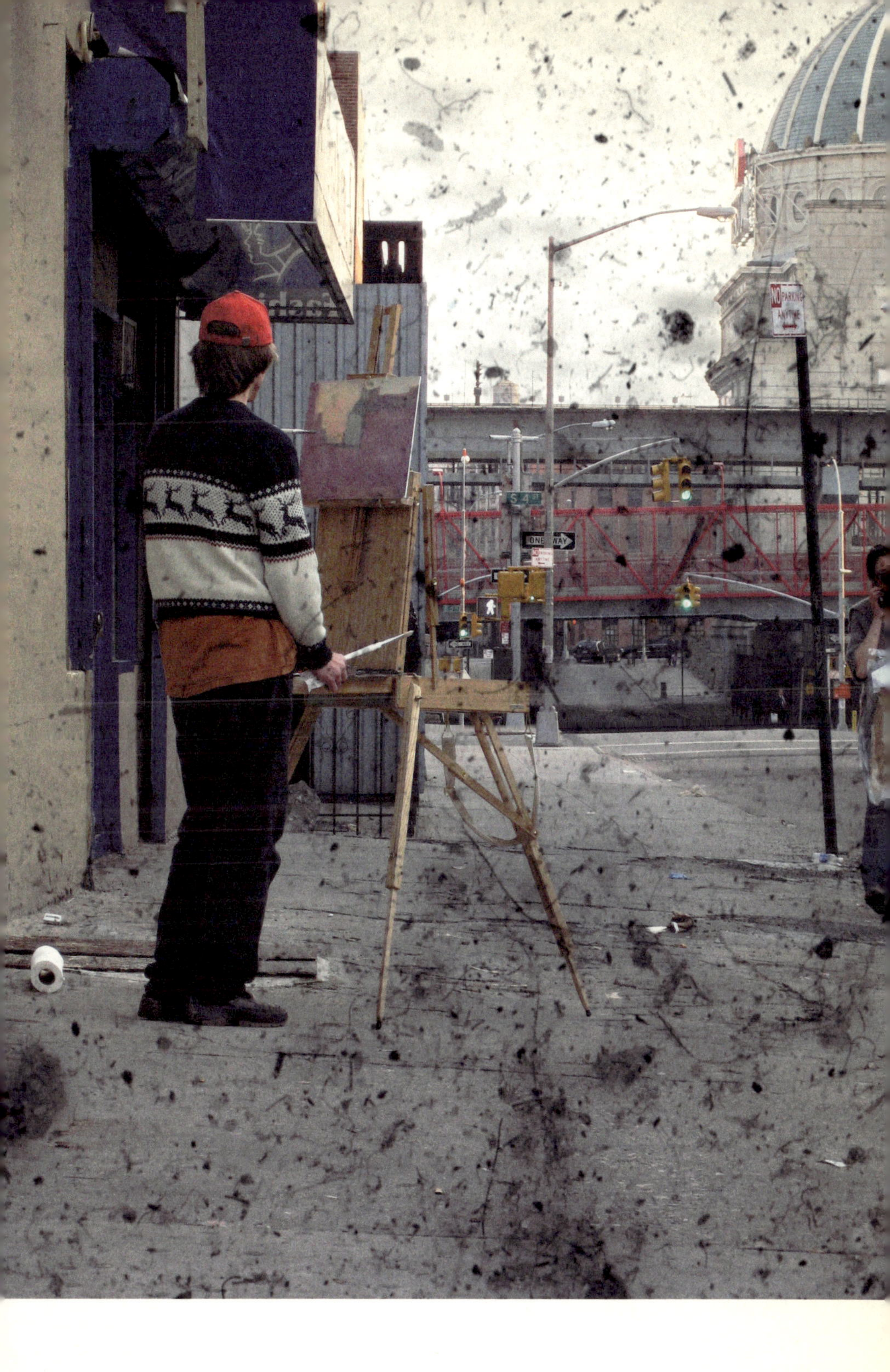
NO PARKING ANYTIME
ONE WAY

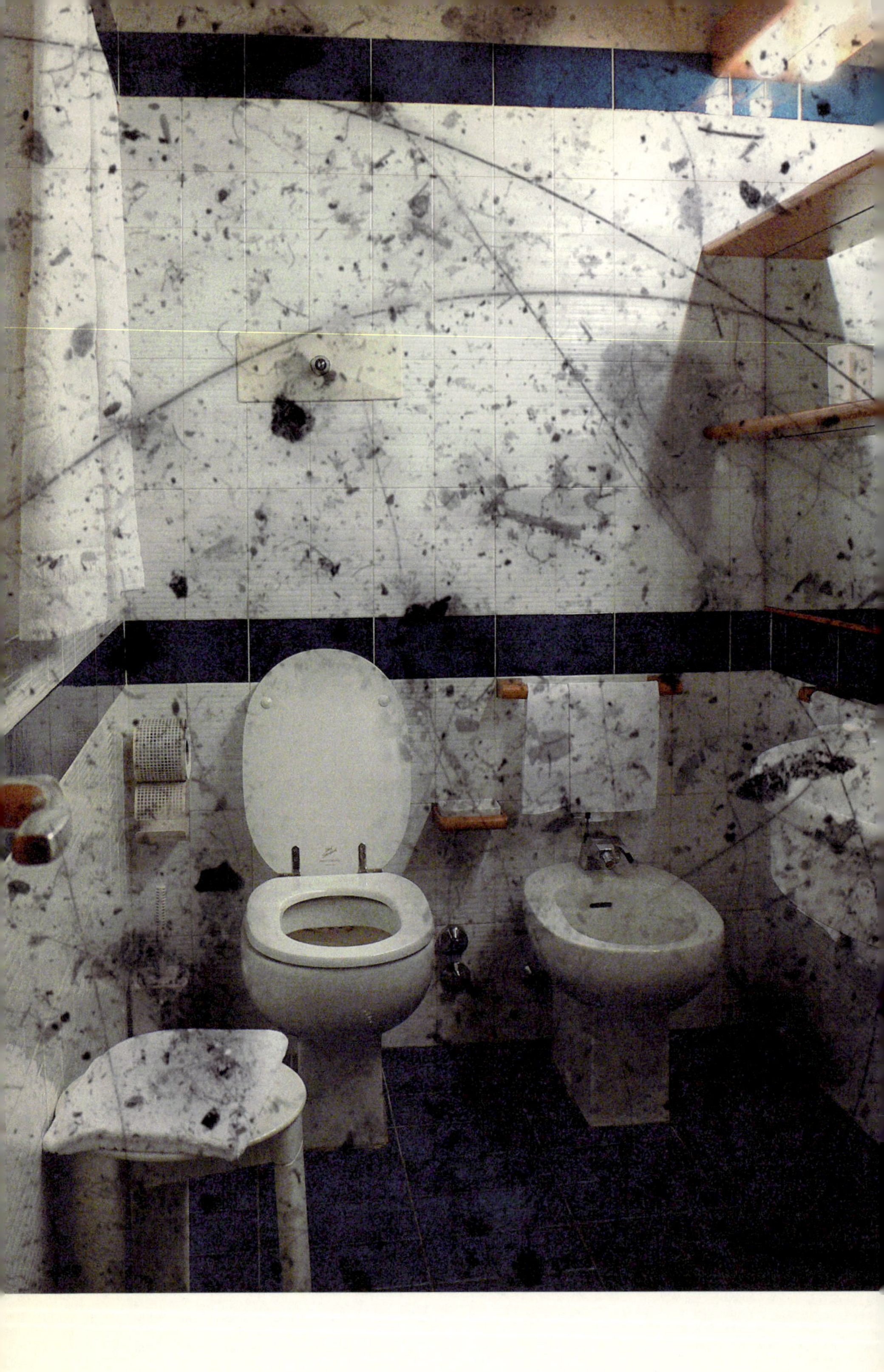

360
transbud Gdańsk S.A.
04858 309 07 14, fax 04858 306 69 64

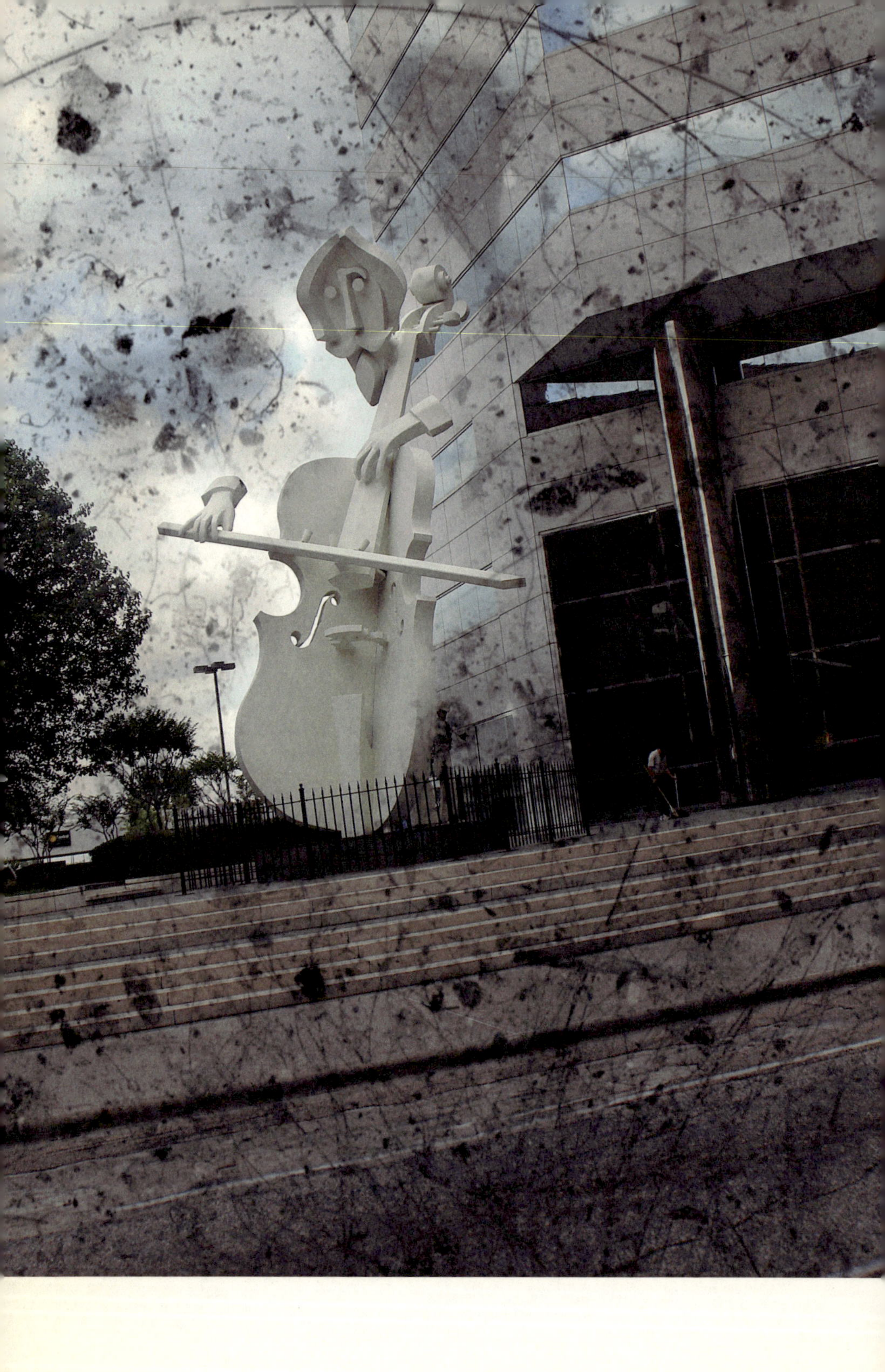

Art and Shock—The Reversal of Reversed Reality

Black humor, sarcasm, obscenity, and shock were once used, in the arts, to subvert political and moral conformity. But what effect do these strategies still have today? Comparatively the popular media machinery produces more intense stimuli and binds psychic energies: in talk shows, the psychopathology of everyday life has become entertainment, in the tabloids, political transformations surface as events abbreviated into images, and in films, historical traumas appear as well-narrated, comforting stories. Klaus Theweleit explores a current dilemma, and discovers points of departure in the underground comics of 1960s and 1970s San Francisco. Where satirical tactics contribute to a loosening of the social body, and pornography is encountered as a means of critical cognition.—*dk*

The most enlightened, hallucinatory view of the world of the second half of the twentieth century, especially the American world and all its insanities, was developed by a closely knit group of American comic artists from San Francisco in the 1960s. What Robert Crumb, Bill Griffith, Kim Deitch, Gilbert Shelton, and around twenty other cartoonists brought to paper in this city around the mid 1960s in their self-produced and distributed comic books, at first in black and white, and then color, can today be seen as a collection that violated basically all existing taboos that had existed until then in America—especially when it came to the representation of things sexual. Or as the author Patrick Rosenkranz termed the work of this San Francisco comics underground, America's only real revolution during the twentieth century. A fan's exaggeration or a justified evaluation? That's one question. It is no question that these comics had exactly the effect they wanted: they quickly tore down all forms of sexual restriction, not just for the generation of those directly participating in San Francisco, inadequately described as Hippies, a culture of notorious drug eaters that in the course of the dissolution of conditioned body limits and personality structures also dissolved the structure of *the love object*; the claim to personal possession in the sexual realm disappeared for around a decade from the behavioral repertoire of a large part of the first American post-war generation, as a whole understood as a *great opening.* "Open up your mind": bodies and their perceptive apparatuses opened to an uncensored representation of all conceivable or inconceivable forms not just of the sexual, but also of life in general. Aldous Huxley's drug book *The Doors of Perception*, provided the name for a musical flagship of the changing drug and sex culture: The Doors.

If it was said of the gay and/or transvestite cast of the New York underground from the same period that their consciousness raising work helped America decisively "to get rid of its Puritanism," this would have to be said to an even greater degree about the San Francisco comics underground. This scene, in contrast to the New York

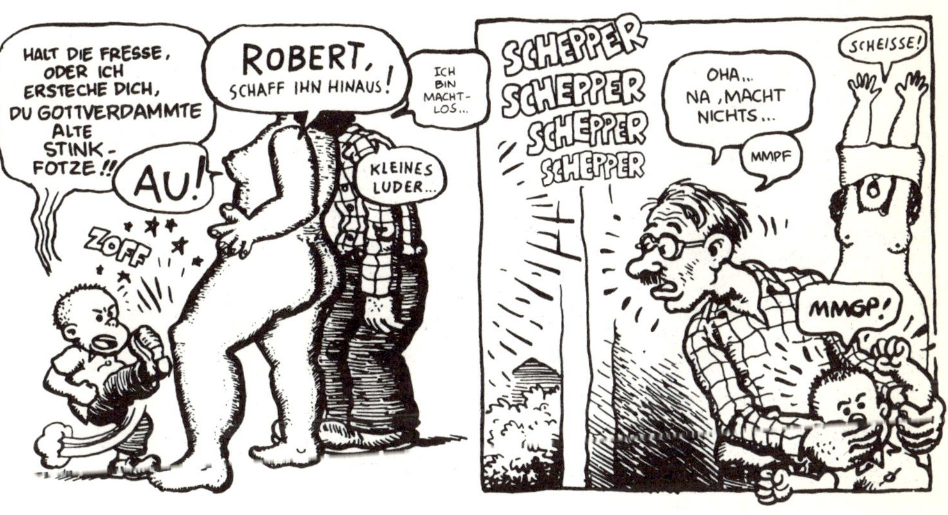

Robert Crumb, Aline Kominsky, "Aline & Bobs spassige Spielchen," in Aline Kominsky-Crumb, Robert Crumb, *Schmutzige Wäsche Comics*, 2002

scene, was rather heterosexually oriented; in its later phase, as a series of women artists joined in, lesbian as well. Comparable to the sexual reorientations, a kind of competition reigned between the New York and the San Francisco underground around the "right" or "harder" drugs: heroin in New York, LSD for San Francisco. Lou Reed vs. Robert Crumb (where the people with the needle also surface). All relevant Americana, new and old, materialized under Robert Crumb's pens. He transformed in the three decades from 1962 to 1990 into *America's most significant sociologist*: no field research in the realm of so-called subcultures or other social "shifts" can hold up to Crumb's account: particularly not with the totality of what all the comic artists from San Francisco produced in this period of time. But, hardly anyone born after 1980 knows these comic artists and their work: not even those

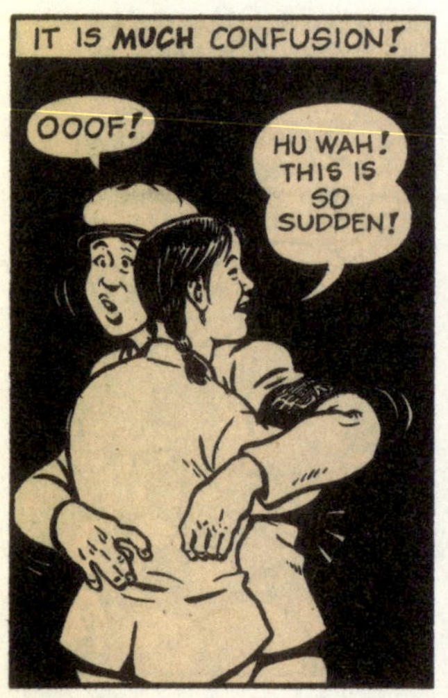

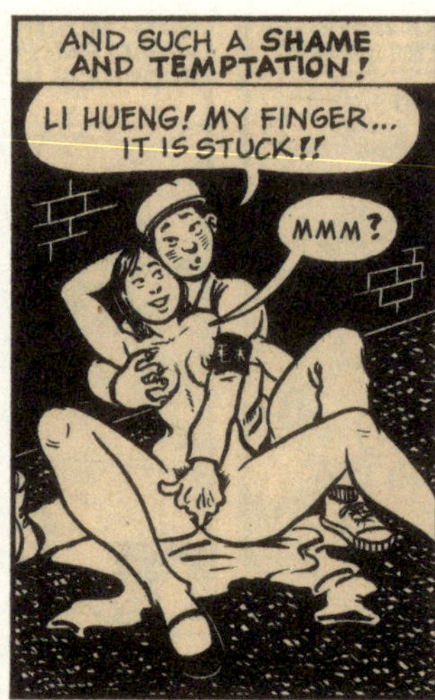

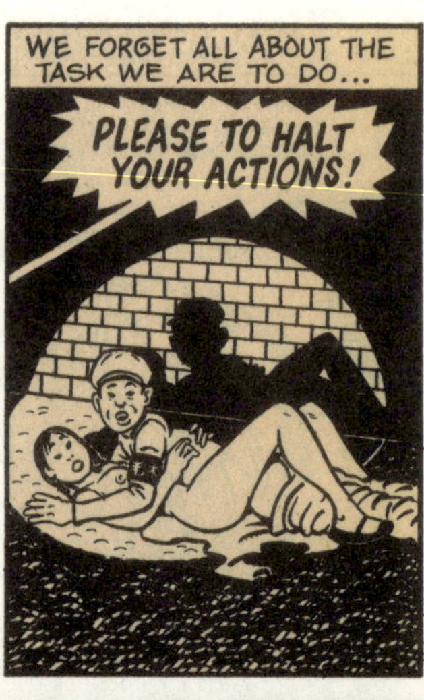

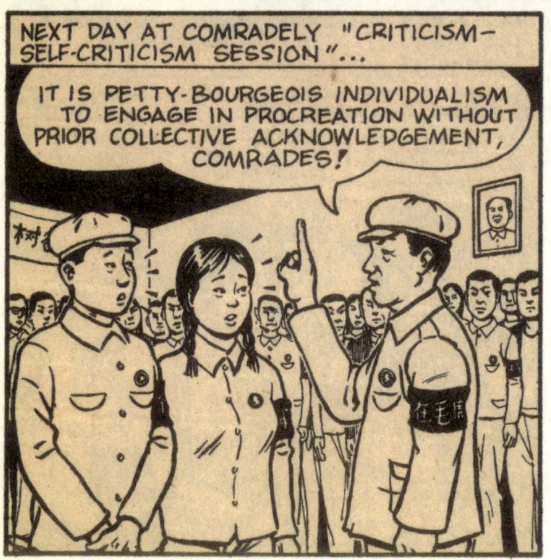

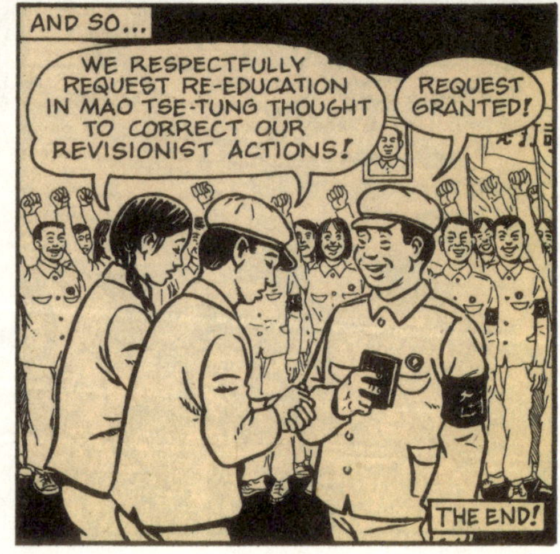

Jay Kinney, "Red Guard Romance,"
in *Young Lust*, no. 5, ed. Jay Kinney, 1977

who are particulary interested in questions of the popular culture underground. Somehow an obliterating wave seems to have crashed on top of these works and this phase of our "culture."

This raises various questions: about the origin of the American Puritanism that is today again so dominant. Did it simply resurrect? Furthermore, the question of the tenability, or as one says today, sustainability of such "revolutions" in artistic realms. There is the question of the decreasing effectiveness of taboo violations, legal violations, outlawness, racy anarchy. To be more precise: is the power of such shock today basically used up? Are transgressions and taboo violations that work with shock still effective in any way as artistic strategies? Who is reached by transgression in the age of a general hard-boiledness, when the "forbidden" is omnipresent in the media? What has changed in the perceptual apparatus of the younger generation? What role is played by the sexual, and what role is played by the arts and by the media through which it comes to us?

Looking through my underground comics for forms of sexuality, I quickly find: sex with animals (Bill Griffith, Kim Deitch), in the latter two monkeys, Hans and Fritz, doing it with their German animal trainer Freda; all kinds of chaining up in the direction of S&M; lesbian love between a white and a black woman, a blonde and an Indian; lesbian Amazon tribes in the South American jungle; a female Tarzan, black, beautiful, and man-killing (all specialties of Trina Robbins, who had the comic thought bubbles come not from the head, but from under the skirt of one of her heroines); all sorts of transvestites; blow jobs; fucking couples in mock Wilhelm-Reich-dialogs; gay pirate ships, where sex and violence are inextricably linked (Clay Wilson), complemented by a gang of female pirates with breasts as long as baseball bats; sex with aliens, a fat black woman abducted by Martians, whoa! Fritz the Cat fucks a crocodile (until the farting Steffi Strauss, who's too stupid for him, puts a stop to it with an ice pick in the neck: Trotzky's death, transported to the sexual madness of Crumb's 1970s San Francisco); young Chinese men and women who without Mao's bible in their hands fuck, are caught, and are forced to do a public "self critique"; Bill Griffith's absolute lust man Claude Funston, who fucks everything that comes before him—in and out—especially the sheep Susi; the sexual rendezvous of a sea researcher with a salamander-like being (lech) on the bottom of the ocean. Later she keeps it as a pet in the bathtub and animates students to join it in the tub; alien-like body entanglements with lovely women from other galaxies that have to be killed (Möbius); sex games between parents where the children get involved (damn brats!), and so on.... And a total dose of political incorrectness: Crumb draws what will happen when "niggers" take power in America—because they are too stupid to do it alone—together with the damn Jews: an unholy alliance of slaveholders, black torturers, and Jewish rapists.

These are drawn without any fear of being accused of racism, for a comic wit pervades all these productions. He demolishes the sexual or political Puritanism built into us with our upbringing, and—the decisive thing—this still works today, at least for my eyes and the constitution of my mind. The *comédie humaine* and the human tragedy are equally present, drawn precisely in detail: that is the requirement. The dramaturgies, the bodies, and the objects are the way they are "supposed" to be. It is a film drawn of what *cannot be seen* in the cinema.

If we ask about the psychological authorities that the artistic violations are directed at—forty years ago or today—we find ourselves on unsure territory. Surely, it can be said that for the first post-war generation, who grew

Kim Deitch, "Simian Sin,"
in *Young Lust*, no. 4, ed. Jay Kinney, 1974

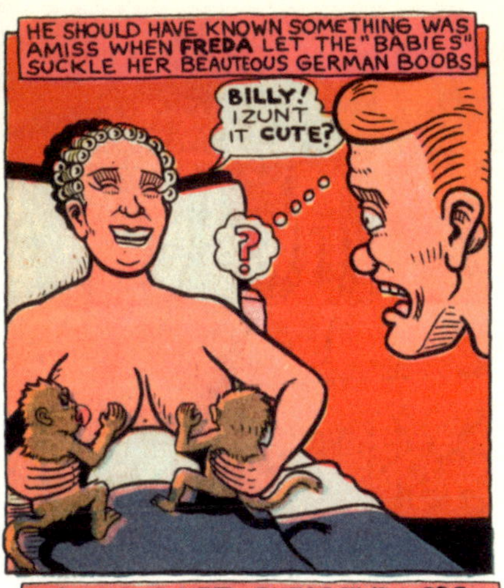
HE SHOULD HAVE KNOWN SOMETHING WAS AMISS WHEN **FREDA** LET THE "BABIES" SUCKLE HER BEAUTEOUS GERMAN BOOBS
BILLY! IZUNT IT **CUTE?**
?

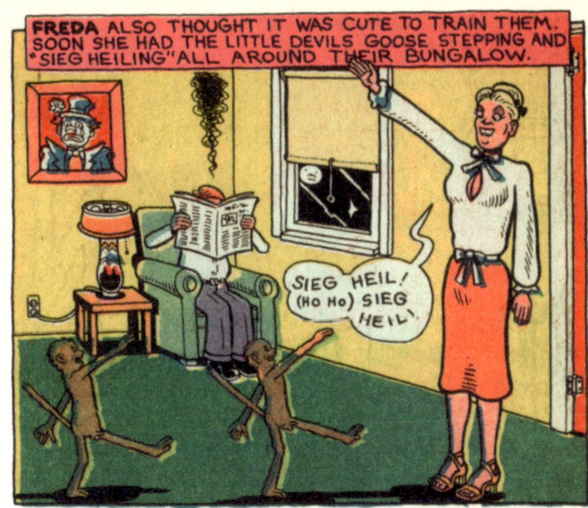
FREDA ALSO THOUGHT IT WAS CUTE TO TRAIN THEM. SOON SHE HAD THE LITTLE DEVILS GOOSE STEPPING AND "SIEG HEILING" ALL AROUND THEIR BUNGALOW.
SIEG HEIL! (HO HO) SIEG HEIL!

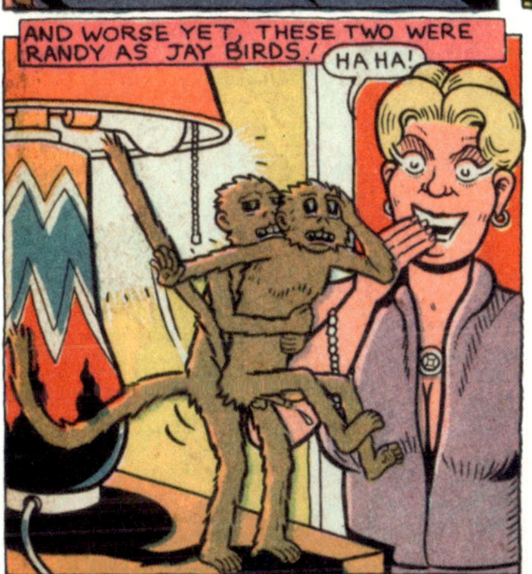
AND WORSE YET, THESE TWO WERE RANDY AS JAY BIRDS!
HA HA!

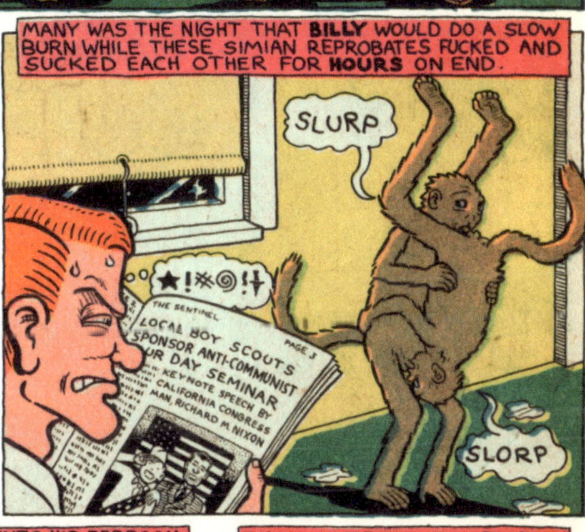
MANY WAS THE NIGHT THAT **BILLY** WOULD DO A SLOW BURN WHILE THESE SIMIAN REPROBATES FUCKED AND SUCKED EACH OTHER FOR **HOURS** ON END.
SLURP
★!※◎!‡
THE SENTINEL
PAGE 3
LOCAL BOY SCOUTS SPONSOR ANTI-COMMUNIST UR DAY SEMINAR
KEYNOTE SPEECH BY CALIFORNIA CONGRESS MAN RICHARD M NIXON
SLORP

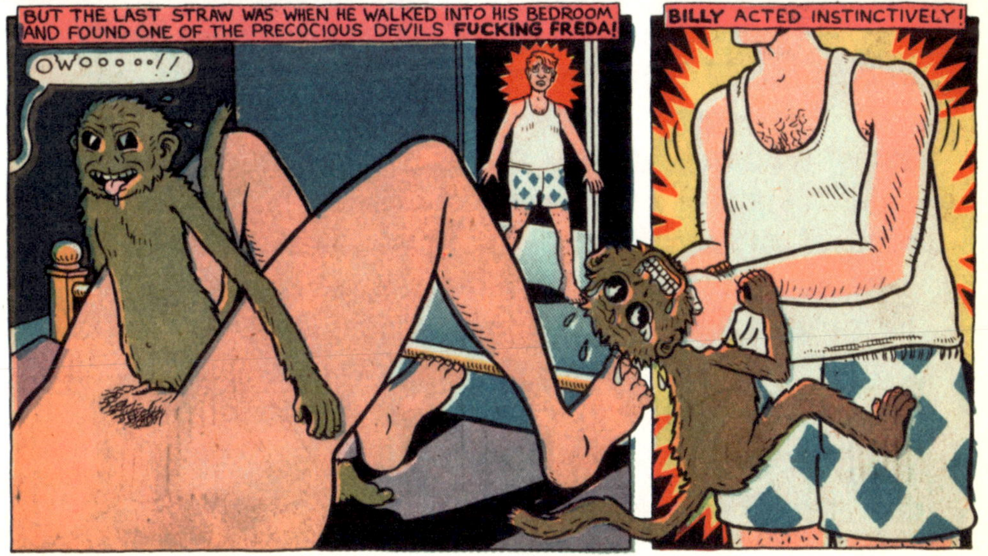
BUT THE LAST STRAW WAS WHEN HE WALKED INTO HIS BEDROOM AND FOUND ONE OF THE PRECOCIOUS DEVILS **FUCKING FREDA!**
OWOOOOO!!
BILLY ACTED INSTINCTIVELY!

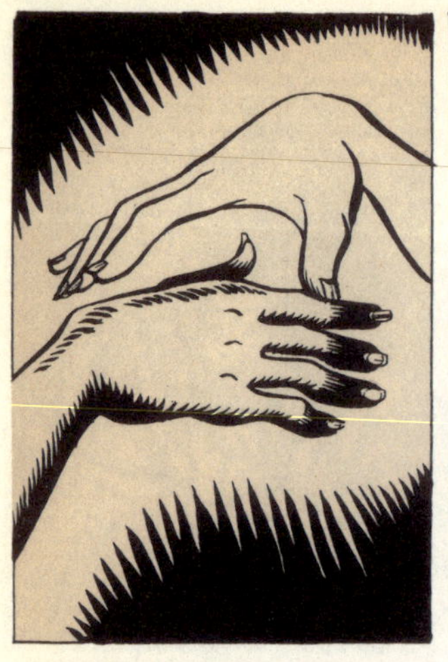

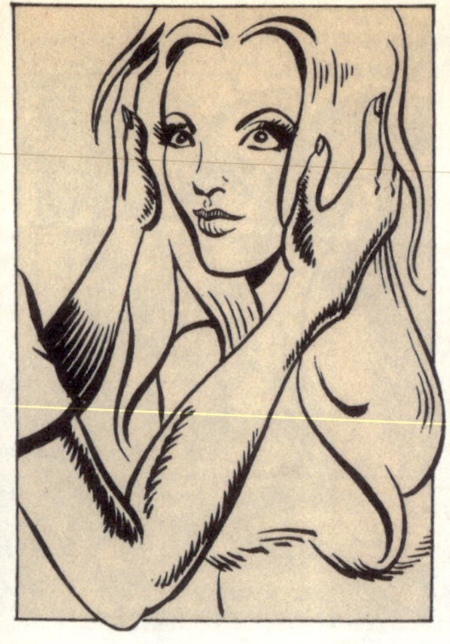

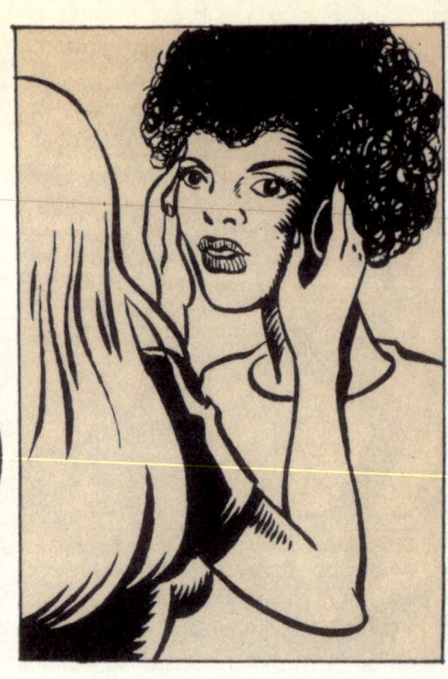

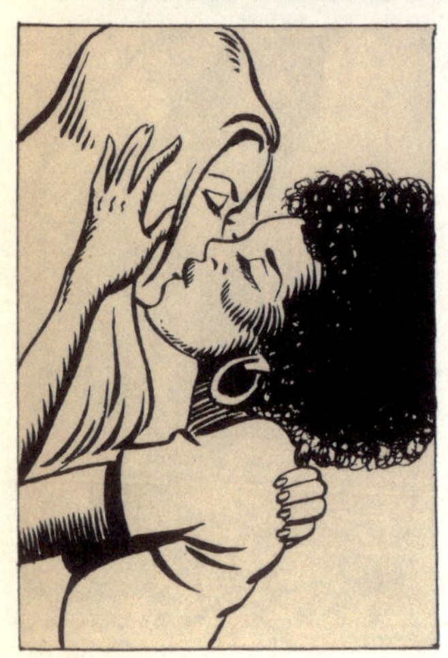

Trina Robbins, "Fox," 1972,
in *U-Comix*, Sonderband Nr. 13, 1977

up with many taboos on sexuality and rules on proper moral behavior, the tearing down of these rules and the massively rigorous refusal of the commanding "morality" of their parents' generation had a huge affective profit—on an international scale.

To state that the only half-fixed superego structures of an entire junior generation collapsed in one fell swoosh would be somewhat oversimplified. The superego—if we want to use this concept—is a multifunctional authority: psychoanalysis sees it not only as the "seat" of parental bans or a punishing conscience, but also as a place of values, the ideal ego and individual self-regulation. In addition, this generation's fears of punishment were physically anchored, literally beaten into them rather than psychologically "acquired." Maybe it would suffice to speak of a rapid resolution of body tension with the continued maintenance of a certain amount of old ideological material. Such dissolution results in laughter, delirium, and pleasure in violation, with a strongly addictive component, especially when experienced as a collective process, and then also staged. As a historical rule, such an outbreak leaves behind a kind of hangover due to its contradictory nature. The level of the delirium and the intensity of transgressions cannot be maintained for years in everyday life, or only for a select few, hard-core professional transgressors, who in this very process become professionals. The others return to a kind of "new normality," completed renewed.

For their children's generation, the result of this process is ambivalent. The loss of a whole series of religious and social proscriptions, which massively decreased the pressure on single individuals to conform in the course of the 1970s to the 1990s, of course also implies a changed relation to the whole complex of "transgression." Where life follows prepared tracks, the necessity of transgressions and outbreak as a personal form of development sinks: new forms of (always necessary) generational conflict have to be invented; a difficult job, for which there are no short cuts or forced time points.

In addition, the paths created by tearing down restrictive walls are not just populated and expanded by the prophets or practitioners of "new freedoms," but also by other beneficiaries, by the producers, traders, and sellers of garbage. There is no social, affective transformation that does not have its point of interface with the market: the marketplace of ideologies and economic markets. Standing at each breakthrough are not just the prophets, poets, experimenters, and dreamers, but also gangsters who check the new gaps for what can be financially milked; who are quickly on hand with new products, who seem to satisfy the ensemble of new "needs," but in fact just exploit them; usually, or almost always with the well-trained use of new technologies. In the 1980s and

1990s this primarily took the form of new media technologies. In the rougher forms of their application, we can regularly find an aggressively anti-artistic structure, whether intended or not—that's what characterizes their potential criminality. The majority of banned video games for example have or had a decidedly primitive design; this is not without consequence and would not be any better, even if these games were more "pacifist" than they are.

As I said, I don't think the transgressions of the underground comics have lost their power or humor. Their artistic verve, their accurate analytics, their sparkling drive towards liberation from constant idiocy all remain fully unbroken. Even their gesture of "you've all lost it" is absolutely convincing and charming. What has however changed is the observing eye or brain that dominates today. It knows all the transgressions undertaken there, or thinks it knows them. And it's right about that, to the extent that *it has already seen, it already knows* everything that dances out of the historical backdrop breaking all sorts of taboos. And has even gotten tired of it. Whether splatter movies, hardcore porn at the video shop, the TV masturbation fantasies of the telephone sex lines. In Germany, we are all familiar with the "ass fuck" rap from Sido and the noise of the neo-Nazi bands, the killer slogans of the hooligans and so on. If in 2007 an eight-year-old schoolboy wakes at twelve thirty at night and stumbles from his nightmare into the parent's bedroom, where the two are lying in the bed and watching a hardcore porn movie that they don't turn off when the little one crawls into bed, that's a primal scene in a not very Freudian sense.

But I absolutely do not think that the bad thing about these productions is primarily that they lead their viewers

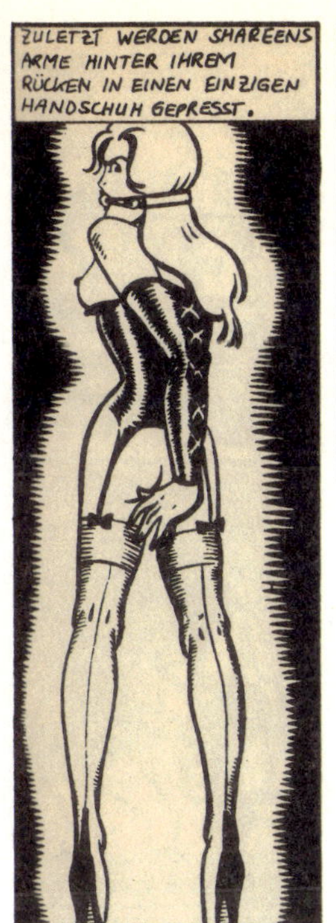

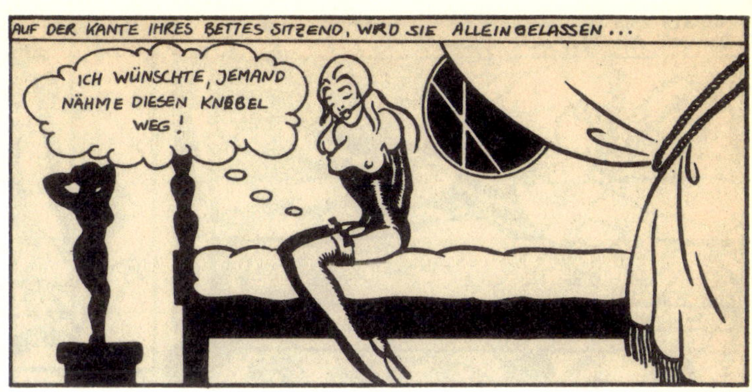

Trina Robbins, "Rawhide Revenge," 1975, in *U-Comix*, Sonderband Nr. 13, 1977

to engage in the acts depicted there, making them copycat masturbators or murderers; the crime statistics alone belie this. No, their criminal potential lies elsewhere, in abolishing the beholder's *capacity for distinction*, caused by a constant overdose of "bad shit"; stupid, violent fucking around, torture without consequences, breasts on spits, ripped open assholes (without it being a concentration camp); senselessly naked bodies in endless processions of affectively fully incomprehensible sexual acts, linked to all sorts of absurd body positions and contortions. The perceptive apparatuses of many of today's youth are pasted over, bombarded with endless amounts of "bad shit"—sometimes at a very early age. Many have no orientation in their ability to take up "sexuality" or "violence," and thus in the psychological processing of human relationships. So, they react with numbness, or identification with the aggressor. A large part of today's twenty to thirty year olds (never mind the younger ones) live in a state of excessive emotional demands transported by the media.

It is not the forbidden "suppressed" that comes out in these media productions. No, the notion and/or the fact of the suppressed plays almost no role at all in their psyche. They know all the crap, they carry it about with them in their minds and are now either dependent on its consumption (addicted) or bored; that is, they are out

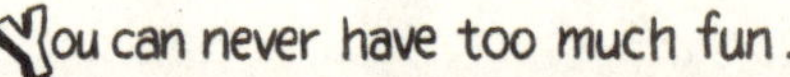

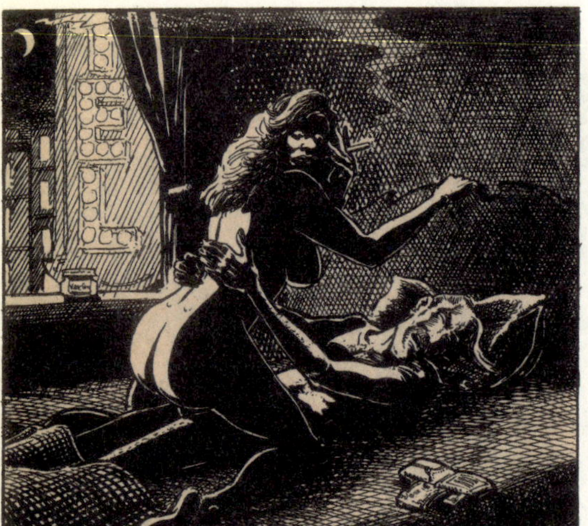

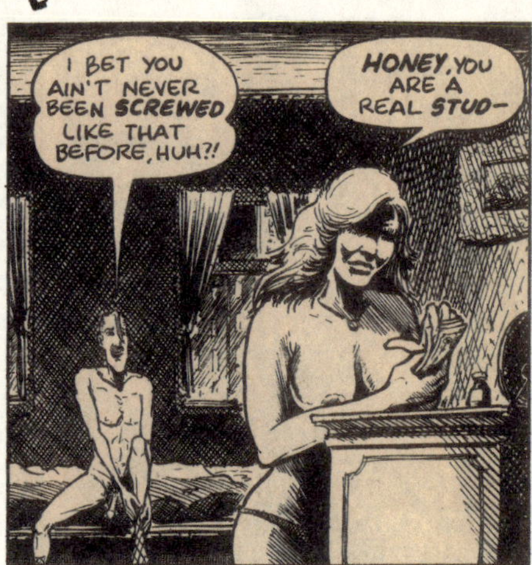

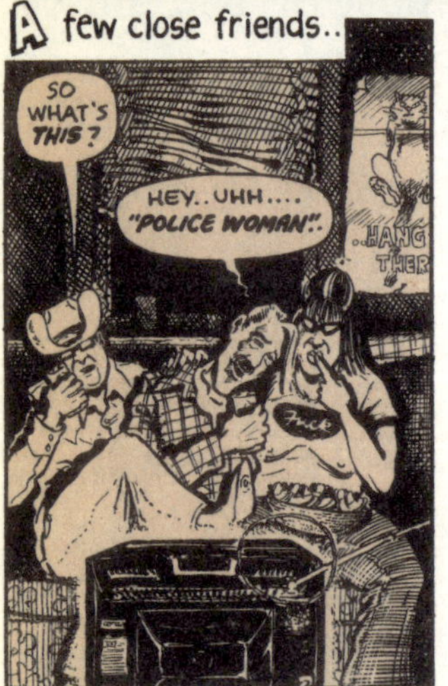

Bill Griffith, "Too Much Fun," in *Young Lust*, no. 5, ed. Jay Kinney, 1977

of its reach and push aside "the stuff." But as a consequence they do not really look when media comes before them in the cloak of aggressive transgression, or to be more precise, attacks them. The reasonable ones just pass by it, or check it off in the category "that's crazy nonsense, leave me alone with that." While the addicts notice indeed that there is a potential here that could criticize my behavior, my addiction; so out with it and in with the next violent porn movie. It at least underscores my state as one of *normality:* for everyone I know consumes it like me—Hot! (with our heart pounding in our pants). The other there, the artistically "good things," in contrasts, just want to convince me that I'm gaga. (And they might well be right. To hell with it. "Intellectual crap." I'm too stupid for it. Ha ha. We all agree.)

This would also mean that shock material that is exquisite in terms of quality does not reach either the relatively rational beholders or the passive-dependent rest, apart from a small circle of artistic schooled or crafty people. The criminality of those serving the market users has guaranteed that the perception of the artistic quality of such products among the younger generation has all but died out. The aggressive liberatory aspect that was there at a certain historical moment has not been censored away this time. On the contrary. It's been taken to the extreme and made cheaply available to everybody. In particular, the organs of perception have been capped for all those towards which these arts, the underground comics, could direct themselves. Their "revolutionary potential" is simply overlooked. This is true of most productions today that rely on breaking rules. Where there is no (fixed) psychologically anchored canon of rules,

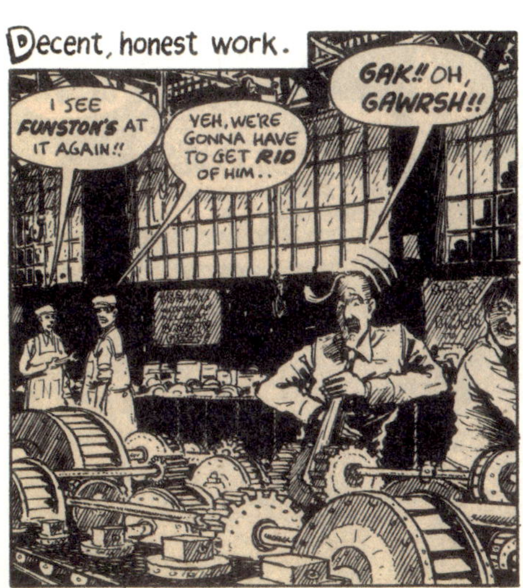

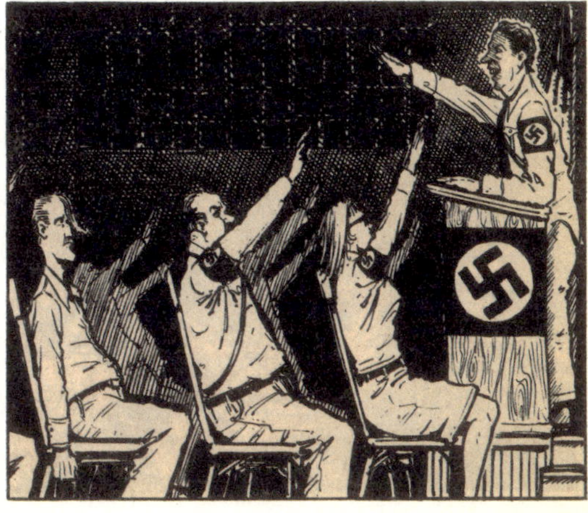

nothing can be properly "violated." Unless, if the fuses blow, we call the referee an asshole: primitivist, autodestructive.

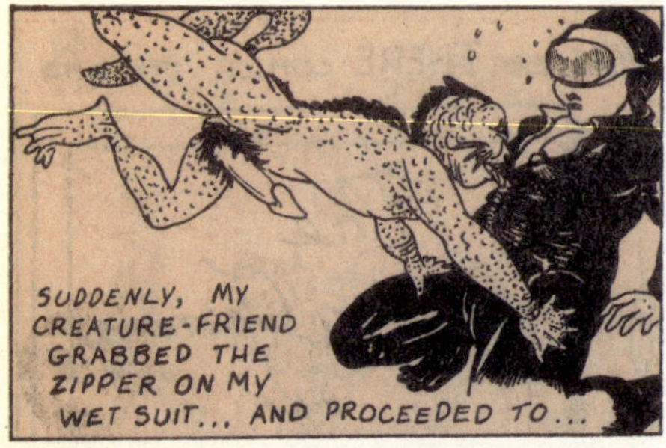

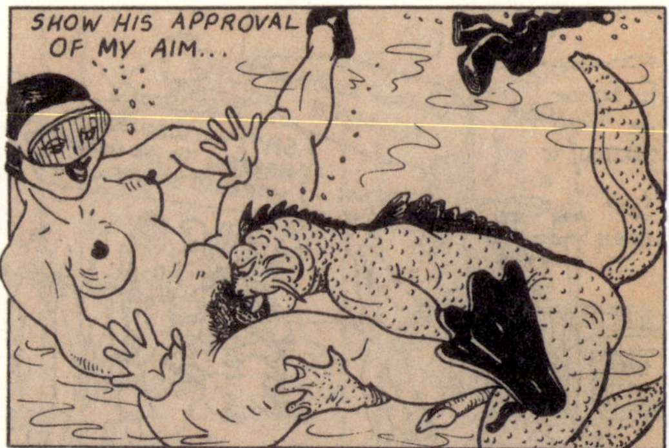

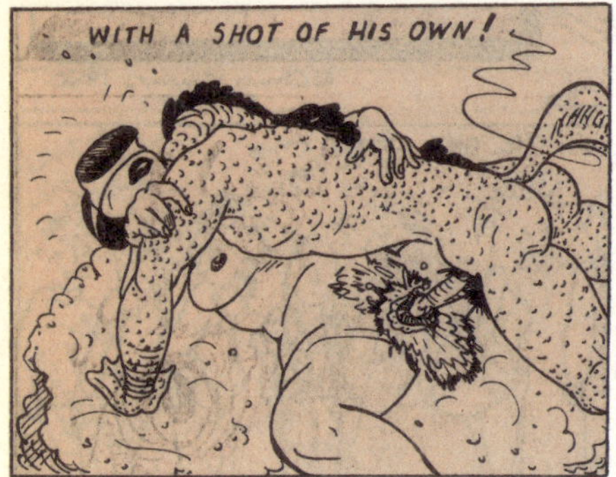

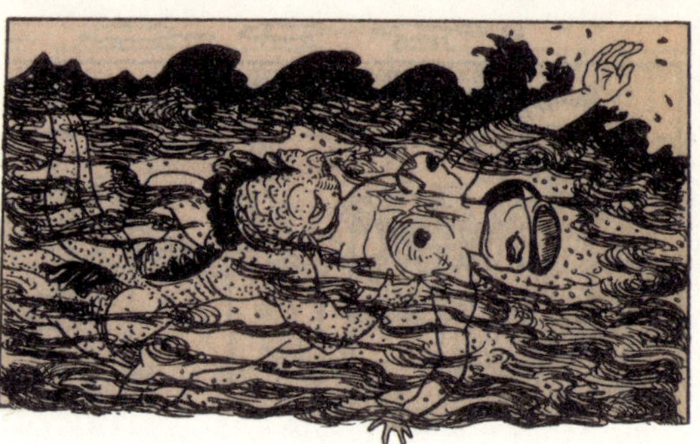

Rocky Trout, "The Fishy Facts of Life," in *Tits & Clits Comix*, 1980

What to do? The painter Blalla W. Hallmann, himself strongly infected by drugs and the comics underground by his San Francisco stay in 1968 (followed by a drug clinic and similar misfortunes) drew a special (and perhaps in this field only possible) conclusion: raising the dose of transgression to such an extent that just looking away doesn't work; because what is already visible in his images on first glance demolishes in a single second the massive overall "understanding" that we all lug about as a kind of self-protection. So a "second look" has to be risked. Hallmann's cycle of Hitler pictures from the 1990s might just show a "way."

We learn from Hallmann that what goes with Hitler are little innocent girls that suck on Führer dicks in all innocence. *Ihr schönster Tag* (1991) in a field with dandelions. And Hitler's hand jerks up. *Heil!* Such images: *Onkel Wolf zaubert!* (also from 1991) show exactly the constellations concealed by the Nazi staging. They present that one can only get to that cunt Hitler by adding the people of cunts along with him under his shower of piss. A Warholian "piss" painting of a different kind, German degenerating de-arting, End-Art, not *Endsieg*. Hallmann concisely shows that Hitler cannot be shown without pornography. Pornography not as material for masturbation, but as a cognitive instrument, even if crude one. But this was also done by the comic artists in their own way.

We recognize in the light of this knowledge that any approach to the Hitler figure that considers itself "serious" truly deserves to be called "pornographic." Pornography in a sense as pasting over. An undertaking like the Hitler movie by Joachim Fest, Bernd Eichinger, and Bruno Ganz pursues the (old) German pornography of aggressive pasting over reality. It's not fake to paint Hitler fucking a pig; what is fake is giving a prominent actor a mustache and Hitler costume and letting him speak "original" Hitler

Trina Robbins, "Fox," 1972,
in *U-Comix*, Sonderband Nr. 13, 1977

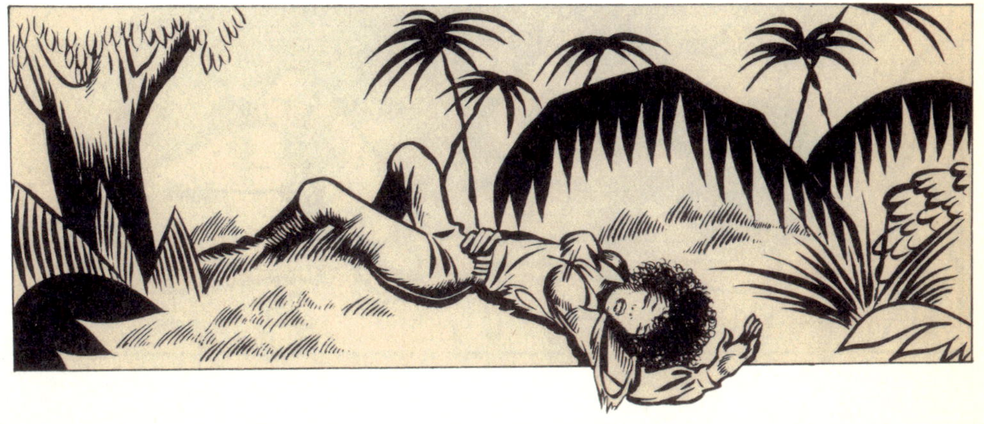

sentences. Or showing "Hitler" in statesmanlike clothing on a magazine cover. Or just showing "Nazi documentary footage" on television. As if Hitler were a "person," and not the longed for, loved incarnation of German piggishness of the 1930s and 1940s. Whoever simulates the neutrality of "clean documentation" by presenting mere archival material of the Nazis is a pig.

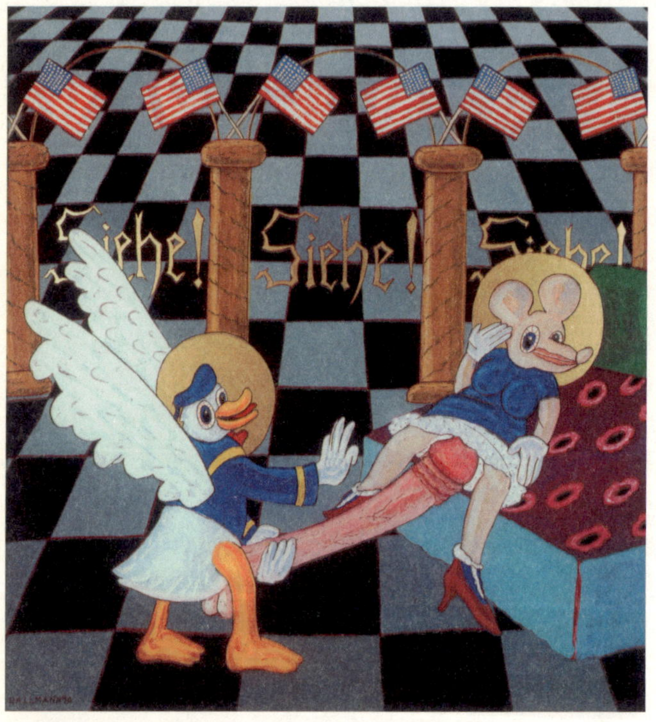

Blalla W. Hallmann
Siehe! Siehe! Siehe!, 1990

The image of a jubilant German human formation with arms raised on the street side while their beloved Führer goes by, means: the German community, united in jubilation, man and woman, are fucking the pig up the ass. The jubilation and the clean white *dirndls* are there to hide that (for the stupid, not-master-race rest of the world); but also to exhibit it for all those in the know, for the feverishly undertaken collaboration: here, the Jewish world-pig is fucked, and we know it and want it. Whoever doesn't show that, but Hitler "in a suit," is the real pornographer, an active prolonger of the specific German piggery still present today. Whoever conceals this core, the conscious transgression into all realms of the truly forbidden, into the realms of shared sexualized criminality *in awareness of full immunity* "we are annihilating a people, we can do that, and that's hot," whoever does not show that becomes himself a pig. The pig places Hitler in the series of (half marveled) great criminals of history, makes him like a man like Napoleon, makes a demigod (albeit a negative one) of a filthy pig. Above all, he refuses to take a look at the psychological and physical state of "the German" in the first half of the twentieth century, which intended nothing less than the destruction of European culture (as far as that existed): a total mockery making harmless the apotheosis of a life in criminal transgression, sexual acting out: hey neighbor! Heil! Hot! A life in a state of legally permitted (divine) superiority over the rest of the world (Untermenschen, niggers, insects, pests).

If Hallmann adds to this constellation the new savior, Donald Duck, who with a meter long cock fucks his Daisy and nails Mickey Mouse to the cross and/or waves a swastika flag and has the empty earth "occupied," he is in fact able to remove the veil covering our gaze, so that a few scraps of thought can find their way into our brain whorls. Works that are only acceptable at the price of their own borderline, as Hallmann himself showed. The transgressive artist is close to psychosis.

It's a matter of definition whether this is understood as individual or "social," but I do not see a fundamental theoretical difference between psychic appearances in the individual or social groups. The psychological mechanisms approach one another, only their intensity differs. I would indeed distinguish the hallucinatory clarity from psychosis, more precisely: from the state of acute psychotic phases. The first leads to a kind of beatitude (as in the late Nietzsche), the latter to serious illness (as also present in Nietzsche). For an artist there is a gradual transition; the balance that success or failure depends upon. With too little intensity the transgression cannot be achieved; with too much, it threatens to become self-devouring. The transgressive artist verges more closely than ever before on psychosis.

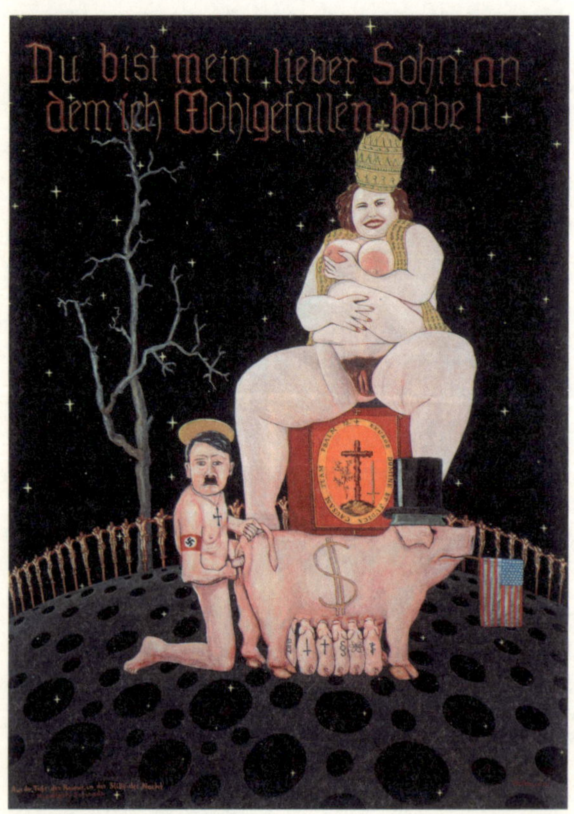

Blalla W. Hallmann
Aus der Tiefe des Raumes, in der Stille der Nacht—Moonlight Serenade, 1991

Journey Through the Country

Seamless and with rounded corners the window-frame flows around the view, as on polished rails things glide by in it according to their role. Things move exactly as expected, those that are near quickly from one side to another, those placed somewhat further away take their proper time to give up their position, while those destined to shape the horizon persist as ordered in the illusion of their motionlessness. Unchanged they seem to stay there, bound to the spot, until suddenly they are no longer to be seen, and one did not even notice how that came about, there was so much beauty to look at everywhere, glacier-promising distances in every direction, flower boxes in front of the facades of houses that provide the red accents rapidly passing by, and brown deer made of painted concrete in the gardens that have inched close enough to our window to catch us by surprise, and corn fields and yellow hiking trail signs and noise-protection walls colorfully painted by officially approved artists. As usual everything here is in order, the conductor comes on time, the river, too. It shows up in the lower half of the window, and the corresponding bridge will be there as well. We must cross this bridge, that is clear to us, to reach the place that we have declared as our wished-for destination to the ticket machine, and look, the river is there. If one had not been taught about the river at school, one could examine it with the help of maps that are hanging here and on which we can study the stretch that we wanted to travel. No different from the expectations that we brought with us, things move within the frame, we calculate where we are now and what will soon appear in our window as a sign of our former presence and passage. And there the blue rectangle with the familiar white letters appears, briefly enough to win our entire attention, yes, everything is in order, it was the right one. The remaining railway station hardly differs from the others, but the sign was there, it showed us that everything is taking its correct course, the view is beautiful, as we all know, we learned that at school. Guests have been taught the same thing in brochures and in films which hardly differ from what is taking place in the frame of the window. Zoning regulations will preserve the mountain view. There are no people to be seen, and the window before our eyes, before our view, is spotlessly clean, as if not one single raindrop had ever touched it, and even if one were to imagine that there must be a seam there in which once the glass was placed, one fails to find it, at first one does not even, however briefly, want to believe it. Not even the least puff of air comes from the other side, and if the air here right next to the window moves it is only the imitation wind of our journey, an artificially created circulation that only makes it clear that there are no seams, for it is only there in compensation for our well-being.

Through many journeys and advertisements we have come to know this country, we have often seen it in the window of the train and on the highway, in the window of the car, in which the highway also moved. The fact that this country offers us a view disturbs no one here, it's hardly noticeable. We lose track of space outside the window, we rethink it ourselves, a little bluish coloration of small sections is enough and the obligatory classical perspective trick is there, the trees have to hurry, the houses turn as on a string, the grass in the foreground slopes away and the sun hops from one side to the other. A calm occurs, everything points to the hoped-for relationship between both spaces, the one which seems to stand still and the other which hurries past. Yet one does not want to keep them apart, the view is so lovely, one is happy in it, one likes feeling like a geranium, it is a lovely feeling. The space that seems to be at rest here seems to be moving when seen from the other side, one knows that, and for that reason prefers not to think about it. Luckily, wherever one is, space appears perfectly seamed. How comforting that is. Many fall into a cozy sleep at once, their heads leaning against the frame, which, without sound, flows in its round corners around a view of the country which we expected and which came and which moved as the country which we know does not move. Trees in our country have roots, after all, mountains are immovable, and houses are built on solid foundations. Exactly that comforts us, that we see the country as it can not be, that assures us that it is not as we see it, that is a peculiarly profound comfort, for we have known for a long time now that what runs does not move. That which stands still around me is not to be kept, why even try, things are in their proper place, that has been taken care of, I don't have to examine that, I don't have to have seen it. So one dreams away, one dreams: I am the one, I make the difference, I decide where I get off and wherever I get off reality changes and respectfully lets me determine what runs away and what remains.

Here at home everything is in order, we sit across from each other without looking at one another. We look at the lovely view from assigned seats for which we have paid the prescribed prices and it seems, such is the feeling at least, that seen from this fully air-conditioned narrowness it would be somewhat risky to enter the view, it is good that we are inside. To enter your own view would be to fall out of the frame, and what if the view is not as fully air-conditioned as it appears? Might one not stumble unknowingly over the cable with which the green color of the grass has been regulated? Perhaps the flowers have a gray pasteboard side and behind the half-timber facades of the houses there is nothing but a scaffolding beyond which the refuse has been heaped in towers, and what if the hiking trails never lead us over the horizon? The view is set in motion for an exactly measurable length of time, from below comes the simulation of archaic trembling, which puts the minds of the passengers at ease. Communicating from their thighs they answer E-mails or type SMS love-messages with their thumbs, read historical novels and sleep. They play cards. Now and then the train suggests a slant, toilets are standing ready where the soap never runs out and the water never dries up, and below the toilet bowl a film is being shown, one sees the sleepers there hurrying away, so quickly that one doesn't really see them, and should something contrary to all expectations not function perfectly one says here: you're in the wrong film, but the films are in general precisely selected, the projector functions without friction or sound, between films there is no gap, no tears are ever visible, and if you lift the toilet lid the wind of the journey greets you from there as well, an anachronistic sentimentality. Through the empty center in which one could move freely but which no one here does, unless someone has pressing business on the toilet, there comes, at regular intervals, an employee disguised as a foreigner, who brings refreshments: synthetic snacks and drinks at astronomical prices in order to emphasize the fact that this is the last place on earth, the last inhabitable oasis, all the money that one spends here is in a sense saved, one might as well leave it here, outside no currency will be of further help, so it is better to spend everything here, quickly and altogether without pain, and in return, as a reward, one gets something sweet.

Bodies in Search of Matter—A Portrait of Yves Netzhammer

The work of Yves Netzhammer plays out in drawings, projections, and installations. This variety of media is telling, for the artist crosses, combines, superimposes, and mixes familiar, socially canonized symbols to produce contradictory and yet unreal scenarios. In so doing, he uses human, animal, organic and inorganic figures like an open-ended alphabet. Tim Zulauf has put together a "portrait" made up of literary and philosophical quotations that refer not to an external biography, but prefer to follow a conceptual direction. This compilation surpasses any one single issue, and is at the same time a revisitation of existant themes in Netzhammer's work, and an outlook on their potential development—a processual portrait that crosses areas like "criteria of identity," "scanning knowledge," and the "politics of sensation." The video stills are taken from the work of Yves Netzhammer.—*dk*

My two hands began a struggle. They shut the book in which I had been reading so that it wouldn't get in the way. They saluted me, and chose me as their referee. [...] Faced with this distress, had I not had the liberating thought that it was my own hands here struggling, and that I could pull them apart with a slight tug, thus ending all struggle and distress, had I not thought of this, the left would have been broken out of the joint and thrown from the table, and then perhaps the right, with the victor's lack of restraint would have attacked me like a five-headed Cerberus, biting my attentive face. Instead, the two lie on top of one another, the right stroking the back of the left, and I, the dishonest referee, nod at this.

Franz Kafka, "Oktavheft D" (1917), in *Beim Bau der chinesischen Mauer und andere Schriften aus dem Nachlass* [The Great Wall of China and Other Unpublished Writings], Frankfurt am Main: Fischer, 1994, p. 104.

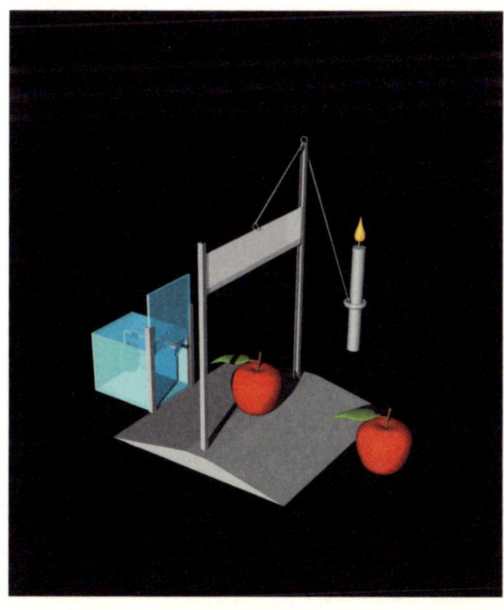

I find that my very formation implicates the other in me, that my own foreignness to myself is, paradoxically, the source of my ethical connection with others. [...] I am wounded, and I find that the wound itself testifies to the fact that I am impressionable, given over to the Other in ways that I cannot fully predict or control. I cannot think the question of responsibility alone, in isolation from the Other; if I do, I have taken myself out of the relational bind that frames the problem of responsibility from the start.

Judith Butler, *Precarious Life: The Powers of Mourning and Violence,* London-New York: Verso, 2004, p. 46.

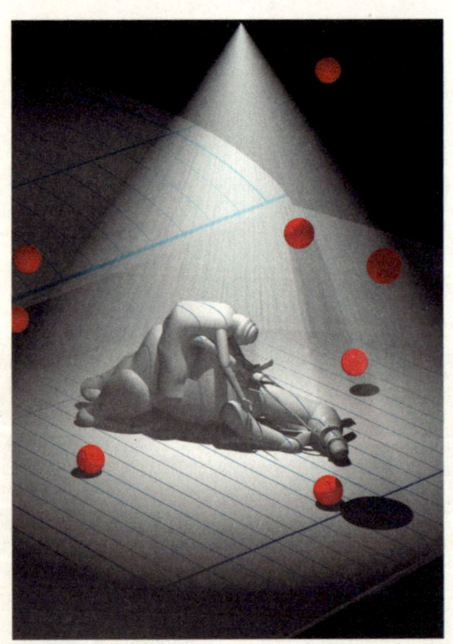

"Another person can't have my pains."—Which are *my* pains? What counts as a criterion of identity here?

Ludwig Wittgenstein, *Philosophical Investigations* [Philosophische Untersuchungen, 1953], trans. G.E.M. Anscombe, Oxford: Basil Blackwell, second edition, 1958, p. 91.

I have lost in the process of eating and drinking and rubbing my eyes along surfaces that thin, hard shell which cases the soul, which, in youth, shuts one in—hence the fierceness, and the tap, tap, tap of the remorseless beaks of the young. And now I ask, "Who am I?" [...] As I talked I felt, "I am you." This difference we make so much of, this identity we so feverishly cherish, was overcome.

Virginia Woolf, *The Waves* (1931),
London: Penguin, 1992, p. 222.

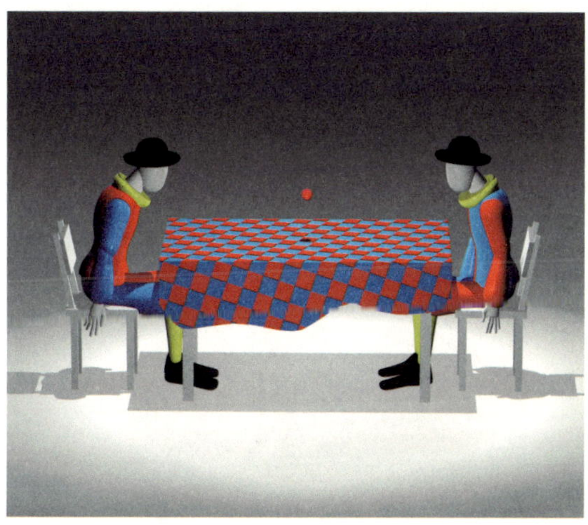

In fact, in an essay entitled "Peace and Proximity," Levinas makes plain that "the face is not exclusively a human face." [...] Here the term "face" operates as a catachresis: "face" describes the human back, the craning of the neck, the raising of the shoulder blades like "springs." And these bodily parts, in turn, are said to cry and to sob and to scream, as if they were a face or, rather, a face with a mouth, a throat, or indeed, just a mouth and throat from which vocalizations emerge that do not settle into words. [...] Thus the face, the name for the face, and the words by which we are to understand its meaning—"Thou shalt not kill"—do not quite deliver the meaning of the face, since at the end of the line, it seems, it is precisely the wordless vocalization of suffering that marks the limits of linguistic translation here.

Judith Butler, *Precarious Life: The Powers of Mourning and Violence,* London-New York: Verso, 2004, pp. 133–4.

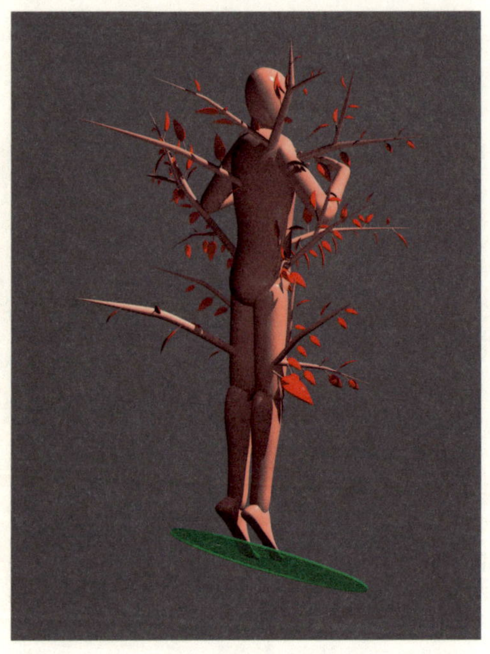

Think, too, how one can imitate a man's face without seeing one's own in a mirror.

Ludwig Wittgenstein, *Philosophical Investigations* [Philosophische Untersuchungen, 1953], trans. G.E.M. Anscombe, Oxford: Basil Blackwell, second edition, 1958, p. 98.

In the ever denser darkness, the horse pushed onward towards us—not galloping, not at a trot, but moving at a leisurely pace, and behind it the swaying wagon with the silhouette of the coachman high on his mount—and the speed or slowness of the wagon's motion stood in precise relation to the denseness of the darkness, so that the wagon, if it had stopped, would have been swallowed by the darkness, but since it moved forward, it constantly balanced the degree of increasing darkness with the degree of proximity, but also due to the increasing darkness retained the same vagueness, so that when it was finally close before us only gained in size, and otherwise remained foggily smoldering in the deep twilight just like the rest of the time.

Peter Weiss, *Der Schatten des Körpers des Kutschers* (1960), [The Shadow of the Body of the Coachman], Frankfurt am Main: Suhrkamp, 1964, p. 92.

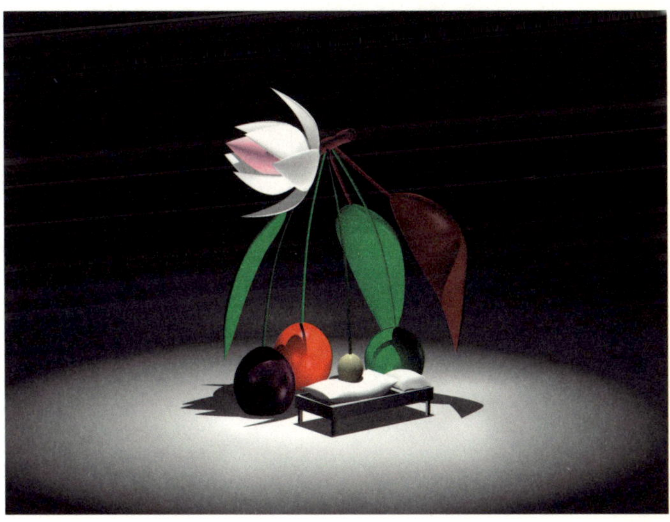

We now come to the question of the image, or the transition from perception to mental representation. In the present experiments this process is accompanied by the translation of tactile into visual data. It occurs when the child attempts to derive either a mental image or a drawing involving vision and movement, from tactile perceptions governed by perceptual activity of a tactile-kinesthetic order. [...] The image is a product of imitation. It is in fact an internalized imitation, one that can be made without retort to external gesture, though it is at first associated with such gestures, as in the ludic image or deferred imitation.

Jean Piaget and Bärbel Inhelder, *The Child's Conception of Space* [La représentation de l'espace chez l'enfant, 1948], trans. F. J. Langdon and J. L. Luzner, London: Routledge and Kegan Paul, 1956, p. 40.

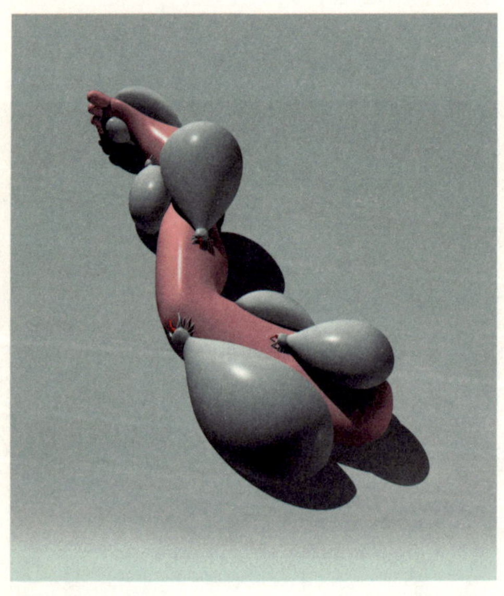

Suppose, however, that someone were to draw while he had an image or instead of having it, though it were only with his finger in the air. (This might be called "motor imagery.") He could be asked: "Whom does that represent?" And his answer would be decisive.

Ludwig Wittgenstein, *Philosophical*

Investigations [Philosophische Untersuchungen, 1953], trans. G.E.M. Anscombe, Oxford: Basil Blackwell, second edition, 1958, p. 177.

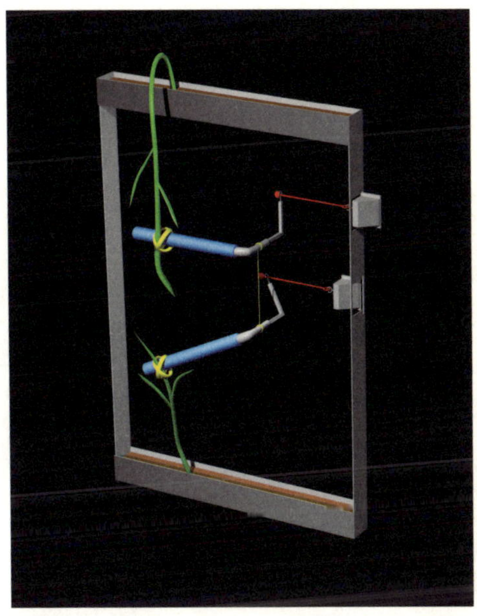

Between the alleged colors and visibles, we would find anew the tissue that lines them, sustains them, nourishes them, and which for its part is not a thing, but a possibility, a latency, and a flesh of things.

Maurice Merleau-Ponty, *The Visible and the Invisible* [Le visible et l'invisible, 1964], trans. Alfonso Lingis, Evanston: Northwestern University Press, 1968, pp. 132–3.

We give one another some superficial bit of ourselves—just a bit of skin, a nothing, a tiny fragment that we are able to give at the time. But the other carries it unconsciously with him. And when he is suddenly lonely, he remembers that he has a piece of a different, dear person in himself, and if he looks closely, it has grown and become a part of him, is in all and all in him, and he is not alone.

Robert Musil, second of three letter-drafts to Liesl, June 1908, in *Briefe* [Letters] *1901–1942*, ed. Adolf Friesé, Reinbek bei Hamburg: Rowohlt, 1981, p. 55.

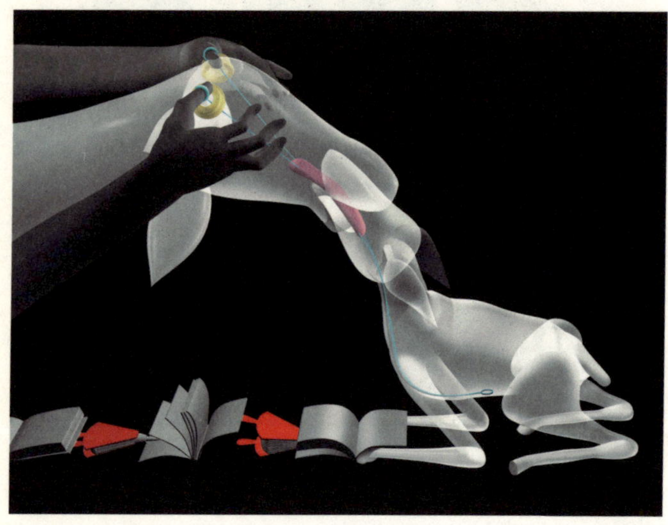

I took the print of life not outwardly, but inwardly upon the raw, the white, the unprotected fiber. I am clouded and bruised with the print of minds and faces and things so subtle that they have smell, colour, texture, substance, but no name.

Virginia Woolf, *The Waves* (1931), London: Penguin, 1992, p. 164.

What I would propose in place of these conceptions of construction is a return to the notion of matter not as a site or surface, but as *a process of materialization that stabilizes over time to produce the effect of boundary, fixity, and surface we call matter.* That matter is always materialized has, I think, to be thought in relation to the productive and, indeed, materializing effects of regulatory power in the Foucaultian sense.

Judith Butler, *Bodies that Matter: On the Discursive Limits of "Sex,"* London: Routledge, 1993, pp. 9–10.

After that he began waking up in the morning with a transparent jelly like a tadpole's tail all over his mouth. This jelly was what the scientists call un-D.T., Undifferentiated Tissue, which can grow into any kind of flesh on the human body.

William S. Burroughs, *Naked Lunch* (1959), London: Flamingo, 1993, pp. 110–11.

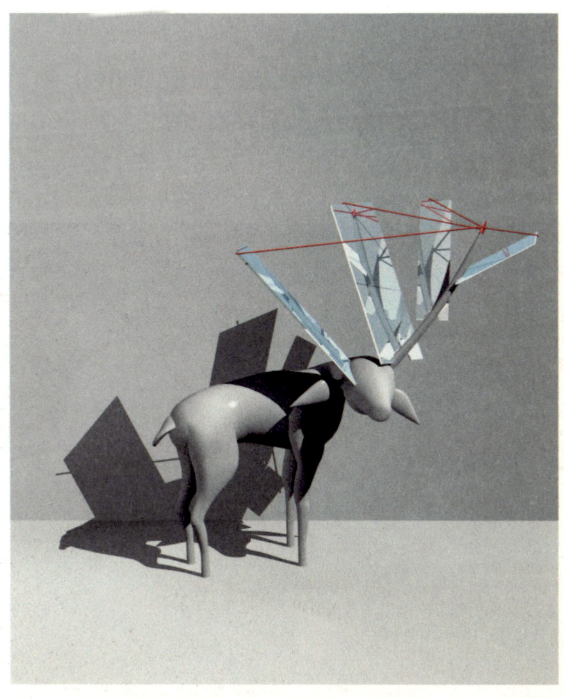

I shall never get out of this! There are two of me now:
This new absolutely white person and the old yellow one,
And the white person is certainly the superior one.
She doesn't need food, she is one of the real saints.
At the beginning I hated her, she had no personality—
She lay in bed with me like a dead body
And I was scared, because she was shaped just the way
I was. [...]
She wanted to leave me, she thought she was superior,
And I'd been keeping her in the dark, and she was
resentful—
Wasting her days waiting on a half-corpse!
And secretly she began to hope I'd die.
Then she could cover my mouth and eyes, cover me
entirely,
And wear my painted face the way a mummy-case
Wears the face of a pharaoh, though it's made of mud
and water.

Sylvia Plath, "In Plaster" (1961), in Sylvia Plath, *Collected Poems*, ed. Ted Hughes, London: Faber and Faber, 1981, p. 159.

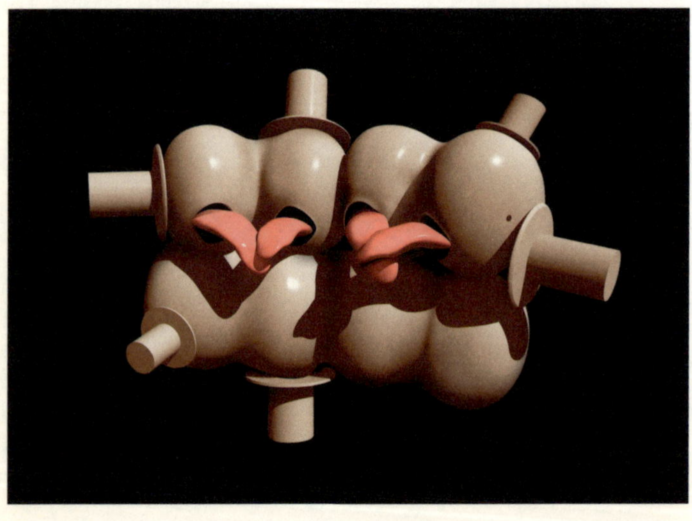

"When I touch this object with a stick I have the sensation of touching in the tip of the stick, not in the hand that holds it." [...] Does what I say mean "It is as if I had nerve-endings in the tip of the stick?" *In what sense* is it like that?—Well, I am at any rate inclined to say, "I feel the hardness etc. in the tip of the stick."

Ludwig Wittgenstein, *Philosophical Investigations* [Philosophische Untersuchungen, 1953], trans. G.E.M. Anscombe, Oxford: Basil Blackwell, 1958, pp. 161–2.

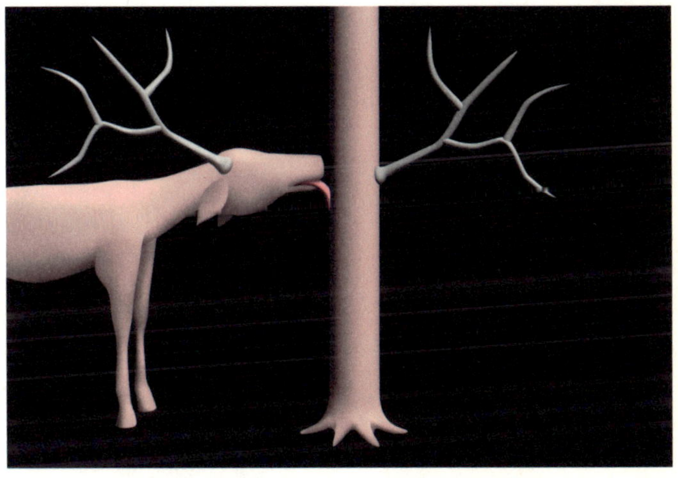

Conversely, if it touches [the body] and sees, this is not because it would have the visibles before itself as objects: they are about it, they even enter into its enclosure, they are within it, they line its looks and its hands inside and outside.

Maurice Merleau-Ponty, *The Visible and the Invisible* [Le visible et l'invisible, 1964], trans. Alfonso Lingis, Evanston: Northwestern University Press, 1968, p. 137.

This trivial gesture, which I begin, is continued by another part of myself; without anything interrupting it physically, it branches off, shifts from a simple function to a dazzling meaning, that of the demand for love; I am about to tear open the other's opaque body, oblige the other (whether there is a response, a withdrawal, or mere acceptance) to enter into the interplay of meaning: I am about *to make the other speak.*

Roland Barthes, *A Lover's Discourse: Fragments* [Fragments d'un discours amoureux, 1977], trans. Richard Howard, London: Penguin Books, 1990, p. 68.

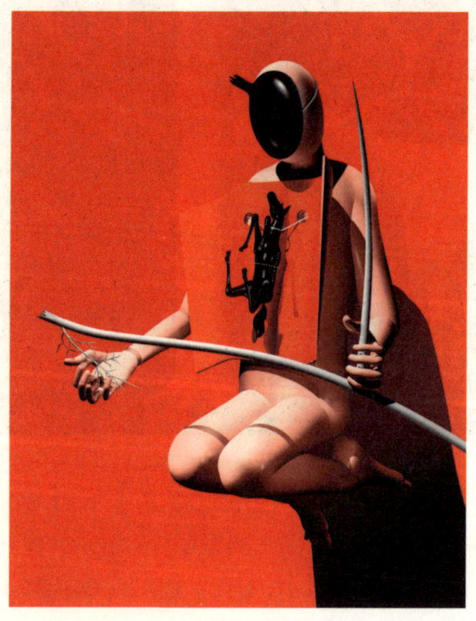

What sort of issue is: Is it the *body* that feels pain?—How is it to be decided? What makes it plausible to say that it is *not* the body?—Well, something like this: if someone has a pain in his hand, then the *hand* does not say so (unless it writes it) and one does not comfort the hand, but the sufferer: one looks into his face.

Ludwig Wittgenstein, *Philosophical Investigations* [Philosophische Untersuchungen, 1953], trans. G.E.M. Anscombe, Oxford: Basil Blackwell, 1958, p. 98.

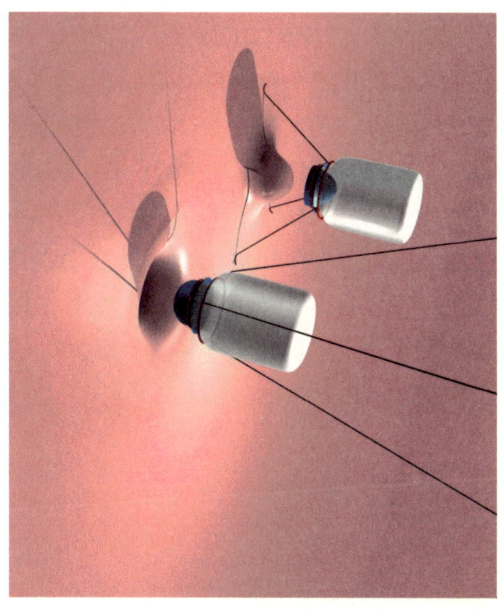

But I can throw up my arm in a particular way when somebody jabs me, and this act too would allow the observer to state that the movement of my arm "expresses" or "articulates" a pain that I felt. But this time there is no unbroken chain of cause and motion. A kind of wedge interrupts the chain, a codification that gives the movement a specific structure, so that for those that know the code it is considered appropriate to communicate the "meaning" of pain. The knowledge of this code, and not a theory, gives the beholder the right to say that the movement "expresses" the pain that I felt. [...] It is a gesture because it represents something, because at issue here is giving meaning.

Vilém Flusser, "Geste und Gestimmtheit," in *Gesten: Versuch einer Phänomenologie*

[Gestures: An Attempt at a Phenomenology], Düsseldorf-Bensheim: Bollmann Verlag, 1991, pp. 10–11.

The gesture is the exhibition of a mediality: it is the process of making a means visible as such. It allows the emergence of the being-in-a-medium of human beings and thus it opens the ethical dimension for them.

Giorgio Agamben, "Notes on Gesture," in *Means without End: Notes on Politics* [Mezzi senza fine: note sulla politica, 1996], trans. Vincenzo Binetti and Cesare Casarino, Minneapolis-London: University of Minnesota Press, 2000, p. 58.

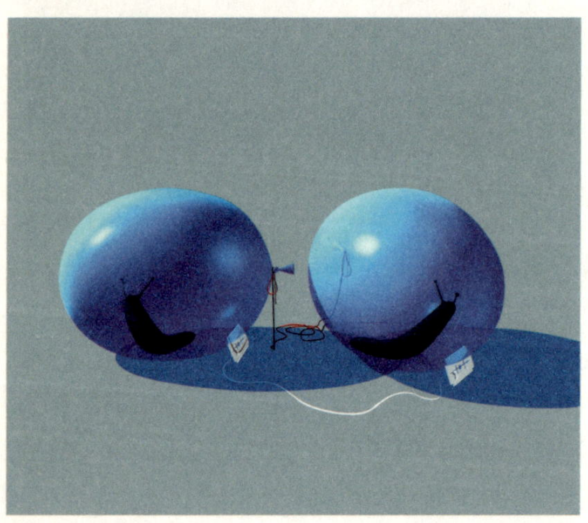

There is no law that is not inscribed on bodies. [...] From birth to mourning after death, law "takes hold of" bodies in order to make them its text.

Michel de Certeau, *The Practice of Everyday Life* [Arts de faire, 1980], trans. Steven Rendall, London-Berkeley: University of California Press, 1984, p. 139.

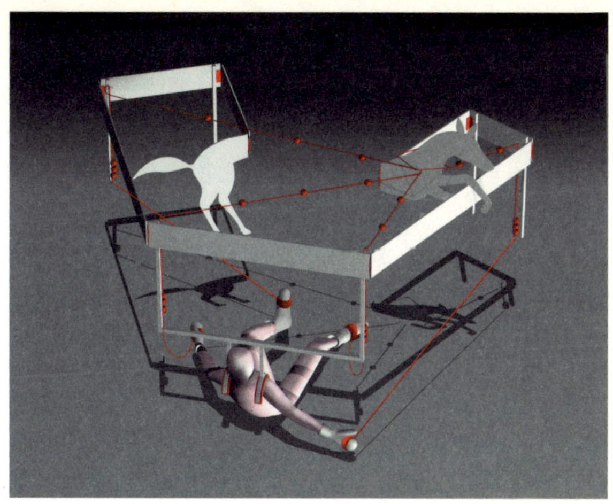

The mechanism of "pathic projection" determines that those in power perceive as human only their own reflected image, instead of reflecting back the human as precisely what is different. Murder is thus the repeated attempt, by yet greater madness, to distort the madness of such false perception into reason: what was not seen as human and yet is human, is made a thing, so that its stirrings can no longer refute the manic gaze.

Theodor W. Adorno, *Minima Moralia: Reflections on a Damaged Life* [Minima Moralia. Reflexionen aus dem beschädigten Leben, 1951], trans. E. F. N. Jephcott, London: New Left Books, 1974, p. 105.

The negro who, brought home from the world exhibition and gone mad from homesickness, performs in the midst of his village, with a most serious face as custom and duty dictates, among the lament of the tribe, the tricks that charmed the European audience as African conventions and traditions.

Franz Kafka, "Oktavheft G" (1917/1918), in *Beim Bau der chinesischen Mauer und andere Schriften aus dem Nachlass* [The Great Wall of China and Other Unpublished Writings], Frankfurt am Main: Fischer, 1994, p. 188.

There can be no two cultures which are completely identical. To believe that it is possible to create a black culture is to forget that *niggers* are disappearing, just as those people who brought them into being are seeing the break-up of their economic and cultural supremacy.

Frantz Fanon, *The Wretched of the Earth* [Les damnés de la terre, 1961], trans. Constance Farrington, London: Penguin Books, 2001, p. 188.

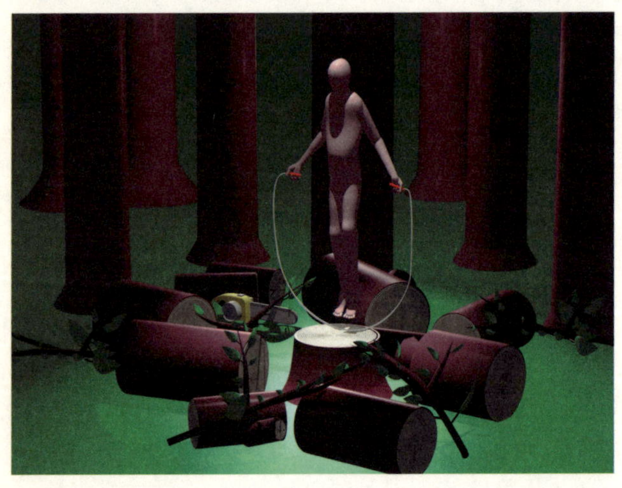

The media's evacuation of the human through the image has to be understood, though, in terms of the broader problem that normative schemes of intelligibility establish what will and will not be human, what will be a livable life, what will be a grievable death. [...] The task at hand is to establish modes of public seeing and hearing that might well respond to the cry of the human within the sphere of appearance, a sphere in which the trace of the cry has become hyperbolically inflated to rationalize a gluttonous nationalism, or fully obliterated, where both alternatives turn out to be the same.

Judith Butler, *Precarious Life: The Powers of Mourning and Violence,* London-New York: Verso, 2004, pp. 146–7.

Yves Netzhammer, videostills

Die begehbare Falle, 1999
p. 113
Süsser Wind im Gesicht, 2004
p. 114
Die ungenauen Körper, 2007
p. 115
Die Zeit bis eine Form entsteht, addiert mit der Zeit, bis die Form zerstört ist, 2003
p. 116
Die Anordnungsweise zweier Gegenteile bei der Erzeugung ihres Berührungsmaximums, 2005
p. 117
Grosse Spiegel werden verloren: Informationen von Abwesenheit, damit Anwesenheit entstehen kann, 2000
p. 118
Die begehbare Falle, 1999
p. 119
Junge Äste ahmen alte Geweihe nach und alte Geweihe junge Äste, 1999
p. 120
Junge Äste ahmen alte Geweihe nach und alte Geweihe junge Äste, 1999
p. 121
Wenn man etwas gegen seine Eigenschaften benützt, muss man dafür einen anderen Namen finden, 1997/99
p. 122
Wenn man etwas gegen seine Eigenschaften benützt, muss man dafür einen anderen Namen finden, 1997/99
p. 123
Die umgekehrte Rüstung, 2002
p. 124
Grosse Spiegel werden verloren: Informationen von Abwesenheit, damit Anwesenheit entstehen kann, 2000
p. 125
Grosse Spiegel werden verloren: Informationen von Abwesenheit, damit Anwesenheit entstehen kann, 2000
p. 126
Übungen machen Meister, die sich nicht an ihre Anfänge erinnern, 2000
p. 127
Die Anordnungsweise zweier Gegenteile bei der Erzeugung ihres Berührungsmaximums, 2005
p. 128

1998
Markus Stegmann
Wenn man etwas gegen seine Eigenschaften benützt, muss man dafür einen anderen Namen finden
"The artist's universe is memorable in an aloof, sometimes repellent sense, and yet when looked at, the fantastic transformations in this universe trigger emotions—not least sympathetic ones—in the beholder. The visual worlds are ambivalent: smoothness and sterility make us shudder; the unexpected mutations on the other hand cause a curious intimacy and emotional investment. Being simultaneously repelled and attracted is an important experience of reception. The sequences deal with people, animals, and things. Wondrous mutations are a key theme throughout the little pieces. One important group of motifs, for example, are hands performing a task, another people or dolls moving in bare rooms. Then there are animals [...]. Grotesque, intricate, opaque events are taking place here in a private, secluded world."

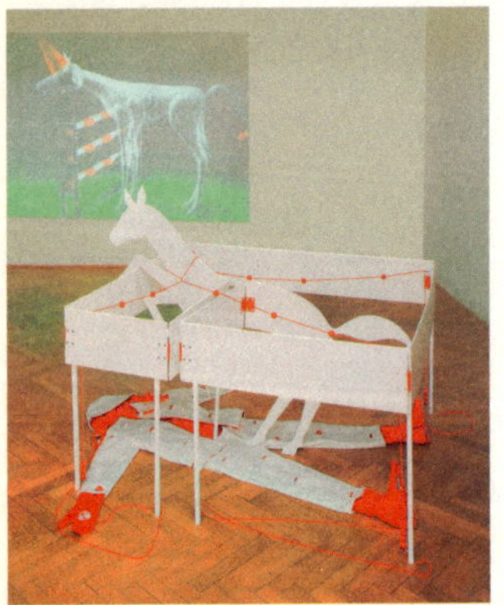

Übungen machen Meister, die sich nicht an ihre Anfänge erinnern, 2000

2001
Stefan Zucker
Tages-Anzeiger
"He succeeds in creating a parallel world with animals, people, and plants, a world with its own laws that still engages in a dialogue with existing reality. People become objects, objects mutate into animals, animals melt into body parts. What disintegrates again becomes something new; everything is in constant osmotic movement. Netzhammer's animations are simultaneously exploration, instruction, and seduction in a world where borders blur, a world in flux."

2001
Wulf Herzogenrath
Kunstzeitung
"His almost mirror-like, smooth visions of a future artificial world with robots and animals are full of sex and irony: cool creatures [...] transform themselves in a virtual world that makes all sorts of allusions to our own reality."

2003
Andreas Jürgensen / Simon Maurer / Tim Zulauf
The Surprising Displacement of the Predetermined Breaking Point of a Branch Grown under Optimal Conditions
"Netzhammer's chains of actions are reflected in the foundations of sociopolitical structures: they clash with conventional, everyday usage of signs and become artificial drives and imaginary structures in the data space of low-threshold resistances. Caught in the process of metamorphosis, pictorial conventions give off burning secretions. As signs and emotions, they burn on our skin, and they target the longings and fears our society uses to separate bodies from each other, to isolate ideas, and to create the sense of self. They hit us where we are most sensitive: in illness and love, sexuality and death."

2003
Peter P. Schneider
Züritipp
"With Netzhammer, a person is what he becomes through perception: a store of senses and a body of language. He sees, hears, touches, smells, and tastes, lets impressions flow into his memories, stacked in the form of bricks. An art(ificial) figure, similar to the wooden puppets used for anatomical drawing, absorbs the surroundings: mountains fold like the hands that the figure spots on its own body. An interplay of interior image and exterior view, of perception and figuration is set in motion."

2003
Gerhard Mack
NZZ am Sonntag
"As unusual as his images and figures may seem, they are not without tradition in art history. 'I'm not a good exhibition-goer, but I always come upon related material,'

Netzhammer says. Already in antiquity, Ovid created a monument to the principle of transformation in *Metamorphoses*. The artist is always thrilled by the convincing compositions of old Indian drawings; whenever he speaks of Museum Rietberg, his breath quickens. Similarities can just as easily flash up in four-hundred-year-old mannerist drawing or in the work of Matthew Barney and his play with power codes."

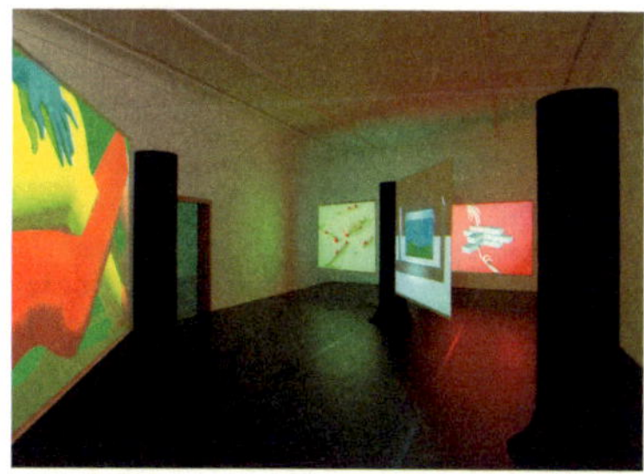

Videoskulptur, 2003

2003
Barbara Basting
Tages-Anzeiger

"The computer animations' cool mood and their spatiality, so sparse in terms of texture and surface detail, promote an effect of aesthetic alienation; just enough to ban the uncontrollable, vulnerable, tabooed juice-flow of natural bodies from the picture. He thus constructs antiseptic experimental arrangements born of the spirit of the laboratory. At the same time, Netzhammer does everything to reintroduce a sensation-saturated physicality by way of association. The fascination of his videos, the delight in watching them originates from the difference between one's own body perception and the model world on offer, where sensations can be rediscovered or even sharpened. Netzhammer radicalizes and heightens micro-moments of sensation, drills into the deeper sediments of the body's memory."

2003
Claudia Spinelli
Weltwoche

"A quiet melancholy pervades Yves Netzhammer's visual world. His protagonists are imprisoned in the finiteness of their body, and the signals they receive are nothing more than the echo of the impulses they themselves broadcast. [...] Netzhammer's sequences of images grow uncontrollably like tumors, mutually determining and constantly generating one another. Where is the artist headed? Of course Netzhammer's visual signs, as artificial and model-like as they may be, are refractions of an actually existing world. Only that the meanings, stimulated by always new combinations and shifts, keep multiplying. The images revolve around fundamental conditions of human existence."

2003
Angelika Affentranger-Kirchrath
Neue Zürcher Zeitung

"In the work of the Zurich-based artist, born in 1970, the word plays a central role—although he mistrusts it. It causes unease, initiates stories and leaves them as an open ellipse, it clearly belongs with the images and links up with them to form a visual language that is difficult to access. [...] Although digitally generated and strangely artificial in appearance and language, these actors are surprisingly fitting as projection figures for the beholder. He recognizes them as his stand-ins, reduced to a pictogrammatically abbreviated form, moving in a world that is no longer controllable. [...] While walking through the filmic path [...] we slowly delve into Netzhammer's calculated and yet suggestive universe, which awakens emotions and enthrallingly communicates existential content, using a cool aesthetic."

2003
Catherine Riva
Le Matin

"Netzhammer spends [...] his time in eluding our expectations, in modifying perspectives. In the world which he displays, the trees are made out of bricks, bricks which they lose like leaves, and the leaves are like small graves within which a story is entombed. Tanks are running over the bodies like insects on corpses while strange little submarines are delving into the wounds. He steals blind parrots which utter forth sententious phrases. He depicts the day and the night, because the landscapes slide sometimes in a bright room, and sometimes in a dim room. The bodies dislocate, the protagonists and their universe fuse together, mix and become entangled, and then they come loose again, like single-celled creatures who are victims of a mysterious randomness."

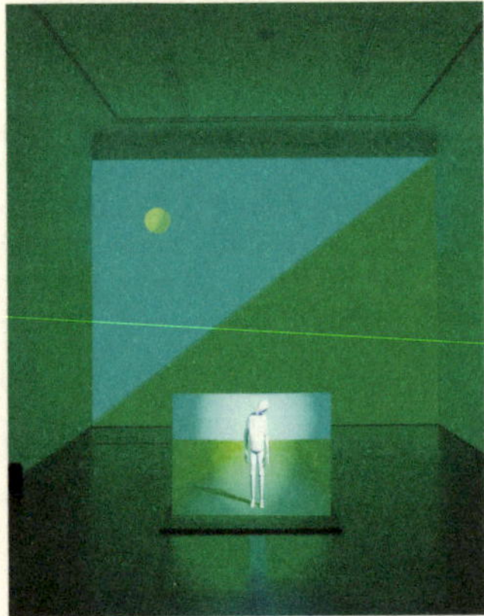

Am Horizont können wir unsere Sinne ablesen, 2003

2003
Anna Schindler
Kunstzeitung

"Using drawings, videos, and installations, Netzhammer transforms our familiar everyday environment into a surreal cosmos: he blends human bodies with flora and fauna and lets arms end in snouts and horse's hoofs. The computer animations contribute in their own way: one visual sequence floats into the next like an oil stain that spreads on the water, always changing shape. [...] Netzhammer's fantasies are sometimes not without brutality, but in their suffering, his protagonists remain faceless: they are not individuals, but computer-animated bodies, not men and women, but mannequins. [...] Under a clinically smooth, cool surface, Yves Netzhammer tells serious stories of life and death, uncanny metamorphoses of our reality. They only become bearable in their alienation."

2003
Silke Hohmann
Frankfurter Rundschau

"[Netzhammer] is one of the few multimedia artists who use the computer not merely as a tool, but have developed their own formal language on the computer screen. With their sober tone, his film sequences and images are reminiscent of informational graphics or representations in textbooks. Netzhammer's human figures, without any individual features whatsoever, have the charm of the first man-machine visions from the days when a computer had the computing power of today's telephones. Ironic references to his chosen medium, however, are not Netzhammer's thing. After all, anybody can be funny on the computer, but developing serious or romantic content with animation programs demands courage. Despite their formal reduction (possibly even because of it), his figures have a subtle air of melancholy and ponderousness. For Netzhammer's naked, smooth, genderless hominids are boiled down to 'the human individual as such,' and, as we know, they don't have it easy."

2003
Beate Ermacora
Das Gefühl präziser Haltlosigkeit beim Festhalten der Dinge

"If we want to approach Netzhammer's visual world verbally, technological and scientific terms come to mind. He sets into motion endless viral chain reactions through the encounter of people, instruments, trees, birds, spaces, and other elements, which never find their way back to the point of origin. Every touch results in drastic changes."

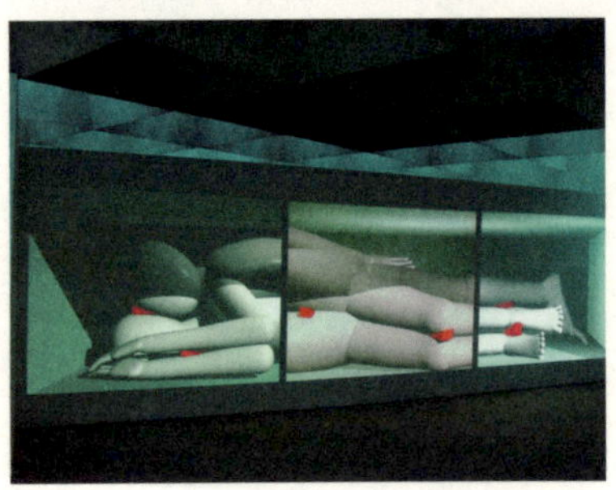

Das Gefühl präziser Haltlosigkeit beim Festhalten der Dinge, 2003

2003
Heidrun Wirth
Kölnische Rundschau

"The figures are constantly changing—genderless and faceless, pink as if made of celluloid, sometimes reminiscent of the mannequins by Oskar Schlemmer or De Chirico."

2004
Gisela Kuoni
Kunst-Bulletin

"The beholder is drawn for no explicable reason into Netzhammer's visual world and visual events, because unknown to the beholder, they are his or her own visual world and visual events. The beholder surrenders to the poetical, often moving narrative flow without losing perception and alertness, as if in a delirium. Netzhammer does not numb us, he animates us to think for ourselves, using the unusual logic of the path behind us. This path is full of speed and surprises. Within seconds, it leads astray, but just as quickly new and surprising turns open up. With lightening speed, they lead us on, awaken memories and confirm our own insights. His videos are not a way of passing the time, they touch on the existential."

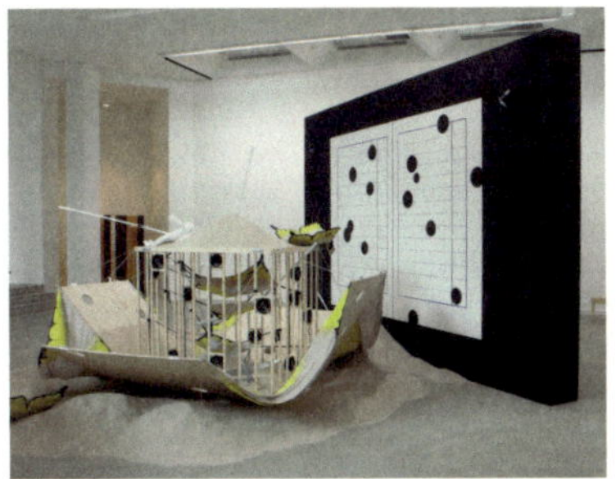

Süsser Wind im Gesicht, 2004

2005
Claudine Metzger
Sturzenegger-Stiftung

"In spite of the technological artificiality of the images that Yves Netzhammer develops as drawings on the computer, they are dense in terms of emotion and hit right at the center of our emotions. Their artificiality and media reduction enable the artist to create personal metaphors for not representable processes that we associate due to our habits of vision and our life experience with elemental, difficult-to-grasp human emotions and states of being like love, affection, illness, injury, pain. In his almost surreal, mysterious, quiet and disquieting images, Yves Netzhammer knows how to show how close soundness and injury, connectedness and separation really are."

2005
Frank Laukötter
The Arrangement of two Opposites while their Maximum Contact is under Generation

"The pictures [...] are thought-images. Thinking in images is testing actions in images. The animated and animating pictures experiment with those of reality. Art tests the world. 'Animation is documentation' is a corresponding motto of Yves Netzhammer. The aim is potentiality as reality, grasping the world via the model of the world. Aesthetic experience replaces experience. Nonetheless, the described experiences of the modelled figures inside their modelled world apply to the relationship of real people to themselves, to their real environment and their real fellow humans. Neither the image sequence discussed nor the following film sequences can do without references to reality (9/11 really live)—or to the stage of media reality (9/11 on all channels). The figures in the image world of the film are de-individualized actors. As such, they are figures that represent humans outside the image world of the film: They are abstract characters. Through their actions and fates they visualize basic traits and their dramas."

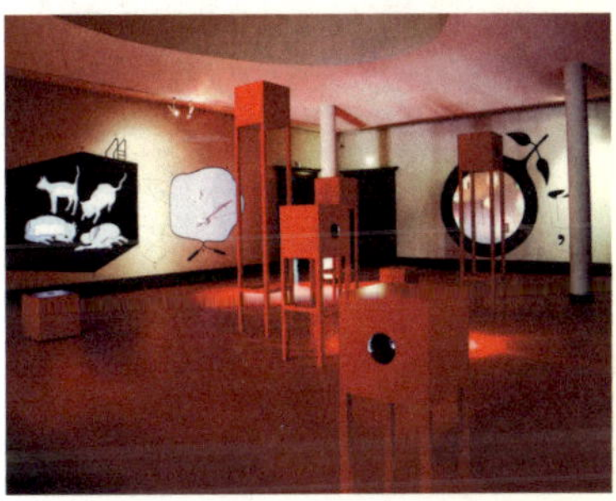

Die Anordnungsweise zweier Gegenteile bei der Erzeugung ihres Berührungsmaximums, 2005

2006
Tim Zulauf
Unfassbare Abnutzungen. Überlegungen zum Materialitätsbegriff von Yves Netzhammer,
unpublished lecture

"What is immediately evident when we encounter Netzhammer's works is the fact that his visual world is a world of signs. This means that the movements, figures, and spaces of this visual world are recognizable and legible. Apparently, Netzhammer does not seek images that try to invalidate the sign itself. The reverse is the case, to the extent that he assumes a reflex-like reaction to signs or the emblematic. In this, his work is fundamentally different from those that, in the tradition of suprematism, art informel, or postminimalism want to present 'the material' as a presence, as the effect of a pure present. [...] 'Materiality' in the sense offered by Yves Netzhammer [...]

remains somewhere between a movement that cannot yet be read as a gesture, and the use of sensations that 'are used against their nature,' or have no inherent nature of their own as of yet. Materiality is the possibility of material, the possibility of the presence of an unknown form of sensation."

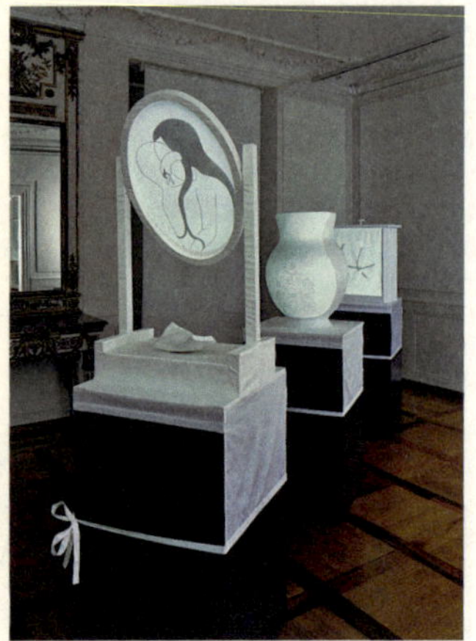

Gefährdete Liebschaften, 2006

2007
Nils Röller
ZappingZone

"Netzhammer's figures [...] use instruments as 'pure' means. The figures move in a state of underdeveloped perception. Their movements are controlled by the artifacts. The jump rope, the record player, the wheel chair on the street pavement control the figures' movement. The instruments are not mobilized by the figures; instead, the instruments make use of the figures, and help them in discovering themselves. The treatment of pure means presumes that instruments and techniques are conceived as condensations of human habitual behavior in which the development of civilization has inscribed itself. In so doing, Netzhammer's figures operate in an epistemologically testing fashion: they explore themselves. They discover their functions by trying out instruments, allowing themselves to be directed by them, investigating their own essence."

Further reading

Yves Netzhammer—Das Gefühl präziser Haltlosigkeit beim Festhalten der Dinge, exhibition catalog, Krefelder Kunstmuseen/ Kaiser Wilhelm Museum, Stiftung Wilhelm Lehmbruck Museum, Duisburg, Bielefeld: Kerber Verlag, 2003.

Yves Netzhammer—The Surprising Displacement of the Predetermined Breaking Point of a Branch Grown under Optimal Conditions, exhibition catalog, Helmhaus Zürich, in collaboration with Institut für moderne Kunst Nürnberg, Nuremberg: Verlag für moderne Kunst Nürnberg, 2003.

Yves Netzhammer—The Arrangement of two Opposites while their Maximum Contact is under Generation, exhibition catalog, Kunsthalle Bremen, eds. Wulf Herzogenrath and Frank Laukötter, Nuremberg: Verlag für moderne Kunst Nürnberg, 2005.

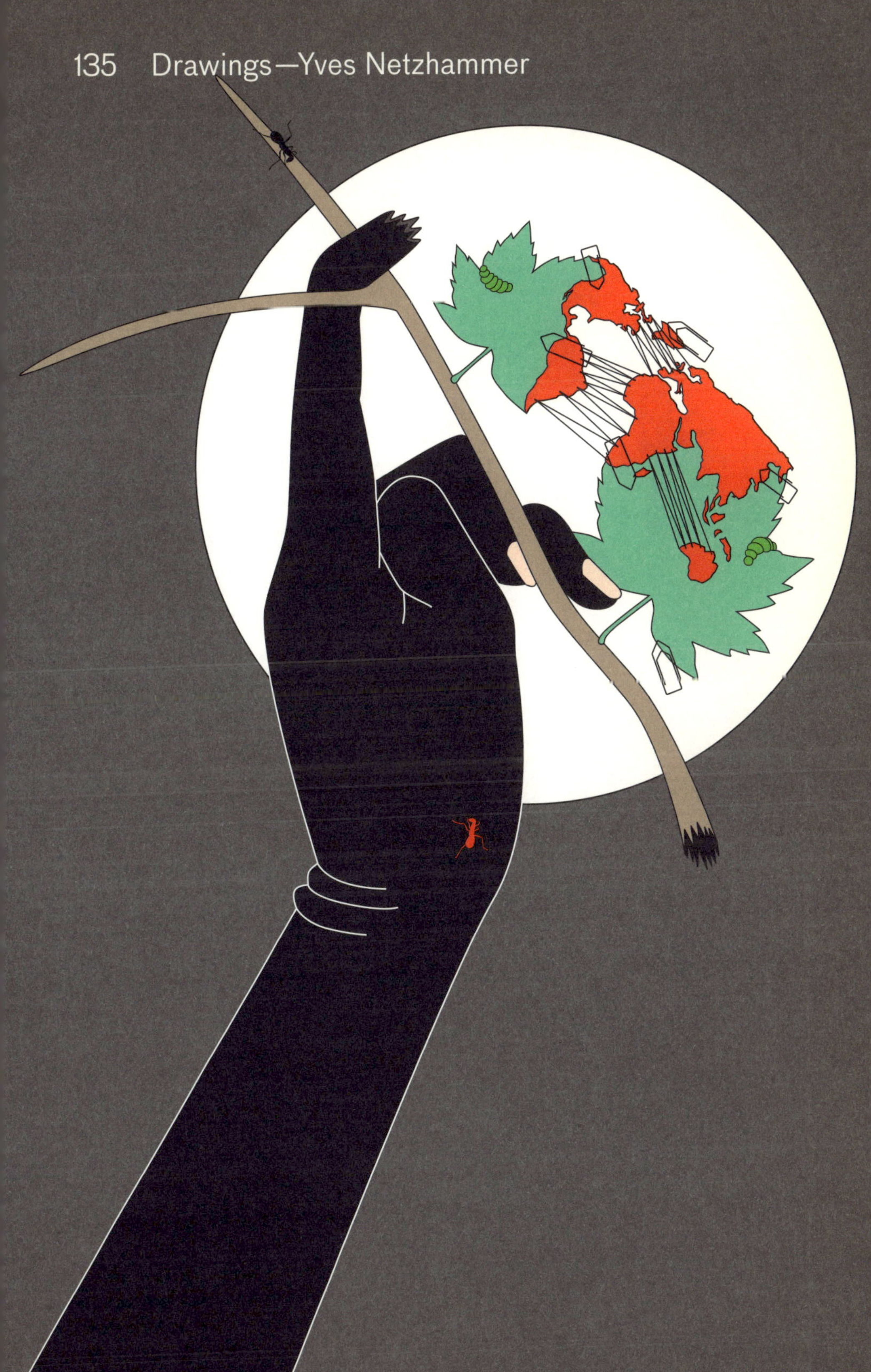

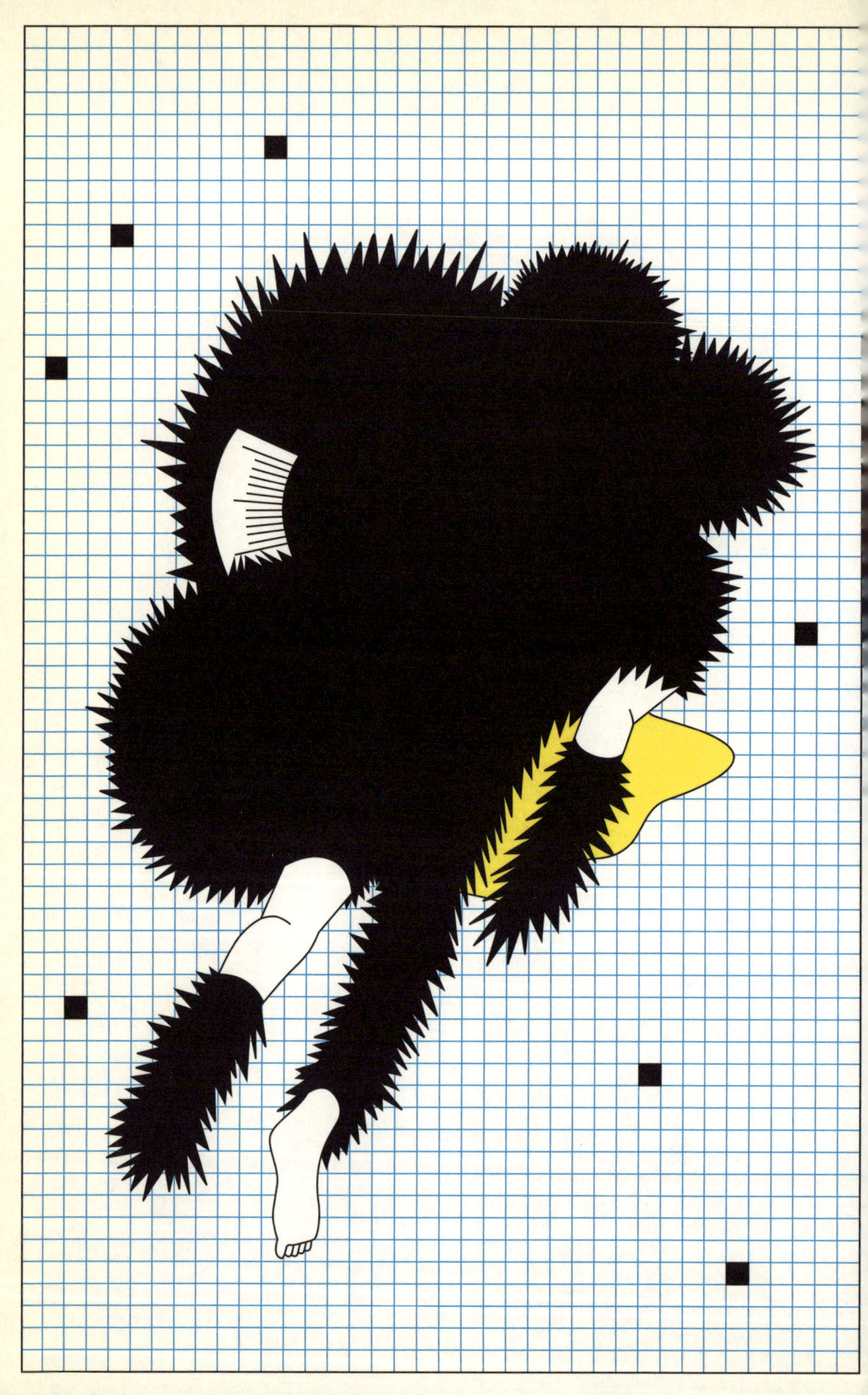

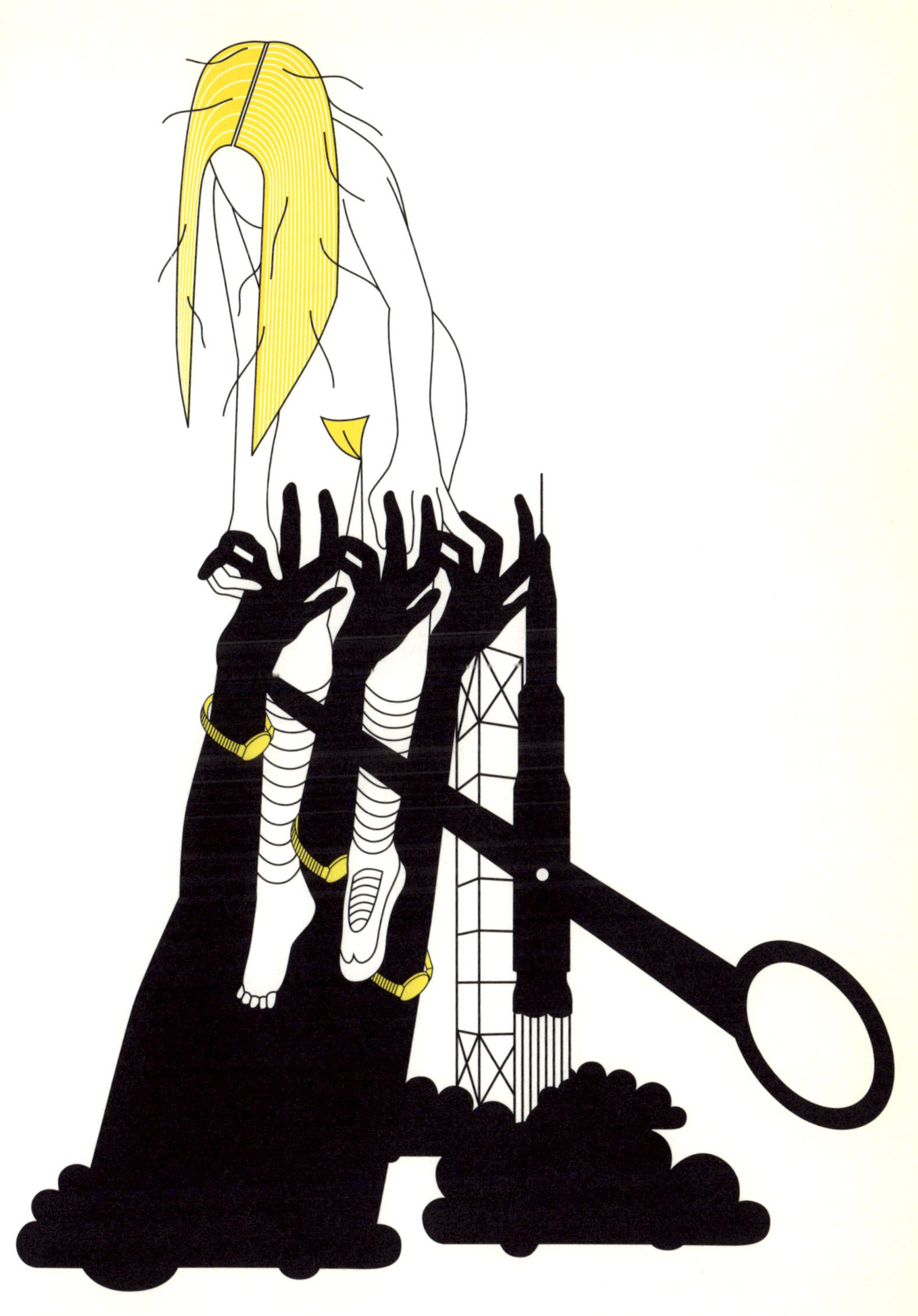

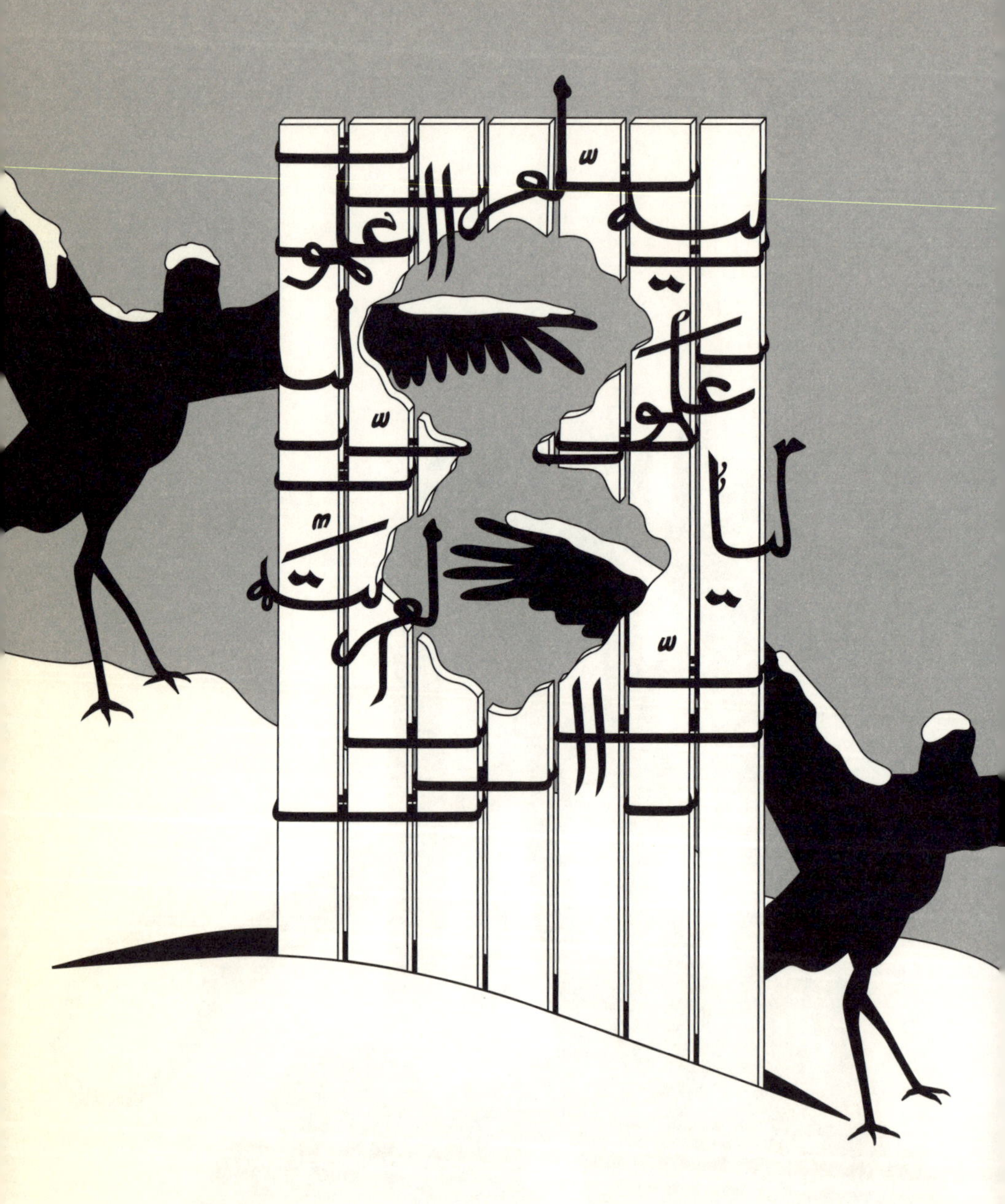

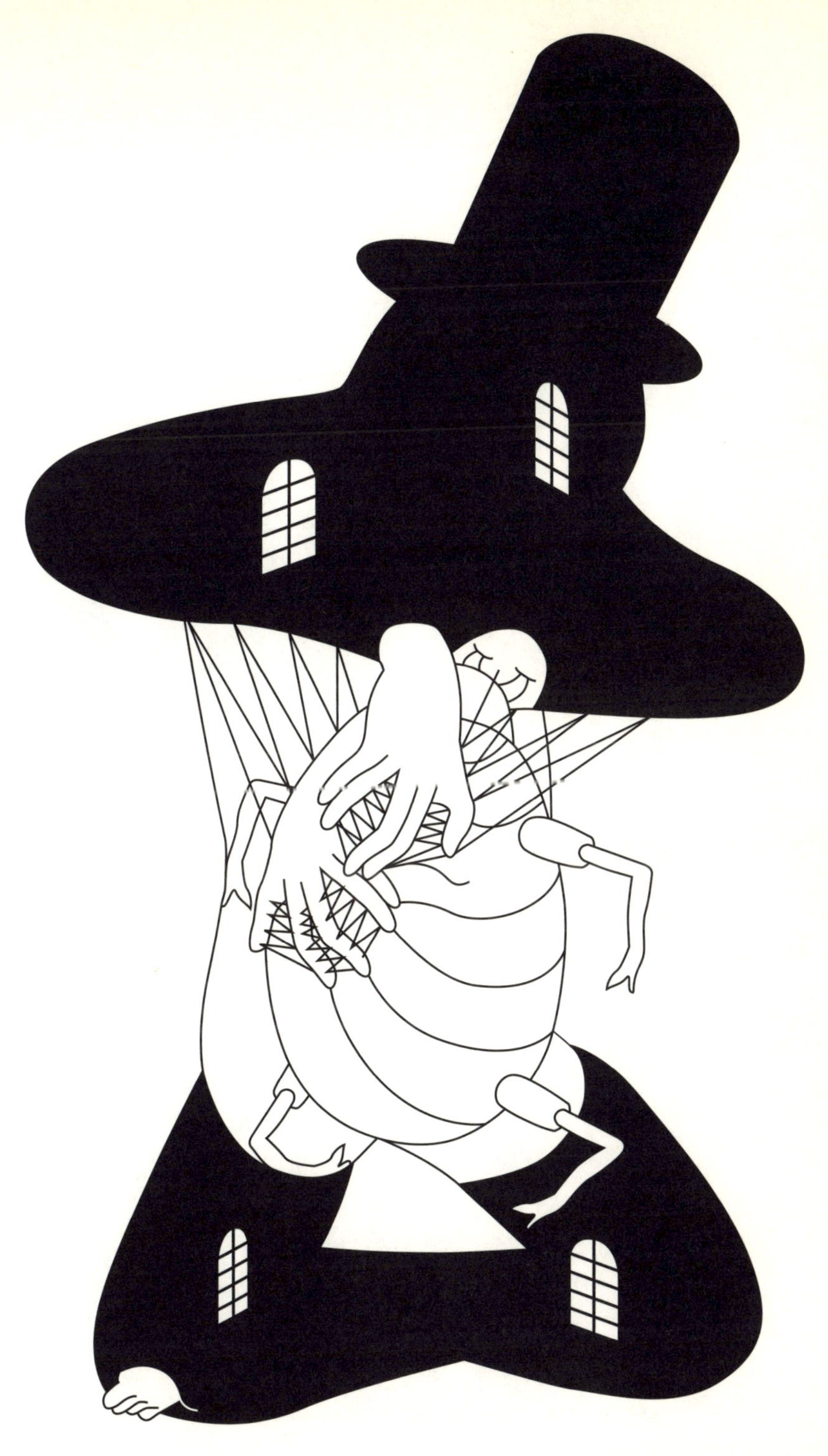

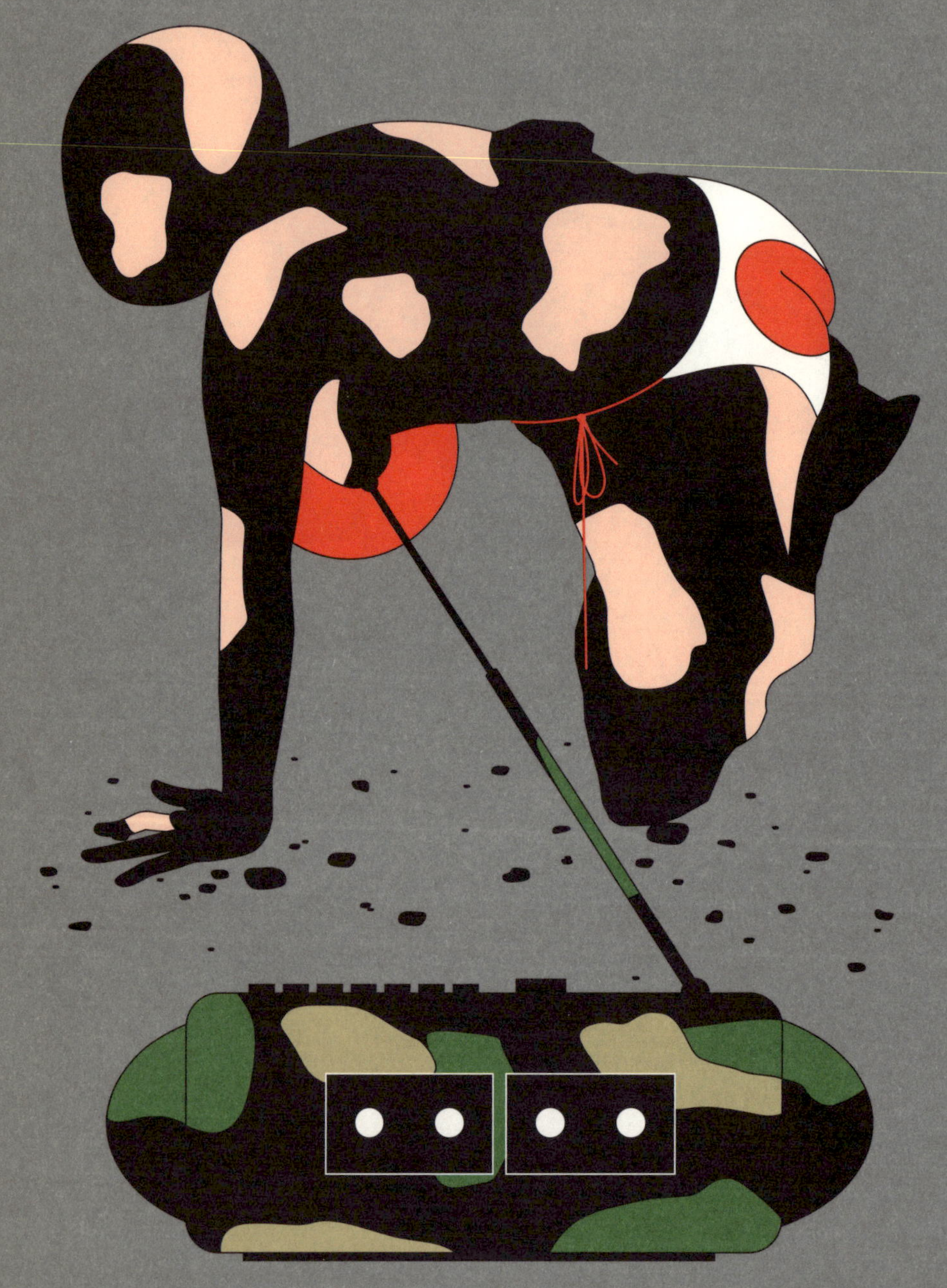

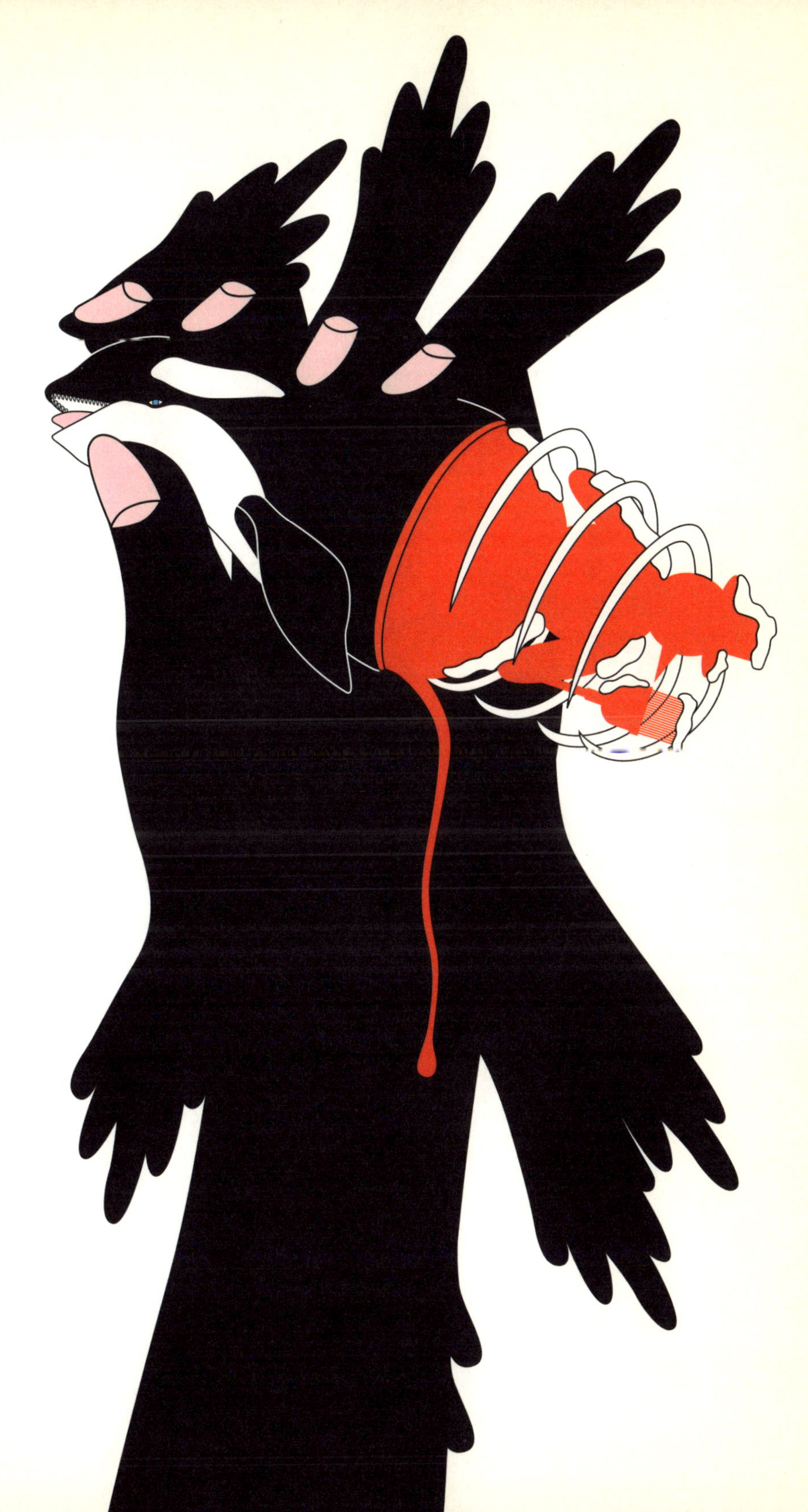

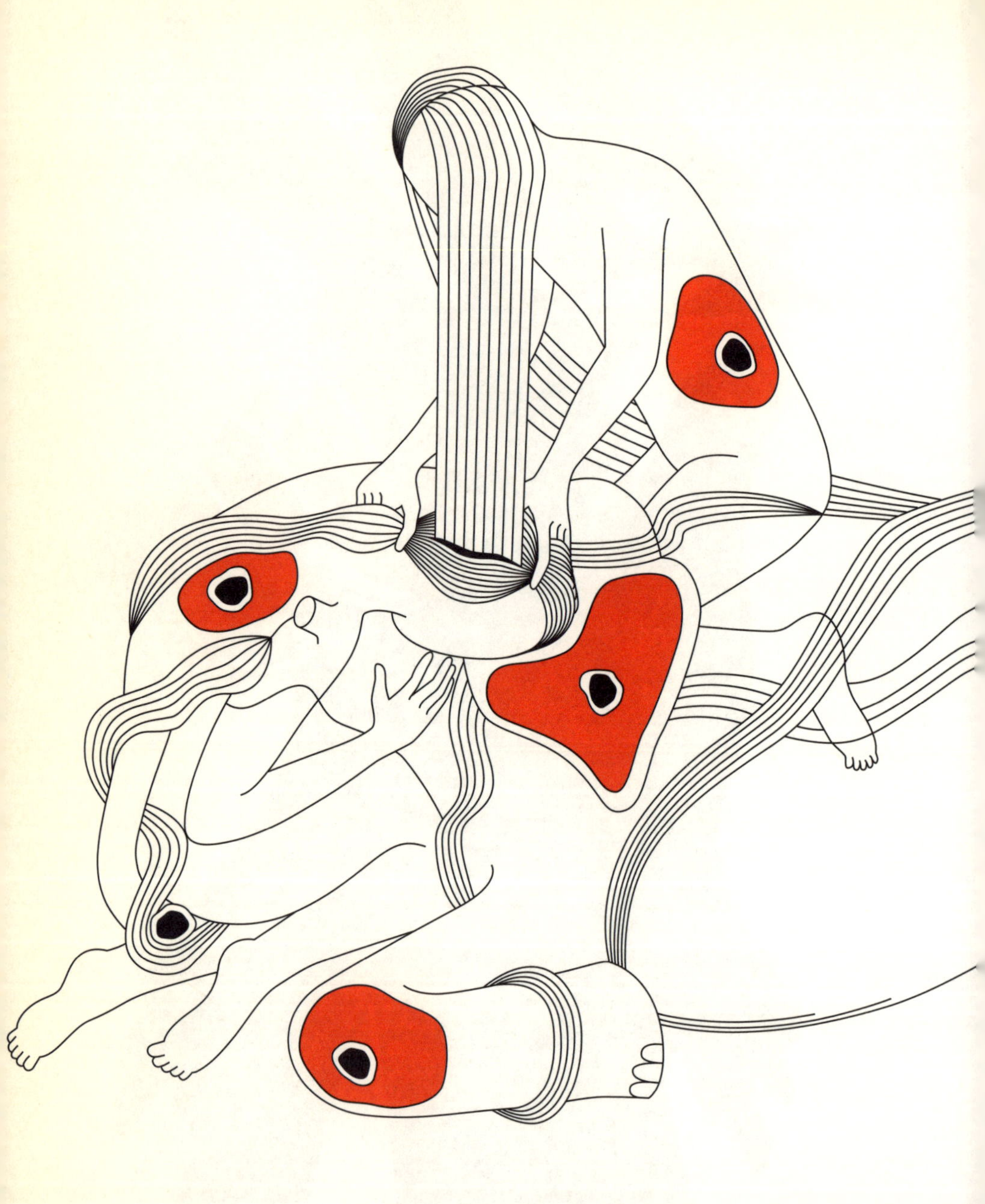

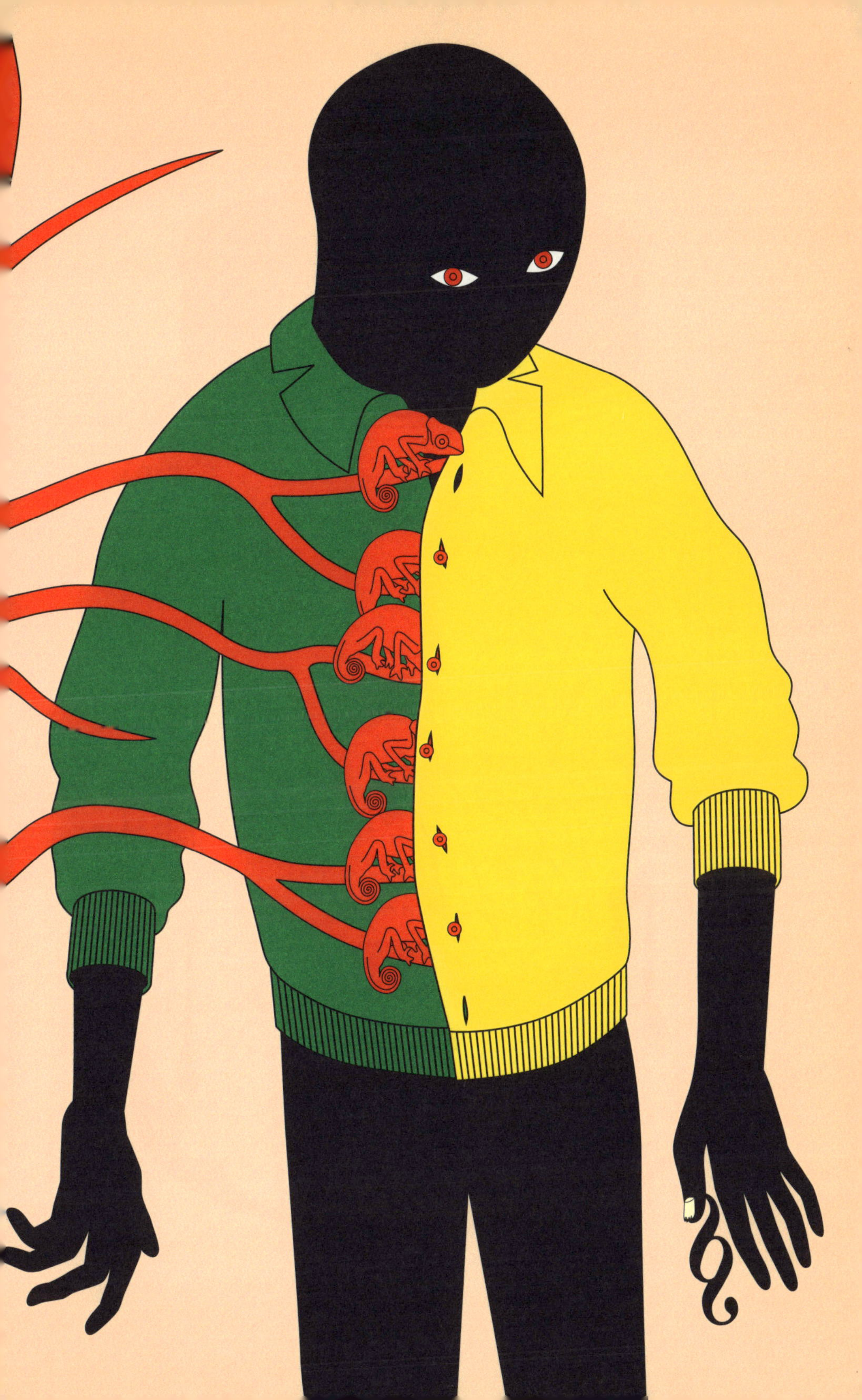

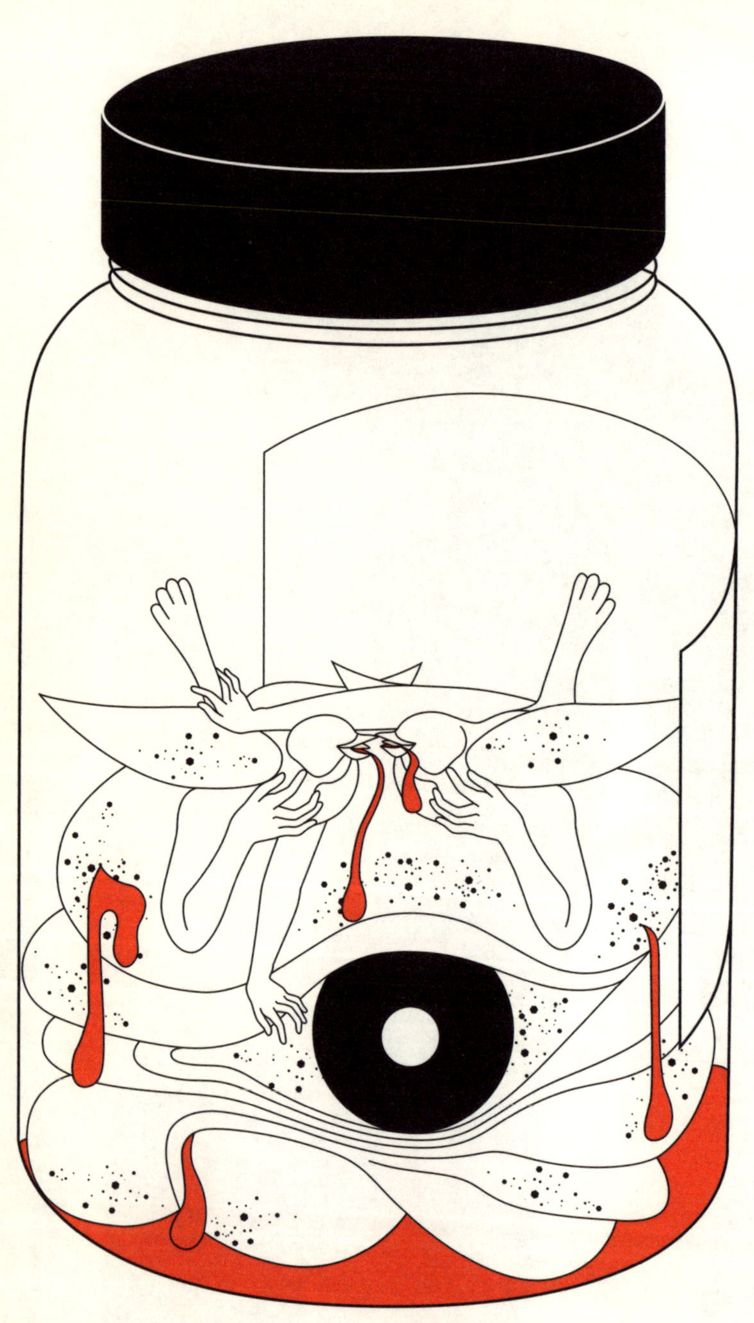

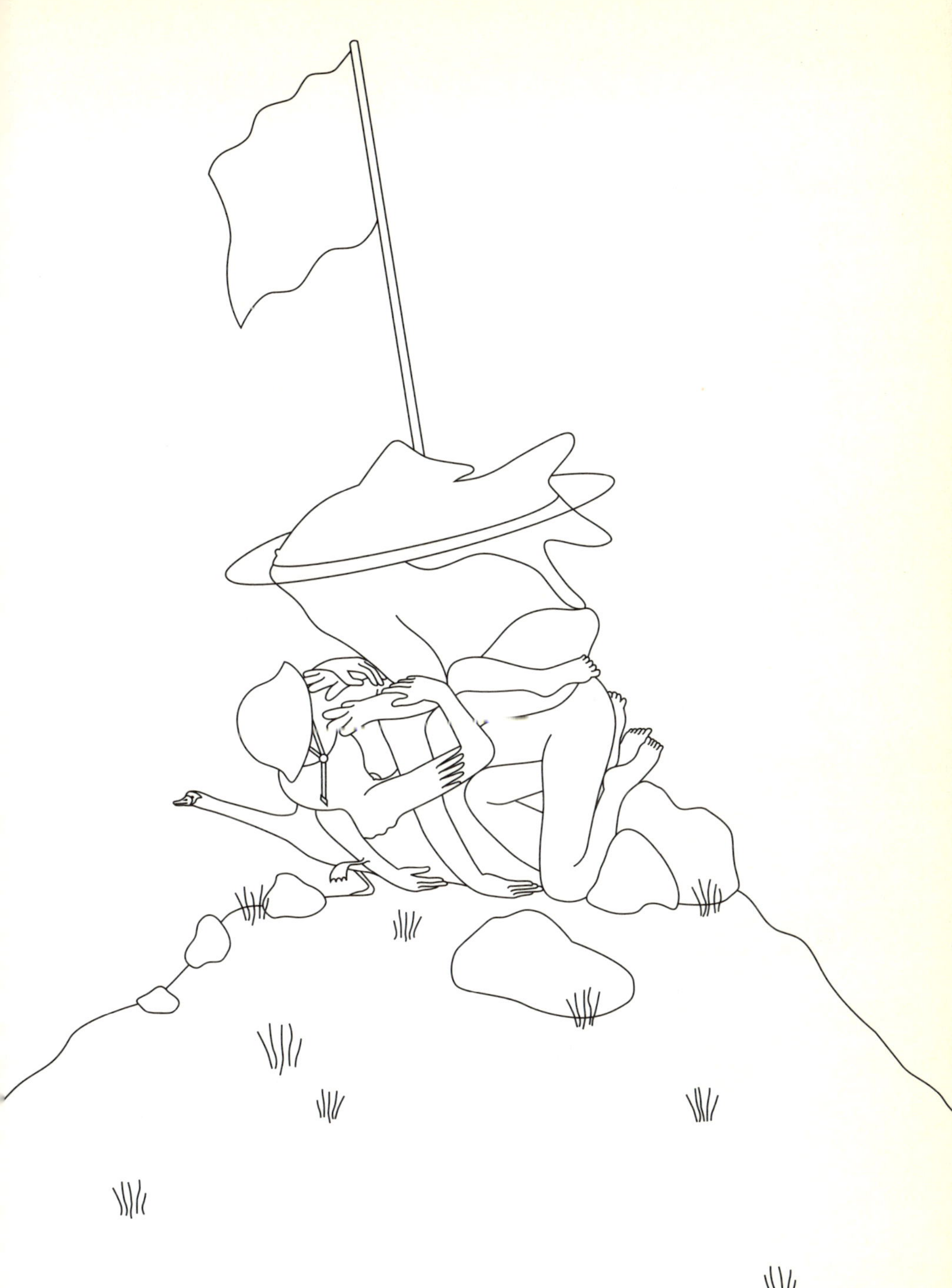

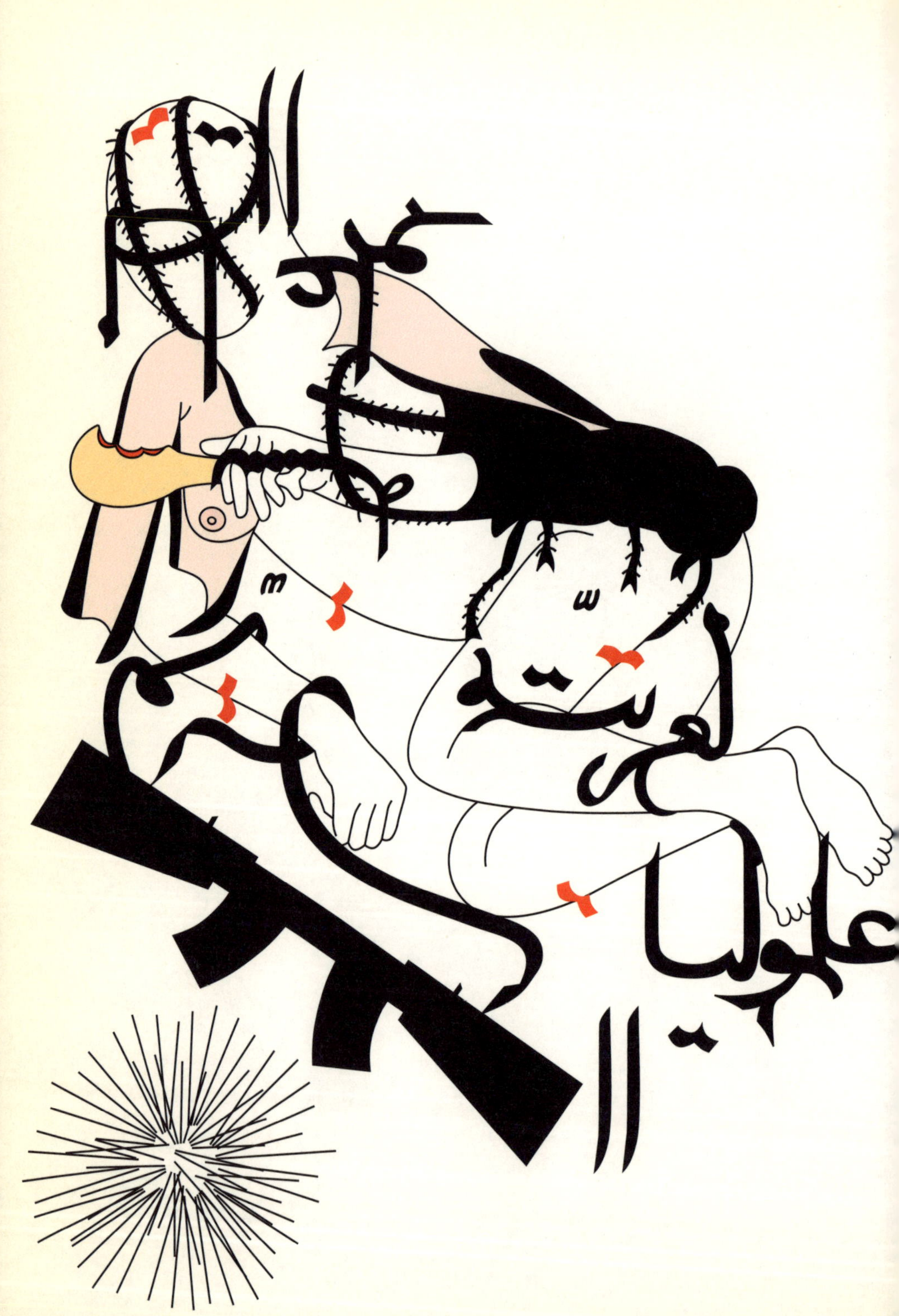

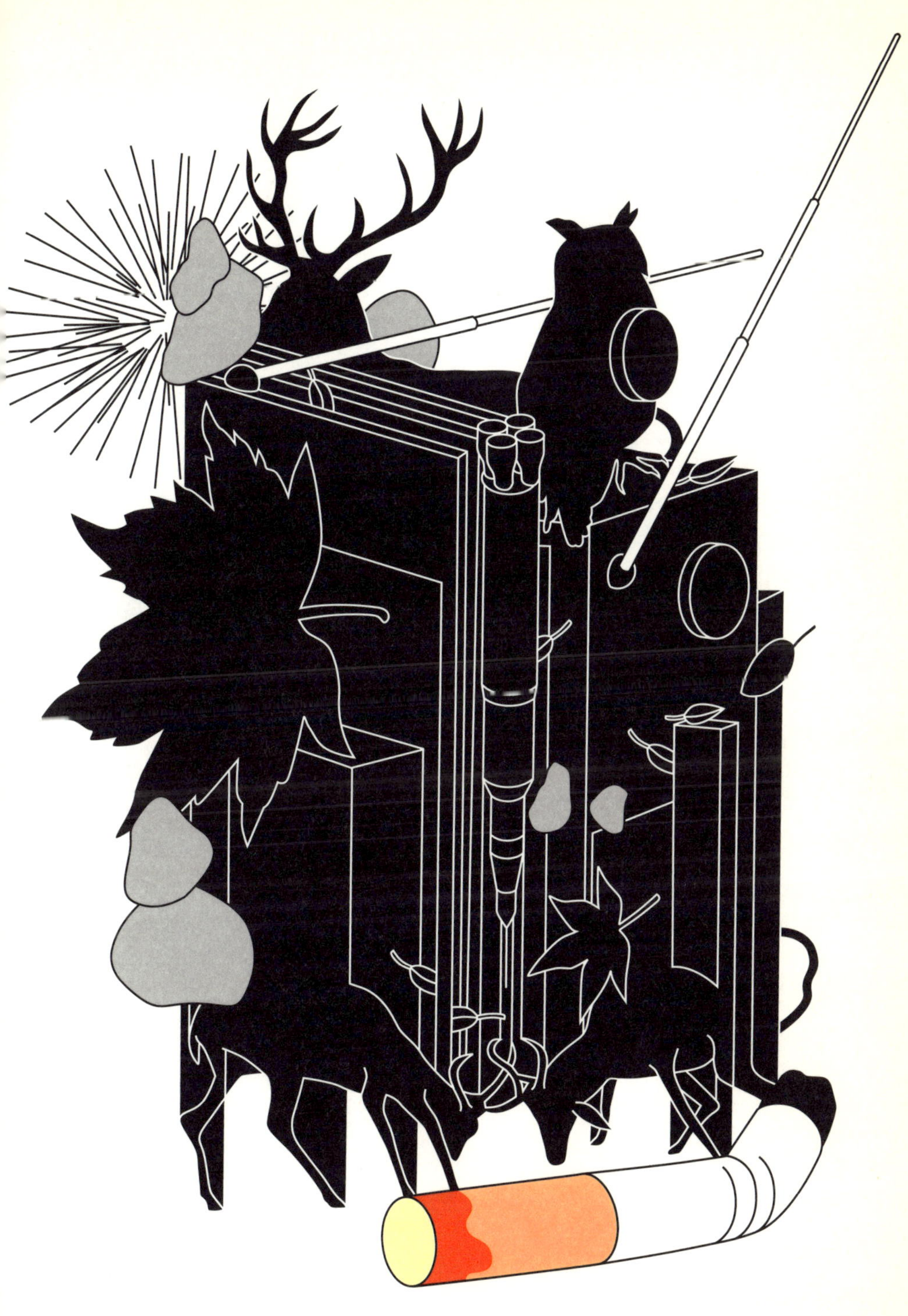

Animality and Humanity—On a Shifting Relationship

The animal refuses comprehension. Sometimes entirely foreign, sometimes an over-domesticated, excessively familiar life form. As soon as we see it, it becomes a mirror. But precisely for this reason, it seems scarcely possible to find something real behind the metaphors. The mirror will not stop reflecting distorted images, as in our approach to animals, our darkest fears alternate with scenarios of reconciliation. In the following conversation with the editor, Ludger Schwarte explores the contemporary relevance of this special relationship, this dilemma. While noting the brutal mechanism that fixes the positions of animals and people in a power politics of living beings, he also points to new approaches that might be able to straighten out the mirror. Roland Lüthi contributes an associative visual essay.—*dk*

How would you define the contemporary relevance of the relationship between humans and animals?

The issue is relevant for three reasons: there is an everyday practical reason, a scientific reason, and a philosophical reason. The everyday practical reason is that animals in their wildness, in that which they once were, are becoming purely imagined beings. Pets in turn are seen by many as a toy or a psychological substitute and precisely do not contain the otherness and danger that was once tied to the animal. The animal moves out of the lifeworld, it becomes alien, and for this reason dubious.

The scientific reason is that the animal is no longer just an object, as was usual since the scientific revolution of the seventeenth century; an object on which one tests scientific methods, from which knowledge is squeezed out by subjecting it to experimentation. It becomes increasingly a stockpile for the production of human organs, it is short-circuited with the human. For example, the pig becomes an organ provider for the human.

On the one hand, from a scientific view the dividing line between animal and man is disappearing. The human body and the animal body are fused. On the other hand, to the same extent bodies are beginning to dissolve. Living beings are increasingly seen as cell groupings that consist of genetic codes and to the extent that this is the case, they become manipulable and artificially breedable. The direction that is becoming clear with gene technology is one where living creatures cannot only be crossed or domesticated, but every form of living being can be produced by combining various genetic codes or inventing them. Biotechnology presents itself here for artistic fantasies.

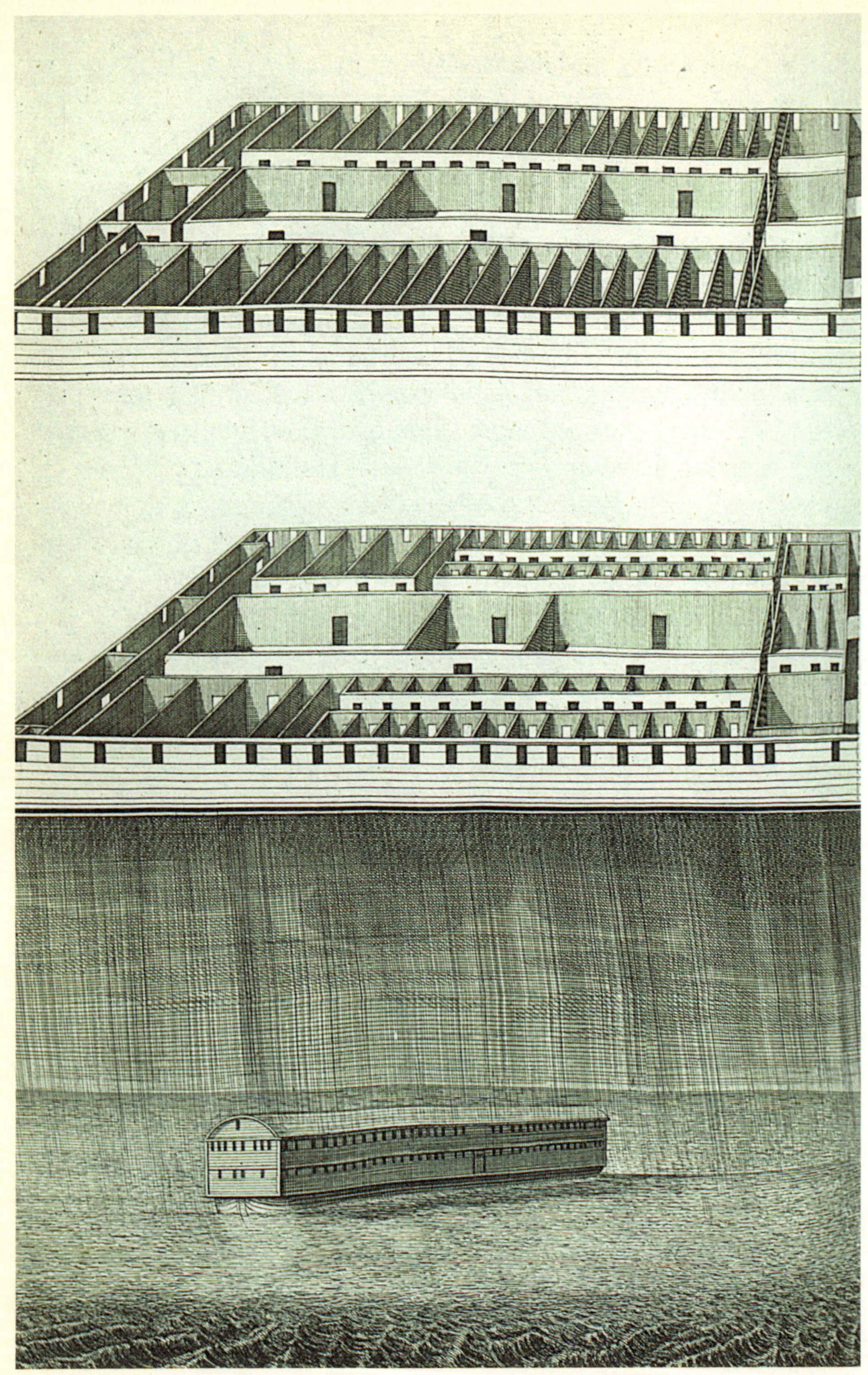

1 Perspectival View of Noah's Ark

The third is a philosophical reason: for centuries, the animal has surfaced in philosophical texts, forming the background before which humanity develops itself and develops a concept of itself. This begins with Aristotle and goes through Descartes to philosophical anthropology that began in the mid-twentieth century, and at the center of which is this man-animal question.

Most recently, however, there are increasingly efforts to reconceive the relationship between humanity and the animal and in general to think about what characterizes the animal. Giorgio Agamben's book *The Open* is such a work. In Agamben, in my view this still lacks differentiation. At the end of his book, he is more interested in humanity and in the animal in a very Heideggerian understanding of existence as something derived from language. He adopts very traditional positions, while he is certainly cognizant of the problem. Much more interesting on this path is a very late work by Jacques Derrida with the title *L'animal que donc je suis* from 1999. To my knowledge, Derrida is the first philosopher who deconstructed the animal concept. He established that something like "the animal"—a concept that would apply to all living beings—does not exist, and he points out that the most various, divergent life forms exist; the life form of a cat is quite different from that of an amoeba or an earthworm. A general concept like "the animal" does not do justice to all of this. There is no possibility to name a criterion that links all these forms of life. For the very first time, the concept "the animal" has become quite questionable. It is often assumed to be self-evident, and especially by philosophical anthropology that always just believed that humanity is the questionable, the not-determined animal, of which we cannot say what it is or what kind of future or developing form it is. It has always

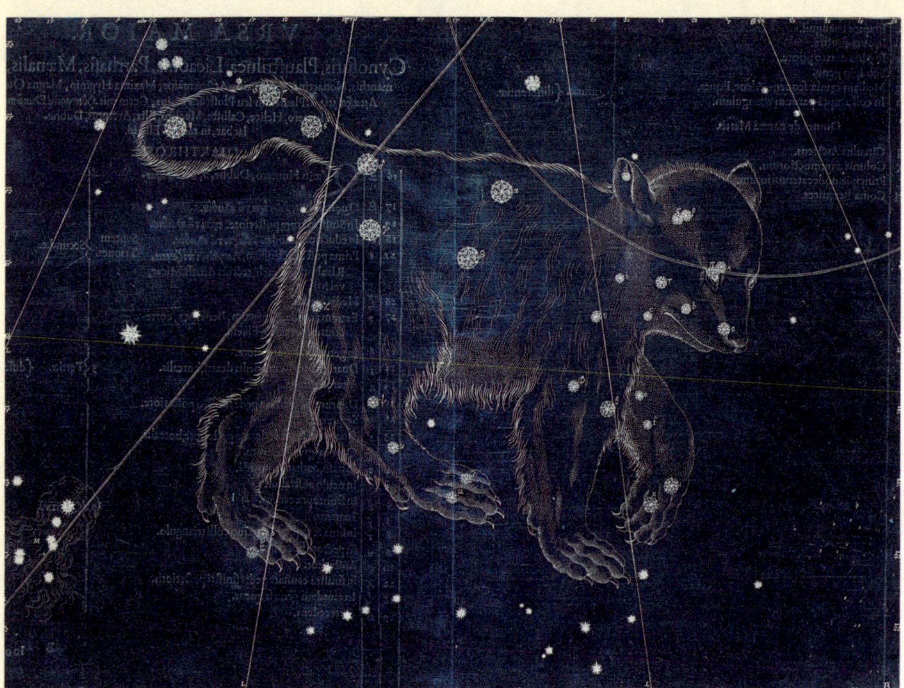

2

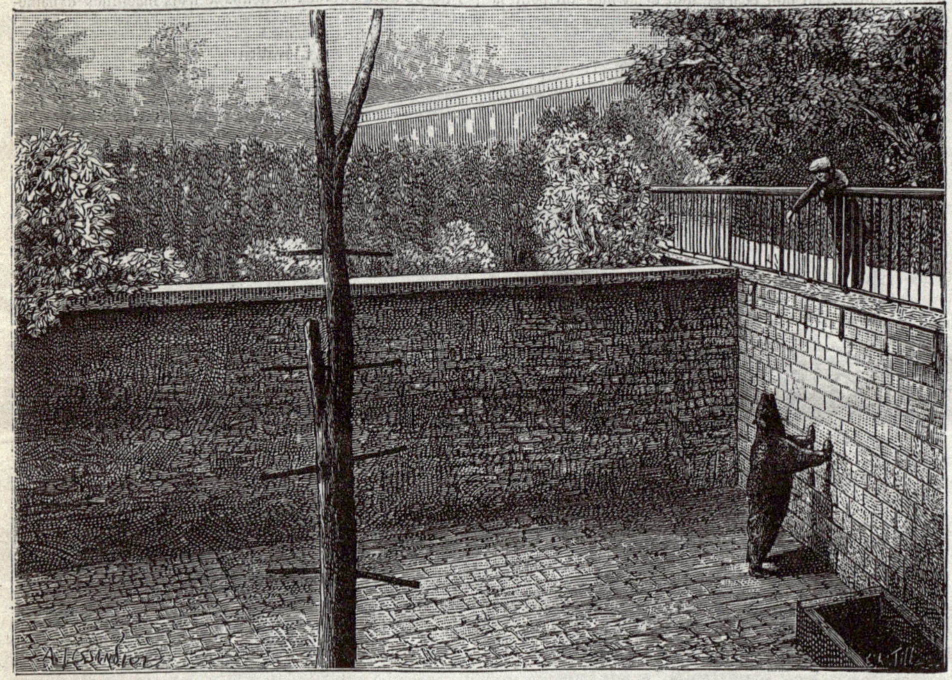

3

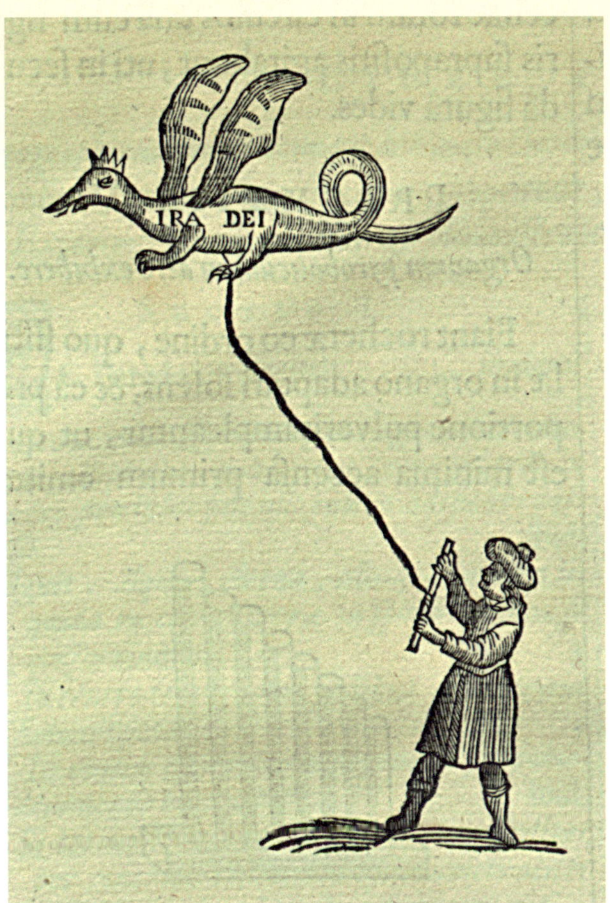

4

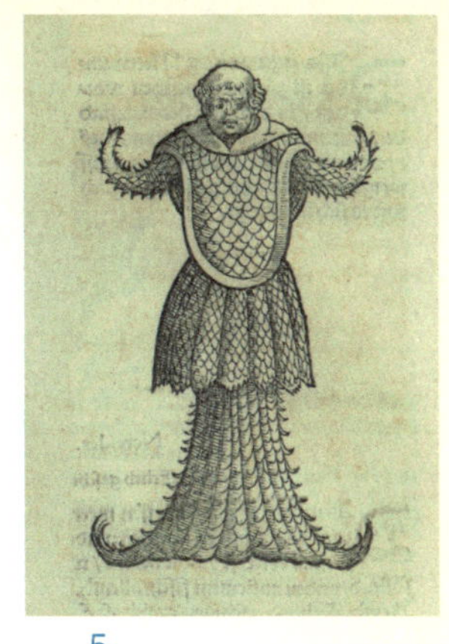

5

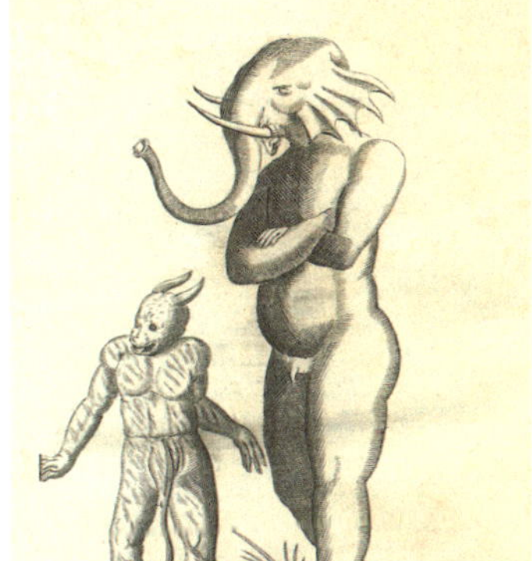

6

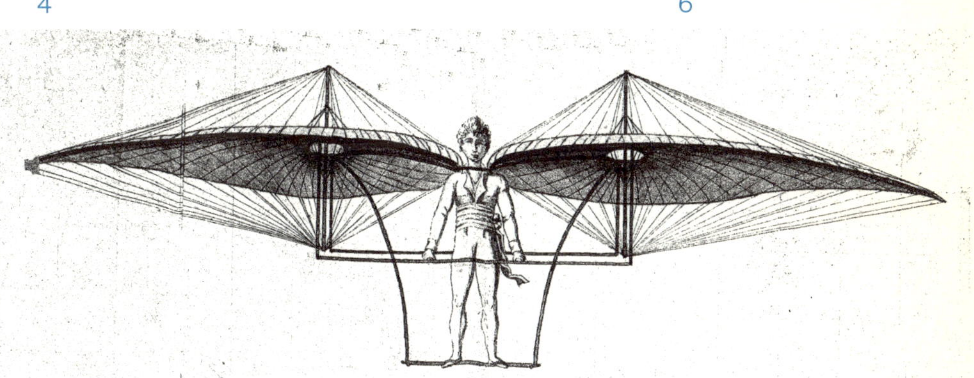

7

2 The Great Bear
3 Bear Ditch at the Botanical Garden, Paris
4 Kite in the Shape of a Flying Dragon
5 Monkfish
6 Boy with Elephant Head/Horned Newborn with Broad Mouth
7 Jakob Degen's Flying Machine

been suggested that for all other living beings the question is already solved, that in other words it is self-evident what we mean when we say "the animal." If we take all three reasons together, in addition to perhaps also questions of animal ethics and animal rights debates, then we have to reconceive entirely the relation to other living beings.

> *So there is a kind of rethinking, so that the animal itself is becoming questionable.*

Within philosophy, in simplified terms a distinction can be made between two breaks: on the one hand in Aristotle, where for the first time the notion of *zoon alogon* emerges and at the same time the human being is called *zoon logon echon*. What we understand today as animal—the form of life contrary to the human—is for the first time termed by Aristotle vaguely as a living being without "language" or "reason." But the human being is also a living thing that is termed by Aristotle a "reason-possessing" living thing or a "political animal." In both cases, Aristotle applies this concept of *zoon* to humanity as well.

At the same time, the Greeks had no unified concept of the animal. There are various terms that depend on the context, but which also implied quite different life forms. *Zoon*, living things, for example could also include the human, and was thus not the animal in contrast to humanity. *Bios*, life form, was another concept, or *therion*, a third concept used for a wild animal. At the same time, in Aristotle there is also the notion that animals always have a soul, that they can perceive and have imagination. This idea of animals having a soul is maintained into the early modern period, and Descartes—rightly or wrongly—is often cited as the person who was the first to heighten the man/animal opposition, saying that animals are in principle just mechanical bodies that function according to mechanical rules, extension without a soul. He is the first one who formulated the idea that there is a fundamental opposition so drastically, at a time when only traces of such ideas can be found in other thinkers. As a whole, this leads to the fact that the animal can without more ado be only compared to man by way of corporeality; as something that has no soul and with which one can thus experiment. This is the time of the rise of the experimental sciences, which Descartes' thinking helped advance, among other things.

Darwin marked the second break in which the opposition between animal and man, built up through reason and possessing language, is blurred. Suddenly, the familial resemblance moves to the foreground, the descent of the human from the primate. For this, a biologically inspired philosophy is constructed that continues to maintain a strict opposition between man and animal—homo sapiens sapiens. As a rule, this runs also through categories like language or reason, things that have nothing to do with the body.

The attempt was always made to emphasize the fundamental otherness of humanity, and in turn it becomes interesting that this otherness of the human is becoming dubious, in just the moment when one seeks to understand the animal as a creature, when solidarity with the animal is the goal. This arises with the debate about animal rights, but is also the reason why thinkers like Agamben and Derrida make their way back to the biblical sources of our understanding of the animal where both is grounded: on the one hand the similarity as a creature —animals as co-creatures—on the other hand the rule of man over animal. The definition of the human as ruling

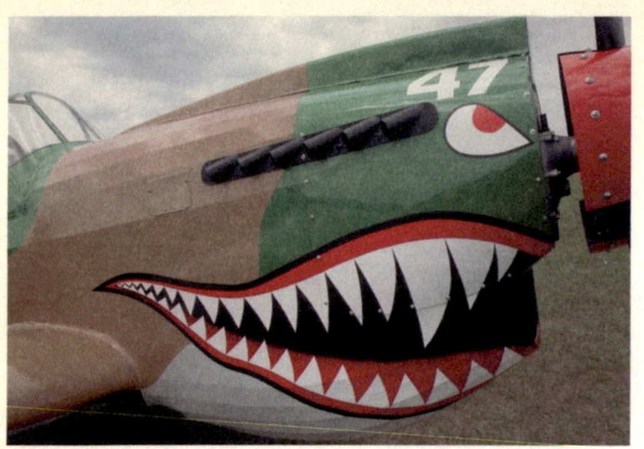

8

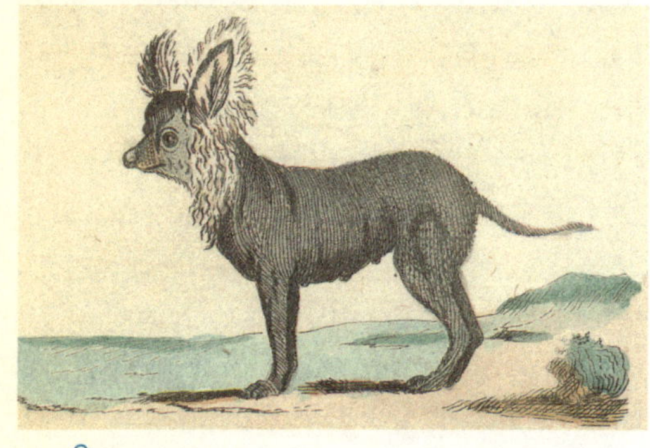

9

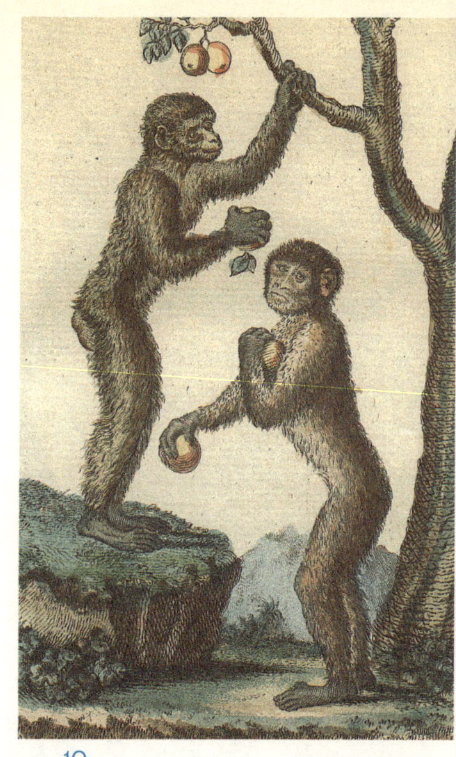

10

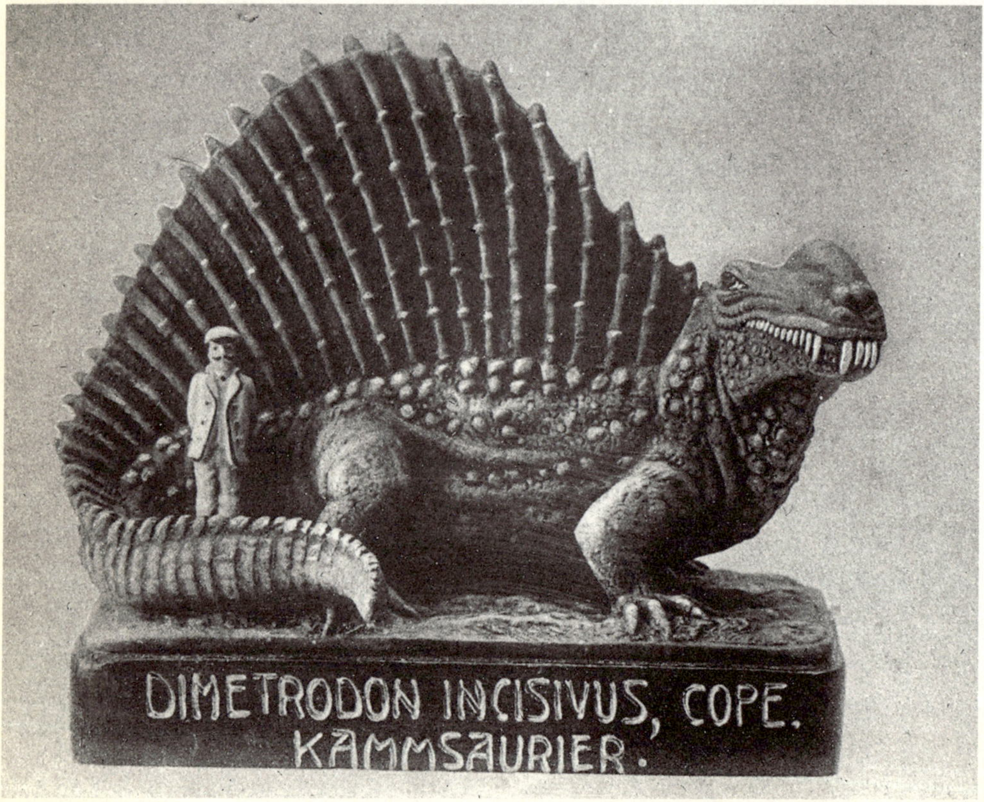

DIMETRODON INCISIVUS, COPE.
KAMMSAURIER.

11

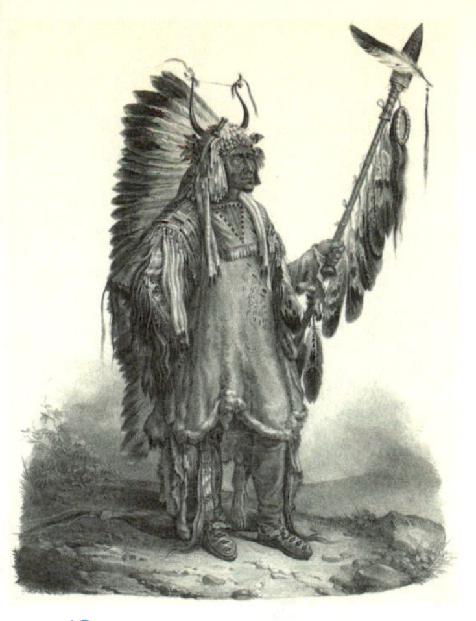

12

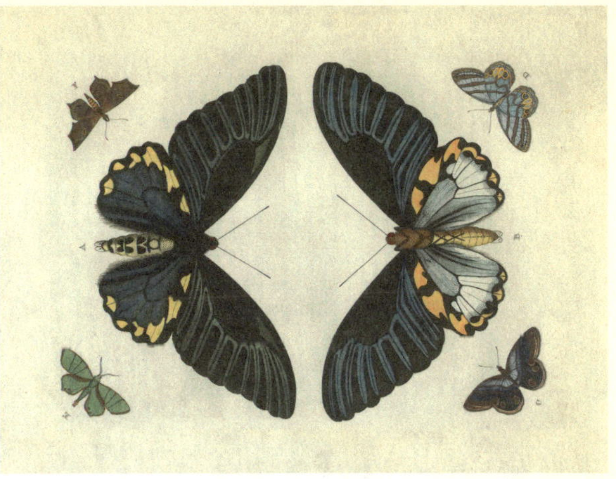

13

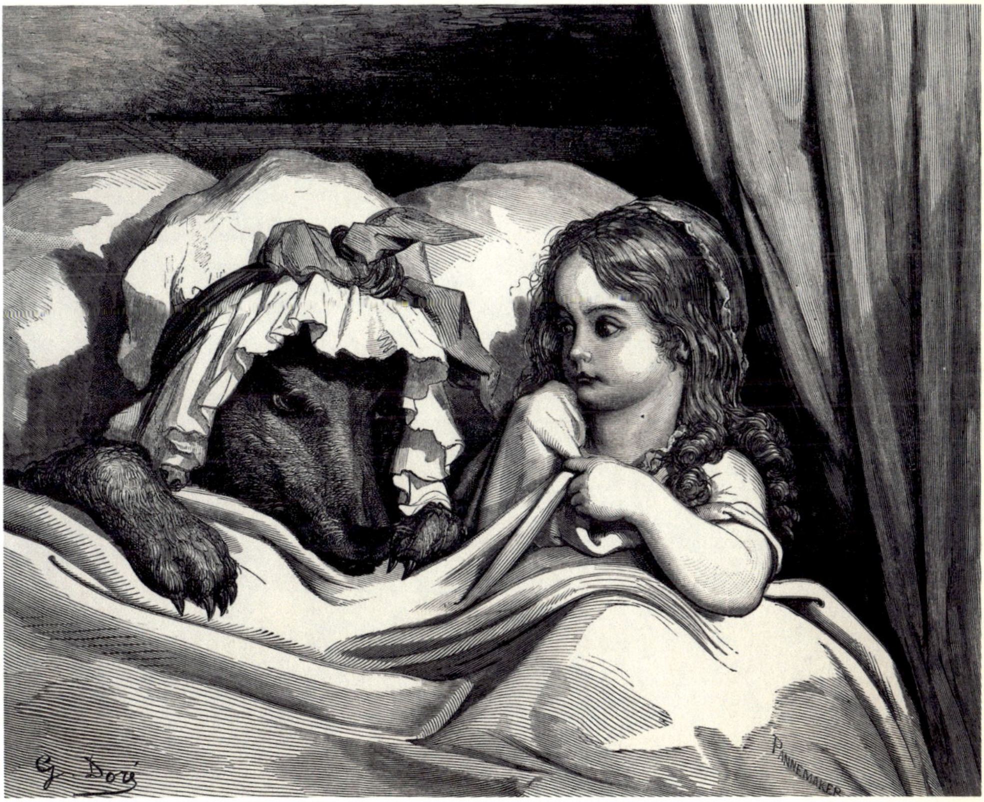

14

8 Painted Engine Cowling of a Loehle P-40 Aircraft
9 Turkish Rascal Dog
10 Male and Female Anthropoid Monkeys
11 Model of a Crested Dinosaur Compared to the Size of a Man
12 Mandan Chief
13 Male Hypolitus, Herfe, Ilyrias and Manto Butterflies
14 Little Red Riding Hood in Bed with the Disguised Wolf

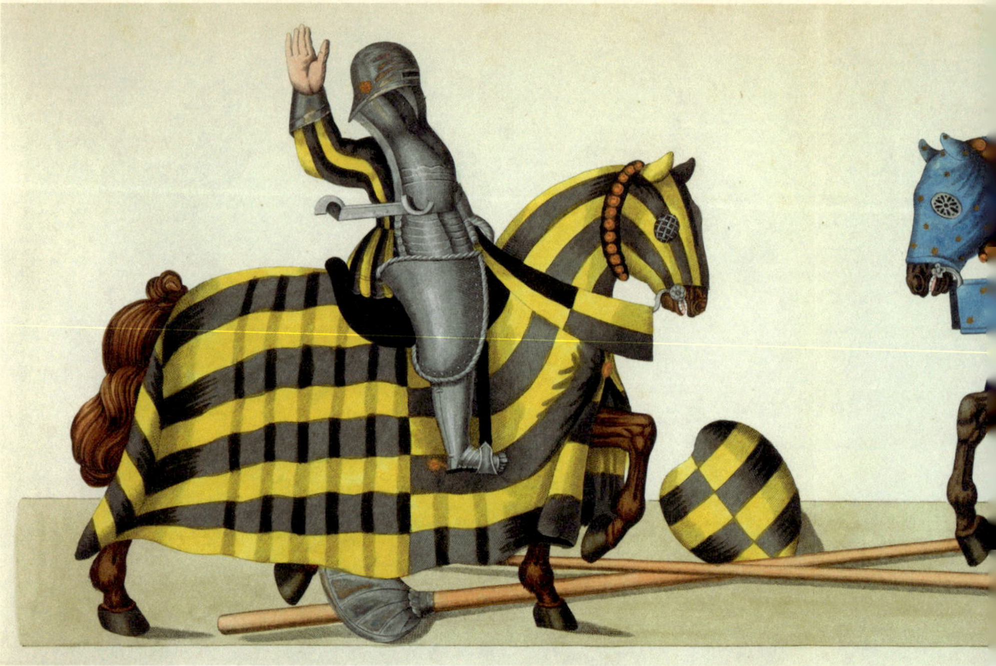

15

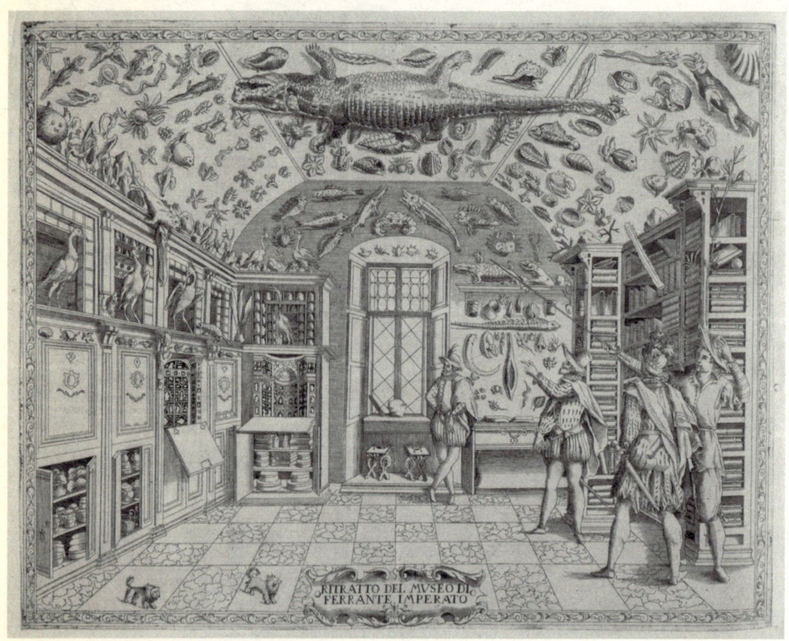

16

15 Two Knights at a Tournament
16 View of the Cabinet of Curiosities of Ferrante Imperato, Naples
17 Le Doubler (Equestrian Figure Riding)
18 The Killing of a Giant Alligator
19 Experiment in the Sorbonne Laboratories Concerning the Muscular Force of a Crocodile's Jaws
20 Grimaldi and the Nondescript in the Pantomime *The Red Dwarf*

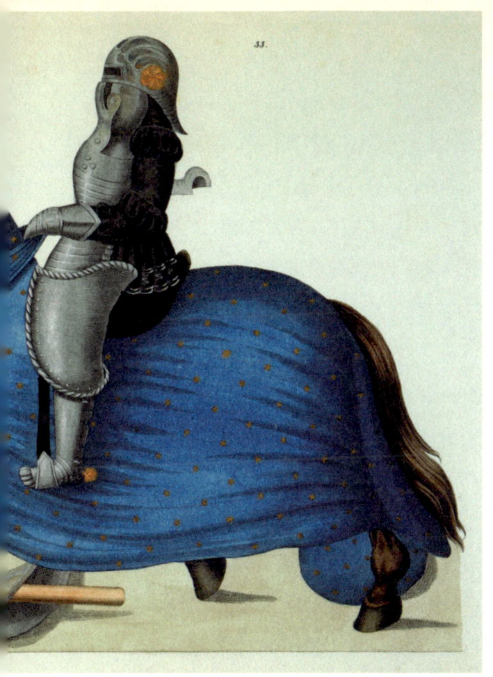

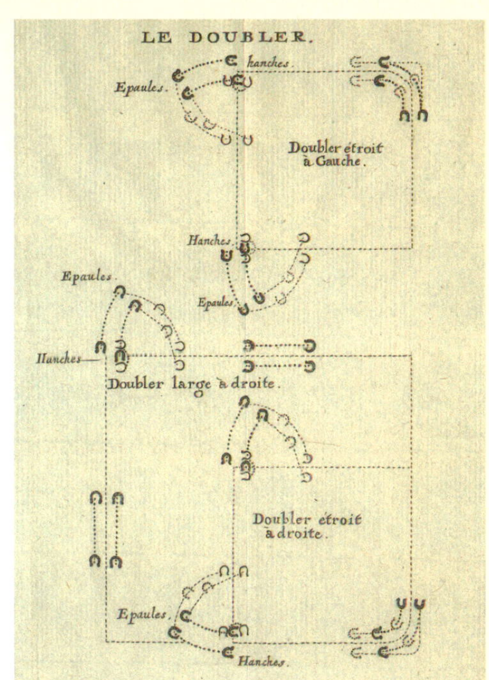
LE DOUBLER.
hanches.
Epaules.
Doubler étroit à Gauche.
Hanches.
Epaules.
Epaules.
Hanches
Doubler large à droite.
Doubler étroit à droite.
Epaules.
Hanches.

17

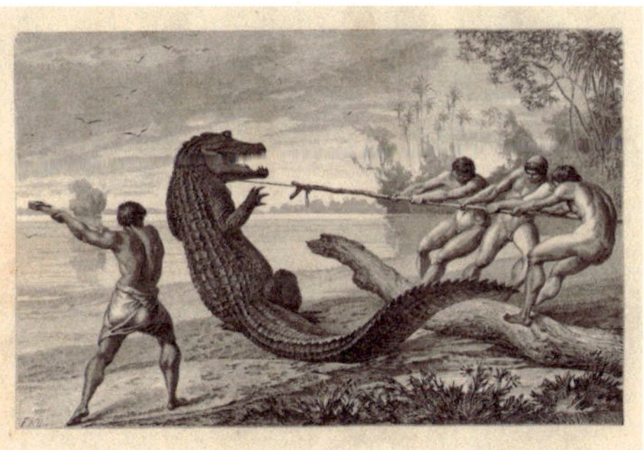

18

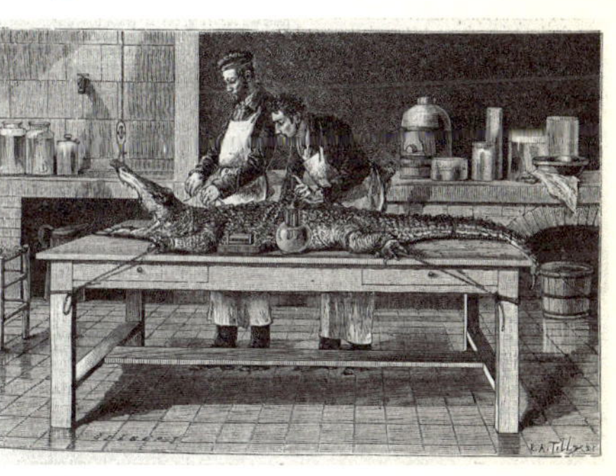

19

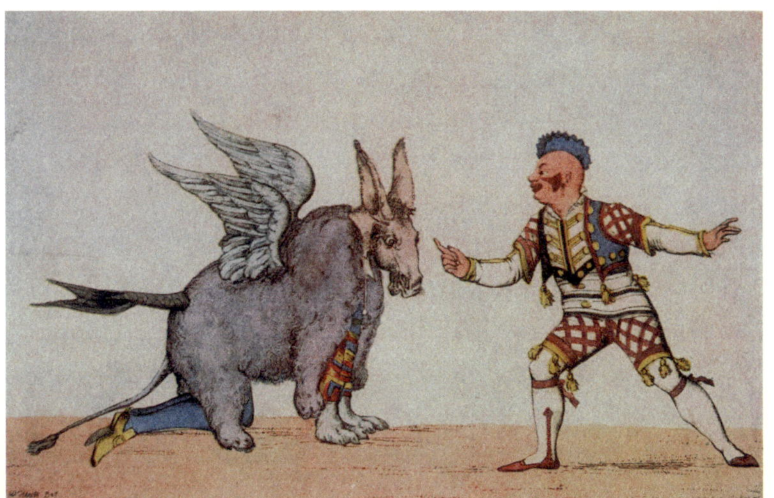

20

by reason or language is not least grounded in the biblical texts. But what will become of this domination when the animals disappear from us, and only our own animality remains, so that we realize that we have become victims of our own machinery of domination and science?

To what extent is a fear or concern for humanity for itself inseparable from the animal?

The human self-conception is one that takes shape with the domination of the animal. What then proves to be domination over the animal is the domination of reason, language, and knowledge. We realize that we ourselves are animals to the extent that we are dominated by knowledge that we have built up or support.

But as the animal was the other, it was a sort of mirror of human divinity. Now, not just the concept of God has dissipated with the question of *deus absconditus*, a God no longer accessible. For us, instead the question of a no longer graspable, disappeared animal rises on the horizon: animal absconditum.

Ultimately, I think animal, God, and humanity will dissolve in a construction of knowledge. The image of the bull in cultural history shows how the animal, God, and man belong together. It's clear in the fine arts for example that the animal becomes portrait-worthy, as man searches for himself, assuming the position previously held in art by the divine image. The look in the mirror, as Lichtenberg put it, from which the animal looks back, has for humanity in the meantime become an unbearable glance. This look leads to the fact that we no longer see the difference. This is due to the fact that in meantime the entire relationship has become artificial, dubious. The loss of the category of the animal, the depictability of the animal, is caused by the fact that we have lost divinity as well. If there is no God, there is no animal.

To what extent do we no longer see ourselves when the animal disappears?

Self-depiction or the look in the mirror both suggest a difference. I look at an ideal of myself, or I look at the reality that presents itself to me in the mirror. What is present in the mirror is marked by a corporeality. This corporeality always bears individual traits, so that I recognize myself in it. I individuate myself in a body. That was, among other things, the idea of the portrait, the passport photo, the genetic fingerprint. To the extent that this will be a keyboard for genetic technologies that are manipulable, the handwriting and the face that make me unmistakable no longer exist. The whole problem of individuation by way of corporeality is not just a problem of man and animal, but the individual person in relation to another person. Individuation is always only possible when there is also a generic term, like “human,” “cat,” “dog.” The individual genera dissolve, and thus also the possibility of being an individual.

The animals are thus a kind of matrix that allows for this performance of difference. The animal becomes a factor in humanity’s self-occupation. Is the animal also already thought here?

The question of the difference between man and animal has up to now dominated the animal concept, that is now becoming dubious. It’s time to ask about the form of life

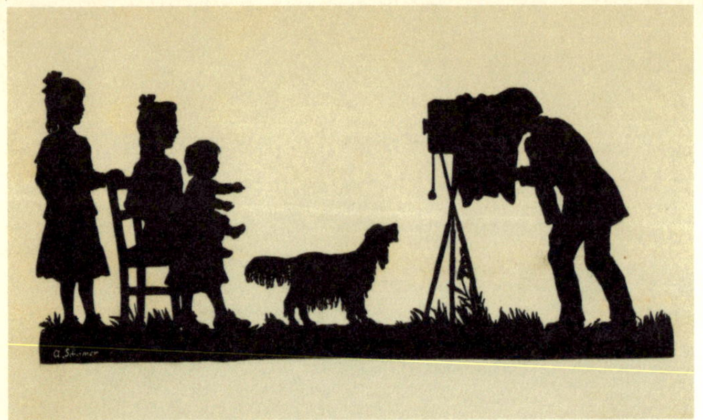

21

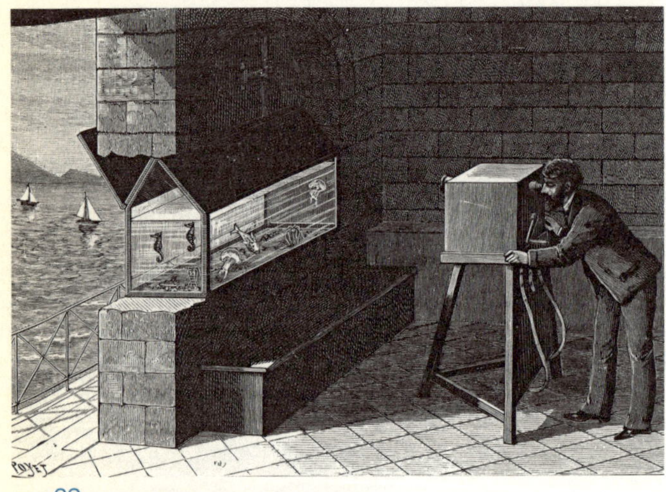

22

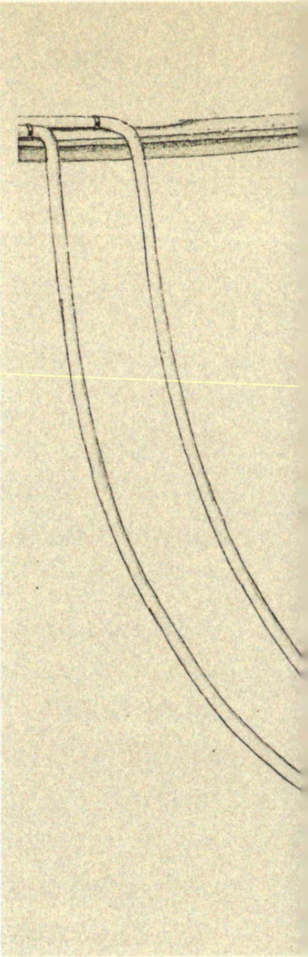

23

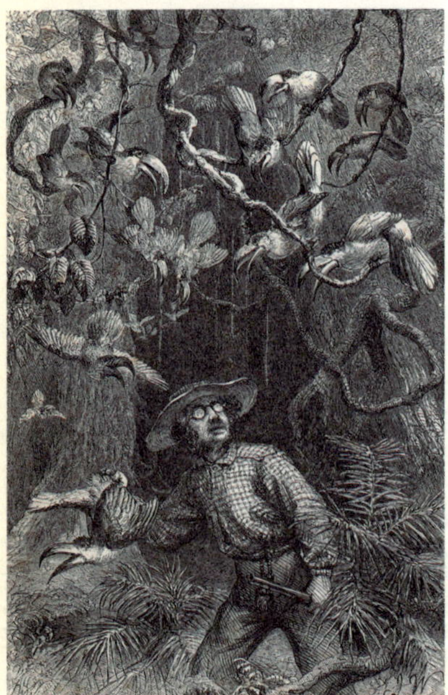

24

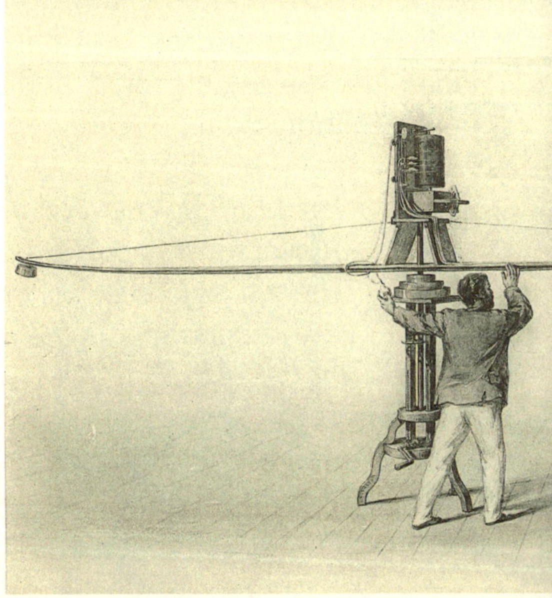

25

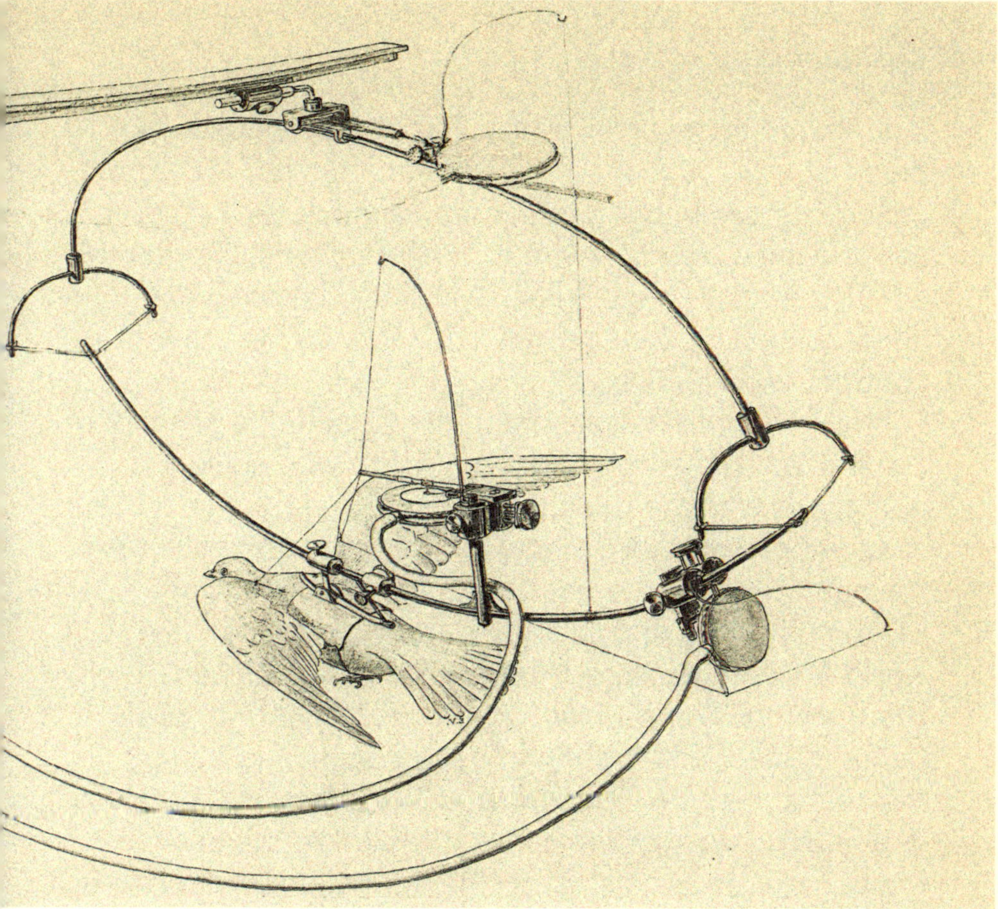

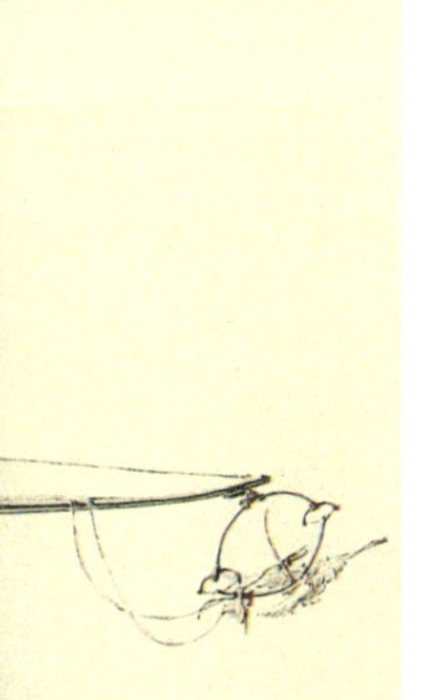

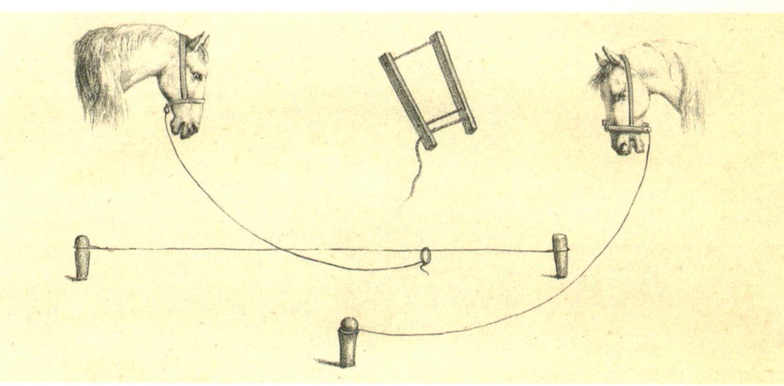

26

21 Postcard of Children Posing for a Photograph
22 Sea Water Aquarium Displayed to Study Underwater Locomotion
23 Pigeon Attached to a Merry-Go-Round for the Graphic Determination of Wing Movement
24 Adventure with Curl-Crested Toucans
25 Merry-Go-Round for the Graphic Determination of Wing Movement (General View)
26 Stakes with a Rope to Put Horses out to Pasture and Halter to Control the Animals

that characterizes the cat, the dog or individual dogs, the singularity of a different life form, and not in relation only to humanity, but to other life forms as well. These shades and differences are to be perceived in a different way. It seems to me the task is to think that, and that animals should no longer have to serve as the other in contrast to humanity.

We've thus come to an interesting point: the concept of the animal always encompassed those who could not rule, those who are ruled by language and rationality. That included always those whom we today mean by the term "human being." In the nineteenth century, it was perfectly natural that lions and giraffes were to be seen in the world exhibitions and early zoos, but also pygmies, African villagers, etc. "Animalistic" was also intended for proletarians, since Aristotle it had been common to equate the animal and the feminine, etc. We should not overlook that in the history of the concept of animal, human life forms have always also been meant that could not rise to what was understood as the "dignity of humanity."

It would now be interesting to deconstruct the question of the animal and to ask to what extent the means of representation and singularity of individual animal beings play a special role in the fine arts. It's clear that there is naturally a whole series of modern artists who in recent times provoke by on the one hand alluding to experiments and laboratory animals, equating them to radical avant-garde practices. On the other hand, animal-human hybrids are being created, animal and technology are linked together, becoming practices of representation and artistic concepts on the possibility of an animal life form.

To what extent does the aspect of the machine or the mechanical apparatus mark a specifically modern discussion of the animal-human issue?

On the one hand, we need to remember that the human-animal story as a cultural technique is always a story of serving and mechanization of various animals. I'm thinking here of farming and cattle-breeding, where animals were already early on put to service in machine-like constructions. This biblical idea of making the animals our subject is also based on cultural techniques. That is an idea that can be found in the critique of the capitalist machinery by Marx. This amounts to describing the phenomenon of alienation of the proletarian, the worker, from the product of his labor as an "animalization." Man here only serves, he is hooked up to the machine, he no longer develops by way of his free activity into or as a human being.

The other aspect is more part of the history of science, Descartes' comparison of machines to animals. For him, animals are nothing but complicated biological machines that can be understood mechanically. He thought here in hydraulic terms, but it can also be explained biochemically, as done today in the laboratory. For modern biology, the rat is nothing but a machine where knowledge is tested and can be evaluated on causal contexts, that provides these contexts and confirms them.

Ever since Descartes there has been the idea that animalistic life forms are nothing but machines and thus knowledge about biological life forms, based on this machine comparison, is only experimentally obtainable in this way in the first place. Only if bodies are to be seen as machines is it possible to explore them in this way, as in modern science.

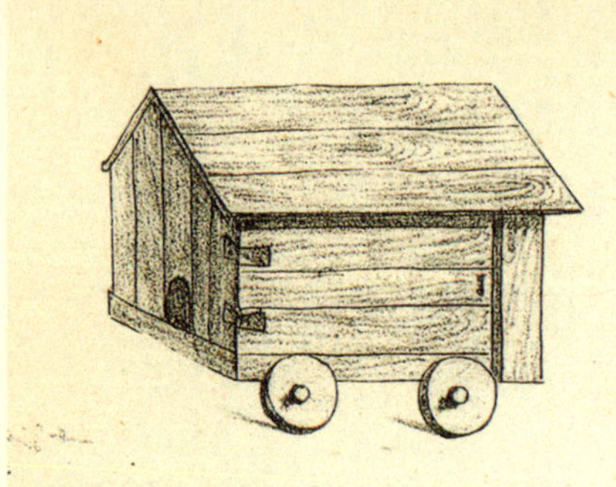

27

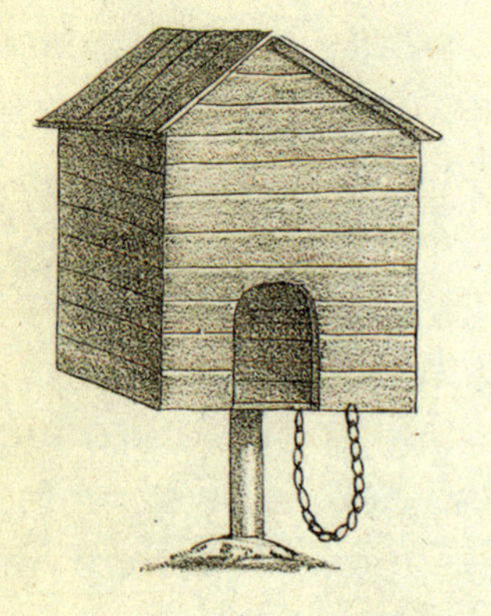

28

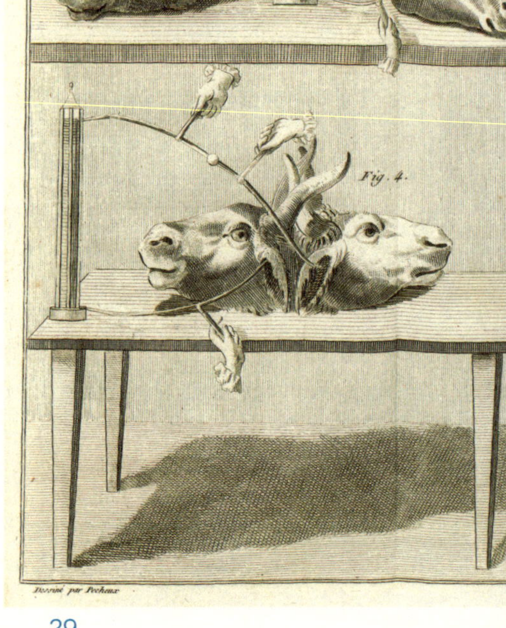

29

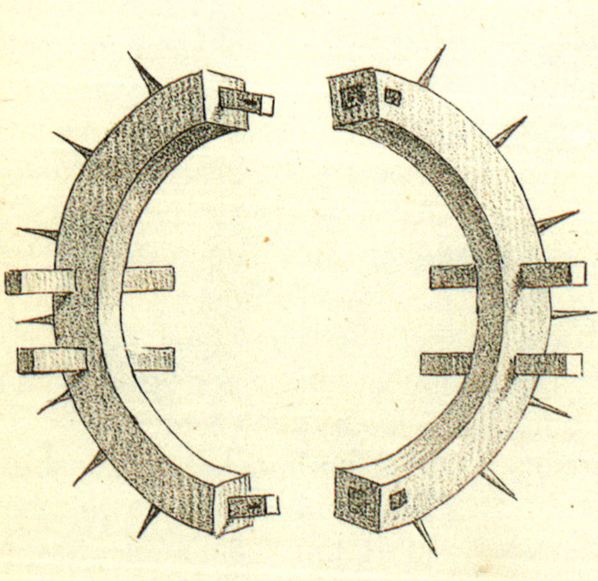

30

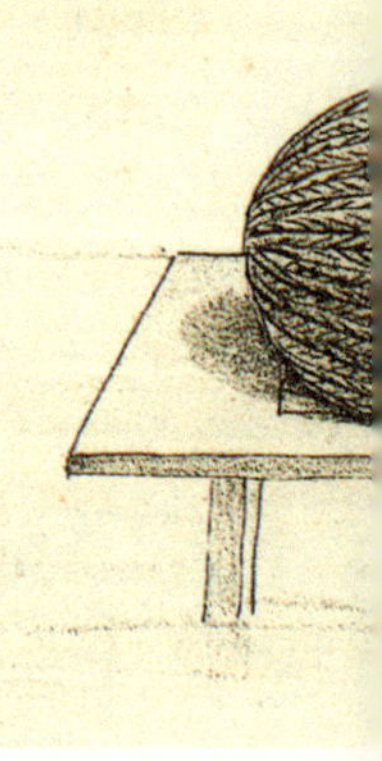

31

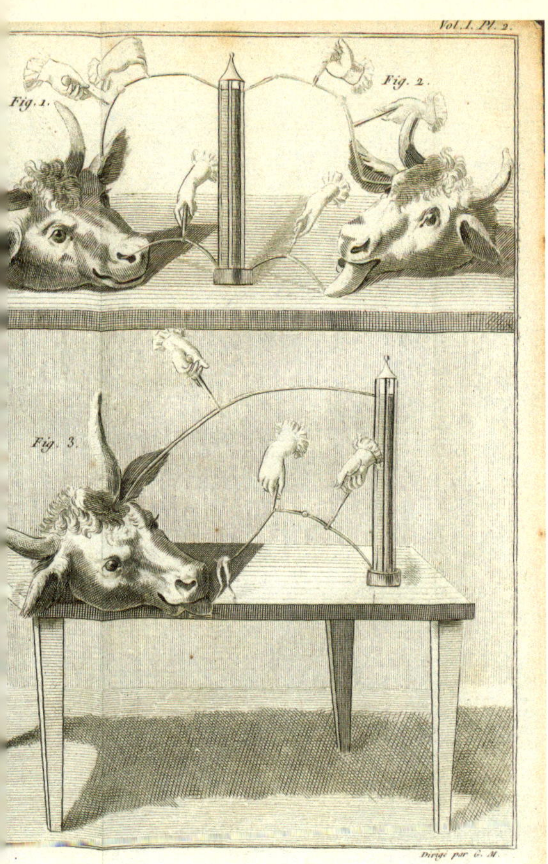

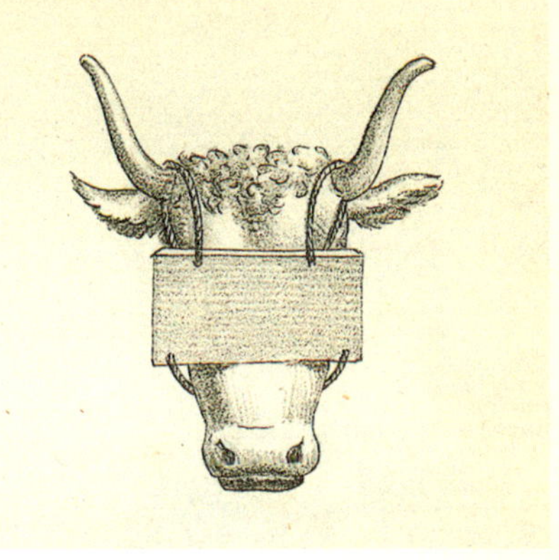

32

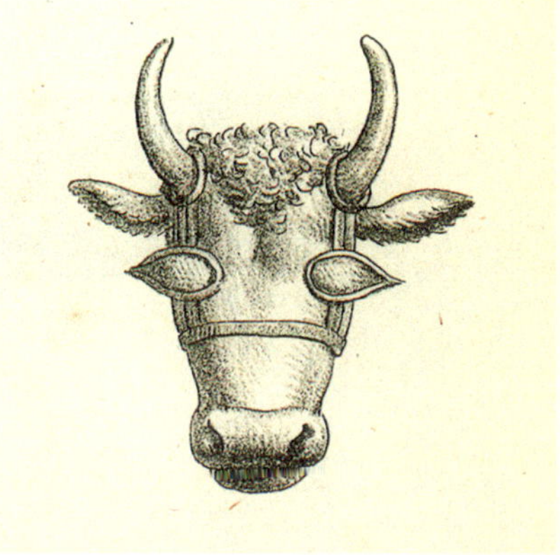

33

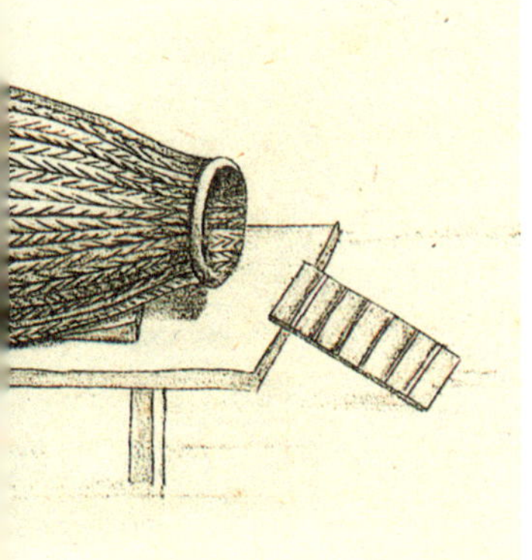

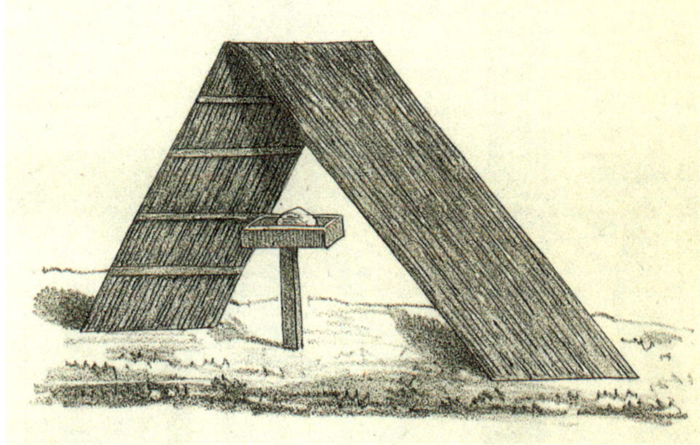

34

27 Mobile Henhouse
28 Dog Kennel
29 On Galvanism Applied to the Head of a Recently Slaughtered Ox
30 Collar with Spikes
31 Ducks' Nest in the Shape of a Pear
32 Eye Screen
33 Blinders
34 Shelter for Feeding Salt to Animals

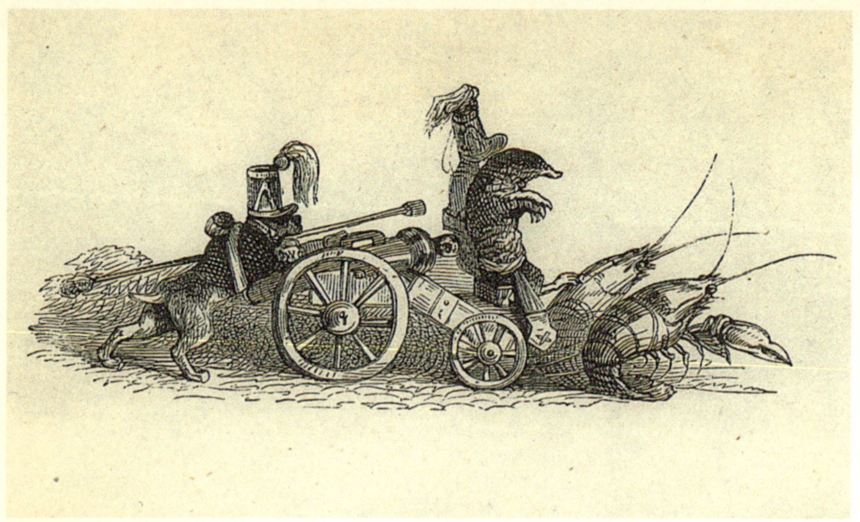

35

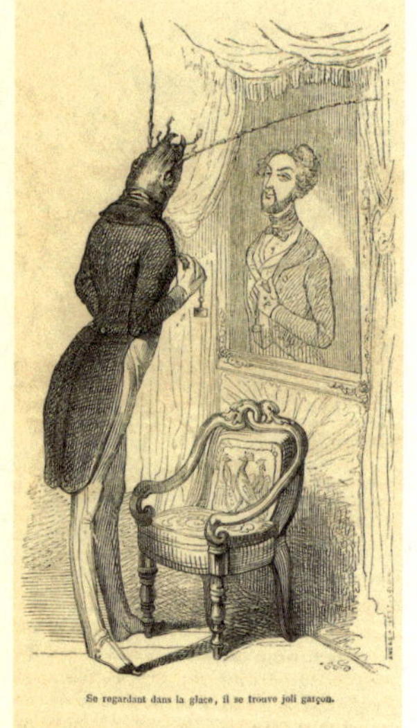

Se regardant dans la glace, il se trouve joli garçon.

36

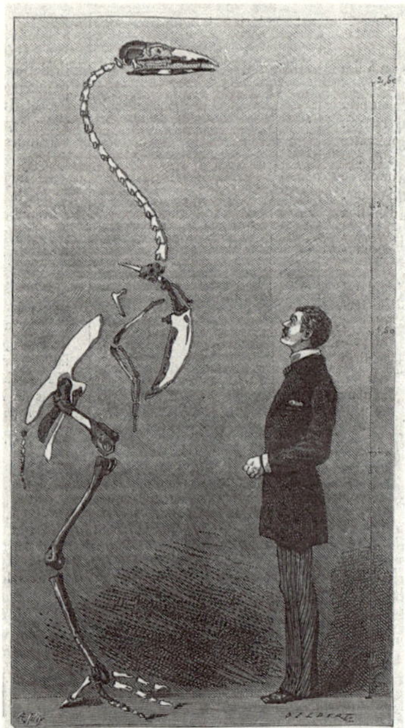

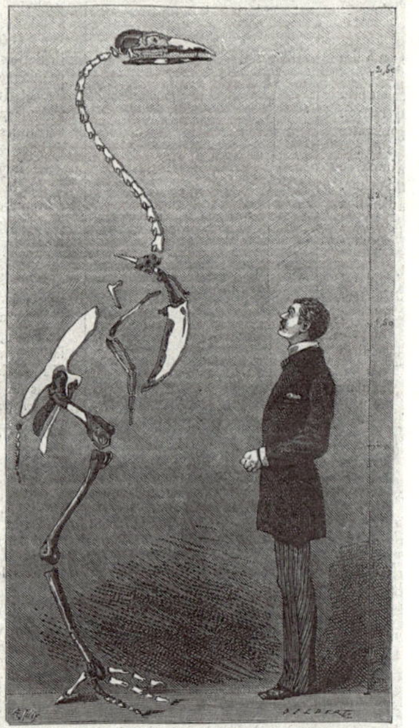

37

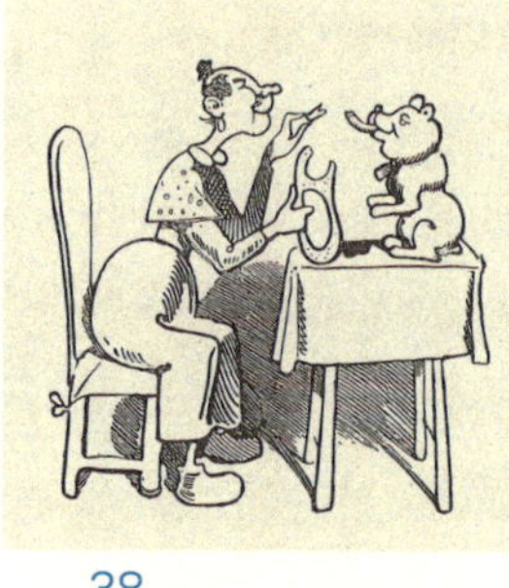

38

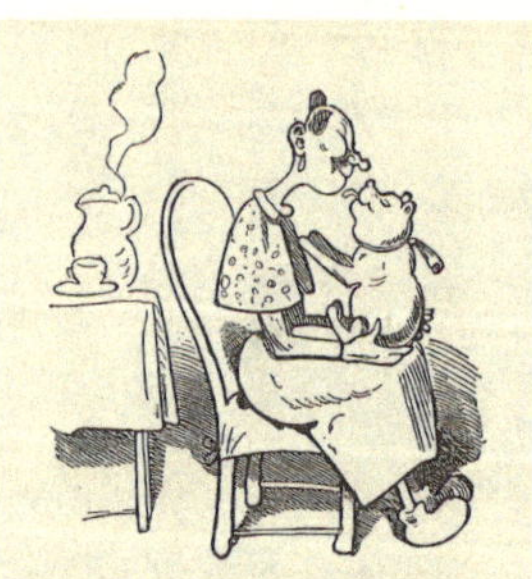

39

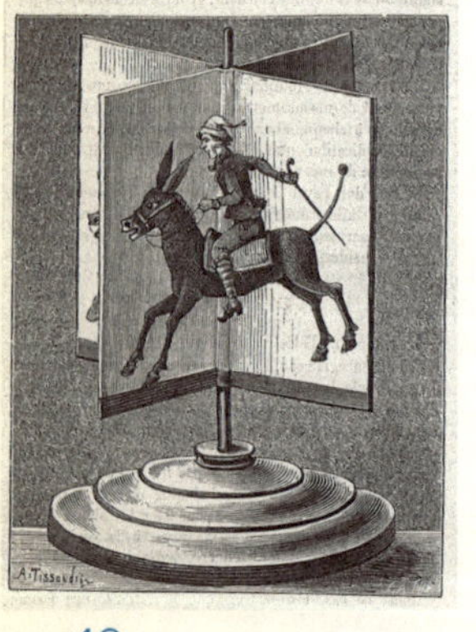

40

41

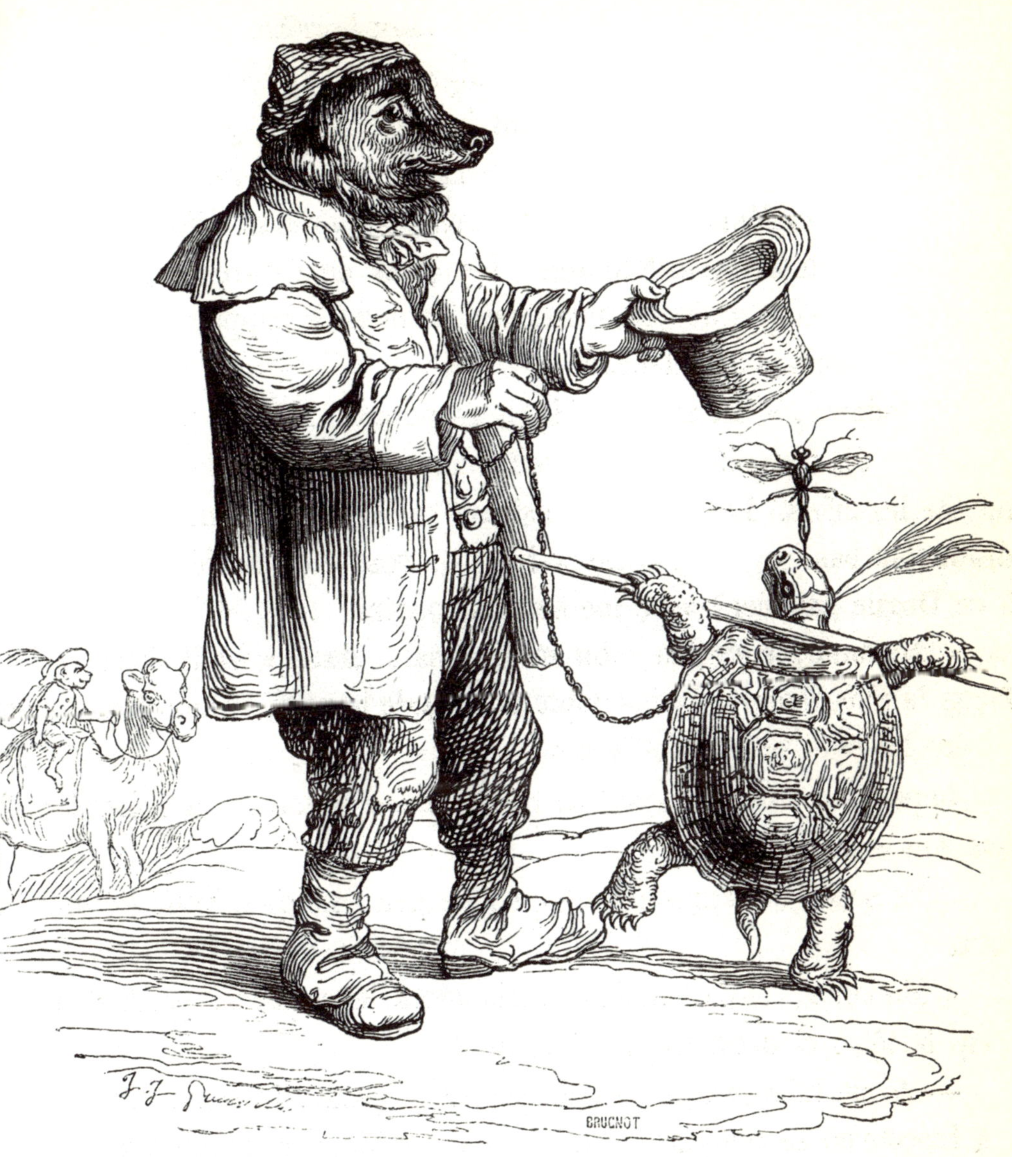

42

35 Vignette from *The Private and Public Life of Animals*
36 Looking at Himself in the Mirror He Finds Himself a Handsome Guy
37 Restauration of the Skeleton of the Eocene Bird Gastornis Edwardsii
38 Fräulein Ammer Kisses and Cuddles Her Pet
39 All Day Long She Feeds Him with Gingerbread
40 Rigolo, the Funny Mule
41 Leg Movement of a Prawn
42 Vignette from *The Private and Public Life of Animals*

On the other hand, these bodies, these biological contexts can be mobilized as machines, that is, individual parts can be removed, replaced, and connected elsewhere. On the one side, people become animals by being connected to machines, as Marx lamented. Only in seeing human and animal bodies as machines can we in this way penetrate them with knowledge and use them to produce knowledge.

This connection of biology and mechanics has led both to a complicated current form, bioinformatics, as well as transforming the notion of the machine. It is naturally no longer the mechanical-hydraulic that Descartes still had in mind. By now, notions of hardware and software have become biologized in such a way that many postulate that they form their own life form or the foundation of our life form. This idea of a matrix or a cosmic program that is evolutionary, that changes, but also rules over life forms, the idea of a super formula that exists in physics today and that regards the universe as nothing but a very complex, complicated machine, assumes a model of the machine saturated with living emergent phenomena. Physics and mechanics show by now traces of life in the models and theories with which they work.

To what extent can the arts add something to this complex of questions, that does not amount to a fantasy of reconciliation between animal and man, but also does not revel in the pathos of an absolute divide?

I find it very stimulating to think of the history of modern art as one of "animalization." Perhaps it is possible to mark here the entry point of modernism, where artistic forms of representation separate from the religious paradigm, from the representation of a religious hierarchy and hierarchy in general. Here a point begins to take form where man no longer had to represent his own divinity, or god as the absolute other was no longer available to him, the evocation of which had been the task of classical art in Europe. Modernism would thus be an art that attempts to secure itself of the animal as the other that represents the precise counter image, but also the mechanical foundation of civilization, the source of the phantasmatic or fantastic.

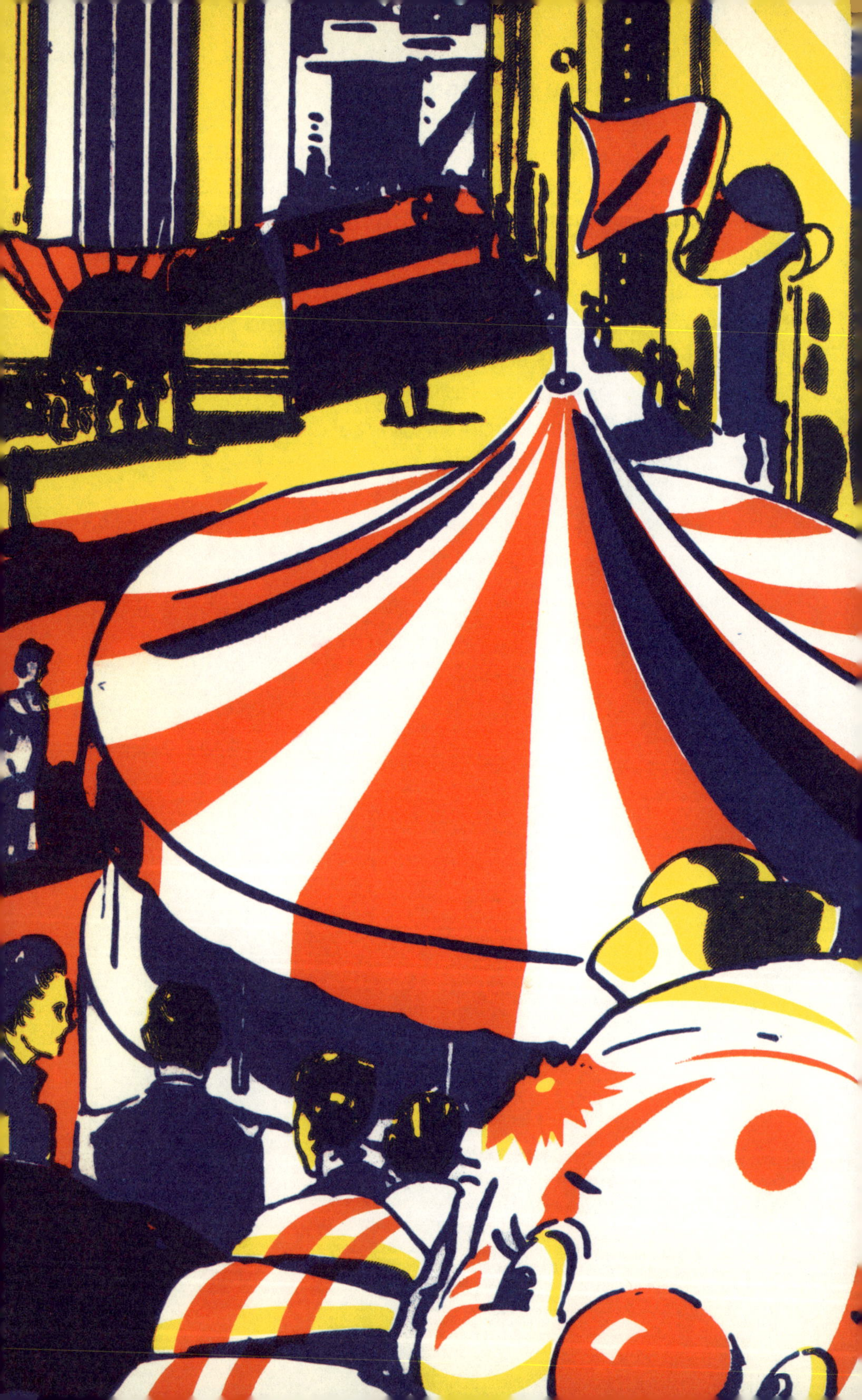

Where Do We Go from Here?—Biennials Today and Tomorrow

In the past years, protagonists of the business world have discovered art as a first class stake. Corporate and private initiatives triumphantly present spectacular art collections and events. And dynamic art fairs—a development that seems to be growing into a downright "fair-mania"—generate such great flows of goods and attract so much attention that the biennials appear unable to keep up with the pace. On the one hand this development can be read as a sign that biennials are becoming less significant than their openly commercial counterparts. On the other, despite ongoing debates about the sense of biennials and, in particular, the questioning of national presentations, both the number of biennials worldwide and the number of countries and regions represented through their own pavilions or exhibitions at the "king of biennials", Venice, have continuously increased over the past years.

So, where do we stand today? A wide range of people from the art world—artists, critics, curators, and gallerists—were asked to submit a statement presenting their point of view, either by commenting on the current state of affairs as described above or by addressing one or both of the following questions.

Firstly, how convincing is the format of the Venice Biennale when it comes to mediating between artists, theorists and the public? Or more generally, under which conditions are large-scale formats such as the Venice Biennale or the documenta convincing in this mediation and under which conditions are they not?

Secondly, is it the task of the Venice Biennale to take into adequate account the changing political and cultural environment in Europe and the world? And to what extent can it respond, if at all, to the needs of contemporary artists asserting themselves in this political, technological and economic environment?—*dk*

Vanessa Beecroft
artist, New York

Biennials as compared to art fairs should be representative of values rather than market giants. Artists should challenge their work at biennials to create meanings rather than respond to a demand, using the space to talk sense, even at the risk of becoming less visible. The number of countries and regions represented by their own pavilions at the Venice Biennale mirrors the world order and supremacy configuration by and large. It mimics the geo-political system of the world where the first world detains more space and more power and the peripheral worlds less space, less centrality and less power of expression. The format of the Venice Biennale cannot be entirely convincing as it is constricted within the perimeters and borders that reproduce the world and the world's politics. An American or English artist has more space and more visibility than an Egyptian (who is given limitations in the materials to use or themes) or an artist from Iraq for example (who is not given a pavilion at all).

The Biennale is usually curated by a leading nation's curator or director, who inevitably represents the interests of his or her own culture. It is not the task of the Venice Biennale to take into account the changing political and cultural environment in Europe and the world in a direct way. It would be interesting to see the pavilions and artists rotating, giving a chance, for example to Iraqi artists to occupy the American pavilion or to American artists to occupy the streets of Venice. This way we may see something that we are not already used to see in fairs, galleries and international collector's homes. In the same fashion, curators and directors could come from a less established environment to diversify the selection of works and artists not to bore the art public with the same context they already view in an ordinary art life of the major capitals of the world.

A biennial may be able to allow artists to assert themselves by creating an environment that does not duplicate the existing world and that it is not celebrative, but different and without borders. Sometime the Biennale could also free the artists from the weight of carrying their already established name, by, for example pulling down national flags and creating a nameless exhibition where the work itself would speak.

Ralf Beil
Institut Mathildenhöhe, Darmstadt

For the Venice Biennale, the situation is similar to that of painting: every couple of years it is pronounced dead, but it remains as lively as it ever was. And just like the existence of painting is hardly threatened by the art fairs, the Venice Biennale will easily outlive most of the art fairs of our time. Just as the comprehensive and high-quality show is played out in the exhibition halls of Art Basel each year, the numerous venues opened up for art in Venice every two years have a completely different, incomparable format. It has long since not only been a matter of the original Giardini with their national pavilions; but, in addition to these, the Arsenale firmly acquired for art by Harald Szeemann in 1999, as a possible place for the condensation of content, and then, not to be forgotten, the whole of Venice with all its churches, palazzi and dormant industrial areas, that also have their magic effect. Douglas Gordon, for instance, struck me for the first time in a lasting way in the exterritorial British Council exhibition, General Release, parallel to the 1995 Biennale in the Scuola di San Pasquale. In 2001 Mike Nelson convinced with his labyrinth of rooms, *The Deliverance and the Patience,* in a shut down beer brewery on Giudecca. On top of that, the apparent anachronism of national pavilions in the age of globalization has in the meantime shown itself to be highly successful. Particularism in the global village is a reality, just as the power of location is more significant than ever in the global "nowhere". It is not infrequent that historic architecture serves as both an anchor and a point of friction, so that the old-fashioned principle of national solo shows nevertheless regularly develops "nucleus qualities". Beyond potential acts of state, here, in the critical engagement with history and the present, extremely intense installations can be experienced. One only has to think of Hans Haacke's German pavilion, Germania, in 1993 or Santiago Sierra's Spanish pavilion in 2003. Repeatedly it is such individual presentations, whether from Gregor Schneider, Janet Cardiff & George Bures Miller or Uri Tzaig, that have made strong artistic positions visible. Clear profiles and directions are possible, especially within the given spatial and national limitations.

Davide Croff
president, Venice Biennale*

The Venice Biennale is something completely different from a fair and there is no initiative here that could somehow be considered to be a fair. But in the past, until the beginning of the 1970s, within the Biennale, there was a so-called sales-office. This was sort of a small way to bring in the commercial side of contemporary art, within the Biennale. Then, because of the difficulties after 1968, that initiative was completely dismissed and for many years nobody was talking anymore about bringing this kind of thing back to the Biennale. Now, these kinds of problems are coming back. There is a debate about the relationship between museums, biennials and art fairs and I would not be surprised if this kind of argument came back to Venice and was somehow debated in the future. What I can tell you is that for the time being I do not see an immediate change in this strategic position. But I cannot commit myself in the long run.

Ingvild Goetz
Goetz Collection, Munich

The dramatically intensified interest in contemporary art, mostly of the pleasing sort, is satisfied by countless art fairs and gallery exhibitions. Only a few gallery exhibitions, and especially museum exhibitions, can dedicate themselves to fundamental questions, whether they are of an art-theoretical, political, social or culture-critical nature. In this context, however, formats such as Kassel or Venice can play a significantly constructive role. Since the pavilions and their national assignments represent a limitation *sui generis,* for me, what has been said applies particularly to Kassel. Today, as in the past, documenta has an almost unique opportunity of laying down coordinates for art and showing ways into its future. This particular role is certainly supported by the fact that for probably no other event in the world do specialists do their research for so long, namely, for four years, selecting artists and art works and putting them together.

If you want to protect art against market motivations and faddish trends, it is precisely events such as Venice and particularly Kassel, with their more profound approaches, which will be increasingly important in future.

Eva González-Sancho
FRAC Bourgogne, Dijon

The art economy is increasingly based on private funding. In this context, any public institution devoted to the promotion and the diffusion of contemporary art, and particularly one that intends to build a collection, faces considerable difficulties in participating in the debate on art. Rather than identifying the reasons for such a situation, it seems more important to acquire new mechanisms of action that allow us to remain stakeholders in the debate. In what way can cultural actors make use of art fairs and biennials as an opportunity to reflect on art, instead of adopting a left over role of spectators and consumers of productions that are dominated by economic power? I do not intend to challenge the format of the Venice Biennale as a means of obtaining an optimal forum between the artists, the art theorists and the public. Rather, I would like to question the form of interaction, as such, that takes place between the art professionals: curators, as well as private and public institutions, all of whom are indispensable actors for an art history in the making.

At present, a considerable number of public institutions are struggling for survival. This fact should not be attributed so much to the decline of the art reception, with its more or less ideological or political causes. Rather, it results from new economic powers with which public structures for art reception and diffusion are seemingly unable to cope. Something is missing here. The quinquennial encounters of the documenta in Kassel, the world-wide rise of biennials in imitation of the grande dame of Venice, or the highly awaited, the must-see contemporary art show at Münster, all of these make up the art market today, and form, at the same time, a considerable part of the art debate, with much the same force as do the leading galleries and the private sponsors and patrons. It seems likely that this new situation results, in part, from the accelerating decline of public influence in European cultural politics—a development that has to be watched. The large-scale format of the exhibitions just mentioned does not, in itself, constitute a major problem. However, given the present economic state of the public institutions, the division between the private and the public sector is more noticeable than ever. The latter is able, only to a limited extent, to participate in the present speculation, and this in spite of the fact that it plays a dominating role in the endorsements of artistic productions. To my mind, the grand art exhibits have to take into consideration this phenomenon. They cannot liberate themselves of the artistic and intellectual responsibility they possess. These important encounters, whether they intend to transmit the pulse of the current art scene (certainly more globalized than ever), or to make an artistic or intellectual contribution to the present creation, should take place in interaction with the political, economic and cultural environment of the artistic realities to which these art events point.

Ulrike Groos
Kunsthalle Düsseldorf

It is part of the nature of biennials that they disseminate a genuinely Western idea and therefore are exported with particular fervor to emerging and developing countries, where, in each of these local contexts, they replace museums and aim at directing attention to each country's present-day, local art scene. Of all the biennials, the Venice Biennale, as the last of the great biennials today, continues to propagate confidently national art. Venice, however, is probably also the only place where this potpourri of nationalities still radiates a certain charm and, although anachronistic in its national structure, still works as a successful model. For a long time, the São Paulo Biennale copied the Venetian model in exhibiting national presentations. The fact that this original idea has long since become a superseded model because of the great migratory movements of the twentieth century, the increasing international networking in the area of contemporary art and the dissolution of national art scenes, was announced and shown in the recent past nowhere more clearly than at the 27th São Paulo Biennale in 2006. Its director, Lisette Lagnado, decided within the framework of a new conception, for the first time in the history of this exhibition, to do without the system of national curators who, in the past, had been responsible for nominating national representatives. Breaking out of outmoded structures and following Lagnado's consistent step toward a comprehensive thematic exhibition, with the participation of international artists, allowed the potential contributors to enter into a stimulating contest with one another. For the future it should be pondered, whether the idea of an art subdivided into nationalities should be allowed to live on in Venice, in the national pavilions built in 1895, which are still used today, and at the same time whether to abolish the large group exhibition in the Italian pavilion. There would then be two clearly outlined models: the Venice model as the only one to preserve the idea of a representation of countries, and the documenta model, which represents a large exhibition format already followed by most biennials. Going beyond this, René Block has described the ideal biennial as a cultural workshop in which a central aspect of this large exhibition, namely, the linking of the local scene with the international scene, would come perceptibly to prominence. Only once such clearly formulated formats have been created do they gain influence as important discoverers and promoters of the contemporary and young art scene and are able to perform persuasive communicative work among artists, theorists and the public.

Paul Groot
Mediamatic, Amsterdam

Venice was once independent, but in the last centuries it has been colonized by its loving neighbors. First it became part of Austria. Later the resurging Italy offended its independence. And now new cultural doges from all over the place have taken it in. For example, the Swiss official participation in the Biennale is perhaps less important than the unofficial one. Of course the Swiss artists competing in the Giardini and in the church of San Stae deserve our attention. But the unofficial participation of Switzerland in the last decade seems much more important. It started with the work of Harald Szeemann who introduced a moral compass that had a strictly elitist, but highly artistic and intellectual character. He purified the Biennale, with its history of false beliefs, from the kitsch-sphere of modernism, so long rooted in the fascist idea of artistic creativity. Together with his friends, he showed us how ambition and a strong artistic attitude could do away with the last debris of modernist poison, creating a real atmosphere of intelligence and creativity. Times are changing. Consumerism has fully arrived in Venice, which has become a sensational public relation cum artistic event. One feels art is vanishing, and consumerist games are taking command. The setting and manipulation of taste looms large. Concurrently, we can witness the introduction of psychological bribery. Recent developments seem not to be inspired artistically, but are driven by blind ambition. Many curators seem to construct exhibitions as a new format, which is mainly echoing their daily reading of the financial newspapers (many magazines act likewise as thinly disguised financial papers). Well, this has brought about the disappearance of the Biennale, and the exhibition in the Venetian labyrinth reflecting and absorbing our insecurities had to vanish. The style of the new cultural doges is straightforward and hard. Could you, *pauvre lecteur,* have expected this? I didn't. It was a surprise for me how the cultural doges translated their ambition from financial newspapers into artistic terms: No longer art values rule, but hedge funds and private equity. No longer the artistic community, but the private equity community rules the artistic game. The killing conditions of the great money banks are today part of the artistic strategy. Everywhere. Look at the German pavilion where Isa Genzken—this greatest artist of all who never believed in art-as-it-is and always looked a few miles ahead—is now presented by the Deutsche Bank! Who is bribing who, and who will be the victim? Artists are no longer in the artistic game, and no longer in relation to the public or the critics. They are in relation to the wolves clad in sheep's clothing—the self-chosen artistic leaders with their new financially inspired artistic formats—who are working together with the great sponsors in the characteristically god-forgotten power game. The task of the Biennale had always been to give room to artists to show their work. If the artists make stupid work, the Biennale is stupid. And if the artists are good, the Biennale is ok.

Marina Gržinić
Institute of Philosophy, ZRC SAZU Ljubljana

In order to try to think of Europe not only as a geographical space, but as a conceptual space, a space that has a specific history—although after the fall of the Berlin wall it is more and more common to say that "Eastern Europe doesn't exist any more"—it is necessary to radicalize this space theoretically and politically. It will be easy to state, similarly as I stated that Eastern Europe does not exist, that Western Europe does not exist, either, or that what is even more fashionable in the last period, that Europe does not exist, but I will state Western Europe does exist, and Europe does exist. What does not exist, and I will make a reference to Bruno Bosteels text "Alain Badiou's Theory of the Subject: the Recommencement of Dialectical Materialism," is Europe as a relationship! Europe exists only as antagonism. What is taking place regularly and also through the big biennials (and other) big manifestations of "world art" is a process I would like to define as a transition from the politics of memory to the memory of that which used to be a political act. Or if I chose to radicalize this statement, I can ask: What defines global capitalism and neoliberal politics today? The answer is the evacuation of the political with processes not only of confusion, through the disappearance of borders and of precise positions, but also of escalation (using the precise military term of the word) of abstractions, evacuations, and empty formalization of protocols of performative politics. It is a war going on, not only for oil, but for the "world(-less) world," which can only be, as Suely Rolnik argued, an ever-expanding territory. What is the specific history of this new Europe? What can we learn from this history? We can learn not to think about this history as individual identity politics, but as something that can produce radical political concepts amongst them, looking historically, those of democracy. Capital emancipates unbelievably. It changes its clothes, and its way of behaving, if we just think of the names given to it in the time we are living in: social capital, inventive capital, the capital that has a special social attitude, the capital that is emancipated in relation to culture etc. These names show the unbelievable flexibility of capital in coping with time. Again, what defines global capitalism and neoliberal politics today? The evacuation of the political. Everything is transferred to art and culture, to some kind of politics of moral ethics and in the last instance it seems that this is about social help. This is how political questions of the world not only in art and culture but also in society are removed. It's almost impossible to do something relevant today in the social and political space of Europe and the world because of fierce censorship through funding etc. installed and constantly reproduced relations of hierarchy, and the interdependence between economic and structural power that demands apolitical projects and (fake) morality. Moreover, the public space is disappearing and private institutions and multinationals, that have money, are increasingly those who articulate, put in balance, sort public needs, histories and commons.

It is about the allocation of capital. Instead of identity politics it is important to analyze the ways we are attached/subjugated not only in our art works, but also in "our" manifestations of the structures of institutional, political and economic power.

Jörg Heiser
Frieze, Berlin

The Venice Biennale is an interesting mirror of the cultural bureaucracies of the countries that participate. Sometimes these bureaucracies produce interesting, "coincidental" results (such as the fact that this year, the three facing "old" pavilions of Germany, France, and the UK, are at last given over to female artists simultaneously, with Isa Genzken, Sophie Calle and Tracey Emin). Sometimes they produce just incoherence, or nothing (think of this year's more than dubious cancellation of David Maljković's Croation pavilion, single-handedly decided upon it seems by incompetent local nomenklatura). The creative output of the artistic director (this year, Robert Storr) and all artists showing (whether within his presentation or outside of it) is ultimately "mediated", for better or worse, by these kinds of bureaucracies. It's like watching a brilliant B-movie on a fucked-up TV set. Which can still be fun, after all.

Even if the Venice Biennale had a single voice unhindered by its own special kind of local nomenklatura within its curated part, it could, in terms of its national pavilions, still only provide an old, oft-refurbished platform for what others —the respective countries—provide. The question remains who has the privilege to provide in the first place: only those countries where either a pavilion is already established in the Giardini (which nevertheless has meant these remained closed, as in the case of Javier Téllez and Pedro Morales, whose Venezuelan pavilion 2003 didn't take place after Téllez withdrew in protest against government politics and Morales' part was censored and eventually cancelled), or also those who can afford to establish themselves in some other part of the City? I for myself had some of my best experiences with "off-site" pavilions (for example, Estonia's Mark Raidpere or Lithuania's Jonas Mekas presentations in 2005). Of course, thinking of all those states who are not represented and all those artists who don't really belong, or want to belong, to any of them, one could simply suggest to do away with the ridiculous nineteenth century idea of "national pavilions" all together. But then we wouldn't get to see how those in power in real-existing nations—whether democratic, pseudo-democratic, or downright autocratic—go about "representing themselves" in terms of art, which is an experience in itself that few other large scale survey exhibitions offer. Oh, the discrete charm of cultural bureaucracy!

Claudia Jolles
Kunst-Bulletin, Zurich

Art as a "first class stake in a game", as mentioned in the introductory question, suggests stock exchange transactions, speculation and money. One thinks of a mixture of power and incompetence, brokering and price manipulation—and does not want to have anything to do with it. Far more exciting is the hypothesis that life in itself is a game in which we act, enthused and burdened by various possibilities and encumbrances. From this point of view, biennials are play-acting stages and can be a genuine enrichment. They entice us to travel to cities where, otherwise, we would never have gone, allow us to sort through a diversity of art presentations and to synchronize what is offered with an often sparse knowledge about the local scene. The mixture of the familiar and the new sharpen up one's own system of reference and make its limitations apparent. In principle, each Biennale bears the signature of the curators responsible. Thus, at the moment, I am interested in whether the rather reticent Robert Storr will assert himself in the Venetian surroundings and whom he will present to us. What does he mean by Think with the Senses—Feel with the Mind? Curare means "to care for", and I expect that those responsible will represent the personal worldviews of artists in public in a forthcoming manner, that the individual character is given a social context and the individual voice finds a collective resonance chamber. In particular, I value clearly contoured exhibition formats such as Manifesta and documenta that are realized with a fixed rhythm by changing teams. Even if once in a while they do not take place, such as last year's Manifesta 6 in Nicosia, this makes something apparent about the current situation in the country concerned, about the possibilities and the limitations of art, about the splintering of individual ambitions and about a dense local bureaucracy against which utopian individual fighters have no effect. Even though culture cannot be thought of independently of market forces, the failure of a planned, large exhibition shows that, without culture, no civilization is possible.

Kasper König
Museum Ludwig, Cologne**

For the fourth time, after a decade, Sculpture Projects is taking place in Münster, this time 007. We, too, are posing the question of where we are standing (or lying) today (yesterday—tomorrow). The Venice format: I like the anachronism of "national" pavilions in the Giardini. Venice is always good because it is the dying, immortal Venice. Don't worry too much. Good art is always the exception.

Elisabeth Lebovici
art critic, Paris

After having acknowledged that the Venice Biennale is presently included in a package entitled "Grand Tour" that comprises the Basel art fair, the documenta, and the Münster Sculpture Project, and after having declared the Biennale—any biennial—comatose in terms of new concepts, models or contents, you have just reserved, well in advance, your train ticket and your hotel room for Venice. Where do we go from there? The invitation to write takes, here, a rather pragmatic connotation: where do you go from there? You go to Basel? You go to Kassel? You know the contradictions; it doesn't scare you, all that seems rather absurd. All these expenses, just to see another "Plate of Humanity", a new chunk of global art? You are at pains to justify your interest with more noble causes than mundane ones but the simple idea of not being "in" upsets you, even if you're incapable of defining yourself within the audience of the Biennale: neither a simple viewer nor an art bureaucrat, neither an artist nor a collector, neither a curator nor—for the first time since quite a long time—an art journalist supposed to account for your journey to your readers, or at least to your employer.

You know that amongst the biennials, Venice, in fact, stays with its own peculiarities, its national pavilions in the Giardini, its Italian pavilion and its arsenal, where one or many curators develop their skills and try to make sense. For you, Venice is a little like the United Nations, an international institution, formed with the aim that the nations live in peace and tolerance and yet continually confronted by war and intolerance. The Venice Biennale is, likewise, a diplomatic event (etymologically, diploma equals passport), with some countries more surely included and others, who strive hard for recognition. Like the UN, the Venice Biennale is neither an assembly of peoples, nor of nations, but of government representatives, who speak the art's diplomatic language. Thus you can say that at the Venice Biennale, the "minorities" are always absent, in the sense that the artists exhibited were chosen by an administration, a committee, a commission, who came to a consensus on their name. The Venice Biennale is an atlas of these consensuses.

It is true that artists and curators have recently tried to impose new rules in the game. To you, the most radical gesture, in this vein, was Utopia Station, initiated by Molly Nesbit, Hans-Ulrich Obrist and Rikrit Tiravanija at the Venice Biennale, 2003: a machinery and a conceptual structure involving artists, architects and theoreticians from all generations in creating a collective process of creativity around the word utopia. "Utopia Station doesn't need an architecture to exist, a simple meeting is sufficient," announced its initiators. This is probably why the station is still on, well out of the Venice Biennale's time and space. In the light of this and as an opposite to the Venice Biennale, you might propose the 15th Paris Biennale (which first took place in 1959): also an ongoing process without a place, without a city, without a space, without exhibition walls, lasting from October 1, 2006 to September 30, 2008. Then the next one will maybe happen, maybe not. The Paris Biennale is going "where things happen when things happen", in order to extract itself from an obligatory visibility and from the policing of invention.

Michael Lingner Hochschule für bildende Künste, Hamburg

In search of another life, more and more people are exploring the virtual world of Second Life. This illusory world visited by millions is an Internet product of the Californian company, Linden Lab. The business consists mainly in selling land in the Second Life world. All the emigrants from the real world have the opportunity of completely reinventing themselves and their existence for the virtual world. This opportunity, however, is mostly used only with regard to outward appearances. The Second Life person is adapted to certain ideals of beauty which deviate from mainstream ideas in the real world just as little as the rest of weborgs' lives. That is at first surprising, since the widespread need to escape everyday reality, just like the widespread use of other surrogates, is also a motive for taking part in Second Life.

But obviously, by now, the majority of globalized people are in a precarious situation similar to that of the man in Franz Kafka's 1922 story, *Breaking Out*, who, in response to his servant's question as to where he is riding to, answers, "I don't know [...] only away from here. On and on, away from here, only in this way can I reach my destination". And when the servant asks further, "So you know the destination," he can only respond, "I already told you, away from here, that is my destination". This urge to make aimless attempts at breaking out merely for the sake of escaping, today masked as tourism, however, is tragically in vain and demands a high price. The eternal escapism costs having to lead an inauthentic life felt to be provisional with, in the worst case, barbaric consequences.

By contrast, an essential cultural achievement of art in the modern age consists precisely in not only giving expression to this desire to escape from the existing world into another one, but also to really make it possible to live it out. However, since in the art world, other worlds conforming to their own laws with a maximum degree of autonomy are no longer being created, but, under the dictates of economic criteria, artistic success is defined only financially, the drift of contemporary art toward having an effect on the public has become unstoppable. In all art genres, modes of play of a somehow (such as bizarre, narcissistic, ironic...) ennobled picture journalism, with certain prestigious qualities and in conformity with social norms and media requirements, celebrate their triumph. At art exhibitions in an international large format such as the Venice Biennale and the Kassel documenta, this artistic mainstream is celebrated and multiplied. Involved in the mechanisms of the art markets, today they no longer function as fora for a specialist public, but as illustrious fairs. Like other offerings for little escapes from everyday life, they are designed and marketed as tourist attractions. Visitors programs and guided tours by the obligatory art communicators serve the purpose of explaining and proclaiming as art these redundant replicas of everyday reality, which can be understood in themselves without any artistic pretensions or simply unmasked as nonsense. Visitors can then fool themselves that they have seen something significant and that the motive and the costs for their tautological trip are justified. As a memento they are sold further explanations in opulent catalogs which gather dust on the bookshelves at home as a kind of discursive kitsch.

The ancient Platonic depreciation of art vis-à-vis reality, as a phenomenon to be entered in the books as second best at best, seems once more to demonstrate its truth.

Michael Lüthy
Interdisziplinäres Zentrum Kunstwissenschaft und Ästhetik, Freie Universität, Berlin

To be sure, the format of the Venice Biennale is antiquated. It stems from the era of competition among nation states in the second half of the nineteenth century when artistic production, as superstructure, had the brief of bearing witness to the potency of each economy. Today we are far removed from that, not only in our conception of art, but also because of the changes in political geography. As far as art is concerned, it hardly maintains a propagandistic relation to the nation in which it was made. The nomadic, transnational artist has advanced to become the model, and art has been discovered as a medium for diverting attention toward cultures standing in the shadows both economically and in power politics. As far as the changes in political geography are concerned, today it is not so much the European nations that are competing with one another, but rather the old continent of Europe with other emerging regions of the world. Insofar it is not surprising that the Venice Biennale, whose location already stands for a declining Europe, is itself under pressure to legitimize itself, to stand out against other art events around the globe, and also to take account of that notorious globalization.

The advantage of competition consists of each exhibition format not having to offer the same thing. The specific potentiality of the Biennale structure lies in concentrating upon individual artistic positions in separate architectural ambiences. Ideally in the national pavilions, aesthetic judgment rules—embodied in the subjective view of each commissioner—that vouches for the validity of presenting a certain artistic position. The public, too, largely decides within the framework of aesthetic judgments: a pavilion is a success, or it isn't. Nonetheless, on the basis of the quality of a pavilion, nobody would like to conclude that the corresponding country is superior. National competition has given way to artistic competition. Thus, the Biennale is willy-nilly banking on singularity. Overarching themes as expected from documenta are kept in the background, at least in the national pavilions (and in the special shows they often seem labored). Aestheticism, however, is not a necessary consequence, as shown by Santiago Sierra's thought-provoking contribution for the Spanish pavilion in 2003. I feel this accent on artistic singularity as a welcome counterweight not only to the overly discursive nature of documenta, which often makes the question concerning the artistic value secondary, but also to the world art trade, from whose pores mercantile lust drips. Of course, the Biennale is not an Arcadia of intra-artistic values, but paradoxically, its historically discredited structure enables an experience of art and an aesthetic judgment to a degree which I find lacking at other large art events and in museums subjected to pressure by private collectors. The specific tension of the Venice Biennale, between structure and experience, seems to me to be worth preserving.

Ken Lum
artist, Vancouver

In relation to the question of how convincing the Venice Biennale is in terms of its mediation between artists, theorists and the public, I am having a hard time with the word "convincing". "Relevant" or "effective" would be more understandable to me, but "convincing"? On a glib level, I can reply readily that I am convinced that the Venice Biennale is always a fun event to attend. A good cross section of the international contemporary art world deems it an important enough event to attend, or at the very least, not to miss. There is always a smattering of interesting works on view, no matter how problematically formatted the Biennale is, with its hierarchical divide between richer and poorer nations' pavilions. (Hans Haacke's beautiful work of broken marble flooring in the German pavilion or Harald Szeemann's ambitious exhibition of Chinese artists are two examples that come to mind.) By the way, while the divide is indefensible, it nonetheless communicates a truth about the unspoken hierarchies that make up the art world at large. And yes, I mean today's art world, even in its globalized form, comprised as it is of an international constituency of artists. The global flows remain largely unidirectional to this day, only the flow charts are longer and they bend a bit more. One only needs to spend a week in Delhi to find out about the dynamic art scene in that city to know this to be the case. But back to the question at hand of how convincing the Venice Biennale is. The question has a nostalgic edge to it. In my mind, it can be rephrased as: how convincing is the Venice Biennale in this age of fallen idealism in art? Or, how convincing is the Venice Biennale given its dowager status in the context of so many more vital biennials and even art fairs, especially those sited in developing localities? Here's my short answer: the Venice Biennale is convincing to the extent that it presents a wide showcase of artists within a miniaturized and replicated model of the larger geopolitical world of competing rich and poor nations. This will remain the case until the structure of the larger geopolitical world is radically changed, such that the divides between rich and poor, and colonizer and colonized look nothing like they do today. At that point the answer to the question about whether the Venice Biennale is convincing, would be simply this—not at all.

Oliver Marchart Soziologisches Seminar, Universität Luzern

The question concerning the social function of biennials, from their function in the area of art to their function in city marketing, has been repeatedly discussed recently. But could platforms such as those of the biennials, beyond these "social" functions, also possess a political function in the narrow sense which further something in the world, and not only in the small world of art? Is there a potential that the thematically focused large exhibitions could radiate into society in order, say, to inject political topics into public debate which otherwise could scarcely become visible? If this question is to be affirmed, then I think that a notion of what an exhibition is has to be rebuilt on the high seas, for such a political function of the public sphere of art would be absolutely at odds with the contribution made by museums and biennials—for instance, to ideological nation-building in Benedict Anderson's sense—as well as with the economic function of the art industry as a market-place where goods and services are traded. Jérôme Sans grasped a tip of this political aspect of the exhibition when he distinguished 'exhibition' from 'ex/position'. The French word, 'ex/position', according to Sans, points to the aspect of ex-position as a positioning and commitment. What a biennial can achieve politically in the most favorable case, if it should set this aim, is a form positioning, of assuming a stance, of consciously taking up a position. But of course not any old position, not even a merely theoretical position, as Sans suggests, but an antagonistic position coupled with already existing, collective, political practices and debates. The political opportunity of a large exhibition lies in visibly marking a counter-position. Only as a counter-position does an exhibition radiate to the broader public. But, at the same time, it will then automatically counter the logic of itself as an institution, since the proper task of every institution consists precisely in domesticating conflicts, which are to be adapted to regulated processes and procedures. The public sphere of antagonism, of positioning, by contrast, interrupts regulated processes, accountabilities, hierarchies and marketing decisions. In fact, every real antagonism makes a breach in the walls of the institution. The ex-position leads to an opening of the institution, leads into the free, open space of the public sphere, leads out of the institutions of art and the art scene and into the debates of the political public sphere. If there is something to be criticized about the institution of the biennials and their present mode of play, then it is this: there is a lack of courage, not only to retell dreams and conflicts thematically and poetically within the protection of one's own four walls, but also to actively generate conflicts and to assume a position within them.

Rita McBride artist, Düsseldorf

Yesterday I flew twelve hours to Las Vegas from Frankfurt. I checked into the Luxor Hotel and turned on the TV in my pyramid enclosed hermetic room. On the internal hotel venue station, a documentary on Las Vegas was attempting explanation; providing tales of mafia and glamour with all the destruction and encompassing fame. It spoke of the time when the stars became the only reason people came to Vegas and how it had left the Casino houses vulnerable and in a compromised profit profile. The Tropicana got tired of paying huge sums to the talent. It cut into the profits and limited the casino's flexibility. The Sands had to agree to the exorbitant terms demanded by the artists. The Golden Nugget was at the mercy of the celebrity's irrational whims. Often the artist would just cancel; then the hotels would have to reimburse the guests and risk disastrous consequences. Without the "stars", no one would check into the hotels and enjoy the casinos; no one would spend money on the one armed bandits.

The infomercial documentary in my room continued; stopping to praise, with emphasis, the break-through innovations developed by Caesar's Palace; going on to explain that the artists had become too problematic and demanding so the casino's created the idea of "venue as act". Theme casinos sprouted up along the strip and people came to participate in the all-encompassing fantasy of the architecture. Then a final breakthrough! Circus-Circus opens on the Strip, with acrobats, jugglers, trapeze artists and "more magicians then you could shake a stick at!", performers without the problem of celebrity. Easily replaceable talent!

I switched off the TV when the docu-commercial sort of ended with a preview of the Luxor's own variety act, Fantasy: a celebrated strip tease show including eleven delectable girls for $45. Funny, I remembered that there was an advertised act called Carrot Top (a "no-name" red-head that did impersonations) for $100. Eleven topless girls have got to be worth more then one comedian? Numbed by the silence turning the TV off had produced; I turned on my mobile to retrieve messages. Message number one: Caesar's Palace had called to cancel the Elton John show I had booked for that night. The twelve-hour notice policy had not accounted for my geography. No matter. My nephew, who was with me on the trip, was secretly happy not to be subjected to The Red Piano after all. I have to admit I am not a fan of Elton John either but it was the only ticket that I had insider connections to (via the LA art world); so in the interest of promised VIP treatment I had agreed to the 250 a pop. Milo preferred to see Cirque du Soleil doing the Beatles. I was dubious but willing.

We headed off for a day tour of the strip, a little overwhelmed, wondering if the whole thing called Las Vegas was better, full of people and in the dark with lights, or empty and bright daylight revealing a little too much. As we walked we began noticing that our Cirque du Soleil wasn't the only Cirque du Soleil in town. There where five others. At this point, I couldn't help but remember the talented tent topped troupe on the beach I had seen in Santa Monica as a kid in 1985. Is it possible that there is that much talent in the world? Yes! I think optimistically to myself. I would wait and see. The show was a bit of a let down. How could they go wrong with such winning combinations? I was of the opinion that the heavy light and sound aspect made it hard for the 40 odd tiny death-defying humans to have any presence. Milo would have settled for a remixed, revamped filmic version of *A Hard Day's Night* in deluxe comfortable seating.

I am left thinking about the Cirque-du-Soleilization of the Art world. Theme-parks (Venice is the original ur-themepark after all) showing variety acts, all with a generous amount of nostalgia for the 1960s like the *Love* show at the Mirage. The pavilions of the Giardini and Kassel's exotic park of Wilhelmshöhe are already so similar in my mind to the landscaping in front of the Venetian Hotel and fantasy gardens of Mandalay Bay that all I need to add conceptually to the scenario are the Artists-as-circus-performers to complete the picture. Mimes, magicians, jugglers, escape artists, clowns, tight-rope walkers and animal trainers; all roles fully in keeping with the present cultural definition of the "artistic persona". From a curatorial perspective there is something quite admirable about the biennial-as-circus construct, with strong democratic connotations, teamwork, flexibility and above all internationalism. One immediately imagines the same "performers" helping to set up the tents, collecting the tickets and after the show, cleaning up as well: troupes of itinerant talent following the biennials from one town to the next.

Tonight we have tickets to the "artist formally known as Prince". Milo is dubious but willing.

Heike Munder Migros Museum für Gegenwartskunst, Zürich

Biennials still promise the possibility of traveling and discovering for artists and visitors—a combination of information and the pleasures of traveling derived today from globalized curators, artists and visitors. For the host countries, this is the hope of being integrated into the leading Western art discourse. It gives countries, which do not (yet) stand at the center of global attention, such as Romania, Lithuania and Cuba, the opportunity, through the national event character, of getting extra money, partners and artists into the country. There is a hope of thus crank-starting the country's own cultural infrastructure and establishing sustainable discourses in one's own country. From the side of sponsors, there is often a desire to get rid of the stamp as periphery and to belong to the greater whole at least as a "bridgehead" (Ulf Wuggenig). One of the most recent positive examples is the triennial in Luanda, Angola which opened in December 2006 on the initiative of its founder, the artist Fernando Alvim. At that time Angola had just four years of peace behind it after more than twenty-five years of civil war. The triennial had the effect of a shiny satellite in the city and, despite its white cubes, was quickly integrated. Alvim refused the simple cultural strategy of globalization and showed also a lot of young art from Angola in order, in the first place, to strengthen the country itself. There were no VIP guests flown in, in masses, for the opening; only individual partners were invited and looked after intensively. These were artists, press people, lecturing curators and former pioneers for this triennial. The power of the triennial which stands for Luanda and does not participate in art tourism, has nevertheless spread by word of mouth. The triennial's maker, Fernando Alvim, was invited to documenta 12 as an artist-curator to present his project, and also as a curator, together with his colleague, Simon Njami, to stage the first African pavilion at the Arsenale in Venice this year. For Angola and thus also for Africa, this is a great opportunity for self-empowerment—and a small step toward the dream of a world without centralized power and borders. As Rasheed Araeen said in 1978 in his plea at the ICA in London, "The myth of the internationalism of Western art must now be destroyed. [...] it is merely a transatlantic art. [...] The present internationalism of Western art is nothing more than a function of the political and economic power of the West which forces its values on other people."

Marie Muracciole Jeu de Paume, Paris

– International exhibitions (biennials etc.) are not to "take into account the changing political and cultural environment" in the world. They are constantly resulting from, and hopefully part of, it. The danger would be to illustrate it.
– Biennials etc. invite curators and theorists to apply and experiment with ideas in the process of making an exhibition. Fairs invite them to theorize.
– A fair is chaos trying to be ordered by the market, a biennial is some order trying to be messed up by ideas.
– You may prefer chaos to the market and to some curators' ideas.
– You may prefer ideas about the situation in art, to art. You may also think that art is making money and making money is art.
– Contrary to the fairs, biennials are expected to make transparent their own history, financial issues, etc.
– Some fairs have the means to look like biennials (e.g. Art Unlimited in Basel), some biennials have the means to look like fairs (e.g. The Moscow Biennale).
– Fairs reflect biennials. Biennials reflect the market?
– Some curators challenge these situations.

– You can find works of art outside the biennials and fairs.
– Collectors (VIP) like to get invited to biennials, curators (Pro.) like to get invited to fairs.
– Art in fairs may be fresh: good to eat but not for long. This can happen also in some biennials etc.
– You may find works from the same artists on both sides, you may like their works here and dislike them there.
– You may find good art on both sides, you may find bad deals, too.
– This all means you have traveled a lot: never complain.
– Let's talk about art.

Hans Ulrich Obrist Serpentine Gallery, London

PARS PRO TOTO:
A Biennial A to Z (fragments)

A. for Archipelago

Regarding the complex question of biennials, it's important not to reduce our reflections to one single model but to study historical and contemporary models with an experimental approach. Édouard Glissant is interesting in this connection: For him, biennials tend to be too much like continents (rock solid and imposing), as opposed to the archipelago (welcoming and sheltering). In his words, "The idea of a non-linear time implicit in this idea, or in this concept, the coexistence of several time zones would of course allow for a great variety of different contact zones as well."

B. for Bridge

The multiplication of biennials/triennials has to be seen positively in terms of the necessary multiplication of centers. The quest for the absolute center, which has dominated big parts of the twentieth century, has opened to a polyphony of centers in the twenty-first century. The biennial as a bridge between the local and the global; on the bridge you have two points, two ends. As artist Huang Yong Ping recently explained: "Normally we think a person should have only one standpoint, but when you become a bridge you have to have two."

C. for Critical Mass

Often the biennial is a trigger for a dynamic energy field radiating throughout a city. This works particularly well when all of a city's exhibitions spaces participate and make a joint effort. A biennial can trigger a lot of self organized side events in a city, warehouse exhibitions, student shows, and counter shows: Parallel realities!

E. for Étonnez-moi

The curatorial position should always be open to surprise. In a now legendary exchange, Diaghilev challenged Cocteau to surprise him. His "Étonnez-moi" will always be important.

N. for New Geographies
(Braudel revisited)

Patricia Falguières sent me the following text message: "Indeed, I think there are a lot of things to be done in this sense, notably to follow and to describe and perhaps to accompany [...] this enormous change we are experiencing. This is an enormous transfer of the centre of gravity from the Old World to the New Worlds, of which we can only guess the shape—in the fog! Obviously the Braudelian parallel imposes itself: I think of the shift of the Mediterranean world to the Atlantic and the Pacific in the sixteenth century (i.e. a shift of a world that is shaped, limited, with its own distinctive architecture, towards an unlimited horizon, punctuated by archipelagos and nebulas as described by Braudel in *Material Civilization and Capitalism*." (SMS of January 2007)

S. for Sustainability

It is important what happens in-between biennials. Ideally, it should be a permanent process. Most biennials are organized in incredibly short time frames and the operation for organizing them gets more and more reduced. Curators need to resist this and find a more reasonable framework. Important as biennials are, the danger is that they can create a firework and then two years of desert. Changing the format and creating interim events, might be very helpful in overcoming this problem. The biennial as a project could build up through some kind of sedimentary levels. This means to avoid the biennial as a *tabula rasa.*

T. for Transnational

Transnational exhibitions seem to be one of the key issues from the 1990s through the present: not to be about borderlines, but actually to become a borderline. In opposing what he called the "irreversible" aspects of globalization (uniformity, homogeneity), Étienne Balibar once described to me the need for artists and exhibitions to become nomadic, physically and mentally traveling across borders; going beyond national boundaries would allow languages and cultures to spill in all directions, to broaden the horizon of translating capacities. "Exhibitions would vanish in their intervention," Balibar used to say, "they would be necessary but without monopoly, they would be borderlines themselves." Thus my earlier accentuation: to become a borderline.

Sandi Paučić
F+F Schule für Kunst und Mediendesign, Zürich

For me as a regular, non-objectively romantic Venice stroller, the Biennale is a welcome refuge from the sometimes, inevitably, encroaching *Truman Show* restrictedness of the Serenissima. The Venice Biennale, as probably the most atmospheric fun fair of fine art, may offer a nice change, but for me it has always been somehow a supplementary program to the city, and not conversely. In its pretensions to being a world power and in its insuperable anachronism, the exhibition is a match for the city where it is held. And like the old Venetians, in the long run the Biennale makers will probably not be able to evade the fight with Istanbul and other emerging powers. And perhaps, when history repeats itself, the Biennale, like her mother city, will sink into imperial insignificance without wanting to look this truth in the face. I always begin my tour in the Giardini. I like the pleasant strolling climate of the national pavilions in the cool shade of the park's trees. These pavilions, in acceptable single doses, facilitate access and thus prevent a premature overloading of the senses. To be more precise, I always first visit the Swiss pavilion to the right of the main entrance. I don't know at all whether only those related to Switzerland do that or whether it corresponds to the intended direction of the architectural arrangement. Perhaps in this receptively fresh position, coupled with the miracle of San Stae, lies the key to the international success of contemporary Helvetian art? Mostly sometime toward noon I pass by the old Yugoslavian building. For me as someone with Croatian origins, it signifies a conspicuous indication of the completely revised concept for the national pavilions. I come from an atomized country whose artistic presence at the Biennale, thanks to the new Venetian foreign offices, has grown—what a tender fruit of war! Shortly before the close I usually reach the Padiglione Italia, as large as a museum, too late to grasp the sense of the curatorial assertion exhibited there which stretches over the labyrinthine arrangement of rooms. I look forward most of all to the Corderie in Arsenale at the beginning of my second day at the Biennale. Usually there are no bad disappointments there because the sacred, early industrial sublimeness of the halls allows me to generously pardon some of the art works and the curators. When, finally, I turn left into the Artiglierie, I walk more quickly because my two-day visit to the Biennale is now reaching its climax and almost its end. I step out into the glaring light and stand in front of my favorite Venetian sculpture, the old, rotating harbor crane which has been rusting for years in Titanic hugeness next to the main basin of the Darzena Grande in the shimmering heat. Here, heated by art and passion, I once drank the finest San Pellegrino of my life with the love of my life on the chic restaurant ship (which later on no longer docked here). It was doubtless the most coherent, most eye opening and the best of all Venetian Biennales.

Stella Rollig
Lentos Kunstmuseum, Linz

Biennials are playing an increasingly significant role as the eye of the needle through which the work of individual artists has to pass into public awareness. In view of an abundance of names, works, projects, exhibitions and publications, which an individual can no longer take in, biennials have left other art institutions behind in relation to the formation of a global canon of contemporary art. The biennials make artists visible and their work negotiable for that critical mass whose attention is necessary for a successful artistic career. What is problematic about this is that a small number of curators serves more and more biennials, which does not further the diversity of the positions communicated. As communicative instances, biennials coin a false image of art in the twenty-first century. They show only a detail which largely coincides with the increasingly numerous worldwide biennials. With their presentation, most biennials confirm a conventional concept of art with a bias toward paintings and objects and are therefore welcome agents for the gallery market. The opportunity of presenting artistic work that critically intervenes, undertakes process-based structural analyses or displays itself in ephemeral presentations is scarcely taken advantage of by the biennials as the only weighty alternative to the art fairs. An important part of artistic practice is thus ignored. The competition among the nations as conceived for the national pavilions today represents only a curious anachronism. However, because it regularly reinforces the self-appointed leading cultural nations of the globe in their obsolete perception of themselves, the buildings on the grounds of the Giardini, together with the surrounding walls, should all be demolished. On the open and freely accessible grounds, a new biennial that has not been seen anywhere else should arise. What a fine thing it would be to want to travel, most of all and out of all the biennials, to the one in Venice—and to do so because of a truly open, free and liberating art show, and not only because of the city, about whose uniqueness one does not have to say a single word.

Nicolaus Schafhausen
Witte de With Center for Contemporary Art, Rotterdam

In comparison to documenta, the Venice Biennale is certainly the less discursive format. The events program and accompanying art-interpretation, which have a central significance for documenta and are directly integrated into the curatorial concept, play a relatively minor role in Venice. In compensation for this, the Venice Biennale is able to address the public much more immediately, even though it does try to do this by generating a critical potential from the traditional format of a show of national achievements. In themselves, however, such large exhibitions are more unwieldy in the communication between art, theory and the public sphere than other institutions, which over the years have worked up a certain profile and, via this profile, are able to develop ties with a public that values a discursive exchange.

The Venice Biennale is a prestigious large format and not a seismograph of cultural and social change. That does not mean that there are no positions present that engage explicitly with the changing cartography of Europe and the world.

Especially the national pavilions must repeatedly pose the question concerning their national pretensions. Nevertheless, the course through the Giardini alone shows that the Venice Biennale comes from a time in which art and hegemonic pretensions were very much brought into relation with one another. Those countries, which do not belong to old Europe and its colonial partners, are marginalized already by their exclusion from the Biennale terrain proper. One can engage with this state of affairs on both a curatorial and an artistic level, but many do not do this.

Christoph Schenker Hochschule für Gestaltung und Kunst, Zürich

The art system is highly differentiated. One pole of the system is formed by artistic work as research, another pole by the sales and service machinery of the "department stores": the art fairs, the biennials, the mega-exhibitions and the exhibition programs of the cultural institution chains. They are strong factors in the worldwide marketing of and competition between cities (the culture economy, tourism). Despite the primarily economic incentive, the occasions for the public are able to function also as a medium of communication. The Venice Biennale with its national pavilions seems to be anachronistic. But what interests us today more than ever, in the process of globalization in a political, ethical and epistemological regard, are the local specificities of thinking and ways of living, of art and culture. Thus, despite the biennials in Asia, Africa and South America, it would be desirable if there were more space for non-NATO art in Venice. At the same time, an up-to-date organization and forms that are adequate to the contents must also be demanded. The Venice Biennale, after documenta in Kassel, certainly would have the potential for reorganization and an openness of the disciplines. But it will miss the opportunity; it is too old. I remember how Harald Szeemann, perhaps the only "master" of large art exhibitions, self-critically asked the artist, Wolfgang Laib, shortly before the exhibition opened, "Have I betrayed your work?" He knew that occasions like biennials, etc., are not the places where artistic discourse takes place. They do not accord with the needs of artists. Beneath the steely framework of the art industry and market, however, there is that delicate, vulnerable network of artistic research. It is anchored individually and locally, but all around the world; it forms itself in micrological work, but opens up the enormous space of the imaginary. Who and what form the nodes of this network? The nodes are the work of artists and their accomplices, and they are the work of the "small" institutions, which conceive of themselves as instruments of artistic research. The discursive field of institutions and accomplices, of studios and art academies forms the framework for the laboratory in which phenomena are made available for what has not been foreseen, for the artistic event. To further these processes and take part in them means to form a critical public sphere.

Katharina Schlieben Shedhalle, Zürich

It is part of the curatorial repertoire to engage in symposia with the format of biennials. This year's Venice Biennale, too, attempted it with a preceding symposium, Where Art Worlds Meet: Multiple Modernities and the Global Salon. With regard to discourses and their spaces, not only the question concerning which discourses take place in which spaces is interesting, but also which spaces produce which discourses. To seek a reflective dialogue with the frame of reference is the starting-point for critical, curatorial practice, which would have to transform the questioning into a performative curatorial practice to open up space for action. Here, curatorial practice can learn from artistic practice. Artists have often presented the prestigious political frame of reference of the Venice Biennale by hacking up floors of the pavilions or questioning the history and politics of national presentation. By virtue of its theme park of national pavilions, the oldest biennial is the witness of a history of exhibition politics for presenting national identities. A questioning of transnational dynamics provokes a curatorial need for action on both a discursive and performative level. Dialogical relations among the pavilions could be set up by, say, reassigning the pavilions for a coming biennial. Nations with a pavilion could pass on theirs to a country without, because of the history of the politics of prestigious presentation. Large formats like biennials have the potential and the responsibility of creating public spheres and drawing attention to bad states of affairs, of enabling intercultural meetings, of developing a dialogue with local contexts, and of questioning transnational circulations. The lack of a mediation—which ties in participants and partial public spheres—runs the risk of the receptive gaze reproducing voyeurism. A critical look behind the contextual backdrops as well as direct, controversial dialogues could create polyphonic public spheres. In this respect Manifesta is more radical. It favors the local contexts and transnational interrelations in its curatorial and artistic program. It does not comfortably set up house, but calls on the initiators, visitors and participants to enter into a dialogue with geopolitical contexts and questions regarding the construction of identity.

Peter J. Schneemann/ Nicola Müllerschön Institut für Kunstgeschichte, Universität Bern

The swan song of the biennial and documenta formats has, in the meantime, become a cultivated ritual. People particularly like to refer to historical functions which today are outmoded: national presentation as the legacy of the display of achievement at the world exposition in the case of the Biennale, and a communicative gesture of the post-war period in the case of documenta. However, neither these arguments, nor the countless, justified references to transgressing the economic limits of attentiveness, have prevented either event from maintaining its significance as a point of reference. There is perhaps no other place where critical reflection on the conditions of the institution called exhibition has been furthered in such a concentrated and lasting way as in the Giardini. The central position of the Biennale in demonstrating new positions has its origin in critical engagement with the continually changing geography of art, with the most diverse artistic approaches of a site-specific way of working. It is no accident that outstanding works by such different artists as Hans Haacke, Gregor Schneider, Ilya Kabakov and Santiago Sierra have arisen in the context of an anachronistic structure. Parts of this fruitful friction are curatorial achievements such as Marius Babias' concept for the Romanian Pavilion. Further evidence for the attractiveness of the predetermined parameters of the pavilions is the observation that the exhibitions in the Arsenale always fade into the background. Of course there is something resembling "biennial art" and one could well ask oneself whether the attractiveness of these surroundings is especially suitable for institutional critiques and whether some of the popular examples for staging pavilions, such as Hans Schabus' mountain, represented merely folkloric interventions in the question concerning locality and identity, that is, whether the Biennale is slipping into becoming a Disneyland of art. The fact that the Biennale happens in Venice of all places, a location that in its magnificent, ruined aesthetic is otherwise no mecca for contemporary art, surely enhances the special attraction of this institution. For the art critic, the Biennale also offers an important mirror of the efforts of cultural policy, of ideological utopias and image-cultivation by curators. Also the mirror image as a distorted image is not to be denied, rather, the "second-order" observer loves this too. Even the new national presentations that do not find space in the Giardini and have to rent a building somewhere or other in the city, can be read as metaphors for changes in the global art world. It is probable that in time, the Venice Biennale will scarcely be able to defend its status as the most important biennial, but nevertheless we do not want to do without it.

Dieter Schwarz Kunstmuseum, Winterthur

I cannot remember ever leaving the Biennale convinced or satisfied. Neither the national pavilions nor the respective overviews at the Italian pavilion or the Arsenale could truly thrill me. So it's the individual works that remain in my memory, since they were able to assert themselves, despite the general leveling context, in that they appeared at just the right time and the right place. With time, I became convinced that it's only the encounter with such individual works that makes the trip worthwhile. At documenta, the other large exhibition, things are a bit different. There was a time—at documenta 5 in 1972—when there was a concentration of great works to be seen. At least that's the picture I have in my memory. It was a happy coincidence that the art that had just emerged in the 1960s, and had already begun to meet with some recognition, here found a large-scale platform for the first time. Four years prior to that, and five years later, the situation was quite different. But we remember from documenta 5 the artistic highpoints, erasing in our memory the palpable confusion in some of that exhibition's individual documentary statements. We should also not forget the numerous critical questions that some documenta artists already directed at the event at the time. As has been shown by documentas of past decades, the times since then have been less fortuitous, and there has been a loss in the ability to concentrate on the essential. At the same time, critical questions posed by the artists to the organizers have increasingly been lacking. This means that attention is directed more and more towards the individual work, rather than the format of the large exhibition. It is only in the realm of detail, and not in grand gestures that there is perhaps something to be observed that can claim to invent a position. Every visit to an exhibition bears at least the promise of a surprise. The outer shell of the exhibition and the media attention that precedes it also foil any real attempt at communication. There are more restful and appropriate places for presenting art than a biennial, like museums. As to your second question about whether the Venice Biennale takes into adequate account the changing political and cultural environment: No, that can't be its task, nor can it be the task of the artists exhibiting there. Art is about art, which doesn't have any "subject matter," as Barnett Newman put it. But it speaks of it, without addressing it directly; it must be seen and cannot be heard. This is the only reason it can assert itself within all political, technological, and economic environments.

Marketta Seppälä Frame, Finnish Fund for Art Exchange, Helsinki

Venice offers in fact a good case study of the tendencies of the global (art-)perspective of today. Especially since the 1990s, the increasingly instrumental nature of the arts has taken the upper hand and shaped cultural development at large. As a consequence, new commercial and governance structures have emerged. Cultural development based on the principle of the autonomy of creative work seems to be no longer adequate. With the discourses of the creative economy, creative industries, content industries, cultural industries, copyright industries, and whatever, objectives and priorities have undergone a change as radical as that of the rhetoric itself. Coming to grips with today's (art-)world is made more complicated particularly by the fact that previous mechanisms come second in the world of global markets and political systems based on supra-national blocks and international markets. In Venice the national pavilions in the Giardini reflect the international politics and formation of the nation-states of the late nineteenth and twentieth centuries. Only the designs, sizes and locations of the pavilions imply changes of political power structures over the years. And since in the Giardini there has not been any space for newcomers, an increasing number of countries are competing with each other in searching for spaces all around the city of Venice, year after year. The city of Venice and the middle-men act in unison, making brilliant use of the mechanisms of cultural industry. Just by lengthening the opening period of the Biennale, its administration makes it ever more expensive for organizers to participate, due to security and maintenance costs alone. In the course of the growing power of the mediating circles the rental costs of the Venetian palazzi are rising as surely as their foundations are sinking. Nevertheless, the organizers of the pavilions or the collateral events—the latter having now to pay a fee of 20.000 Euro+VAT (meaning about 27.000 Euro) only for the collateral status!—have not been able to act in unison to raise any protest. A good question to ask is, why, however, it seems to be a matter of prestige for an increasing number of countries and other organizers to be represented at the Venice Biennale? Is the King of the Biennales just a prisoner of its own historical structure and thus only a sort of amusing relict, the popularity of which is based on something else than contents and quality? Or, by contrast, could it have potentiality to grow into an antidote against uncontrollable commercialization and instrumentalization of the arts—perhaps even by the mutual collaboration of traditional nation-states?

Barbara Steiner Galerie für zeitgenössische Kunst, Leipzig

The Venice Biennale and also documenta have long since become brands which guarantee the appropriate degree of attention. An ever-greater number of visitors are attracted by almost hysterical reportage and the many non-art events around the Biennale. On the one hand, this can be used to communicate art more broadly. On the other hand, I sometimes ask myself how much is communicated qualitatively—in the sense of an intensive, critical engagement. Life style and glamour inevitably superimpose themselves onto the artistic positions and sometimes are even consciously pandered to. I think that large events must be taken seriously with regard to their power to define, but not with regard to their perspectives on content. In my opinion, the latter is generated elsewhere. If only because on the occasion of large formats, too many spheres of interest overlap unfavorably: the politics of prestigious presentation, ideas about financing or generally exaggerated expectations with regard to reception by the media and numbers of visitors. No biennial can avoid a certain amount of reflection on changed social states of affairs. However, in comparison with other biennials, Venice is visibly more anachronistic. In certain parts attempts have been and continue to be made to transcend national borders, whether it be by opening up national pavilions to others and creating additional exhibition platforms, or by extending the principle of the Biennale to the entire city. Unfortunately, this changes nothing regarding the fundamental problem of a display of national achievement and the hegemonic pretensions resulting from this. Presumably also for this reason, China has been working for several years to obtain a pavilion in the Giardini. This competition sometimes assumes absurd traits. I recall two projects which reacted offensively to this principle of the Biennale: Rirkrit Tiravanija's First Royal Thai pavilion in 2003, and Santiago Sierra's Wall Enclosing a Space for the Spanish pavilion in 2003. Tiravanija had taken up the national principle and at the same time frivolously subverted it. In the immediate vicinity to the United States pavilion he built a light platform enclosing a teak tree. The inauguration allowed the usual rhetoric of opening ceremonies to run its course, staged at a tangent to expectations. Sierra allowed only visitors with a Spanish passport to enter and in this way put a mark on mechanisms of inclusion and exclusion. The assertion of the openness of art and participation beyond borders and nations was counteracted by this project. How can a biennial react to changes? The pressure exercised by many emerging nations who also want to participate will increase and thus also the critique. But such large formats are incredibly unwieldy and can hardly really be changed. At the moment the event is being inflated; it is getting bigger and bigger. Perhaps, sooner or later, it will fall apart into smaller units or disappear altogether in favor of a completely new format?

Robert Storr artistic director, Venice Biennale 2007*

As an answer I will repeat an anecdote that I have used several times in this context: A colleague of mine—a very well known, legitimately Avant-garde curator of many years—said to me in light of the upcoming Venice Biennale: "See you at the fair in Venice," which was a Freudian slip. But it was clear that, when a person in her situation, with all of her experience, could make such a Freudian slip, there is a real problem. I think that one of the tasks of anybody now doing the Biennale is to define the work they do and the way in which they treat and present artists, in a way that clearly distinguishes the result from the fair. The fairs have their purpose and the purpose is not entirely just a matter of money. For example ARCO in Madrid, which I have been to several times, is very important for the entire community of Spain in the arts. It is the occasion where people can come to see things that the gallery system is not large enough to bring to them by any other means. Like most art fairs now, ARCO does serious seminars with critics, artists and intellectuals and so on. They have also done exhibitions. Basel now has the Unlimited exhibition, which is a kind of mini-biennial of their own. I am not all opposed to the fairs as such, but they have other motives and the majority of what you see is the taste and judgment of a particular dealer, put cheek by jowl with the taste and judgment of another particular dealer, which is not what curators do. Curators start with the art and they end with the art. They attempt to, if they can, create dynamical relations between works of art, or groups of works of art and other works of art and that is their sole responsibility. Not everybody does it quite that simply but that is what one should aspire to and try to do. I think it is done on behalf of the public and on behalf of the art. If this sounds very idealistic, I am very idealistic. (But having worked for a long time at MOMA, I have earned my idealism in a hard way.)

It seems to me the responsibility of the curators is to make sense as best they can of whatever the givens of an artistic production are, and the time and circumstances in which that work was made, on behalf of the viewer, who they cannot imagine a priori. The viewer can be a truck driver, a millionaire, a teacher or a student. Just another anecdote: The major collector of conceptual art in the United States for many years was a Federal employee and his wife. She was a school librarian and he was a postman. They earned together $50.000 a year, half of which they set aside to buy art. Their name was Vogel. They bought every year $25.000 worth of art, which in those days—the 1970s and 1980s—was a lot of money in that area. They bought Sol LeWitt, Richard Tuttle, Robert Barry, the list is very long. When they retired, they gave that collection to the National Gallery of Art in Washington. So the most advanced collection of the most difficult art was the gift to the nation of somebody who we would call perhaps the "Douanier Vogel".

Birgid Uccia
Gallery Bob van Orsouw, Zürich

It is often claimed that limitless mobility and accessibility, the notorious increasing lack of time, and the domination of the "language of money" has brought about an "art fair-mania." It's true that art fairs represent a huge curiosity cabinet of current art productions and an ideal container for the dynamics of an expansive consumption. On the one hand an immense field of artistic agitation, impossible to survey, while on the other hand a huge army of demanding buyers in the battle for the coveted object. Fairs are like search lights scanning what's available to find the "most wanted." But why do artists avoid fairs like demons avoid holy water, but still consider them biographical milestones? Fairs necessarily subvert artist control, for they decontextualize the works. To that extent, fairs are subversive. They are places where the logic of the market is self-avowed. Here, the mercantile value, constantly condemned, by those stuck in the past, as a curse, becomes a revelation alongside aesthetic value. Not that a biennial or a documenta would think it beneath them to flirt with capital. All the same, they operate under entirely different premises. documenta X for example understood itself as a "political and cultural project," and the 50th Venice Biennale as a "reflection on the politics of art." Inherent to such large events is the possibility of being a synopsis and productive analysis of art practices, launching socially relevant debates and posing questions immanent to art. Even if in the meantime they have come to be instrumentalized by cultural tourism as "spectacle" —and sometimes beginning to believe it themselves—they derive certain demands from their self-justification. Unlike the fairs, the biennials represent forums that pose a self-reflexive exploration of the foundation of their existence. They do this by questioning their instrumentalization of a plethora of significant leitmotifs, articulated in collaboration with artists, architects, theoreticians etc. in manifest forms. Aside from the fact that the art market —in contrast to the oil market—is more pluralistic and more difficult to grasp in its mechanisms, and forms the necessary compliment to biennials. While the latter provide the conceptual and aesthetic ennoblement of a work and its discursive placement, the work must also circulate in an economic circle that signifies an important segment in the field of reception. The respective characters of fairs or biennials can only constitute themselves if there is a mutual distinction of tasks and context and the difference is guaranteed. To cover up this difference would lead to confusion and complete interchangeability of categories. It would be meaningless to say that fairs are becoming biennials and vice versa; it is just as meaningless as comparing the artwork with a barrel of crude oil. Not only does such a leveled scenario fail to recognize the resistance of artists. In addition, there would no longer be any sensible and practicable criteria—neither in a definitional nor a practical sense—to justify the existence of biennials.

Gianfranco Verna,
Annemarie Verna Gallery, Zürich

Experience has shown that it is convenient to have the Biennale every two years and the documenta every five years. Now the year of the Biennale is a special year for art: the year of the documenta as well. When both events take place simultaneously, this explodes the routine entirely, and requires some rather detailed travel planning if one also seeks to integrate Art Basel and Münster Sculpture Project. Of course, it is almost self-evident that on the one hand the priority at all stations is placed on new artistic phenomena, while on the other hand people want to see the same important players over and over. That's why only the days of the openings are available. The time that counts is limited: it's VIP time. The social success of the art system is unmistakable. And art is a multifunctional field, open for numerous kinds of claims. The various goals that owe their existence to the various events are easily appropriated by an overarching goal, degraded to means. This all-purposeness is a flexible result of social practice, and theoretically rather underdefined. Art is a social institution, and obviously here the market is a common denominator. By the way, many consider the biennial an art fair with a different rhythm. In light of pragmatic dominance, it is a difficult task to sensibly demarcate the various roles, and thus distinguish them from the overall context. The chief indicator is success, and the insiders that walk the course claim the authority to decide on this. Is this art of public interest, and to which public do the artists have something to say, something that is also mediated by the theorists? There are various interests, and many of those interested demand and buy representation and profit from art. At the Venice Biennale, national cultural policy also makes legitimate demands. Everyone there promises themselves attention. That this will take place generously and somewhat more over the long term: these marketplaces of vanity should at least be good for that. Maybe art's claim to autonomy is abandoned and disposed of too quickly? It would theoretically not be uninteresting to explore the self-evident truths that allow for a holistic notion of art and are not afraid of self-referentiality. After all, art still refers to itself and generates transformative power from within.

Anton Vidokle
artist, Berlin

The phrasing of this survey questions suggest that the problem (if there is one) is mainly with the competition from the private, commercial sector: fairs vs. biennials, private collections vs. public museums, etc. While these are serious and complex issues, in my opinion they are only symptoms of a deeper shift in circulation and production of art. Its interesting to remember that the public cultural network (museums, schools, libraries, etc.) which most of us have grown up with and accept as legitimized social institutions, came into being during the French Revolution, inextricably linked to the notions of a nation state and a public comprising of citizen-subjects claiming significant political power. In a sense, an experience of going to see a public art exhibition may not have been radically different then voting or going to a public hospital—these were all political exercises of citizenship. While the majority of public cultural institutions have by now perfected the methodology of presenting visual art and have greatly proliferated, the kind of public for which they were invented has largely ceased to exist and has been replaced by audiences for whom the experience of encountering art objects is something closer to consumption and/or entertainment. Somehow the radical political function got detached from the aesthetic experience and now its difficult to remember that the last owner of the Louvre was forcibly evicted and had his head cut off to make "room" for the public art collection. (I wonder if France forgot to mention this to the Sheikh of Abu Dhabi.) Whether this collection contained paintings of flowers or political installations is arguably less significant then the social and political circumstances surrounding its opening to the public.

So in my opinion, the most urgent question facing public art institutions, including national pavilions in Venice, is how can they be more then mere counterfeits of themselves. The question is no different for artists: we do not occupy the same position or have same possibilities to trigger the transformative function that is at the center of the kind of an art practice which we have all been educated (or self-educated) into both privileging and taking for granted; how can we avoid becoming counterfeits of ourselves?

Florian Waldvogel Witte de With Center for Contemporary Art, Rotterdam

The format of the Venice Biennale is delimited by the existing institutional conditions. In the obsolete concept of national pavilions, the art lives and tries to survive amidst a *mise en scène* of notions of competition and rivalry in the form of exorbitant decoration. The selection and design within these environments constitute a conventional form of cultural practice and production. It is thus not surprising that the country commissioners prefer a conventional and schematic exhibition format following historical conventions. Academic notions of curating produce only a limited vocabulary of formats, structures, and strategies of presentation. Particularly problematic is the notion that every exhibition context is simply adjusted to already existing formats, for these formats are not neutral, nor is there something like general validity. Such a notion negates the reality of art works. They become giardini-food.

Rein Wolfs Boijmans van Beuningen Museum, Rotterdam

At the moment, the art business is in a state of intelligent camouflage: the point of this camouflage is optimizing the numbers of visitors and creating economic value. Besides this method of camouflage, a method of adaptation is practiced. Biennials become more and more like art fairs, and art fairs more and more like biennials. Today, a successful art fair requires the general ambience of a large curated exhibition, with conversations, film screenings, lectures, and high power special shows. Fairs are becoming like exhibitions, mobilizing the critical intelligentsia to increase their economic power. Biennials increasingly find themselves overshadowed. They are usually based on traditional structures and represent one possibility for public funding to assert itself in marketing location. They thus camouflage themselves, in part unconsciously, as art fairs, and seem like ennobling shop windows of exhibited goods for the buying-hungry crowds of collectors. How does this affect the self-justification for a biennial with so much tradition like Venice? What is clear is that the structure of the national pavilions competing for attention is becoming with each burst of growth more global, but at the same time also more and more like an art fair. A little comparison: in bicycle racing, the various drivers ride the entire season for a multinational sponsor. Only at the Olympics are the bikers with the same passport brought together in their own national teams. In this way often conflicts of interest arise, where the bikers have to decide to either support their national teams or their sponsoring groups. At the Venice Biennale, something similar already happens. A top group emerges in the international curated exhibition, and a colorful group of qualitatively very different runners up in the artificially constituted national pavilions. Who has the greatest chance of winning? Where does one want to be as an artist? With this mixing and temporary perversion of interests has the biennial of all biennials lost its justification for existence? No, I just think that its significance is caught up in development, and will ultimately culminate in a highly diverse large exhibition with various offerings for different target groups. First there is professional audience, interested in the curated exhibition and highly critical, then there is the tourist audience, interested in national identities, and thirdly, an audience of collectors interested in economic and other values.

Tirdad Zolghadr art critic and curator, Berlin

Although your questions seem to suggest otherwise, to account for the needs of artists is not the same as accounting for changes in the world at large, from Europe to America and beyond. To argue that a biennial has to account for changes in the world at large is a preposterous platitude that leads to the megalomania of so many catalog intros. Catering to changing needs within the arts, however, would imply something much more tangible. It would involve painful questions addressing cultural capital, material remuneration and (un)paid labor. It would imply a genuine self-reflexivity in terms of the biennials' role in perpetuating precarious working conditions and the ideological underpinnings thereof. It would equally imply a reconsideration of conventional divisions of labor between curator, critic and artist —this might unearth the fact that all professional sectors of the art world are actually quite happy with the exhibition industry as it is today, but it might (also) reveal some inspiring forms of dissent. Addressing artist's demands would also, finally, imply a less coquettishly critical production of discourse that ultimately only serves to highlight the critic-curator's political credentials. In other words, it would have to go further than this blurb would allow.

*The statements by Davide Croff and Robert Storr were registered at the Biennale press conference in Paris in March 2007.

**The statement by Kasper König was characteristically sent in on a postcard.

Viewpoints

1. Lake

What is a view and how does it view us? Remember? The sun was shining. You must remember. Say something. Can you see? Wait, isn't something there? Something is shining. Perhaps a genuine viewpoint. Isn't there against the sky a sky, and another beyond it?

2. Railway Station

Numbers, stags, blue vaults, sleighs which rush to the ceiling, come. Let us say farewell to the departing. They're going home. To their own countries, to their own landscapes. Hurry. It can happen again at any moment.

3. Time

Everything in its own time. Still three more, still four more times to sleep. When you fall into time, you touch bottom. There you lie comfortably, and the views come. They come in time. In the gaps between day and night, between light and darkness, between red and blue. Where you are is still nowhere. Shall we leave the views a bit incomplete? Like your heart?

4. Blackbird

The sky clouds, the swallows have delayed their morning rounds till the lower reaches of noon. Then for a moment the sky is free of swallows, and on the roof of an old schoolhouse a crow sits next to the pole with the warning sirens, black and much too large up there. Three red roses have bloomed in a yard, the first of this year. Now to the right from the elderberry the beginning of a blackbird's song. At once Peter and Carina are there, they come with the blackbird. Father and daughter listen to the blackbird. All the blackbirds of the world. There is not a single blackbird that without them could sit on the branch of a tree or on an antenna and sing. As soon as one lifts its voice Peter and Carina join in listening. Father and daughter, the original and its falsification. They will now hurry out again, stepping out of the door. In the shop on the corner buy a liter of milk. Soon we will get to see them. Carina will decide to take her purse which they bought yesterday at the flea market and will hurry to go out, to breathe the free air, to pick out a toy. Which toy from her flock should she take? Maybe the loyal servant Heinrich calling out from behind: the coach is breaking! Though it is really his heart bound in its iron ribs. Or the girl with a piece of apple in her throat? That thinks she is dead and yet can't be sure if she will not once again wake up one day. That girl with the black hair and the white skin that can't remember who she is. Should Carina take her? Will she be able to breathe again? "If you only knew, my love, whispers the girl, I am in a so-called waking coma, have been for centuries now. Sometimes I think I am here on earth in order to manifest this condition."

Carina can't decide. She has hung the purse around her shoulder. She will take it with her to kindergarten, sleep three or four more times, then take an apple, a handkerchief and a chair fit for a dollhouse. Although she does not have such a house, she doesn't play with dolls, knows nevertheless father, mother, child. And a chair is always a good thing. Which does not alter the fact that she still must hurry out now to the corner store where the blackbird sings and buy a liter of milk, if such stores still exist. Until recently they used to exist. And she must accompany her father, take her purse, and pick out a toy from her flock that should breathe the free air again. Everything into the purse that tomorrow or the next day she will take with her to kindergarten. Then she will take an apple and a handkerchief on which a child is pictured getting up in the morning, brushing its teeth, combing its hair, packing its purse and walking out of the house. Then it waves. At the edge of the handkerchief a name has been embroidered: Carina. But the child on the handkerchief is a boy. He is wearing shorts. They are as short as his hair. She draws the purse out again, she goes off, she comes back, without the purse, without the girl and without Heinrich, whose heart has been torn apart, which she does not want to see.

Now they are going down the stairs like the boy on the handkerchief. In front of the house with both feet on the ground, the door has snapped shut, Carina turns around once again, looks up to the second story. There she sees Heinrich standing at the window and next to him the girl with the swallowed bit of apple, and the pale face, and she feels as if they are weeping. Carina waves, her father is holding her hand, they step away, they see the blackbird, it sings what it has to sing. And wasn't there yet another blackbird that many years ago once responded: I am your mother?

5. Trees

Antennae are the blackbirds' trees. Father and daughter remain standing. They must hasten to greet the blackbird, hasten to fetch the milk and not forget to fetch fresh air. A sky free of swallows. Whether it will rain? The three roses are glowing from their yard. And don't three roses likewise glow at the head of the bed of the half-dead Valentine? On that day in 1914 when somewhere else the First World War broke out, as people say. Though no one knew then that that war one day would have such a name, that it was the first but would also be only the first. When it, like Valentine, like Snow White, like Carina and the loyal servant Heinrich would be displayed and lie pale as a sheet in the margins of history books. Surrounded by other historical events and their epochs. And as soon as this chapter is finished, as soon as the book can be put aside, there comes this pounding on the plaster walls of time's division, on the doors of the solitary confinement cells. One, the World War counts and already the Second comes. Three, cry the roses from the foot of the death bed of the woman, of that Valentine that someone has painted for us here on the horizon. On the horizon that is so flat and white, so thin and that imperceptibly divides the earth from the sky and both from "still nevertheless" and "already no more." There someone is lying, there someone is dying, the horizon is a line in which someone goes under and what remains is an image. This line at sea level, this cut between life and death, between image and image, sky and earth, that sets doubling in motion and shadowings, the blind flecks and the white surfaces. The roses, the blackbirds, the ages, they see and they see: The painter was there, he slit open the horizon, no, he was not there, he only let death in, the unspeakable event in the camp; and disappearance.

6. Earth

We stand here on the earth and can't escape the horizon, that flat-lying place of rest. That is a rip. Right in front of you and lying at your feet. The rip of landscape, view and ground. Beyond the mountains daily rise. Yet there is something odd in their solidity, something beyond it, they seem to float and have lost every hold. WHERE THE DEAD ONES WAIT/FOR THE EARTHQUAKES TO COME. While we turn white, thin as a line, and as soon as the heads of three roses appear at our feet we go into the surfaces, we turn into the images and are numbered like that First World War that only then broke out. Or was it only fantasy that went by? Hurrying and high up where a look, like the song of the blackbird, dissolved into the view? Can you see anything?

7. Sky

But still before we let a word be said, let us translate it. Hurriedly, hurriedly. It should not nest here, should not try to stay and if possible not touch any thoughts. Here there is no vacancy for a word, every word must wander, go further, get lost, you, you word, let yourself be said in other native tongues, do what you want. The main thing is that you don't stay. Or have we in our way called you? What do we have to do with you, what have we lost with you? What do you want to tell us that we don't want to let ourselves be told? And what really is the name of the man to whom everyone refers when they talk of freedom? Here, exactly here, the translations fail, here the translations recount what occurs to them and what appears impossible to translate: Here, please, let no language come close, we want to let nothing come to language here. Better to die in the flatlands and breathe the mountain air once again.

8. Sea

Let's replace translation with tradition, tradition with traduction. Let's deal with the uncarryoverable views that enter flesh and blood. And deal with their dream to be carried over. True to more than one memory. To that of the other, the other memory. Carried over from land to water to sky and mountains, the vociferous and reciprocal exchange absolutely without reciprocity right to the sea. The sea of drifting times and languages. Oh, look, they have their eyes open. One-hundred-, two-hundred-year-old rose eyes, always wide-open and red. As soon as they appear the horizon stretches into the distance, the walls become pale, a place of rest clear, there someone is lying, there someone is dying. Before they are carried along the beautifully painted horizon to disappear, in each sight, each insight. What more do you want, one horizon in place of another? Does the sky rhyme then with the earth and both at once?

9. Eye

I have seen everything.
No, you have seen nothing.
Switzerland I have seen.
You have seen nothing.

Pop Emotionality—A Portrait of Ugo Rondinone

One of the most agile of the mid-career Swiss artists, Ugo Rondinone has become famous for his atmospheric installations. In the often intricate interarticulation of architecture, sculpture, object, drawing, light, and sound, they resemble perfectly-arranged film scenarios, where the screenplays are strangely empty of action. In this text, transcribed from a conversation with the editor, Bice Curiger illuminates facets of Ugo Rondinone's career and explores the conditions and surroundings of his work. The spectrum she provides wanders between scenes plucked from recent history through important stages in the artist's career to intimate glimpses behind the scenes. Throughout the text, Curiger taps into their shared experience, for her professional career has long been associated with the work of Rondinone, from exhibitions like Oh! Cet écho! (1992), Endstation Sehnsucht (1994), to Freie Sicht aufs Mittelmeer (1998).—*dk*

Contemporarily Propagandistic

I first noticed Ugo Rondinone's work in 1985 at the Christmas exhibition in Lucerne. It was a huge work on paper showing the head of a great mind of the eighteenth century, perhaps Diderot. I was vexed by this work, because it was so different. It seemed confident and, without being loud in a vulgar way, clearly demanded attention. In other works by Ugo, too, I saw right from the beginning how he expanded something small, like a pen drawing of a landscape, into a large format. It was like the optical effect when looking into a moving spiral: if you look long enough, and then turn to look at something else, say, a tree, then the tree also expands. Such ingenuity was rare in Swiss art. It had something "contemporarily propagandistic" about it, meaning that Ugo was familiar with engineering a message. He has always used all media and materials in an unusual breadth, from drawing to sculpture to paintings to installations. He quotes and appropriates everything to then immediately adapt it for his own purposes.

Cooperation

I must have met Ugo at some point between Shedhalle and Walcheturm, that is, between the mid-1980s and the early 1990s. I remember that Andy Stutz—whom I've known since the mid-1970s—once told me about an artist friend of his: this artist turned out to be Ugo. One of my first collaborations with Ugo was in 1994 for Endstation Sehnsucht, my first exhibition at Kunsthaus Zurich. There was a "mean" technician there who was known for having violent outbursts. I told him I wanted dividing walls in the exhibition. The walls were suggested to Ugo: Janine Antoni on the one side, Ugo on the other. He had first choice and simply couldn't make up his mind. He was told that he had until 7am the next day to decide. Well, Ugo is always late... He arrived at 11am, and the wall was finished, but of course he wanted it shifted by ten centimeters. As I said, it was my first exhibition and then my first confrontation with Herr Hurter, who went berserk, and I—as a woman, too—had to calm him down again. But because he was a great car enthusiast, we could connect about Gabriel Orozco's work—the famous halved *La D.S.* which was also being shown there.

Curators

Harm Lux showed Ugo Rondinone in 1990 at Shedhalle in Zurich, in the exhibition Stillstand Switches, where his work could be seen already in the 1980s with exhibitions like Harm's Spiel der Spur (1988) or Junge Schweizer (1985). What was new at that time was also the exchange between the Geneva and Zurich art scenes. For example, Sylvie Fleury's works could be seen here for the first time, but also Thomas Hirschhorn's. Harm always also included international circles at the same time, Russians next to Canadians and New Yorkers, and so on. His curating was incredibly important in Zurich, where he began working in the mid-1980s. At Shedhalle, Ugo also showed his first dark romantic installation *If* with ink running from the wall and hanging leather straps, crumpled pieces of paper, and Polaroids on the floor. Later it was another Dutchman, Rein Wolfs, who showed Ugo at Migros Museum. Ugo started relatively early to move both in the local and international scenes (he had the Zurich studio on West Broadway in New York in 1998–99). Christine von Assche of Centre Pompidou, for example, was interested in his work as early as the mid-1990s. In 1998, she bought the huge installation *The Evening Passes like Any Other...* with the white floating rocks from Freie Sicht aufs Mittelmeer. After that, there was also an important exhibition in Paris. Then, Paolo Colombo from the Centre d'art contemporain in Geneva started getting enthusiastic about Ugo. After all, it wasn't so common in the mid-1990s for a Zurich artist to be shown so prominently in Geneva. Then, Beatrix Ruf organized the impressive exhibition Guided by Voices in 1999 at Kunsthaus Glarus, with a large filmic installation and the first examples of the "talking" trees. We could go on and on mentioning other curators and their exhibitions like Eric Troncy, Klaus Biesenbach, and Laura Hoptman, who were also important for Ugo's work.

Beginnings

Around 1990, at the start of the reorientation of the Walcheturm—which has always been an association with a not-for-profit status, an alternative art space or a small Kunsthalle—Ugo most likely passed on his perceptions from Zurich and Vienna (where he had been a student) as a suggestion to Eva Presenhuber, who at the time was the director of the space. Certainly the aim was to mix local artists with international ones. For example, the Austrians Heimo Zobernig and Gerwald Rockenschaub showed here, and from 1995 onwards Franz West. Then also Peter Fischli and David Weiss. They started off with Sonnabend and Monika Sprüth, and in Zurich they didn't have a gallery; or Jean-Frédéric Schnyder... At the time, galleries weren't as numerous in Zurich as they are today, but interestingly enough, when the market collapsed in 1990 and the boom of the 1980s had come to an end, several young galleries opened in Zurich. In Cologne, galleries were closing, but in Zurich a few started to open. For example, at that time, Bob van Orsouw put on exhibitions in his apartment, Marc Jancou and Hauser

& Wirth, then very young, started off in west Zurich, where the Kunsthalle had also opened its doors. So while everyone else was in as state of panic, things were just getting started in Zurich. That was an anti-cyclical movement. Of course they profited from the fact that there were people who could be persuaded to support these projects financially. Eva through various channels got other generous people involved in Walcheturm, who could absorb quite a bit. It was a non-commercial space that had been in existence as an association for decades: and now they wanted to give it a new push. That contributed to this mood that made the little Zurich miracle concrete at a certain moment. This was visible not just in Walcheturm, but that was certainly an important site that influenced things.

Connecting Art Scenes

At Walchetum, something blossomed once again in the 1990s that occurred repeatedly in Switzerland from time to time, at the Kunsthalle in Berne and Zurich Kunsthalle, and in the museums supported by the progressive bourgeoisie and exceptional individuals in Zurich, Basel, and Lucerne, which actively influenced the zeitgeist. Walcheturm was a really vibrant place, and its audience was made up of people from all walks of life. That is perhaps something that is typically Swiss. In other places with strong art academies, where there was training for artists and where they were coached to be professional, there was always a strong, but perhaps also somewhat restrictive discourse. In Zurich, on the other hand, there was a free transition from the subculture to the art world, a shared consciousness of belonging to a free space beyond the political restrictiveness, i.e. the question, "Is it permissible to be an artist—isn't that just bourgeois decadence?" When in the 1990s the internationalization of the art world made itself felt, a cosmopolitan flair and a certain nonchalance entered the scene. What earlier had been the Swiss art world's Achilles' heel, its reputation for being full of autistic artists and loners, now suddenly received a collective push thanks to a liberally anarchic charisma. Quite naturally, connections to other scenes were made. What was interesting were not the people from Düsseldorf who had come to Zurich, but people from the Netherlands and from Vienna. Pipilotti Rist, who incidentally in 1992 showed her *Nett, dass Du mich begleitest durch die Kanalisation* at Walcheturm, had Viennese roots through her studies at the Hochschule für Angewandte Kunst from 1982 to 1986. It's possible that the Zurich art scene connects easily to the Austrian scene, because in recent decades it has also worked in the knowledge that it is a marginal but well-informed special case. After all, Beatrix Ruf, who is German, studied in Vienna. She took over Kunsthaus Glarus from 1994 to 1998. And on the connection to Holland: there we have the already mentioned Harm Lux and Rein Wolfs. But it also worked in the opposite direction: artists like Bob Gramsma or Urs Fischer studied in Holland.

Busy Body I

I always thought it was funny that it's possible to speak of Ugo's beelike industriousness. It's paradoxical: he's so industrious at representing standstill, capturing inertia, even paralysis. Ugo often drew one's attention to others, and even today he will often ask, "You know so and so?" I have always liked his interest in other artists. When I was preparing for the exhibition Freie Sicht aufs Mittelmeer, Ugo told me to visit this guy Urs Fischer in Zurich-Seefeld, and I did. At the time, I had already seen a work by Fischer at Migros Museum. I liked him, but it was too late, there was already a long list of artists for the show. But he was also interested in older artists like Hans Josephsohn. Once we visited the Josephsohn Museum in Giornico, where my mother was from, together with Andy Stutz. It is always something special to look at art with artists. Ugo took a lot of photographs there.

Subculture

The role of subculture is a very interesting aspect, that is to say, all the things that Ugo brings together there: gay subculture, music, fashion. He once gave me a book about the slacker movement, also a kind of subculture. Also interesting is his connection to John Giorno and thus the Beatniks and the New York school of poetry, underground in the real sense of the word. Warhol was the first artist to do this, Polke too. There are a few figures in post-war art who referred to or simply included the specific attitudes and ways of living of the so-called counter culture, as it was once was called, as a matter of course.

Corporeality

In thinking about the mood of the late 1980s, the *Parkett* issue of 1991 with Louise Bourgeois and Robert Gober is something that comes to mind. This issue was a watershed in the history of *Parkett*. Suddenly, there was on the one hand this interest in an older artist who somehow had been tainted by surrealism beforehand, and this can be beautifully linked to Robert Gober's art. The body was moved to the center, which was also linked with thematizing AIDS. Gober's work, things like the man's leg growing out of a wall, that wouldn't have been possible five years prior, it would have been too surrealist. The same is true for Bruce Nauman, the skinned animals, suddenly there's something that up to that point had been unpleasantly connoted, as too sticky, feverish, and burdened by all these kitsch derivatives. But very differently than was the case with the neo-expressionists, where the body certainly played a role, think of Disler, Baselitz... Now the point is not individual waste and directness. With Bourgeois, as with Gober, the house, the family as an idea of a place of happiness and unhappiness moves to the center. Before then, this had not been articulated with this strong super-individual impetus. As far as Ugo was concerned, it was not necessary for him to fix the topic again after that. He finds a way into the issue in the same way he gets into everything else. You always have the feeling that he knows very quickly what is being discussed and what is being worked on, so that he can very quickly enter it like a parasite and cloak himself in other disguises.

Motifs

Certain motifs keep appearing again and again with Ugo. For example the tree. It exists in early drawings, bandaged, with voices, right through to this day, the trees in exterior spaces... The clowns have also been appearing for a long time, as drawings and pictures which he made relatively early but never showed to anyone. Then the videos. Finally the figures that appear in the installations. But you never get the impression that a motif is tired out, even though it keeps appearing. On an abstract level, the element of time is present right from the start: the standstill or various forms of time. Ugo creates a space to which you need to subject yourself live, something that has to be experienced in a certain span of time. I think it is important that at the end of the 1990s Ugo himself no longer appears in his installations as a puppet sharing his features. In the video installation *The Evening Passes like Any Other* for Freie Sicht auf Mittelmeer there's a woman. That is one of the first times that another figure appears. The installations become complex environments, the space interlaces and becomes more involved, with sound and picture walls. Ugo gives an incredible number of literary clues, and all the dialogs start to appear in the late 1990s. But we're never in a film, there's no story. I find Ugo's approach very clever and current: for example, I am somebody who goes to the cinema and a week later can't tell the story of the film anymore. I have no sense for stories, but I know exactly what kinds of mood were prevalent. The psychologies of the stories bore me as soon as they are illustrated. It seems to me that Ugo leaves everything out that is not absolutely necessary and would only be tautological ballast.

Pop Emotionality

You never get the impression that Ugo's art makes such existential claims as the "humanism" of someone like Beckett or Nauman. Ugo takes as a point of departure a pop society that isn't brought into play by many other artists. He actually just chooses splinters that have the biggest possible potential of giving you a "push." But that has to be as open as possible. Ugo does not paste everything over with some restrictive sociology or psychology. Our society seems to live in a kind of yearning for the rococo. It is exciting to see how difficult to grasp that is, although it is omnipresent in all those books on youth culture and pop art. On the one hand, there's elite culture, on the other an ethnology of the everyday, but what pop emotionality is remains unclear: a certain emotionality, an emotional state that is not expressive, but has to do with an emotional life, with something like soul in an artificial sense. Yes, all those frowned-upon words. How to describe it? I think we can read Ugo's art as a challenge to intellectual discourses that do not think it worthwhile to engage with a certain pop feeling (or is the pop feeling really just an invention of the industry?).

Busy Body II

As an artist, Ugo takes the making very seriously. You are confronted with a statement where somebody gives all his energy. This industriousness, however, has nothing to do with the exhaustion after giving his all, but in a certain sense he reflects himself in the materials, the way something is made, especially in the more recent structures, the arches, that's state of the art. You know Ugo is the motor behind it, and he is also enormously precise when he awards the production contracts. Like a manager who is looking for the most fabulous car and just at the right moment seeks out a brand that is more innovative. In this respect, he is as industrious as a manager. This industriousness also means to keep informed about what the market or industry have to offer. Ugo's works are incredibly elaborate in terms of logistics and their presentation in the spaces. He usually makes something tailor-made. He is a perfectionist, even if one without any sense for deadlines. An incredible performance.

Mid-career Artist

What is to be expected of Ugo's work in the future? Perhaps not a complete change, as in Sigmar Polke's career around 1980 where there was a precise break: he went on a trip around the world for a year or two and didn't produce anything; before that, he was an ironist, and afterwards an alchemist. It is unlikely that Ugo will return a changed man from a trip around the world, and discover something new; that like a caterpillar he will shed his skin and emerge from his cocoon as a butterfly. I can't imagine that, but of course artists are there to surprise us. They also surprise us by insisting on doing always the same thing, like On Kawara, because it's a life-long task. It shows a certain confidence in a mid-career artist to be able to quote himself. He can once more isolate and increase certain motifs. I felt this with Ugo's olive trees in Battery Park. Although I've seen many trees by him, these have a different effect, well chosen. You are happy that the artist takes the opportunity of using these sunny signs once again, and clarify them with a certain emphasis. The result: signs with complexity. If we think of the bandaged trees that have injuries, then the gnarled things that stand in the cool business world, there could be a certain element of kitsch, but precisely because it is a quotation of a quotation—coming from his own box of quotations—in my opinion the trees subvert the kitsch accusation.

Reception

It is definitely exciting to see all the people who, over the years, Ugo has won over. A whole variety of people, people coming from video art, curators on the lookout for the most advanced things; there are certain moments where the homosexual subculture was interesting as a theme; there are people who are attracted by the romantic, by the pseudo-romanticism in Ugo's work. And his work has a certain openness; it is existential, but also very open.

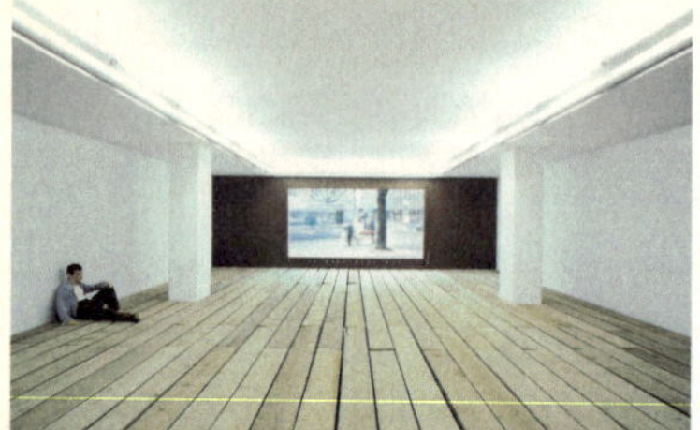

Heyday, 1995

1996
Philippe Régnier
Where Do We Go from Here?

"[...] in the work of this Swiss artist, reality turns out to be plural and contradictory. Necessarily fragmentary, this reality can at best show but several of its faces. Sometimes the latter are even distorted by the roughened surface of the magnifying glass that brings them to the fore. The artist's acknowledgement that he is powerless to change this state of affairs takes the form of a positive attitude based on pleasure and desire. The complexity of Rondinone's work notwithstanding, be it the artistic setting or behavior, the underlying message is one of release, calm and meditation. The serenity and occasional playfulness of an approach that flirts with virtuality, a certain aesthetic frame of reference, are the marks of an oeuvre that fully relates to the ideas of the nineties."

1998
Philip Ursprung
Biografisches Lexikon der Schweizer Kunst

"The figure of the tired clown, this artist's alter ego, embodies the authorial function that has exhausted itself trying to satisfy the insatiable curiosity of the audience. By taking position that the beholder is used to taking, making no attempt to offer anything, just lying there comfortably, he breaks through the customary link between artistic production and reception [...] Again and again, the figure of the artistic author in Rondinone's oeuvre enters the image as a spoilsport, short-circuiting the art system: by electrically hooking up his own portrait to the torsi of female models, or as the negative hero in semi-fictional diaries and comic strips, or as the chronicler and archivist of sheer endless documentations of the everyday world. The Beat culture of the late 1950s serves as a historical reference and formal store for the artist."

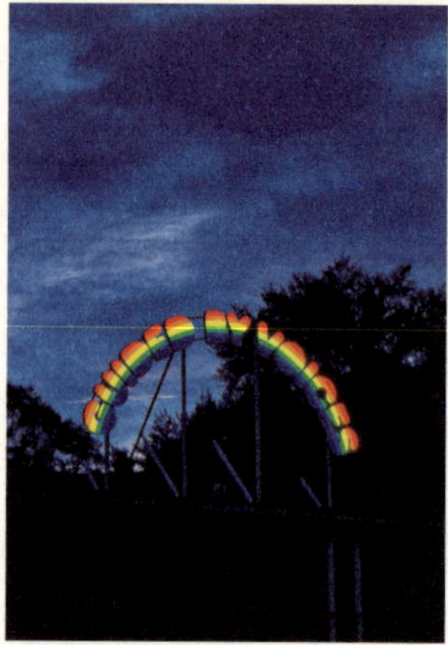

Guided by Voices, 1999

2000
Kathrin Luz
Frame

"Rondinone consciously subjects himself to the fear of a vacuum. He looks for the emptiness of nothingness to show that experience of a world found boring strikes back and leads one to become bored with oneself. Such melancholic moments, romantic longings and nostalgic reminiscences return again and again in Rondinone's work. Whether he represents himself as a deceivingly real-looking plastic mannequin in an easily recognizable pose as a melancholic, draws up a lonely-romantic forest landscape in an old engraving style on large canvases, or—as at the Berlin Biennale—creates melancholic-mental spaces of color and sound, his works always reflect personal moods that between self-pity and self-enjoyment attempt to plumb the depths of what man can take in terms of disappointment and being lost, on being torn and hopelessness, on 'being thrown back on oneself' (Novalis)."

2001
Niru S. Ratnam
The Face

"His work includes landscape drawings, diary entries, documentary video works, photographs, live performances by clowns, wooden constructions, real rocks and polyester rocks, as well as his rainbow signs. Some critics think these works offer autobiographical clues to the elusive Rondinone. The closest we may ever get to him, perhaps, is 'I Don't Live Here Anymore' [...] in which he took 36 existing fashion shoots

[...] and reproduced them with his own face replacing the models'."

2001
Catherine Francblin
Beaux Arts Magazine

"This concerns photographs of female mannequins which are posing in stances which are as suggestive as they are stereotyped. Rondinone replaces the portraits' faces digitally with his own. We can see in this gesture the desire for a change of sex. We can also see with them the desire to change the images, to make them better conform to that which we are,—more human, less authoritarian. Because everything which evokes force and power shocks the artist. And the synonymous values of power and of energy—he opposes the melancholy atmosphere of his sonorous art works, preaches of indifference and passivity."

2002
Éric Troncy
What Is Art (Today)?

"His entire work is based on this tension between supply and demand: it is no coincidence that his alter ego is a clown. Whether he represents himself as a wax figure collapsed on the ground, or as an asexual character in a series of photographs by Jean-Baptiste Mondino for *Vogue*, he is putting himself on stage, using figures somewhere beyond reality, and along with them, the expectations of the art public."

2002
Meghan Dailey
Artforum International

"In Rondinone's hyperreal world, life is a melancholy path of futile searches and broken hearts on a rotting planet. The heady mix of romance and misery is both irresistible and maddening. Yet he tries to reclaim meaning in the meaninglessness of it all through poetry and beauty, which in his work is often conflated with the poetic."

2002
Eva Marz
Süddeutsche Zeitung

"This work is about translating a psychological state or mood into spatial-objective surroundings, and the fascinating thing about entering Rondinone's pure space of art is that its impact is inescapable. Because the art surrounds us entirely, unlike the vis-à-vis of the classical situation of the beholder, it takes hold of us. And for the brief moment of walking among the shiny columns of this implied cathedral of private memories, we feel quite satisfied and safe in a feeling somewhere between monotony and a tranquilizer-like sedation."

2002
Laura Hoptman
No How On

"Do we need any more clues to realize that we are the protagonists, and thus, maybe the victims of Rondinone's scenarios? That perhaps we are being stalked? In a Rondinone environment, lulled by the murmur of voices, the music, the mirrors, the snoozing clowns, we are at our most vulnerable, and cannot help but love it. If our eyes could be observed peeking from one of those one-way peepholes in a mirrored wall, they would no doubt have the same look—excited and scared, trapped, and turned on—as Rondinone's eyes have in his self-portraits."

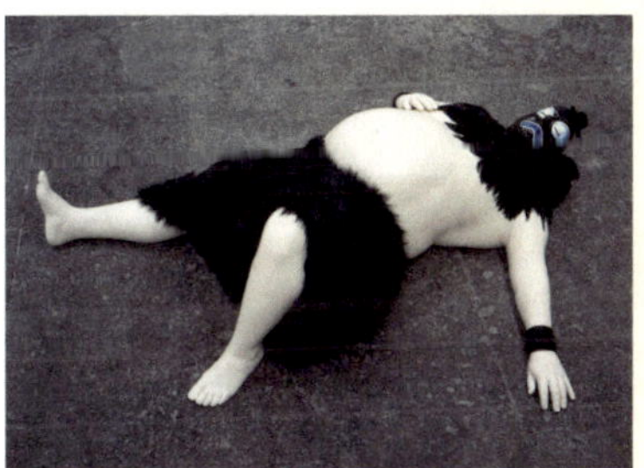

If there Were Anywhere but Desert, Tuesday, 2002

2002
Gaby Hartel
No How On

"[Ugo Rondinone and Samuel Beckett] embark on an investigation into the consciousness of man which, in an unintelligible world, is in a state of constant reconstruction. Certain techniques are called for to carry out this inquiry. Rondinone builds spaces in which he positions his characters, variously mannequins of clowns, himself as clown or shattered mirror images of the viewer. In Beckett's work too, the combination of character and space are the first step towards imaginative departure: 'First the body. No. First the place. No. First either.' (Worstward Ho). From this point on, the author / viewer evokes a store of remembered images. These are then unreeled in minutely varied scenes in an endless loop, comparable to the activity of obsessive diary-keeping found in Beckett and Rondinone. Both artists exercise these processes on our behalf. 'Ideal' conditions are called for to ensure that the audience can physically participate in the journey. Habits of perception must be abandoned, the eye needs to pull into focus and the sense of self, space and time should be thrown into confusion. And crucially, to bring about the ideal speed of perception, the (re)introduction of a slow tempo is called for. 'The mind, slow. The words too, slow, slow,' as Beckett's *Texts for Nothing* hypnotically tell us. In addition, both artists are masters of the hushed tone, and whisper down the thunder of the outside world."

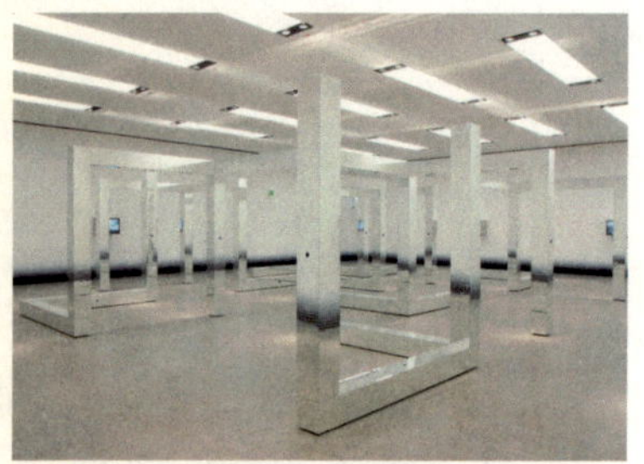

No How On, 2002

2002
Andreas Jürgensen
175 Jahre Württembergischer Kunstverein

"The more artificial the installation, the more direct its link to reality. This seems to be the breathtaking paradox in Rondinone's work: that it is precisely the radically artificial that in computer-manipulated photographic work or in sculptures even touches on the artist himself that defines an authentic sense of reality—it is precisely the extreme artificiality of the artworks that opens the eyes of the beholder for the non-artificial, the normal and the banal in the world."

2002
Pádraig Timoney
Contemporary

"Rondinone's paintings spoil the opportunity of the possible. There is just the relationship of a certain number of colors screened out on an iconic zone, different colours in the simplest positioning of variations. Pure notes, but oppressed by relationship. Never escaping, slickly or fuzzily, from materiality. Tiredness, limpness, misdirection, modesty, haunting traces, emptiness in full light, fully spectacular, apparatus of appearance. A very simple way of making something that doesn't take more than a certain allowed time, aims for and accepts all it can in the space it's introduced to, plays with ideas of paintings as being meaningfully larger than their fabrication."

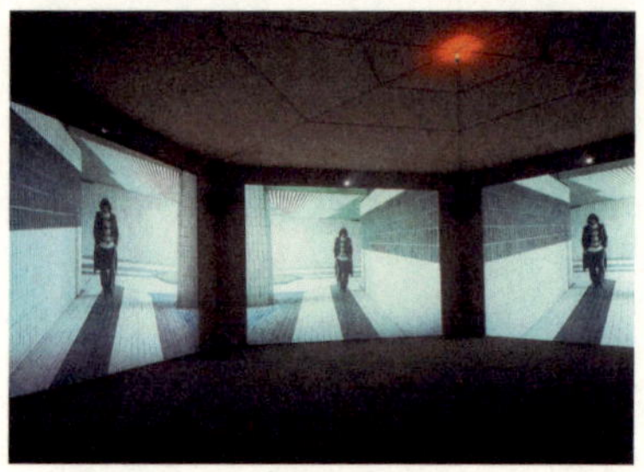

Roundelay, 2003

2003
Markus Boden
Artinvestor

"The artist's technique always consists of a complex system of sampling and quoting."

2003
Gaby Hartel
Roundelay

"In Rondinone, the movement of walking is presented as a psycho-aesthetic act: as an act of reassurance and self immersion, but at the same time as one of flight or an exercise in memory and oblivion of the self. This circling around an empty centre may be regarded as a happy condition. In this respect, Rondinone's 'searchers' form a counterpart to his 'lying figures,' the life-sized clown figures and alter egos of the artist in a relaxed state of waiting or dreaming. They are by now regarded as the 'trademarks' of Rondinone's oeuvre. Focussed on their own mind and body as the only sources of knowledge, they are situated in a kind of limbo, floating between time and space. They often sit or lie in front of shining walls pasted with splinters of mirror-glass, or under the magical glance of hypnotic color circles. This position allows them to embark on a voyage into their inner worlds where we may imagine them as working on the process of self-realisation. This is a central motif in the work of Rondinone and has to be understood as an existential act rather than an act of vanity."

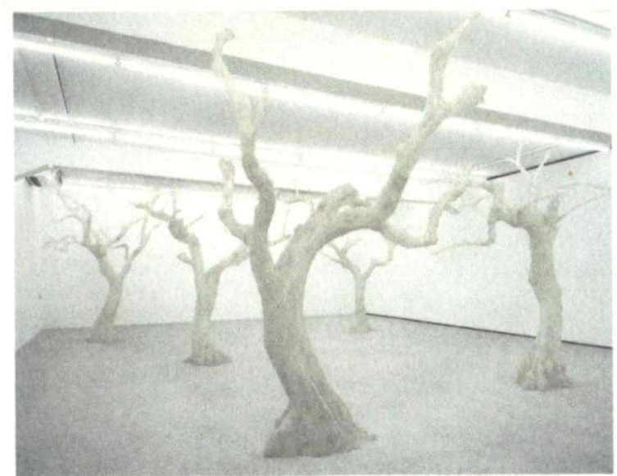

When the Water Went South for the Winter it Carried Us down like Storm Driven Gulls, 2003
Out of Reach until it's Magic We Are Crossing our Own Stony Ocean, 2003
Across Dark Stream of Shooting Stars, 2003
We Sail into Pleasure and Unload our Spacious Soul, 2003
Everything Gets Lighter Everyone Is Light, 2003

2004
Linda Yablonsky
Art + Auction
"'I use all media as a tool,' Rondinone says. 'Every medium has a history.' For him, to be an artist is to address the legacy of each medium in ways that simultaneously subvert and extol tradition—particularly, in his case, the tradition of 19th-century Romanticism and its yearning for an impossible ideal. That impulse, combined with his attachment to the absurdist dramas of Samuel Beckett, gives Rondinone's work an existentialist and rather melancholy tone."

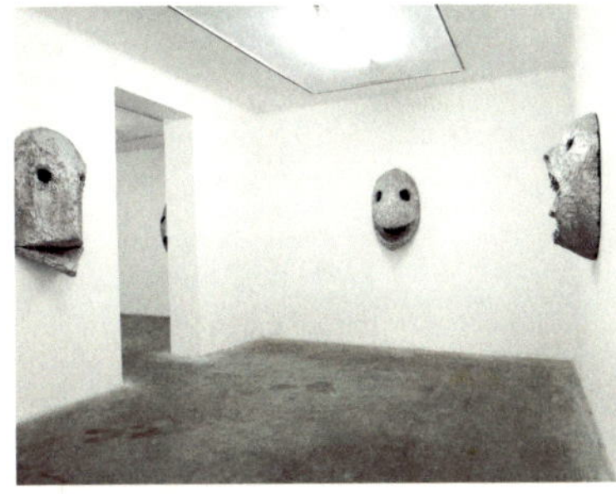

Sunrise. August, 2004
Sunrise. September, 2004
Sunrise. October, 2004

2005
Alison Gingeras
Zero Built a Nest in My Navel
"Rondinone's recent series of mask-like sculptures entitled *Moonrise* is ritually stretched out over an entire year. Produced at a rhythm of one for each month of the year, the features of twelve oversized masks seem to be derived from abstracting human and animal facial features. Hung along the perimeter of the gallery, these impenetrable countenances mutely stare at the viewer, revealing nothing about their identity or possible use. Associated with the performance of sacred rites or celebrations, Rondinone's masks [...] are also meditative devices that bid the wearer to suppress their boredom and sentiment of alienation, and transform their contemplation of the cadence of passing time into an existential exercise."

2005
David Thorp
Zero Built a Nest in My Navel
"Rondinone was brought up in Switzerland, the son of Italian parents. He displays a distinctly Swiss sense of humor that emanates from a prosperous, well-settled generation which has not been disrupted by war. Rondinone shares this somewhat bleak humour with his Swiss predecessors, artists Roman Signer and Fischli and Weiss. It is a humour that cannot really be described as funny, owing more to the tragicomic than farce, and closer to Samuel Beckett's Lucky or Bruce Nauman's clowns."

2006
N.N.
Benezit
"Clowns are recurrent images in his work, but they subvert the traditional view of clowns. They are passive, and do not make people laugh (any more). In his installations, Rondinone likes to set up awkward situations where the clown makes fun of viewers, gets bored and has no hesitation in fingering the object of this boredom."

2006
Martin Herbert
Artforum International
"In locating and arraying object correlatives for daily anxieties, and pressing us through them, he illuminates some kind of path towards acceptance."

2006
Cristina Travaglini/Ugo Rondinone
Mousse
"'My work is simply allergic to the concept of wholeness. All my works acquire their

own independence and refrain from becoming part of a whole. They do not come to stay. They are fickle and subject to constant change. Changing the setting you'll be able to change the meaning and the visual impact of a work. But, after all, I always adopt the same spirit too, even though in different ways: in my case though, the common concept is the concept of nothingness.'"

2006
Stéphanie Moisdon
FROG

"Contrary to surface appearances and remarks, there is no doubt whatsoever for me that the work of Rondinone has no romantic or lyrical connection whatsoever in a traditional sense, and is instead situated precisely in a basic study of the greatest movements of the last century, from abstract to conceptual art. He plays with a certain ambiguity of this question of novelty, renewal, the past and the future. All adjectives such as 'dreamlike' or 'melancholy', which the critics use so gladly for his work, seem to me to be particularly inappropriate.
If melancholy takes on different forms and meanings, it describes in general a state of apathetic despair, of abandon which is close to depression. These things are decisively absent from these works which are as tense as they are also watchful, which play with the conventions of language and of genre and the dogma of the age. Except considering melancholy as a distancing from the conscience which is dealing with disenchantment, this term only describes approximately the principles of detachment in the work in the artist's perception."

Further reading

Ugo Rondinone—Where Do We Go from Here?, exhibition catalog, 23rd International Biennale of São Paulo, ed. Pierre-André Lienhard, Baden: Verlag Lars Müller, 1996.

Ugo Rondinone—Guided by Voices, exhibition catalog, Kunsthaus Glarus, ed. Beatrix Ruf, Ostfildern-Ruit: Hatje-Cantz, 1999.

Ugo Rondinone—No How On, exhibition catalog, Kunsthalle Wien, ed. Gerald Matt, Vienna: Kunsthalle Wien, 2002.

Ugo Rondinone—Roundelay, exhibition catalog, Musée national d'art moderne du Centre Georges Pompidou, Paris, Paris: Éditions du Centre Pompidou, 2003.

Ugo Rondinone—Zero Built a Nest in My Navel, exhibition catalog, Whitechapel Gallery, London, Zurich: JRP| Ringier, 2005.

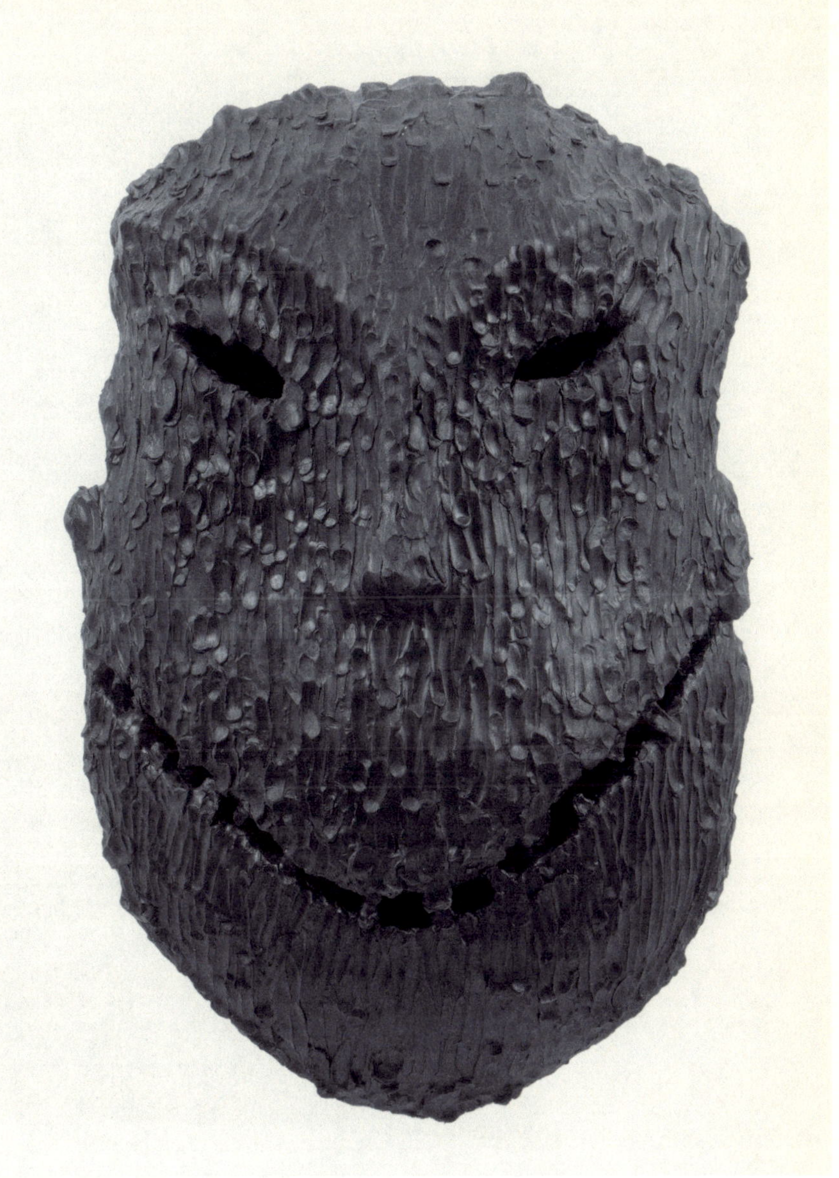

Moonrise. West. December, 2004
Cast polyurethane, black
99 × 67 × 24 cm

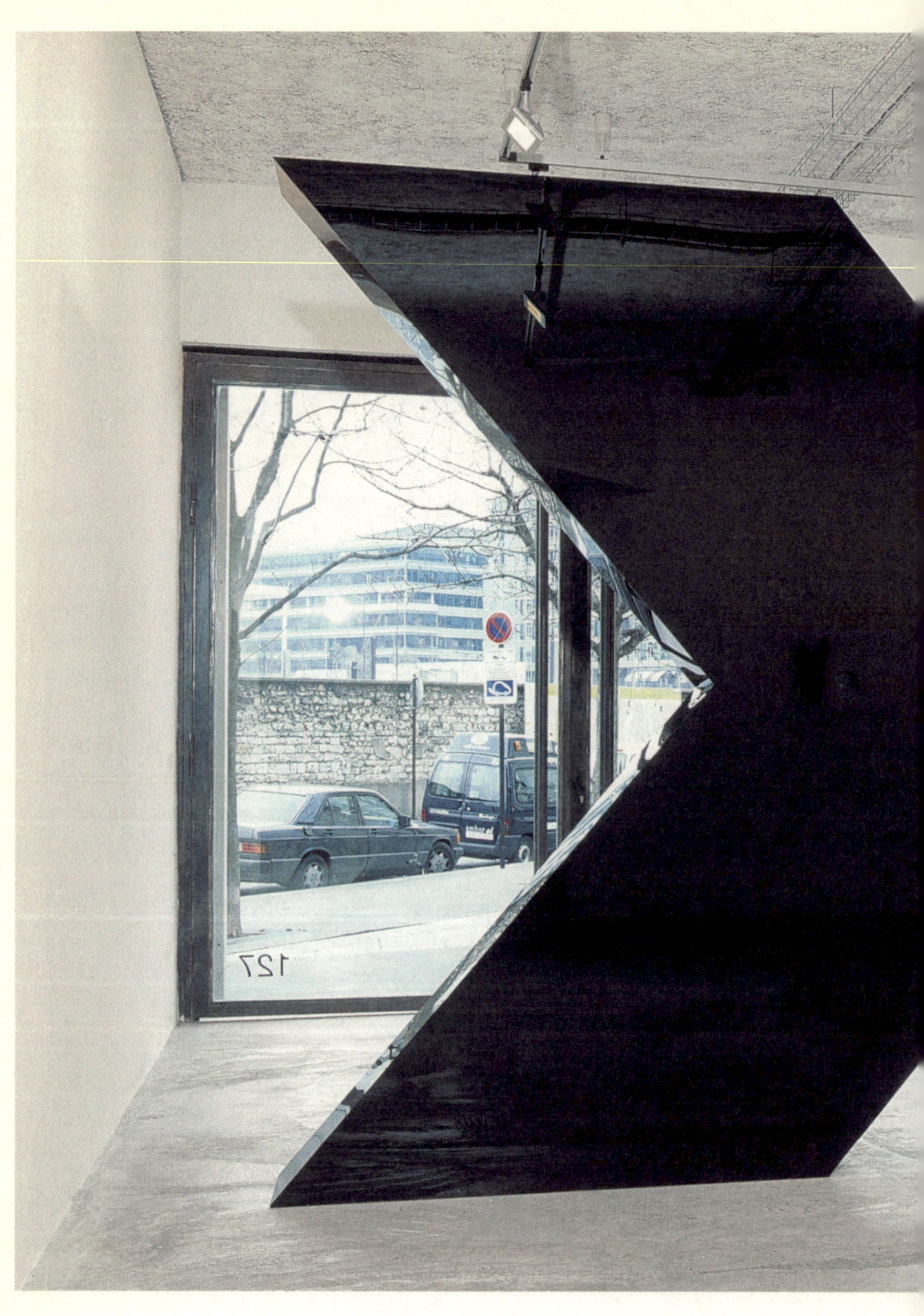
127

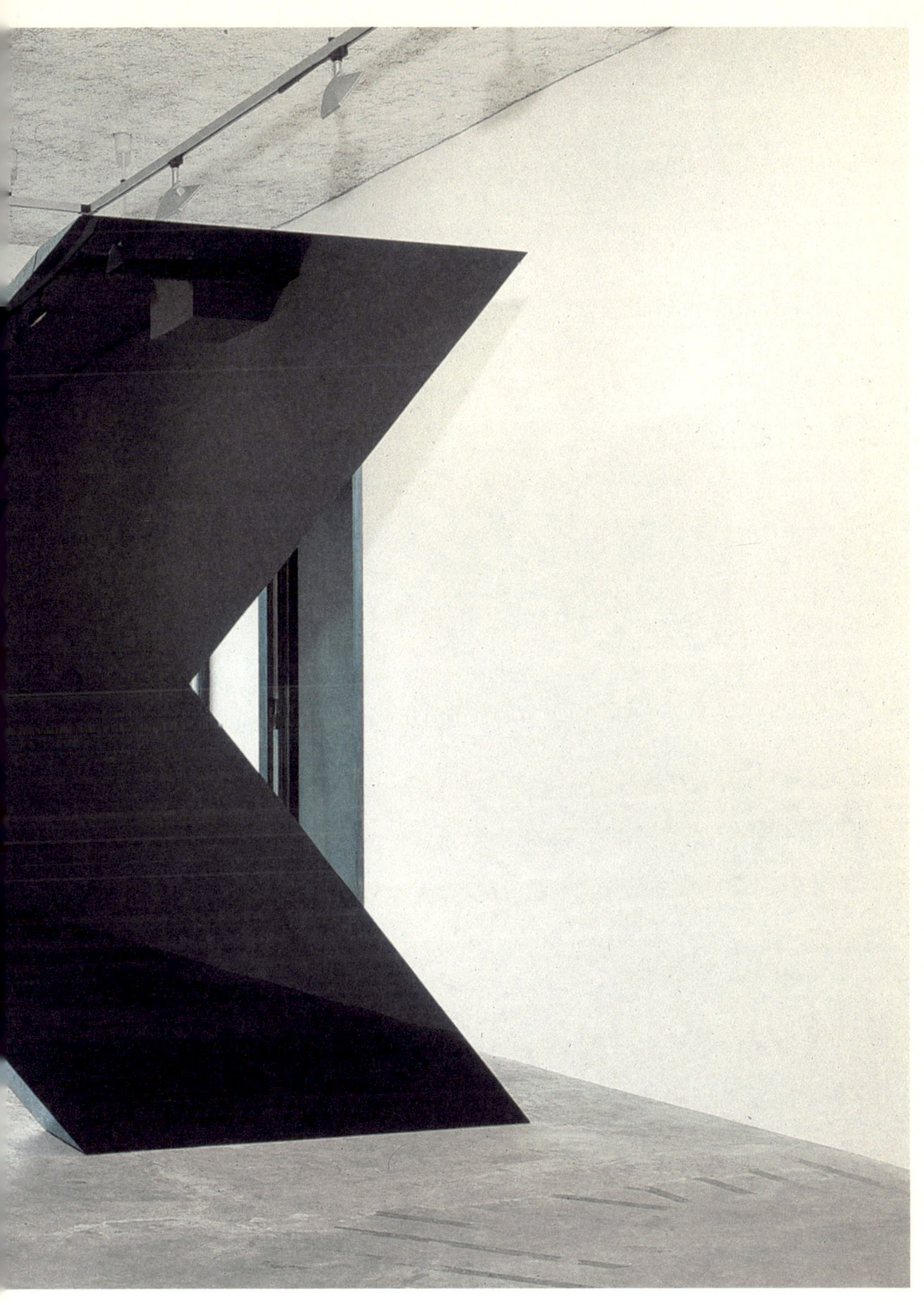

Lessness, 2003
Wood, perspex, speakers, sound
280 × 400 × 40 cm

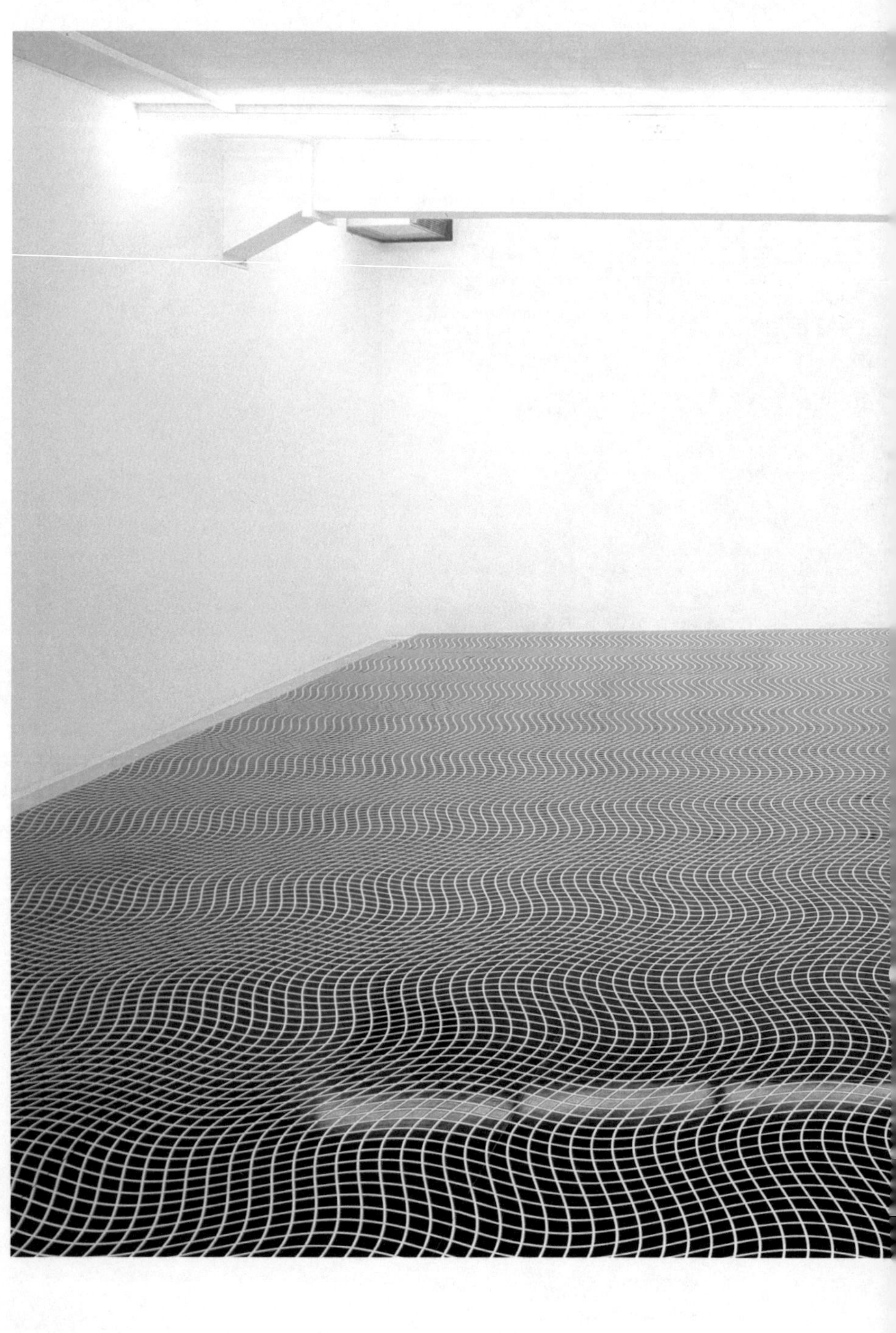

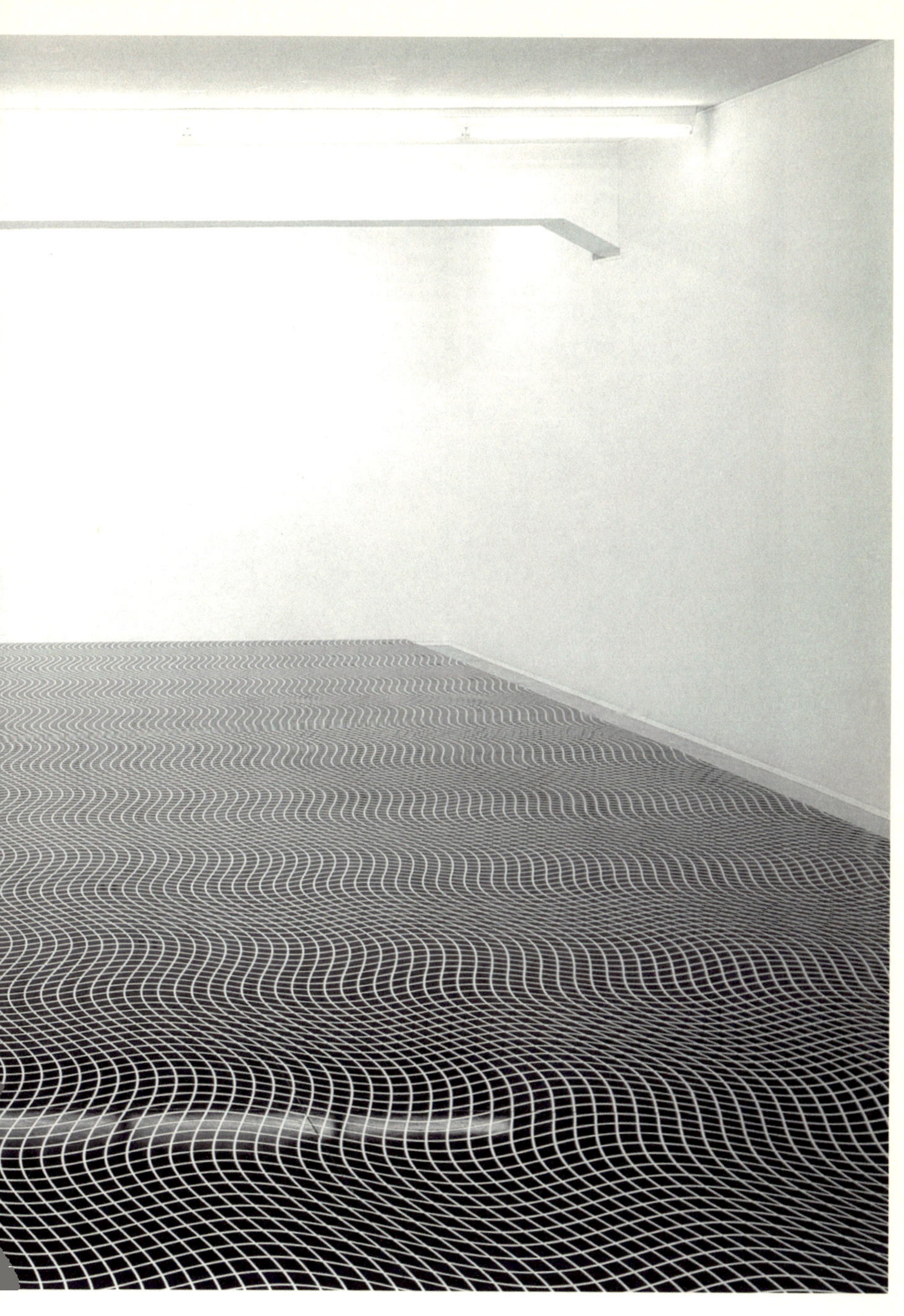

Lowland Lullaby, 2002
Wooden panels, silk-screen printing, polyurethane, speakers, sound, text loop
Modular system

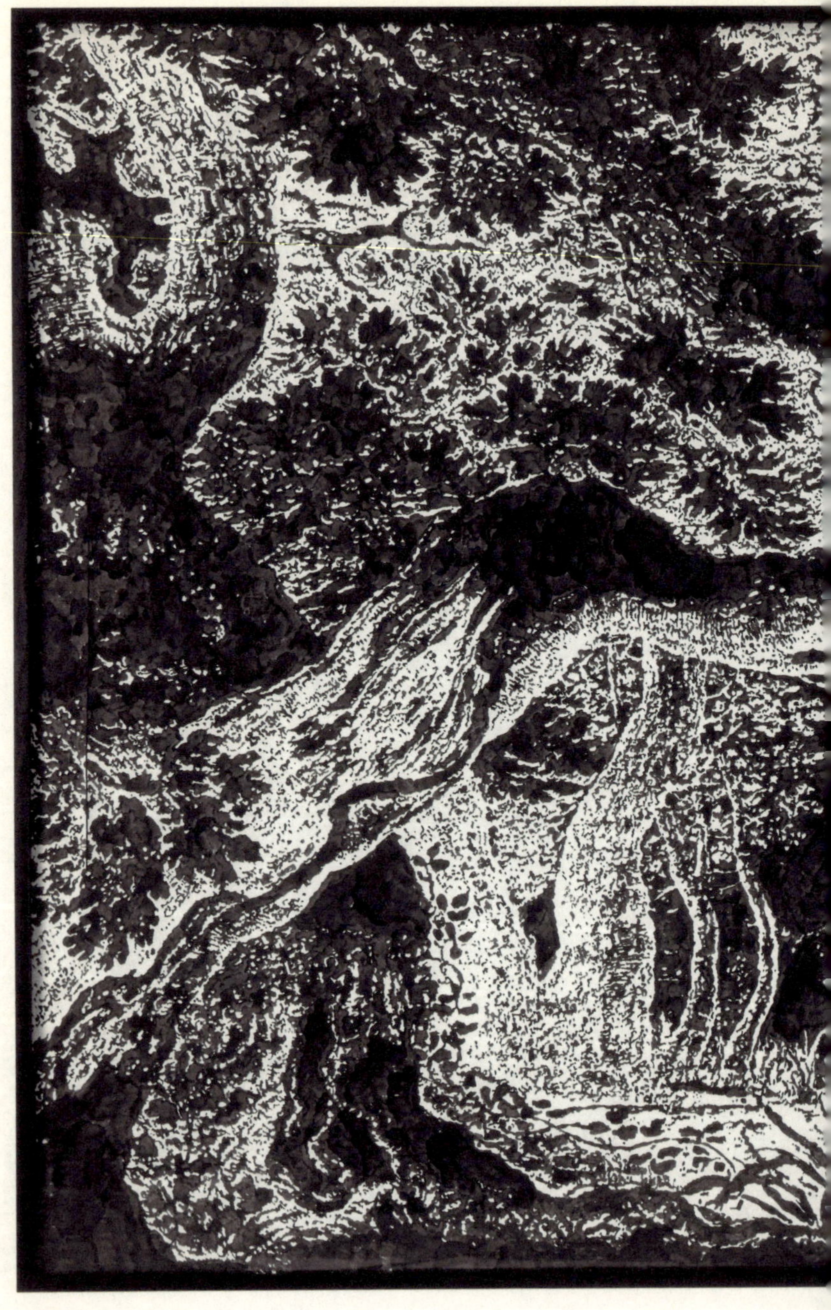

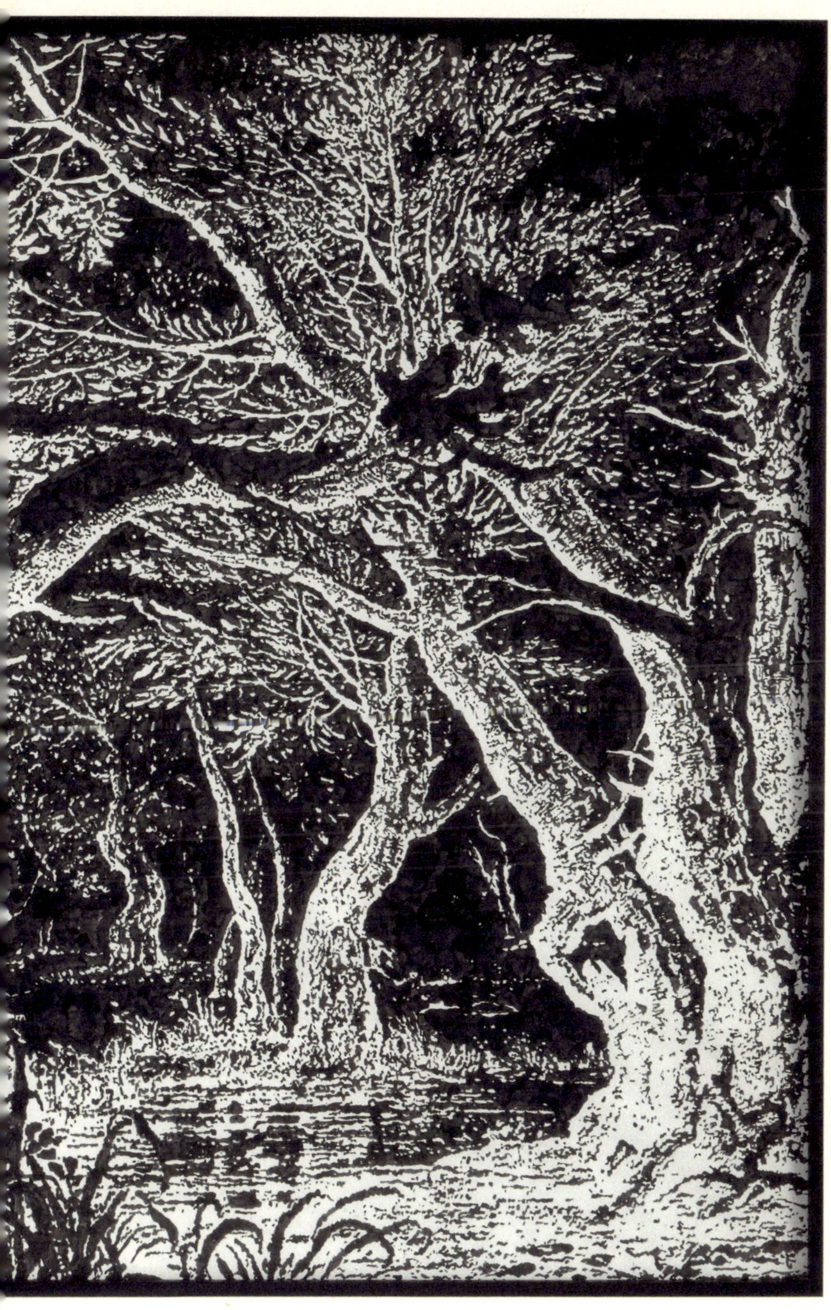

*Dreiundzwanzigsterapril-
zweitausendundnull*, 2000
Ink on paper, wooden frame
200 × 300 cm

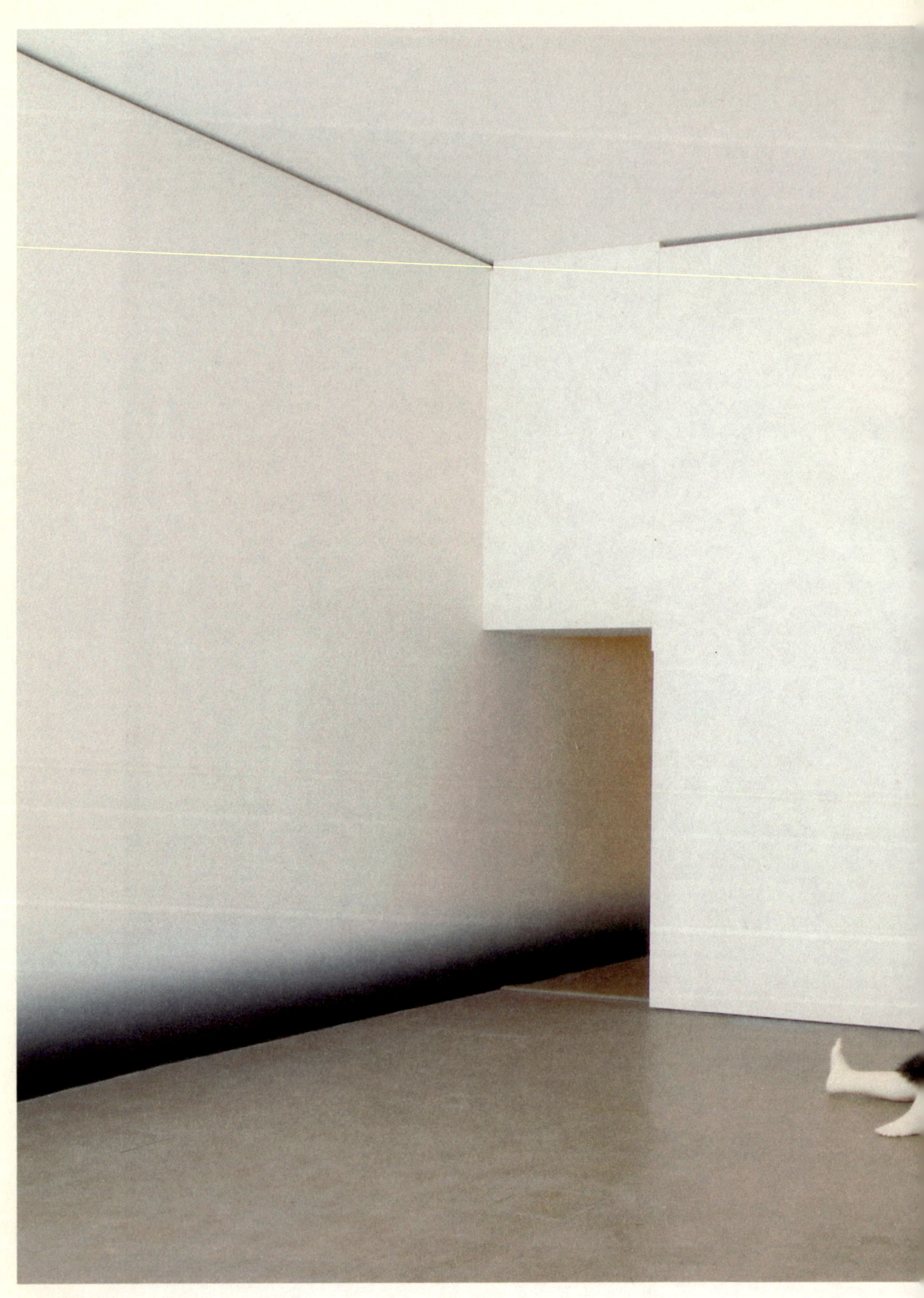

*Siebenundzwanzigsterjuni-
zweitausendundzwei,* 2002
Acrylic mural painting
Diameter 400 cm

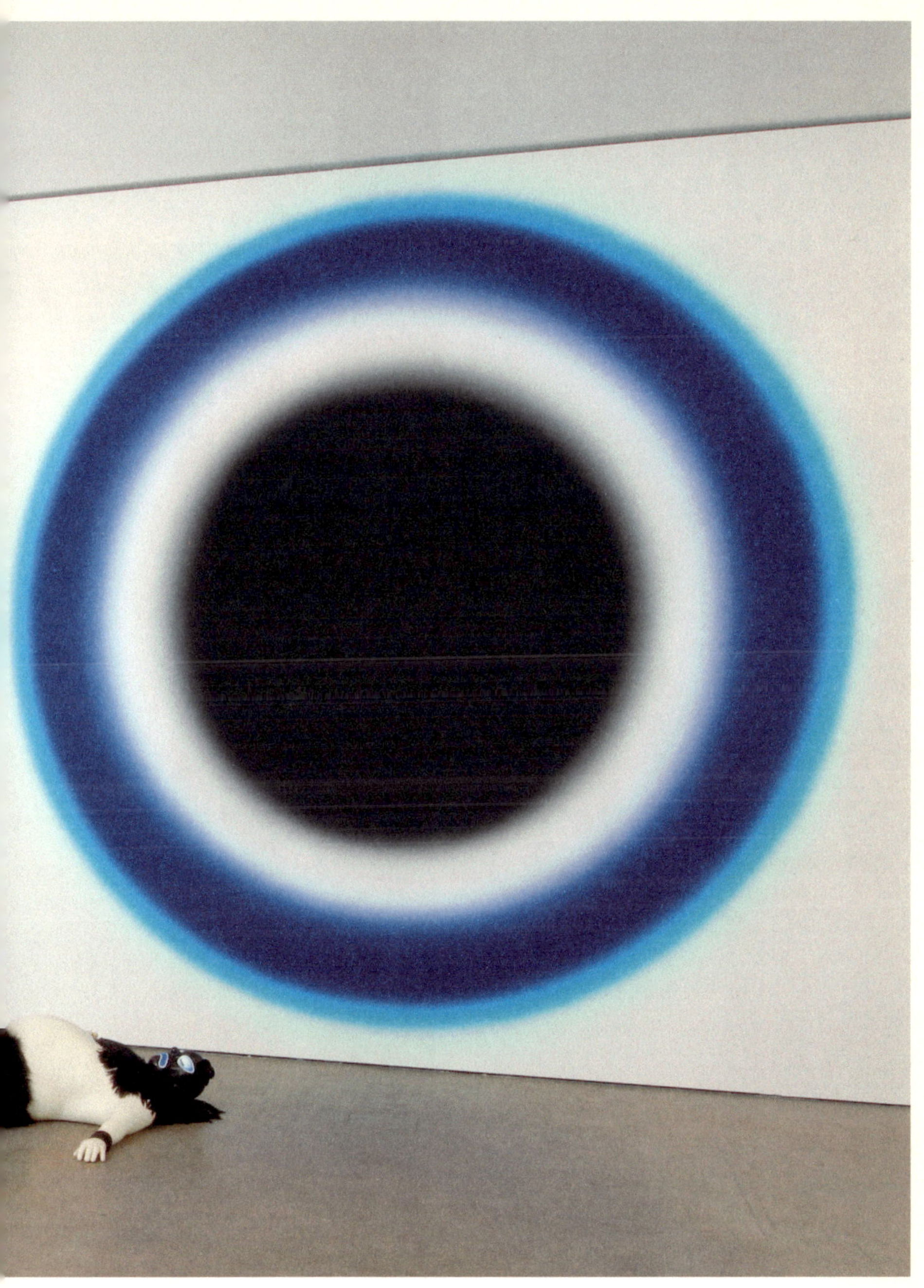

If there Were anywhere but Desert.
Tuesday, 2002
Fibreglass, paint, clothing
51 × 167 × 118 cm

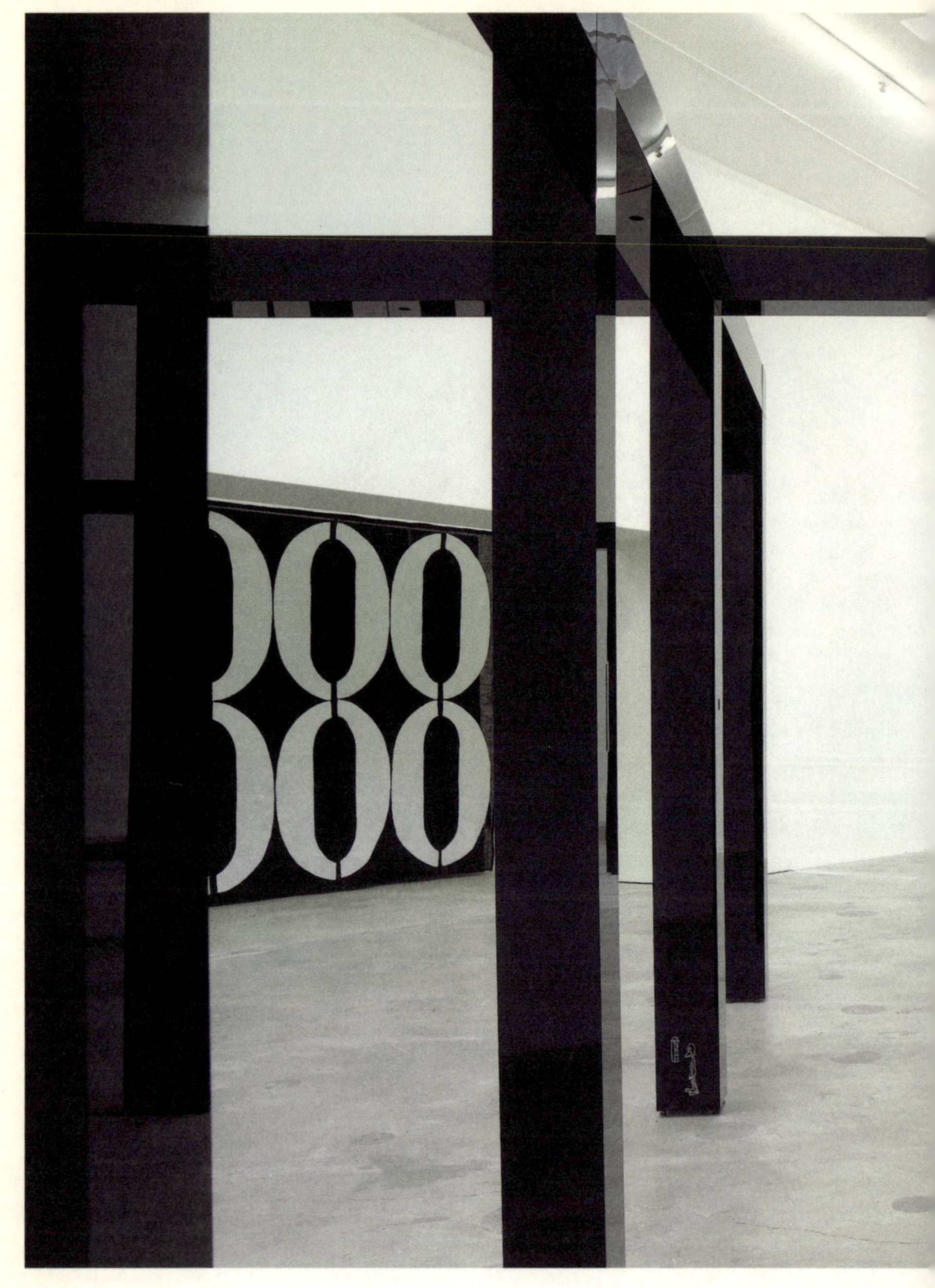

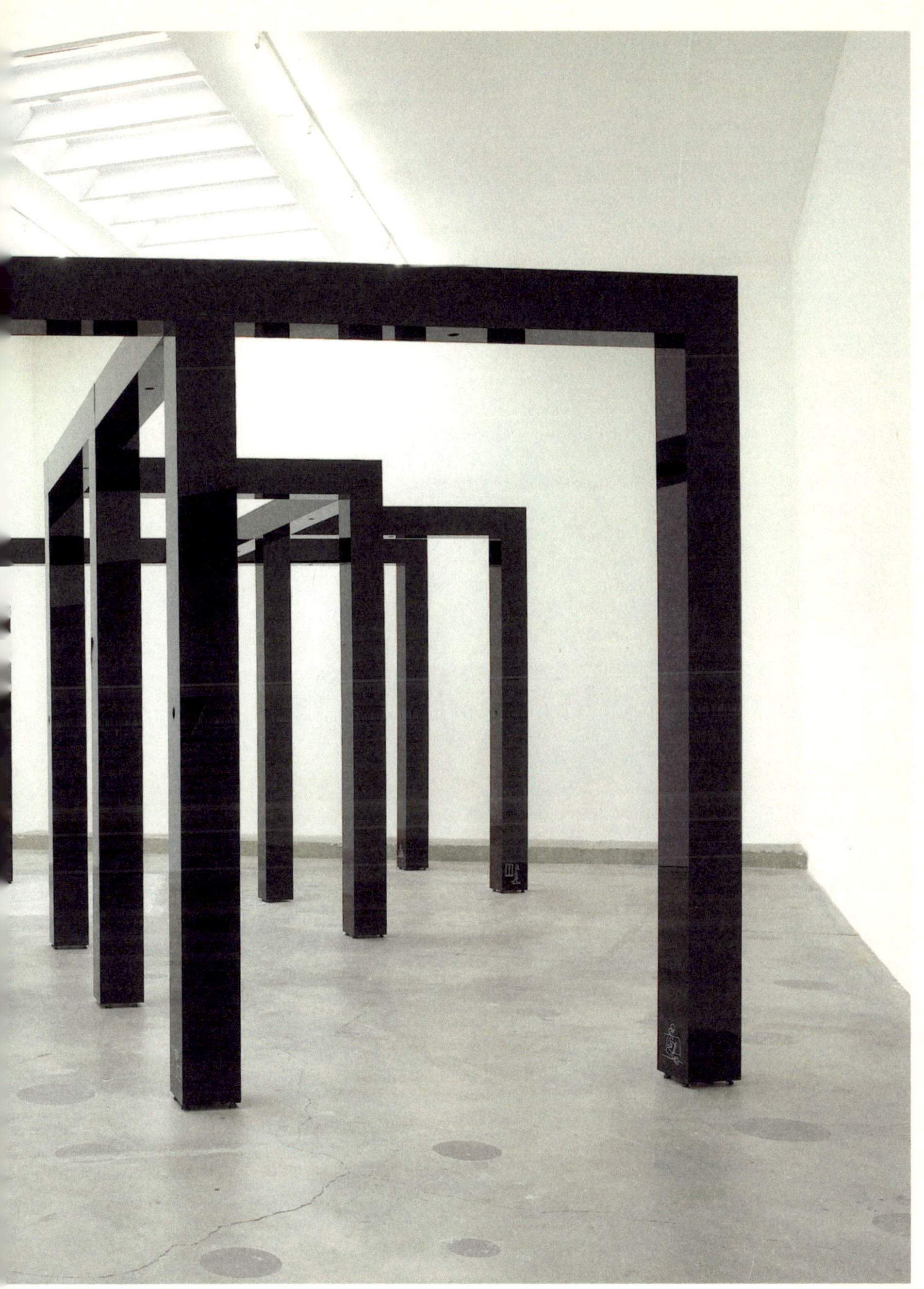

All those Doors, 2003
15 pillars and 14 beams of acrylic glass,
felt tip pen, speakers, sound
Modular system

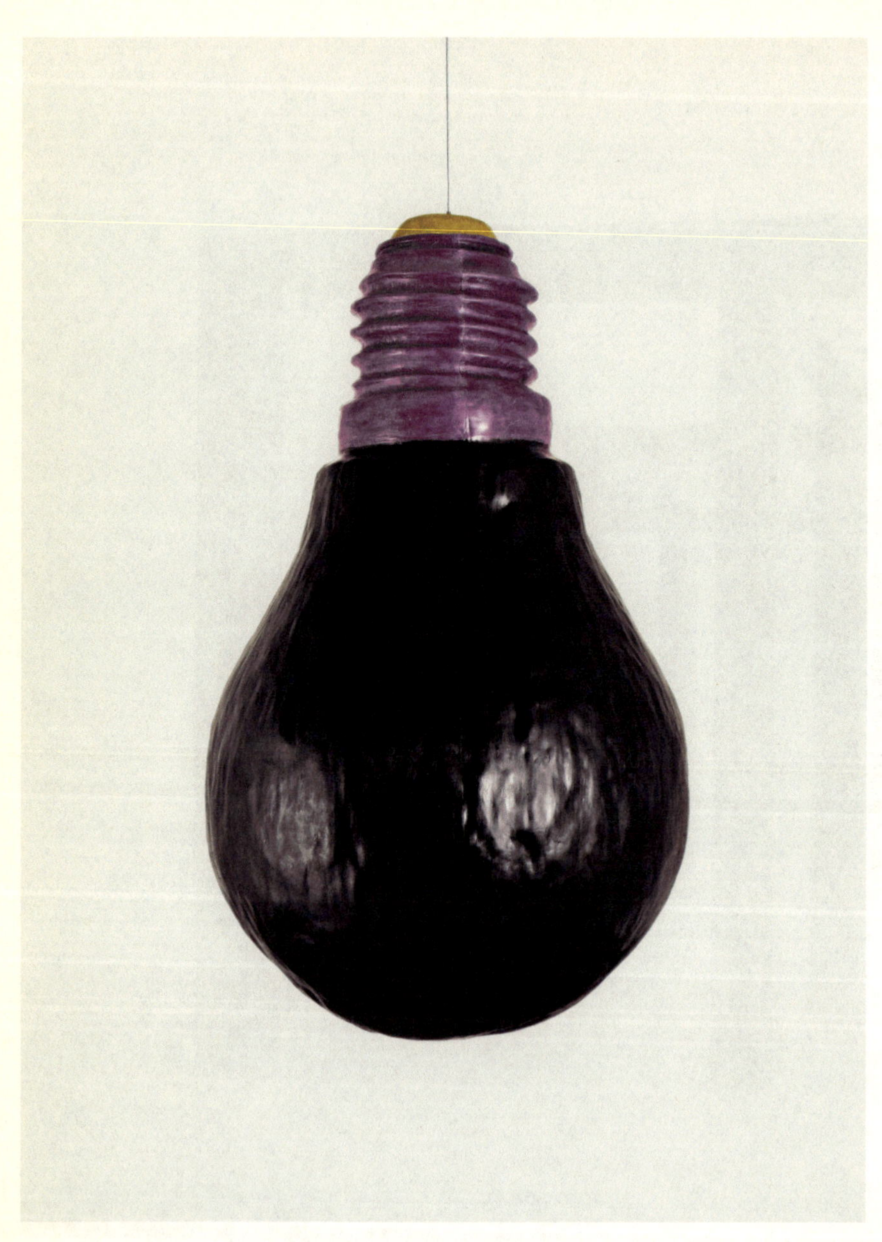

The Third Hour of the Poem, 2005
Cast wax, pigments
140 × 82 × 82 cm

Unexpected Islands of Contemplation—Thoughts About Time

Duration or moment? Whether conceived as an internally expanding horizon, an unbroken line of consciousness, or a suddenly condensed experience, time in art is played as a fantasy about the other in everyday life. Not only since the industrialization, rationalization and administration of life in modernity has time moved into view as an artistic material. In her *tour d'horizon* of European intellectual history, Gaby Hartel explores the transformations of the conception of time from the end of the Middle Ages to high modernism. Roland Lüthi contributes an associative visual essay.—*dk*

> "Unlearn time, so that your face will not wither and with the face your heart."* Can you beat it?
> Samuel Beckett

The end of the Middle Ages—the original setting for Goethe's famous Faustian sigh, "Abide, you are so fair."—provides the first signs of the transferal of the shaping of time and space from divine authority to human hands. Since then, artists and scholars have attempted with the help of alchemy or creative invocation to overcome the time barrier—or at least to counteract it.

For example, the spiral towers of the dreamer Borromini, which became an inspiration for classical modernism, not only conquer airspace, but also generate the illusion that endless time-spaces could be overcome. Borromini's collection of forms was borrowed from nature and marked by amazement in the face of the vast variety of its phenomena, a marveling that also marks the repertoire of the cabinet of curiosities. This penetration of the time barrier as well as the emancipation from the notion that we are all contained within a divinely anointed plan are not just linked to a delight in newly attained freedoms—reinventing oneself each day anew and redefining the world can be a heavy burden. Against this backdrop, it is perhaps no accident that Borromini, following Seneca's model, tried in a dramatic way to catapult himself into timelessness.

It was the Enlightenment that finally demanded of everybody, not just the highly sensitive or creatively curious, intrepidness in the face of the awareness that our existence is both finite and coincidental. Here, the notion of *vanitas* comes into play, the bittersweet realization that all luster and all life ultimately lead to death alone. We know and love the visual metaphors of this feeling, as presented to us in the luscious floral and banquet still-lifes from the seventeenth century that produce a thematic tension with their well-placed skulls, crawling wasps on overripe fruit, or creeping caterpillars. But here, the bitter message of the futility of all our pursuits is consoled with the promise of resurrection (the blossom-eating caterpillar will soon become a butterfly).

Two hundred years later, this offered no solace to the clear-thinking, now skeptical thinkers of the early modern period. The problem had become more drastic, so that Ludwig Tieck's lucid remark, "Only within yourself you carry time, only within yourself fortune and adventure," almost sounds like a threat. For now the responsibility to shape one's life in the best way possible was left to each individual. All the same, alongside this, the individual is granted the chance to "unlearn" time and invent him or herself.

To an even greater extent, twentieth century man feels himself to be a point of exchange among various "selves." In his insightful 1931 essay on Proust, Samuel Beckett describes this phenomenon as a kind of floodgate between constantly renewing, flowing, dissolving selves, where our wishes and desires from yesterday, which appear in multiple, serial forms that constantly fight against time, can only seem musty and wan. As Beckett puts it, man in the claws of the "double headed monster: time" can hardly control its effects, but remains a victim of "time cancer". He is passively immersed in the flow of time, as if he were the scoop on a millwheel. "The individual," Beckett continues, "is the seat of a constant process of decantation, decantation from the vessel containing the fluid of future time, sluggish, pale and monochrome, to the vessel containing the fluid of the past time, agitated and multicolored by the phenomena of its hours." But valuable

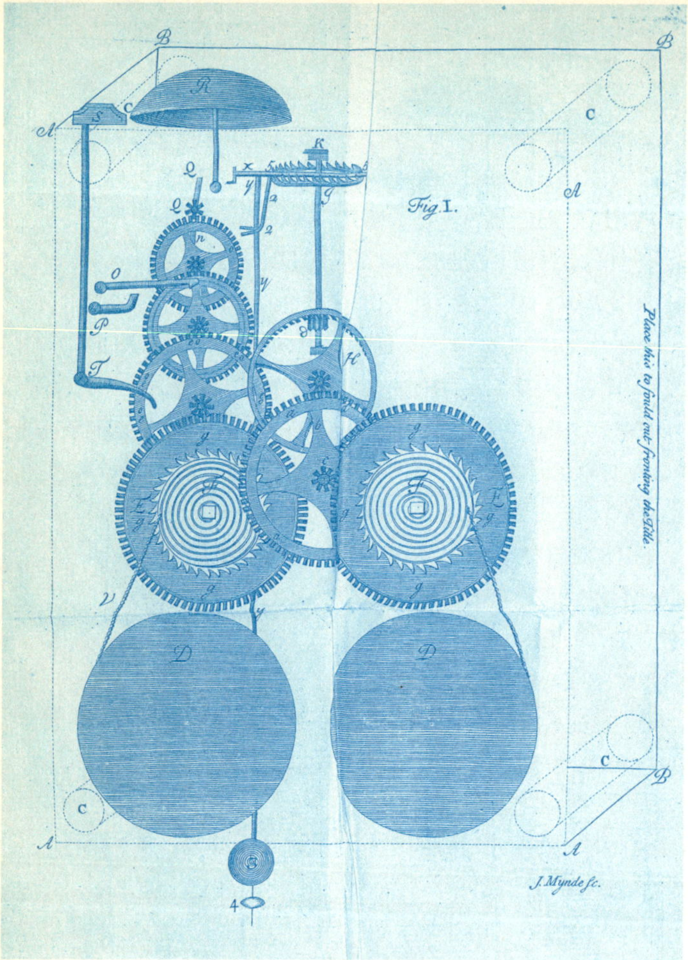

Fig. I.

Place this to fould out froning the Title.

J. Mynde sc.

1

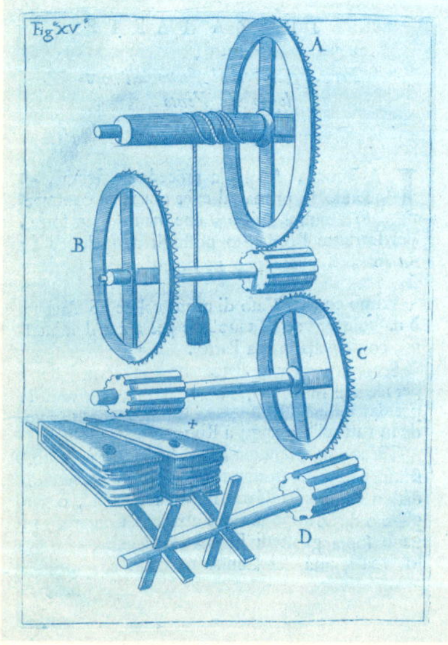

2

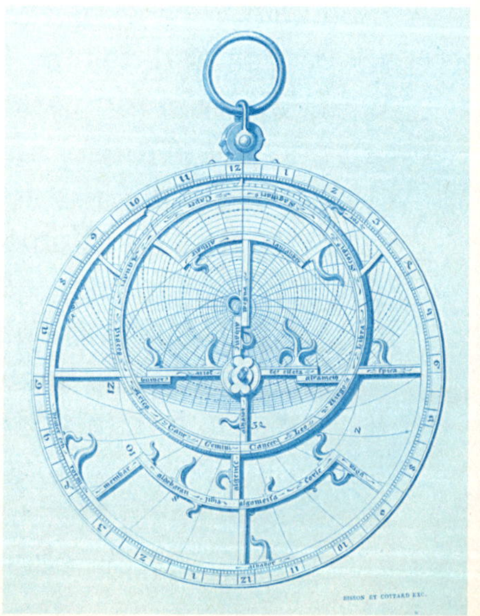

3

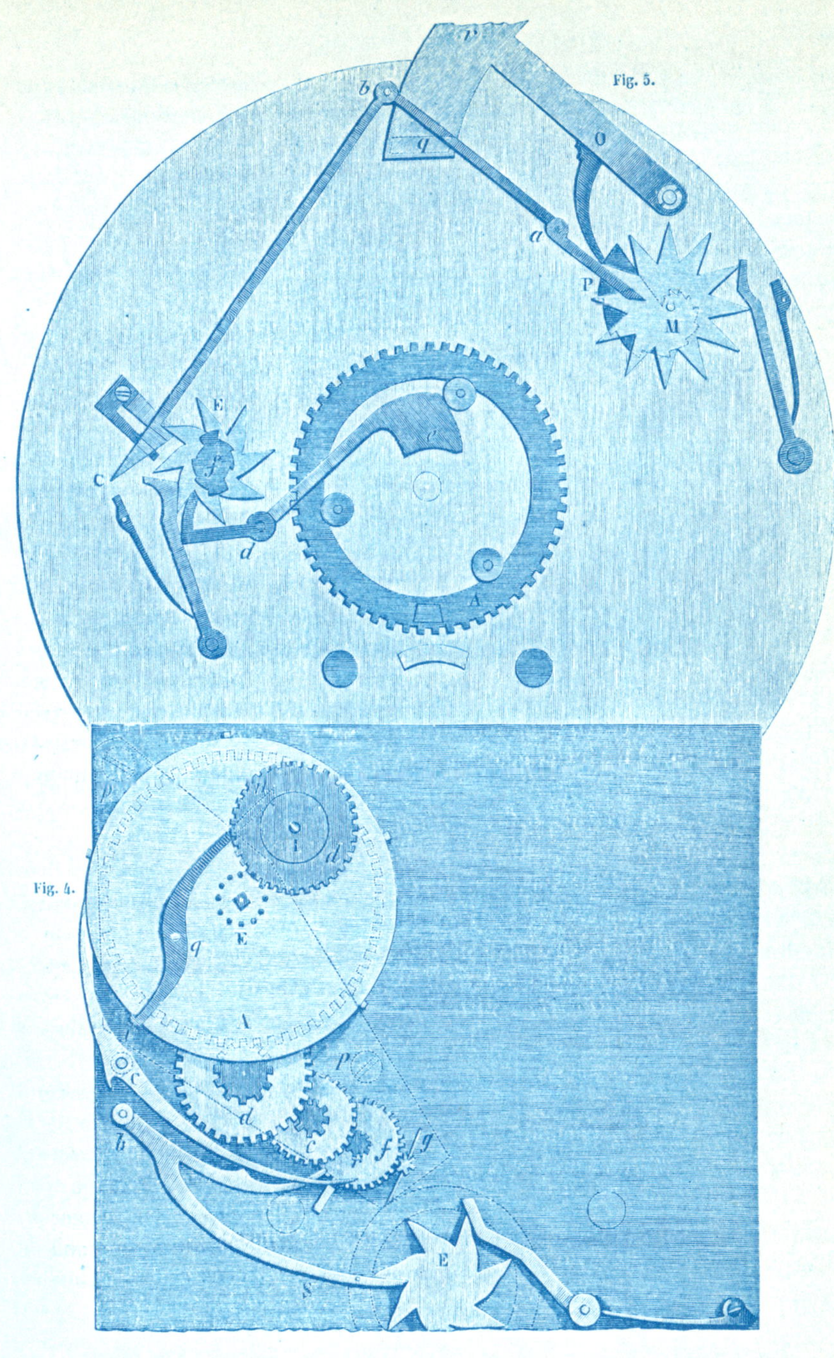

4

1 Stereometric Diagram of a Clock Interior
2 Instructions for Constructing a Wind or Air Powered Clock
3 Sixteenth Century Astrolabe, Back View
4 Astronomical Pendulum Clock with Equation

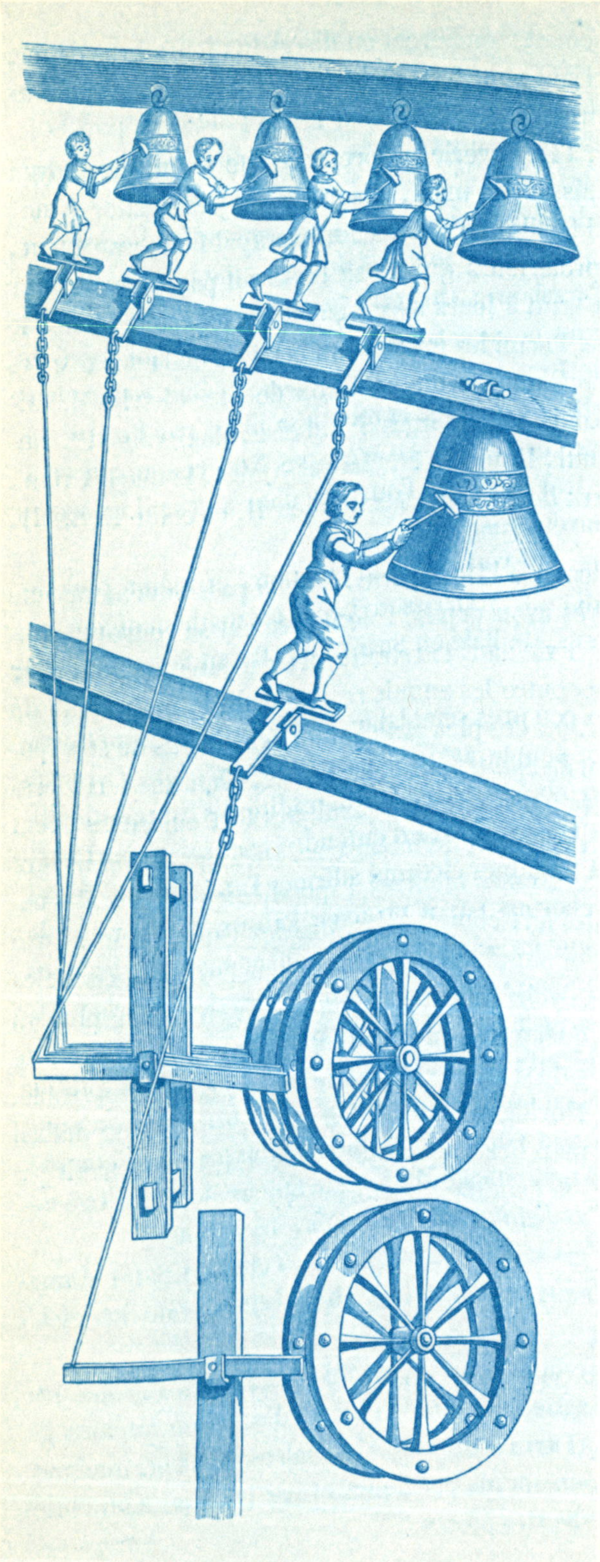

5

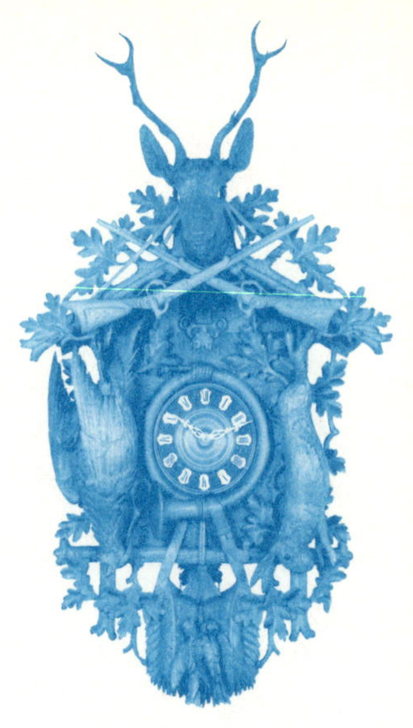

6

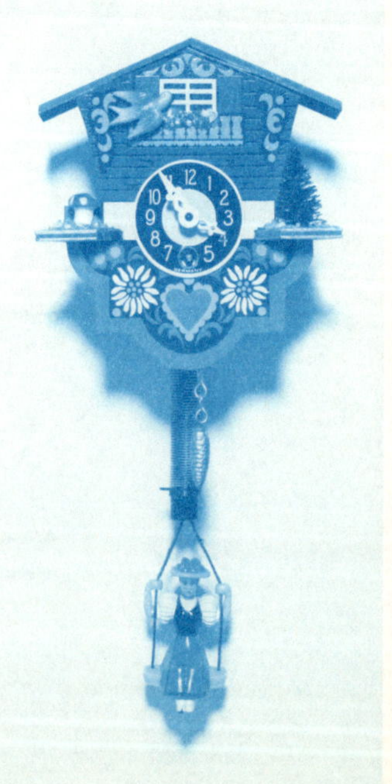

7

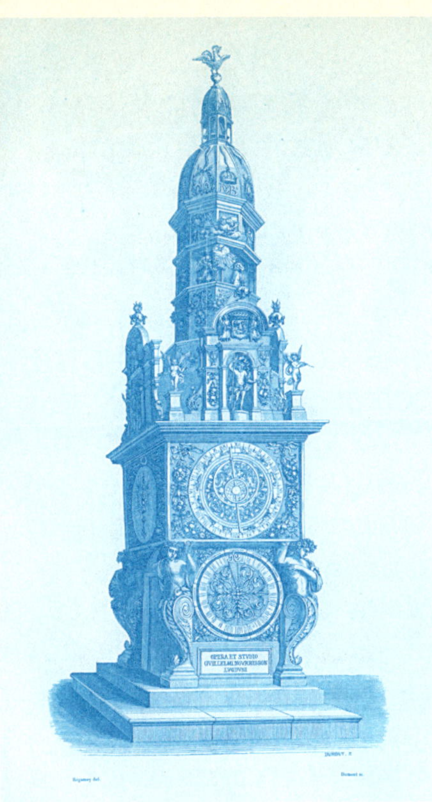

8

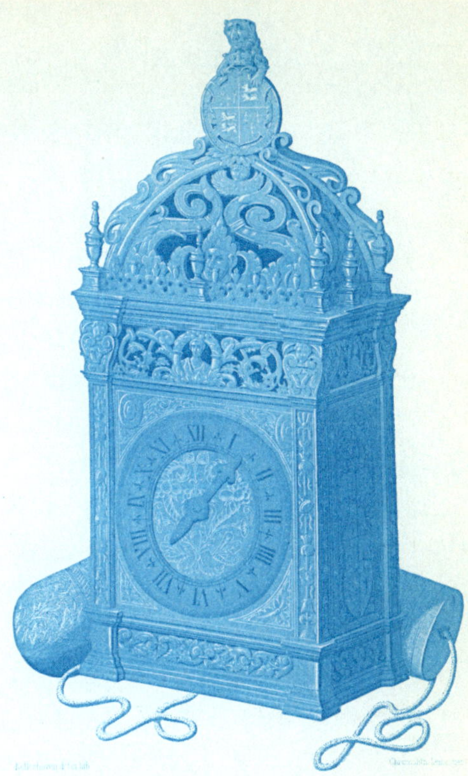

9

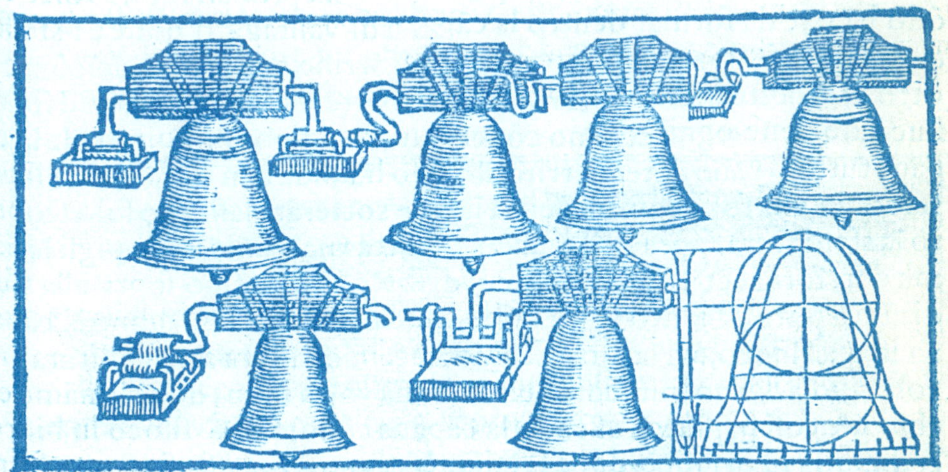

10

5 Chimes of a Liège Church Clock
6 Black Forest Cuckoo Clock, so-called Jagdstück
7 Black Forest Souvenir Cuckoo Clock
8 Astronomical Clock of Saint Jean Cathedral, Lyon
9 Sixteenth Century Weight-Driven Clock Said to Be from Henry VIII, Property of Her Majesty the Queen of England
10 Instructions for Connecting Big Bells, for Ease of Movement and Ringing

flotsam and jetsam flows with it; "astral straws on a time-stream, grit in the mistral," as Beckett writes in 1932 in his first attempt at a novel, *Dream of Fair to Middling Women*. This flotsam and jetsam is the stuff of which art is made. It can be filtered out during the refilling process and reassembled into arcane cabinets of curiosity and unexpected temporal islands of contemplation.

A leap into the present: like snow, cut paper falls from the ceiling. On the floor, a slowly growing white pile of snippets of paper. The view of the snow slows our body rhythm, our breathing, and with it the gaze that now passes over an arbor with black, shiny pillars, where small drawings are discovered. A cartoon duck stages moments in its banal everyday life. Our gaze moves onward, passing over large, dark masks that cover a wall. In the productively slowed-down time it takes to register all this, the viewer also discovers small pieces of driftwood with brief, lyric messages written on them. They seem like frozen flags, petrified in mid-flutter (as can be seen in Ugo Rondinone's installation *Zero Built a Nest in my Navel*). And while the curious eye reads, the visitor suddenly understands what poetry can do: shape the moment and make something non-material concrete, something that people remember when they're alone. In this fashion as well, we unlearn time. For it is a drawn out moment, frozen, and time seems stopped, brought to a standstill, glowing in repetition.

Time regained, *le temps retrouvé*: the twentieth century was modest in the face of the problem of winning time. It occasionally sought—and found—the pregnant moment. James Joyce's epiphanies or Virginia Woolf's "moments of being" are examples of this. This search for the moment that has stepped out of time has a long tradition, as Beckett notes in *Le Monde et le Pantalon*

(The World and the Trousers), "What have the visual arts attempted over and over again? To stop time, by representing it. So much flying, running, flowing, and shooting of arrows. So many collapses, so many ascensions. So much smoke."

This author occupies his cast of characters (and thus his audience) with time in a way that becomes almost paradigmatic for modern man. He does this in several ways, of which the most apparent—and for art history most decisive—is the figure of the stubborn player, the gambler. Recall Bruce Nauman's studio works from the 1960s and 1970s, which owe something to the artist's reading of Beckett's novels. Fond of what he saw as Beckett's systematic nonsense, his way of describing this and of giving it a number of rules, Nauman carried out a couple of performances on the basis of these.

What for Proust's narrator Marcel was a madeleine dunked in tea was for Beckett's protagonist Molloy the strategically varied enjoyment of sucking-stones. But what Molloy gains is not a bittersweet renewed sensation of a time once lost, but a joy in the self-generated energy that emerges in the time-consuming exhaustion of all possibilities of action. Caught in his own self-made time loop, Molloy can thus free himself from "time cancer," (and many other Beckett figures do the same). They all unlearn time by stretching it. In his exploration of Beckett's television plays, Gilles Deleuze convincingly showed that we can imagine the "exhausted" time traveler in Beckett as at once fulfilled and "exhausting." He uses time as a creative material, creating time holes, time loops, time spaces. "Space and body, completed, unchanging, torn from time by the maker of time, protected from time in the time factory," Beckett describes the effects caused by the painting of the brothers Van Velde, and thus characterizes above all—as he ultimately admits—his own obsessions. In such islands of time, man experiences the ideal boredom that according to Siegfried Kracauer is the only state that "provides assurance that one still disposes of one's own existence...."

> *"O verlerne die Zeit, dass nicht dein Antlitz
> verkümmre und mit dem Antlitz das Herz."
> (Hans Carossa)

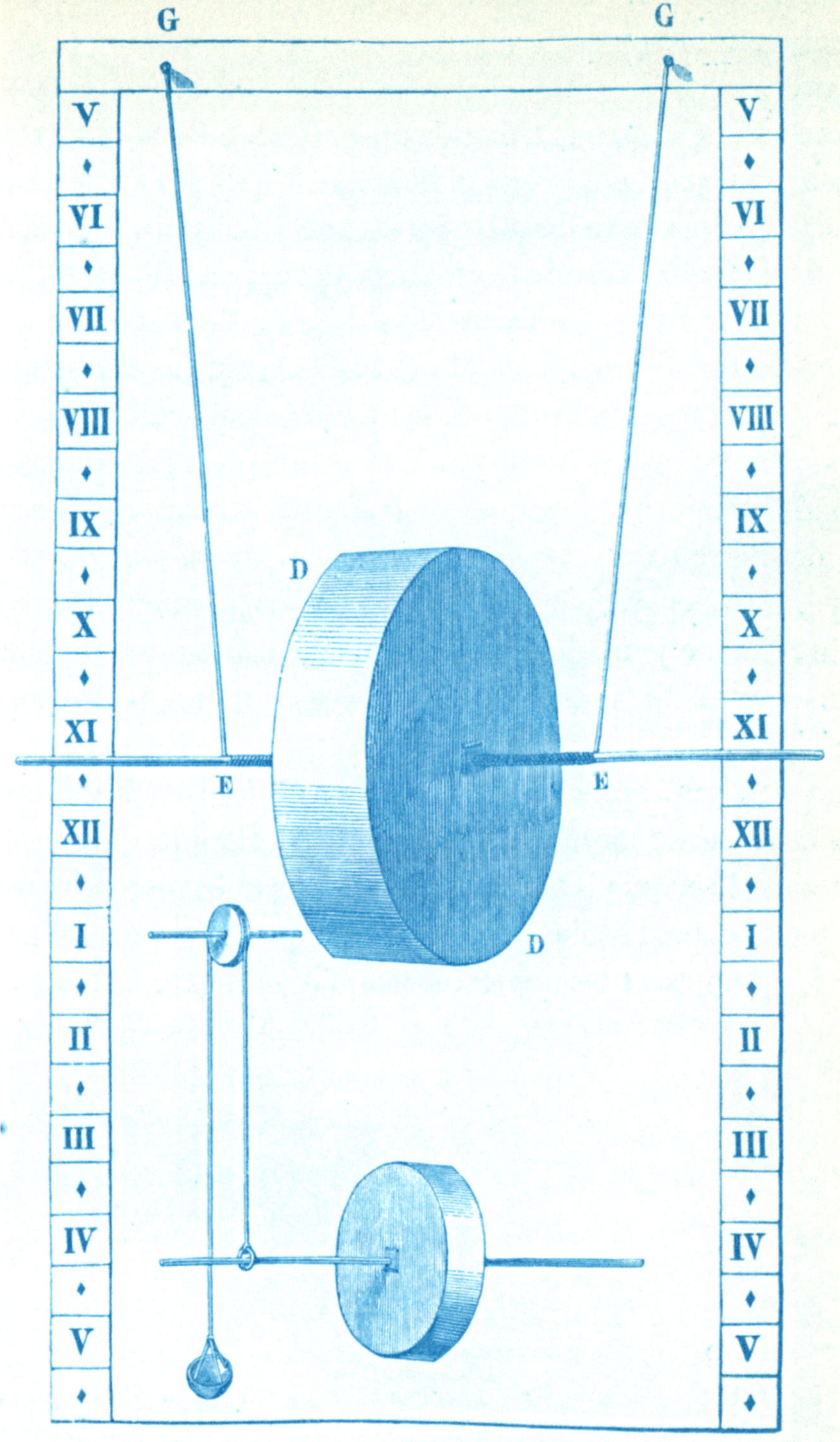

11 Drum Clepsydra (i.e. Water Clock), after Father Alexandre

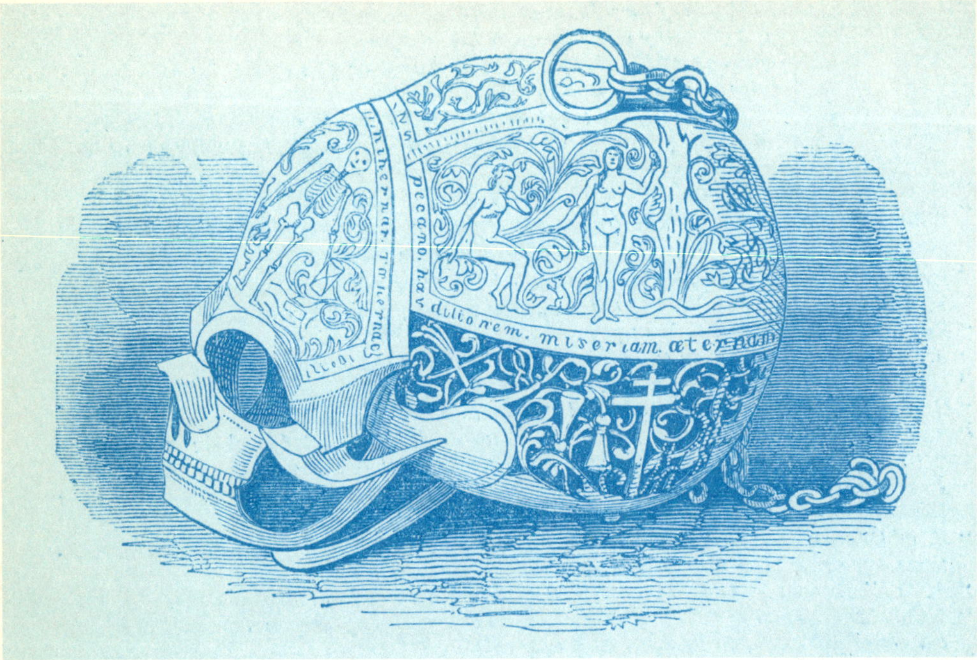

12

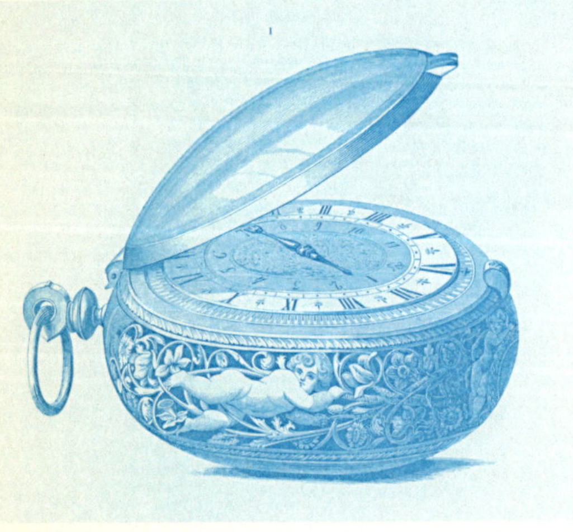

13

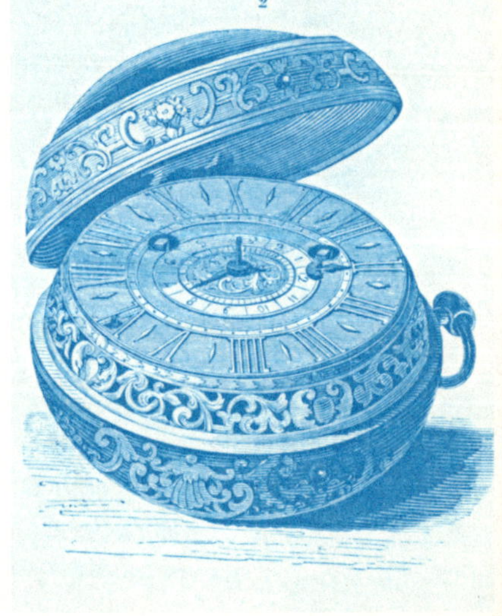

14

12 Memento Mori Watch Given by Mary Queen of Scots to Mary Setoun, her Maid of Honour
13 Seventeenth Century Watch Belonging to Mr Jacquart
14 Seventeenth Century Watch Belonging to Pierre Dubois

The Throes of Time—On Art and Truth

Spectacular images of negative presence like New York's "Ground Zero" or the destroyed Afghan Bamiyan Buddhas are perhaps images for a contemporary elegy. They make manifest events in which time has been suspended in an unreal fashion. The mourning for loss, be it symbolic or real, remains palpable, and continues after the changing rhythm of everyday life has been brutally interrupted. When the daily routine of society as a frame of reference can no longer offer support, everyday understanding retreats, and time appears as a distant horizon. Conversely and suddenly, time also becomes a vortex that devours belief and hope. This ambivalence is a starting point for James Lord's considerations, even if he does not explore the social aspects. His focus is individual: using Alberto Giacometti as an example, he discusses time as the absolute touchstone and ultimate hypothesis for artistic work in modernity.—*dk*

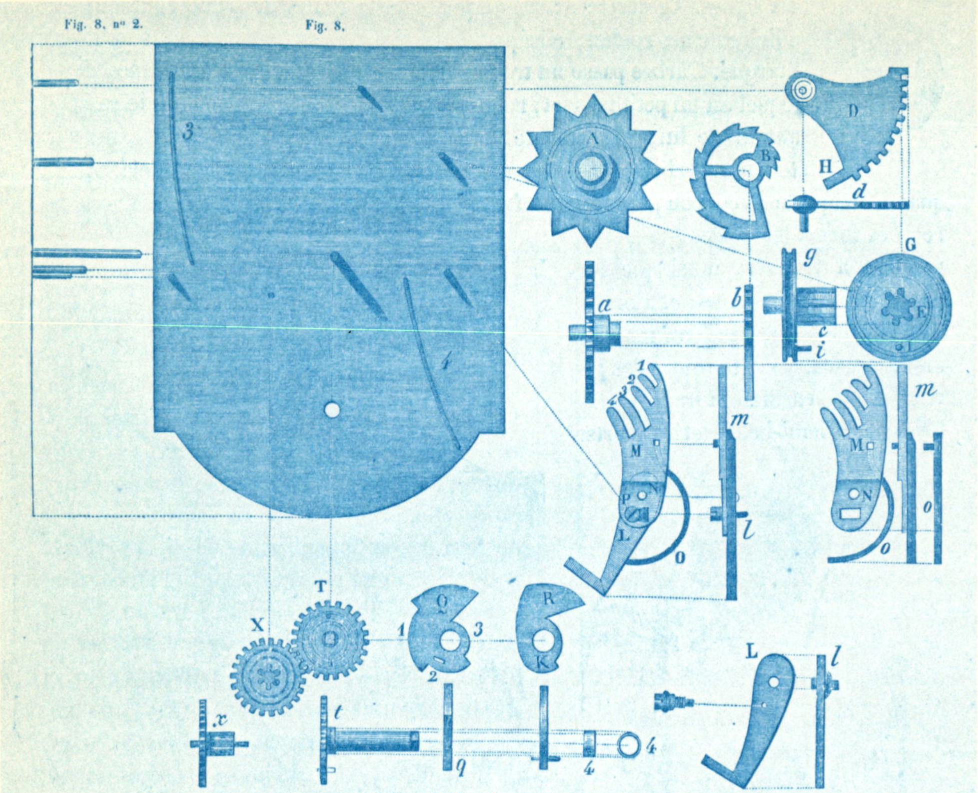

Fig. 8, n° 2.

Fig. 8.

(Fig. 6.)

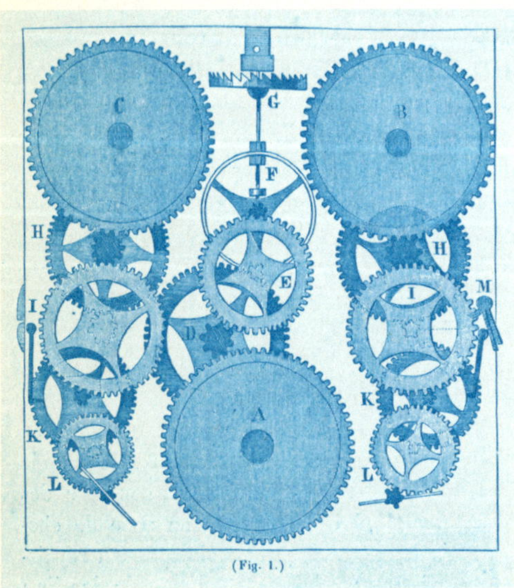

(Fig. 1.)

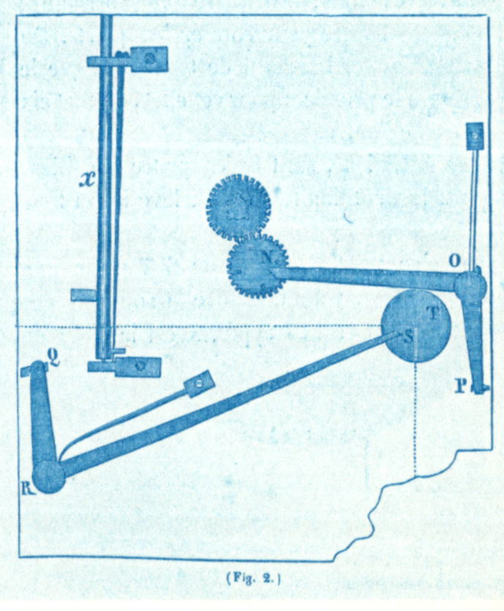

(Fig. 2.)

15 Quarter-Hour Chiming Clocks (three views)

Alberto Giacometti once said, "If I were true to myself, I would bury all of my work so that it wouldn't be found for a thousand years."

What precisely was he seeking to say? What truth to the self was supposedly at stake in entrusting all evidence of his creativity to a putative future?

He also once remarked, "Art interests me very much, but truth interests me infinitely more."

What distinction, what discrepancy may be presumed to set art and truth for Giacometti—or perchance for artists in general—in separate spheres of relevance to the creative act? This, indeed, is a matter that must seem of crucial significance as to logical appreciation of the *idea* animating contemporary creativity and appropriated for its use in order to define the outcome as art. And in the maelstrom of present-day realism—is this *really* neo-realism?—what straw of understanding may one more hopefully grasp, after all, than the wisdom and example of Alberto Giacometti? He was a serious and intransigent thinker, an intimate friend of dialectical ratiocination. One might contend that his existence from first to last was a battle between the biological and the intellectual, an action lost to the former, weaker force only by the bafflement of time. I used sometimes to say that he could conversationally construct the cathedral of Chartres on the head of a pin, then in the twinkling of an eye—and his eyes *did* twinkle—turn straight around and demonstrably deconstruct the whole edifice stone by stone. A man who can do that commands resources of acumen capable of conquering aesthetic retrenchment and making the best—and the most—of the aggressions of time.

For what are a thousand years? One year being a period of 365 solar days—and the sun itself an insignificant speck of incandescence in the incommensurable

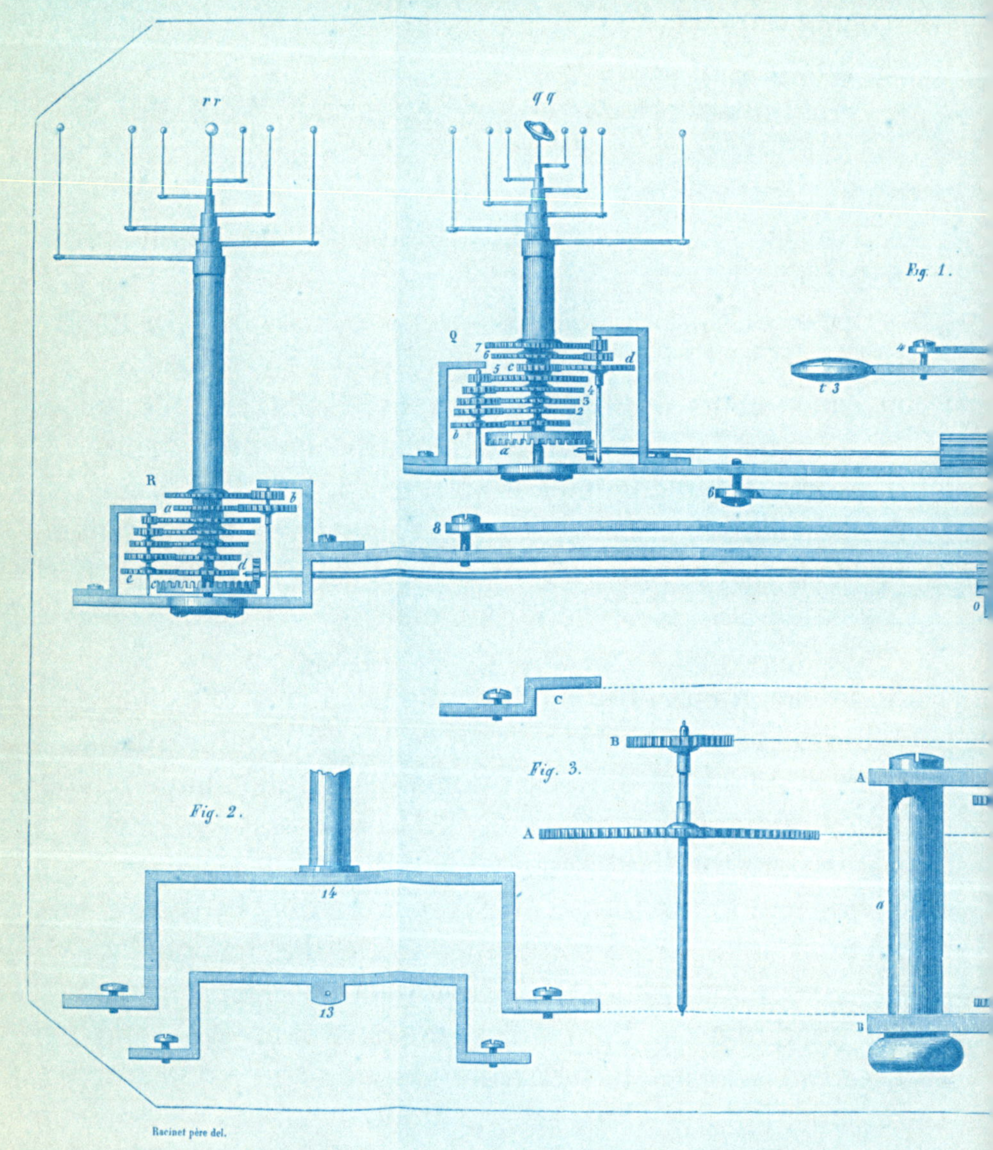

Racinet père del.

MACHINE PLANÉTAI

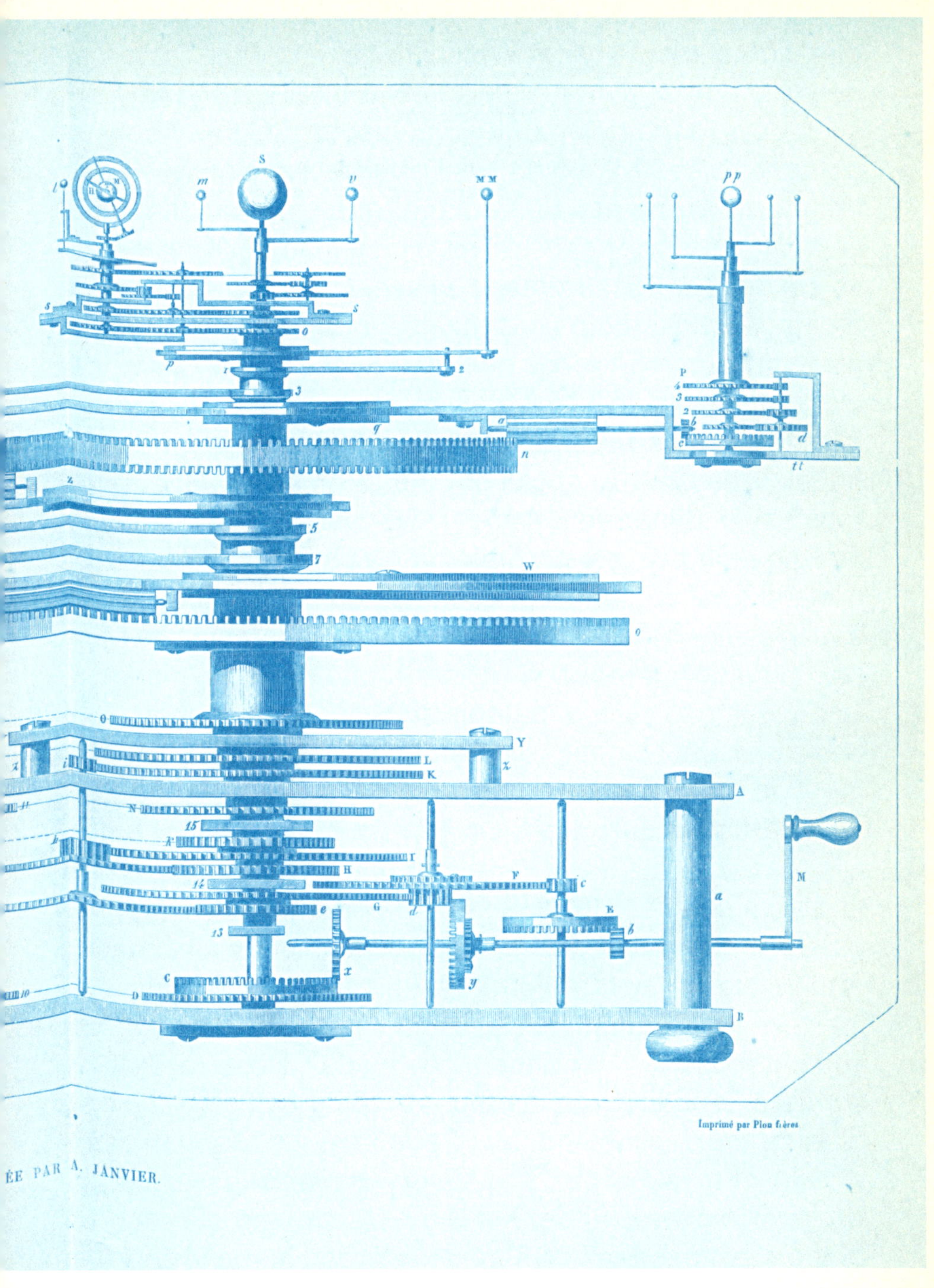

16 Mechanical Model of the Planetary System, Composed by Antide Janvier

question mark of space. What's to be said, then, of three hundred and sixty-five thousand two hundred and fifty such days, each being unique, indispensable and condemned to death even as living beings reluctantly relinquish each instant? No more, after all, than that time is death, and that death is time's inestimable and benevolent desideratum. Perhaps. Given, of course, that we are trying to speak of the unspeakable, of an essence apart from any common sense notion of passing time, from the world of clocks, in which a single event or experience presumes to be separate from another, we are, indeed, hopelessly trying to speak of time as an absolute, Einsteinian dimension. A thousand years, consequently, as a span of being is credible only as a very theoretical projection of present suppositions upon the ideality of a future which is nothing more than the adumbration of a past receding in reality with every rotation of the planet. And yet it is to such a metaphysical speculation that an artist must commit, and commend, his lifework, not to mention his lifetime.

An artist lives in, and by, a relation to the flight of time not shared by the majority of mankind, for his *raison d'être* takes timelessness for granted. The creative act is experientially measurable only by heartbeats, not by calendars. And yet, loving contradiction, artists today often date their works—Giacometti did—and some, contradiction becoming a passion, date them day by day: Picasso. Art survives. It outlives the memory of great battles, schisms of faith, the decline and fall of empires, the Ozymandias wrecks of royal hubris. The history of mankind is subject to the discipline of time, but the history of art is a record of the creations that have made mankind humane and which by that very effect stand aside from mankind's paltry perception of time itself, which has no history.

Other than by creating works of art, albeit closely akin to this instinct, there is but one existential act which vitally encompasses the innate craving to create. This is the compulsion to bring about a self-existence independent of its makers's self-existence, a coexistence, that is, which furthers the subsistence of its progenitor—and not a sculpture or a lyric drama or an heroic symphony—but simply and sublimely a living, breathing, hearing, seeing human life. In short, a child. Now, the sexual act also takes place in a realm of ecstatic oblivion, a space so secret from the couple united by it that its very secrecy secures the inviolable union essential to their climactic fulfillment in the replication of themselves. It's no coincidence that artists so often speak of their creations as their children, even likening the labor of their métier to the labor of childbirth. And neither can it be coincidental that the "children" created by artists receive the wondrous birthright of ideational immortality. Everyday sons and daughters, however, do not necessarily inherit talent, let alone genius. They may want to be barmaids, automobile mechanics, round-the-world mariners, disk jockeys—in a word, themselves, not mere bearers of eminent names. Unhappy facts demonstrate that painters, poets, composers have frequently been incompetent parents. Even the sexual life, not to mention the social life, of the artist must come to an accommodation with the exigencies of his art. Some instances of this accommodation—Michelangelo, Wagner, Picasso, Proust—are as clear as a pane of glass. Others—Poussin, Pascal, Monteverdi, Schopenhauer, Cézanne—leave the issue tantalizingly shrouded in the winding sheet of time.

To be true to himself, then, and to his work, every artist must live for the creative fusion of who he is with what he does. The work he has to do determines the life that

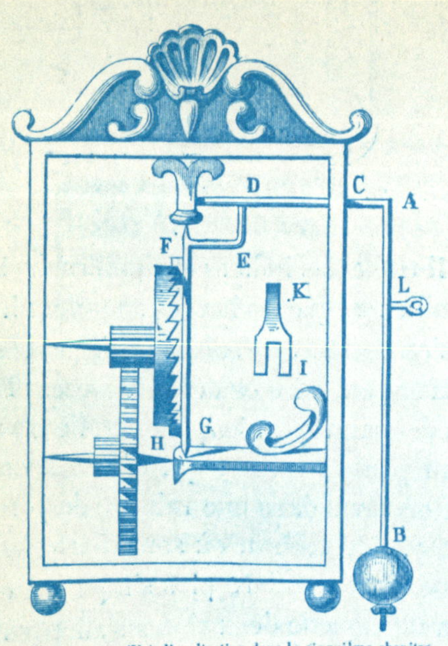

17

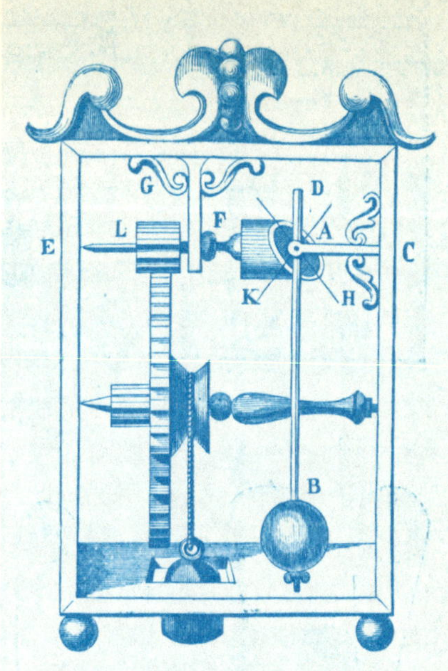

18

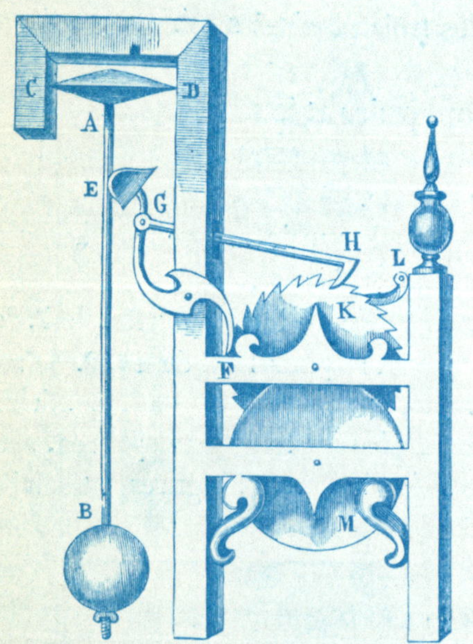

19

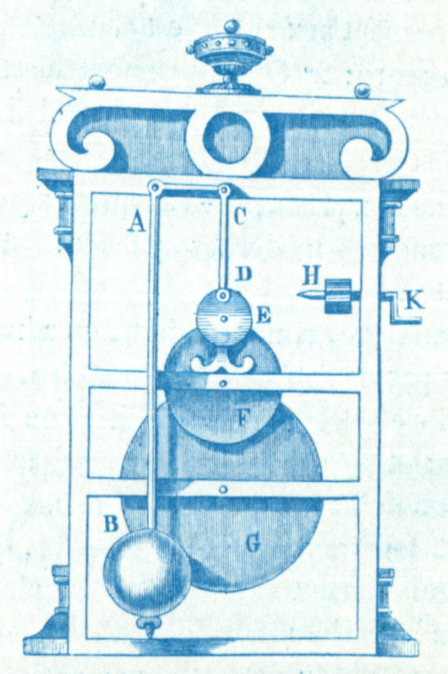

20

17 Clock with Verge Pendulum
18 Unworkable Escapement Mechanism
19 Clock with Pendulum Moved by an Anchor
20 Weight-Driven Clock and Pendulum without Escapement Mechanism, Side View

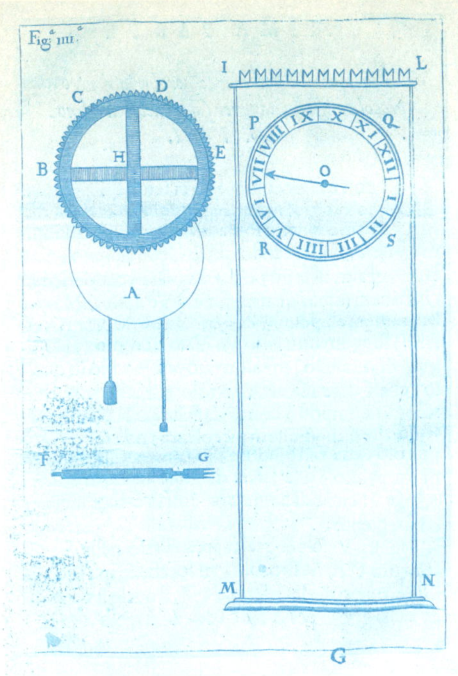

21

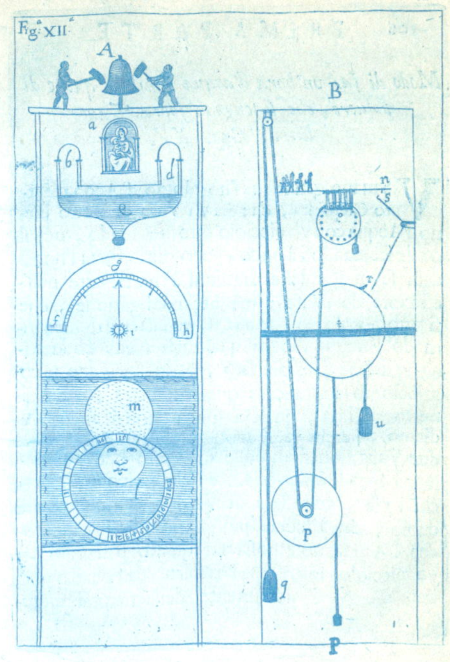

22

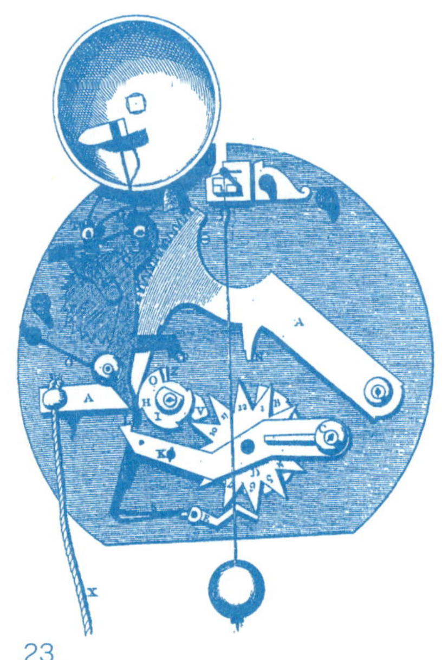

23

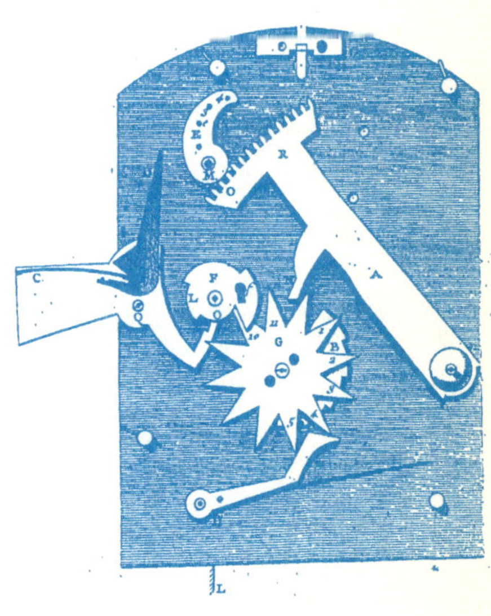

24

21 Clockface Similar to the Ones that Can be Seen on the Fronts of Churches and Towers

22 Clock-Work Resembling the One that Can Be Seen on the Most Famous Venice Piazza with the Moors who Strike the Hours and the Three Magi who, while Passing by, Greet the Virgin Mary

23 Under-Dial Work of All-or-Nothing Repeater

24 Under-Dial Work of Pendulum Clock with Repeater

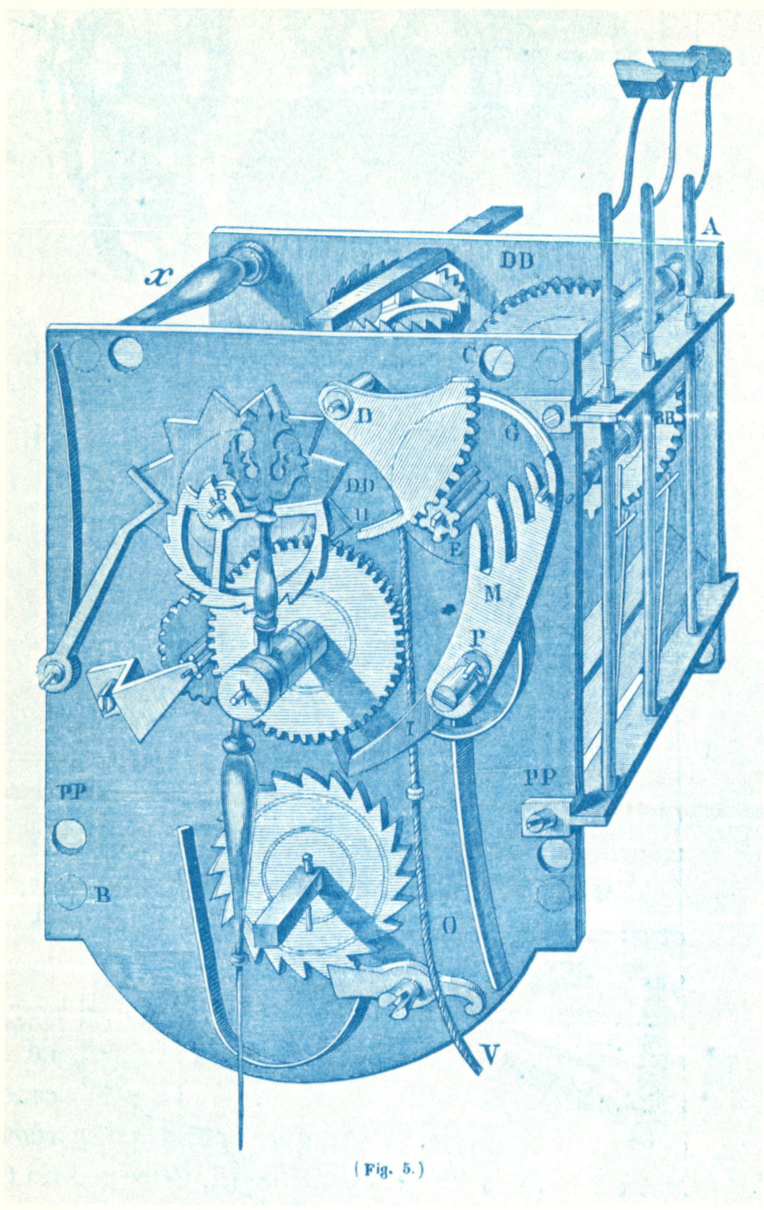

(Fig. 5.)

he has to live. This captivating determinism possesses a creative personality, so to speak, all its own, offering so exuberant a prospect of artistic innovation that it may quite rationally seem so potent with truth as to offer more interest than art itself. A passion for truth embraces a boundless expanse of surmise, of judgment, opinion and intuition, of guesswork, abstraction, predisposition and pure invention so vast, indeed, that it may even presume to take the measure of the universe, a measure, to be sure, theorized by the folly of human hubris in terms of time, which is termless save for the infatuating postulations of art. Truth, 'tis said, dwells in the eye of the beholder, and an artist's eye is conditioned to fall in love with his creations. Every sculptor at heart is Pygmalion, speaking to himself in the words of Schiller's "Ideals."

> Then lived for me the bright creation,
> The silver rill with song was rife;
> The trees, the roses, shared sensation,
> An echo of my boundless life.

So climactic an interest in truth would certainly reward beyond imagining the life-saving interest of art, enriching each and every moment with the approbation of time.

What truth to the self, then, may enjoin an artist to entrust the proof of his creativity to the contingency of burial in time's unverifiable tomb? Must it not be a presumptive self-evidence antecedently accepted as basis for a decisive commitment undertaken in unshakable faith? Burial, indeed, being a manifestation of metaphysical faith and a gesture of practical respect for the ritual assumptions of the afterlife. Ceremonial interment has been attended since remotest antiquity by the premise of absolute and due entitlement to devotional and elegiac

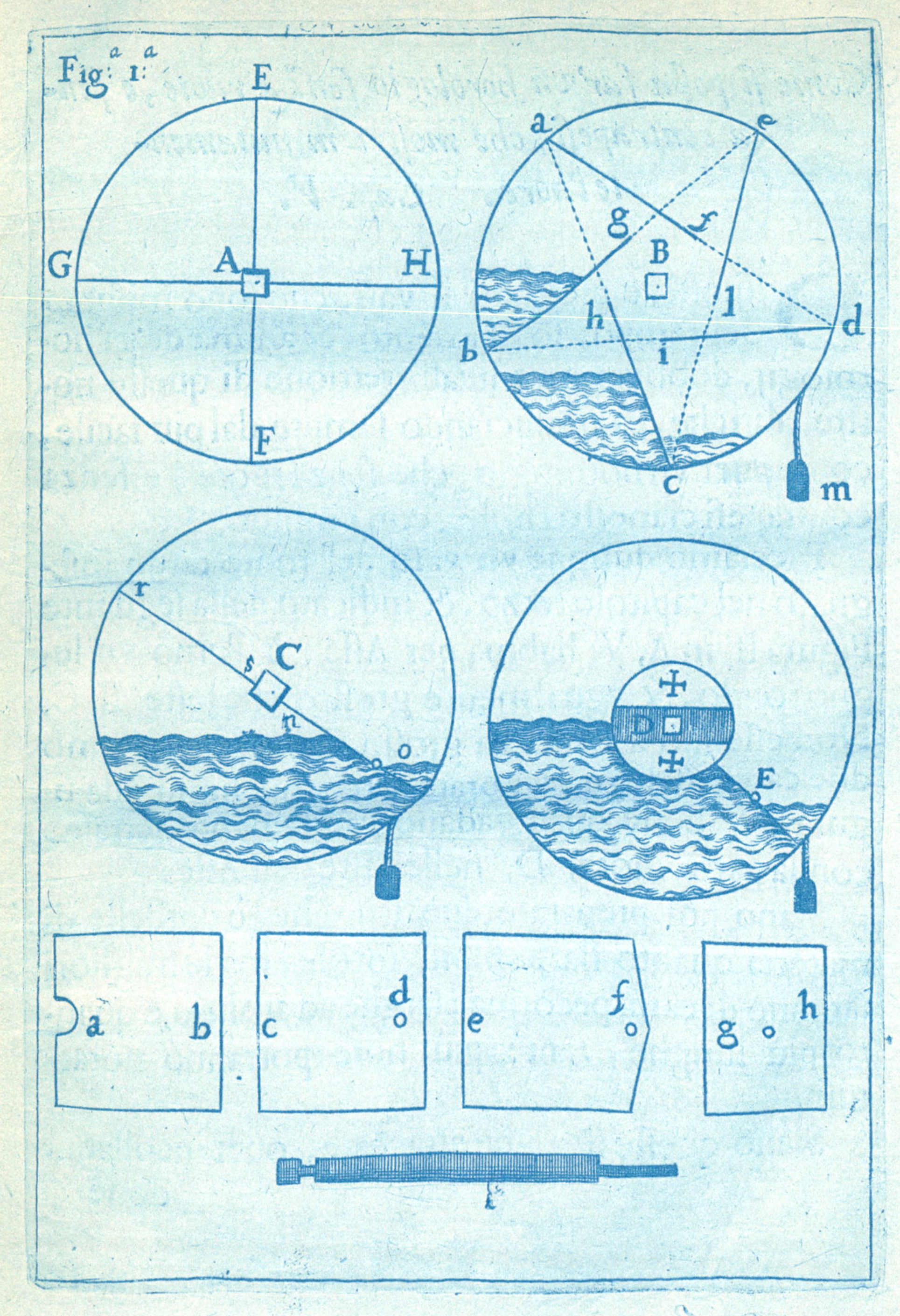

26 Instructions for a Water-Propelled Vessel that Serves to Show and Strike the Hours

observance. Mythic Antigone personified in terms of Sophoclean tragedy the sacrificial *noblesse oblige* toward a respectable sepulcher. Funerary practices of course, even the contemplation of them, entail a reckoning with the eventuality of death. Giacometti, for one, was no stranger to the life-enhancing promise of mortality. He used to say that death was life's most interesting experience, and that the really regrettable thing about dying was that you could only do it once. Such lively composure before the prospect of ending his life's work was actually vital to the production of figures—if only he could create them in likeness of his vision—which would presently be bodied forth as veritable goddesses. For them, indeed, no grandeur of idealistic entombment could ever be too worshipful. For him, moreover, to join them in a transcendent, everlasting hereafter would be merely the human acknowledgment of a superhuman opportunity. He recognized that an artist's works live, as it were, in impatient expectation of the artist's demise. The sedulous burial of art—"for a thousand years"—was nonetheless not intended to be eternal; the goddesses were meant to be found, restored to the verifying light of the workaday world in order to live on in the same museums as those deities of ancient Egypt so admired by Giacometti. And not at all by accident that is what happened. A day by day familiarity with the redeeming godsend of death had brought to life the delightful chance of creating things to beautify the premise of afterlife.

For a man on speaking terms with the man-in-the-street imminence of death it would have been uncharacteristic to fail to scrutinize the perceptible evolution of a future in which he would no longer have a hand or, indeed, so much as a fingertip. Giacometti was too true to himself, and to the supreme interest of truth itself, to dodge a glimpse

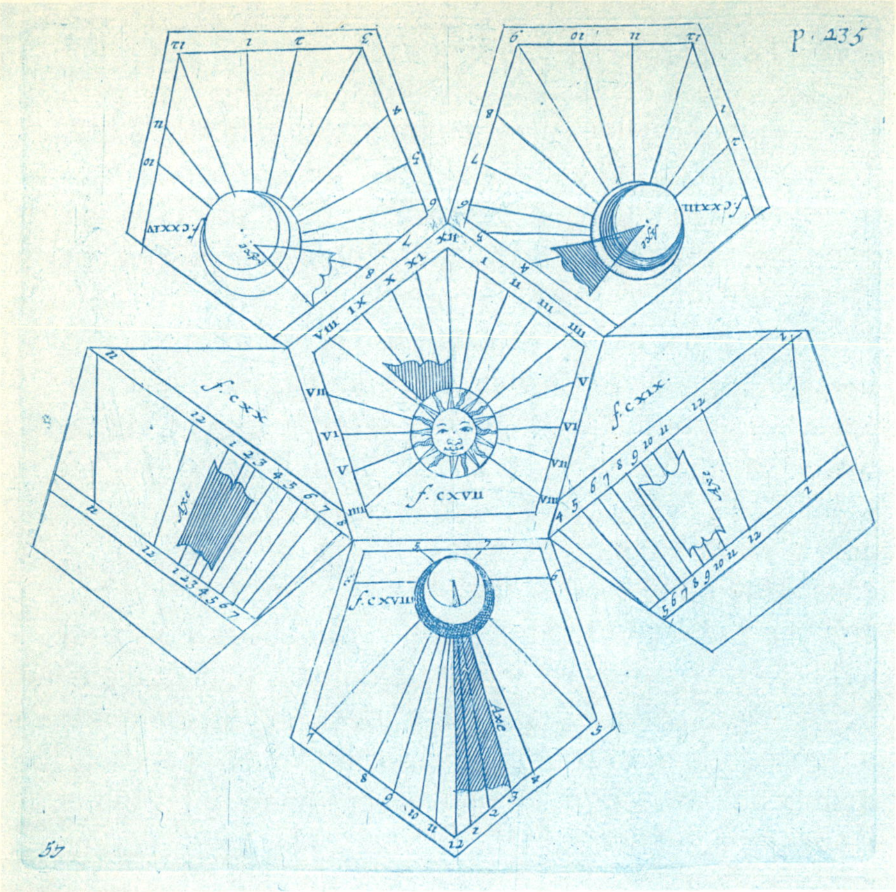

p. 235

f. cxx

f. cxvii

f. cxix

f. cxviii

27

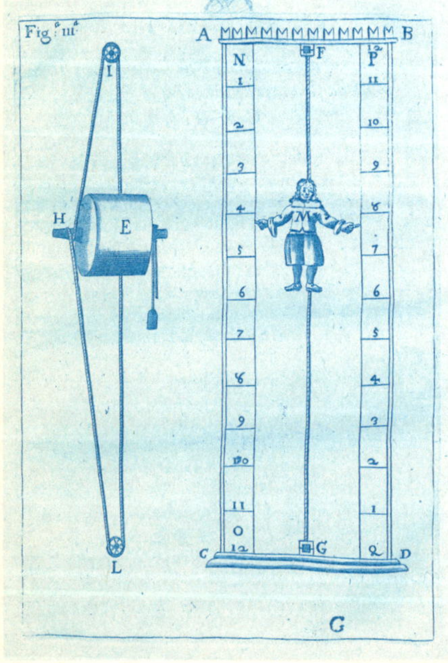

28

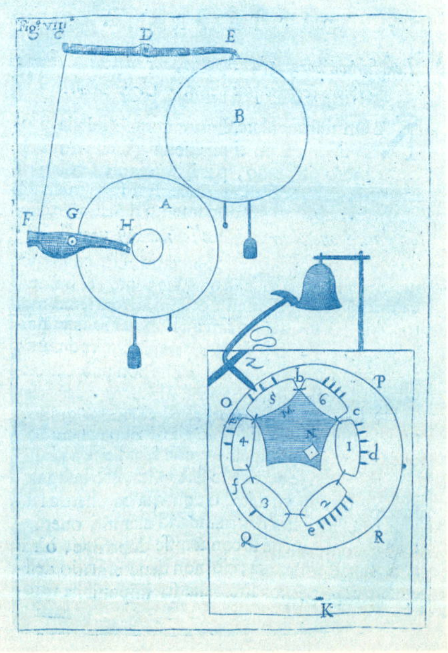

29

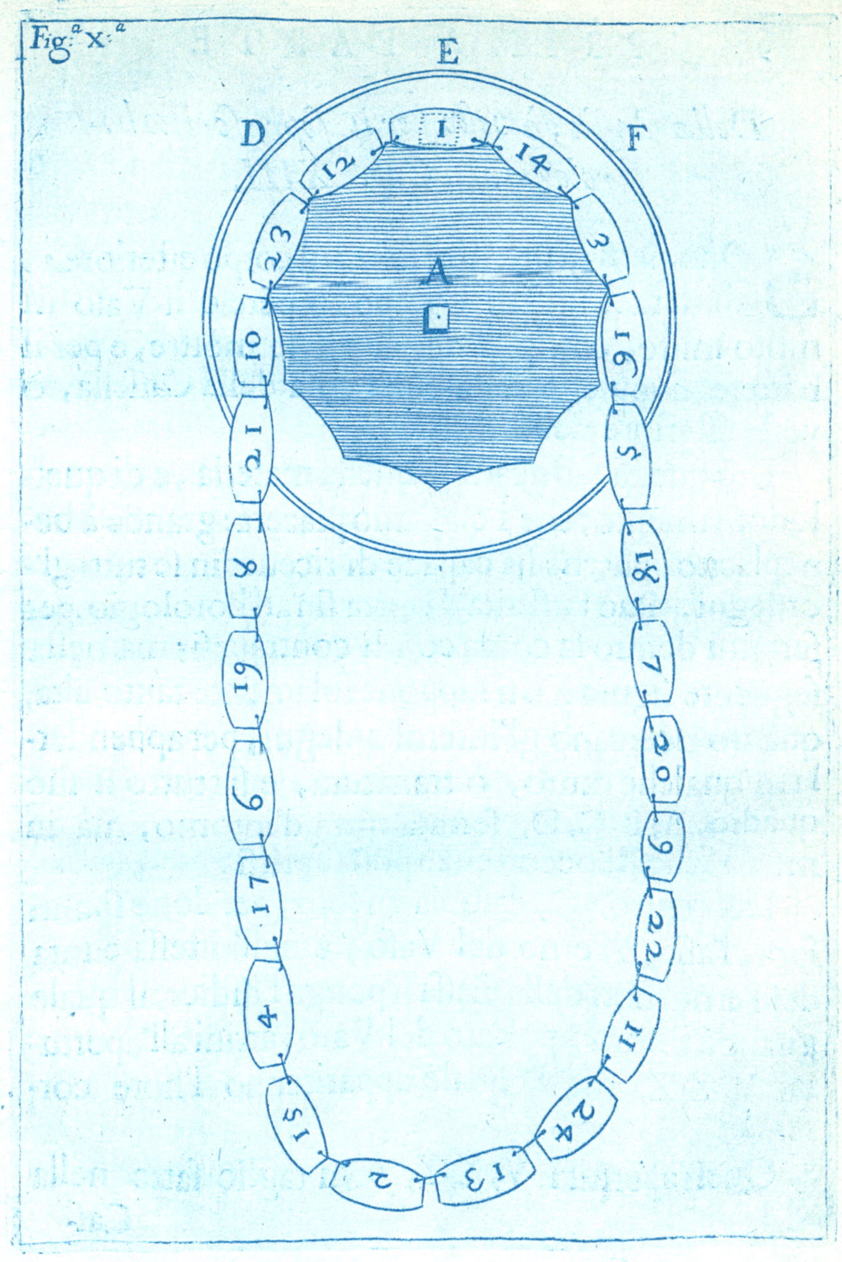

30

27 Instructions for Sculpting Sundial Faces from Stone or Other Solid Material
28 Dial without Wheels with its Counterweight
29 Instructions for the Mounting of Clock-Bells, for Striking the Hours and the Morning Bell
30 Clock Showing and Striking the Hours by Means of One Vessel Only

of the art to come in his—blissful—absence, safe at last from the melee of time in a tomb much like those so presciently prepared in his mythic childhood. What he saw was not a generous, companionable apparition. Speaking not long before he died, he said, "Painting as we know it? I think it has no future in our civilization. Neither does sculpture. What we might call 'bad painting'—that has a future. But what we call great painting is finished."

A melancholy farewell to the creative fatality to which a great man had offered a great lifetime.

But then... it had been high time, indeed, when Giacometti set out on his temporal itinerary, for some artist to try to accomplish as much as he had had the fortitude for—and which no one since Cézanne had had the vision to tackle—and which was accomplished by Giacometti entirely, ineffably in the thankless throes of time. And which, moreover, no artist since then has had the temerity or the mere imagination ever again to envision.

Out of the Country

They met in a café in Kutna Hora, about 70 kilometers east of Prague, a few steps from the ossuary chapel. K. had claimed that, measured as the crow flies, it was the exact centerpoint between Berlin and Vienna, the two cities in which at that moment they were living. This was not actually true, but it seemed to have a good ring to it, at least it was better than Kropácova-Vrutice, where they would have had to meet were they to have had the same length of journey.

K. Milk?
B. Thanks, no. Black. Like the night.
Pause.
K. Didn't you use that once in a text: "On me the sun also shone in the night?"
B. Possibly.
K. I remember. It was one of those Hunter S. Thompson pieces that you used to write. Dreadful.
B. Didn't you do that?
K. I wrote Bukowski pieces. You were Hunter S. Thompson.
B. No.
K. You were. I remember. Hunting for the Swiss dream.
B. That was only an excursion. In the Grissons.
K. No. That was the hunt! You remember that we were at this crash show? You do remember?
B. No.

K. We were. One stuntman climbed up onto a pile of polystyrene cones and the other drove a racing car at it.
B. And?
K. The man on the cones saw the car coming at him, knew that he was about to be run over and...
B. And?
K. Remember. He DIRECTED the traffic. He tried to avert the disaster knowing that it was the disaster, precisely the driving at the cones on which he was standing, that was the actual attraction, the real point of the whole thing.
B. And?
K. Remember! That time we screamed out because we thought we had found it. The dream. The heart of Switzerland, the original Swiss person, what am I saying, the original human being.
B. I only remember that we had a bottle of mineral water filled with grapefruit juice and vodka with us and that we waded for hours through cow shit in order to find some magic mushrooms.
K. Yes. And the farmer's boy who was helping his father slaughter the cows and as we walked past them said: "Daddy, gimme the eye"?
B. That was years earlier.
K. A boy that asks his father if he can have the eye?
B. The eye of a cow.
K. The eye! Don't tell me that it wasn't exactly this image that was the trigger for you to leave the country.
B. I simply wanted to go to Berlin.
K. To be in an enclave. Is that clear to you? From one enclave to another. A smaller one, nota bene.
B. Switzerland is no enclave.
K. Don't you say that, an enclave of freedom?
B. No, you don't say that.

K. Whatever. Wasn't that the reason why you turned your back on your country and went abroad, what am I saying, went foreign?
B. No.
K. Do you remember how we caught trout?
B. No. Where?
K. In the trout hatchery next to the house where we studied for the final Latin exam with H.
B. I remember.
K. Then maybe you recall that we caught and ate two trouts. Maybe that was the reason.
B. For what?
K. To leave Switzerland. Good gracious, don't you understand me?
B. No.
K. WE ATE HATCHERY TROUT!
B. Doesn't everybody?
Pause.
K. You're right, everybody does.
B. Quod erat demonstratur.
K. It's demonstrandur.
B. What?
K. The word.
Pause.
B. Why is Switzerland properly speaking an enclave of freedom?
K. Do you know the theory that freedom will one day become so rare that—as in a zoo—it will have to be locked up and no sooner than it is put in a cage, it will disappear?
B. That is not a theory but a song we used to sing in school camps.
K. In school camps in Switzerland?
B. Where else?

K. Quod erat demonstratur.
B. Trandur.
K. Whatever.
Pause.
B. One thing I remember at any rate.
K. What's that?
B. Ireland and your pocketknife.
K. Pocketknife?
B. You lost your pocketknife in Ireland and then said: I have lost my pocketknife, some day I'm going to lose my country.
K. I never said that.
B. But you did. You placed yourself in the rising sun especially for that sentence, so it would look good.
K. I never did anything of the kind.
B. Against the light.
Pause.
B. It's getting time.
K. Excuse me?
B. It's getting time. To go. My train is leaving.
K. Excuse me? We wanted to spend a weekend here, I've reserved two rooms.
B. M. called, the kids are sick.
K. When did M. call?
B. Just now, when you were on the can.
K. I was not on the can.
B. The telephone was on soundless. You didn't hear it ringing. The kids are sick. I have to go back.
Pause.
K. This is a bitter disappointment. I have made plans.
B. We'll meet some other time.
K. I have made plans. Everything is ready. It took me weeks to organize.
B. The kids are sick. I have to catch the next train.

Pause.

K. Perhaps you're already living it, the dream.

B. The bill, please.

K. You have to speak Czech here.

B. What do you mean?

K. You are living it, the Swiss dream, abroad, with a little family, in the enclave of freedom, with one eye open to disaster. Perhaps you have found it.

An old waiter came to the table, a bent-over old waiter and added everything up. B. avoided looking K. directly in his reproachful eyes. But B. wanted to spare himself a weekend like the one five years ago, when K. was living in Prague and B. in Basel, and for that reason they had had to meet in Braunau, where K. decided to re-live his adolescence and therefore both of them spent two nights standing around the discos of Braunau, B. in tight jeans and a sleeveless T-shirt, K. in pink pantaloons and a smock, talking about girls that they dared not approach, and during the day playing billiards or hunting for the non-existent Antifa of Braunau in order to fraternize with her. A weekend like that or even something close to it.

They left the café without a word and went to the railway station.

K. suggested that they at least take advantage of the situation, of the fact that they were here and that before them lay a grave they could practically enter, the ossuary chapel of Kutna Hora, and if B. refused to play out their important and character-building hunt for the Swiss dream, they could for a moment at least lie down in the chapel and feel what it would be like one day to be buried in the same grave.

Instead B. accelerated his pace.

A butcher approached from a side street, grabbed K. on his sleeve with a blood-splattered hand and spoke at him. In broken Czech K. tried to calm him. A small boy ran up to the butcher, plucked at his blood-smeared coat, held out to him the eye of a cow and blubbered out again and again the same sentence in a horrible language that B. finally recognized as Swiss-German with a Czech accent.

B. moved away slowly toward the railway station, so slowly that a change of position was hardly perceptible with the naked eye.

So doing he passed a man in motorcycle gear that was lying on the ground next to a pair of styrofoam cones and screaming, presumably from the pain in his leg, which was sticking out at an unnatural angle from his body.

In front of the railway station the concrete had been torn open, a large hole had been dug out and filled with water. Trout romped in it, dully observed by an old man with homemade hooks in his hand.

When B. entered the waiting room, he froze: it was swarming with ineptly costumed Czechs, some were rolling wheels of cheese as they moved, others were blowing into alp horns, still others were dipping their arms and legs in great casks of melted chocolate. A few jangled the money in their pants pockets and everyone—women and children included—were wearing glued-on beards and had stuck pipes in their mouths with the heads turned downward. The air had a cheesy sweet stink, the noise level was overwhelming.

B. bought his return ticket from an official sitting behind the glass pane in makeup and a blond wig. B. assumed that this was also part of K.'s plan, the wig was trimmed and suggested a haircut that strongly reminded B. of the haircut of M., his first girlfriend.

Trembling B. got on to the train and rode to his native country which is what he liked to call his family. From K. he would hear nothing more until a postcard years later on which stood a pair of coordinates and a date and below them instructions for B. to appear at the given time and place dressed in nothing but a portable milking stool, strapped to his back.

This B. decided against.

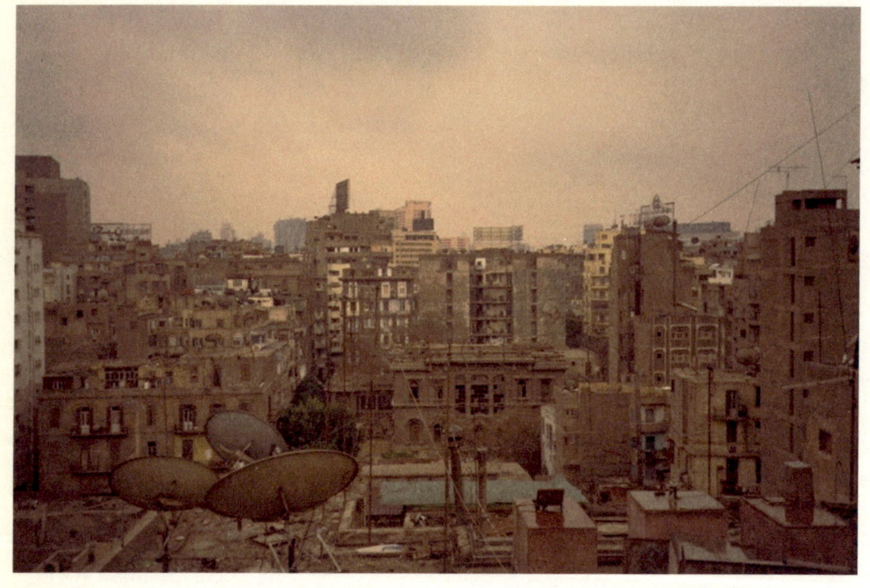

A Surplus of Form—On Some of Christine Streuli's Photographic Vignettes

Christine Streuli is well-known for her complexly layered and densely composed painting. Slowly, her work is moving from the classical painterly formats, expanding beyond the frame into three-dimensional space. What becomes caught in this movement and the visual vortex of her pictorial surfaces are the signs she collects in various environments and geographies recording them in photographic vignettes. Roman Kurzmeyer, Fanni Fetzer and Susann Wintsch engage in a brief email debate about these vignettes and their reference to painting and to cultural context; a conversation based on a few selected photographs that are part of a larger, mostly unpublished body of work.—*dk*

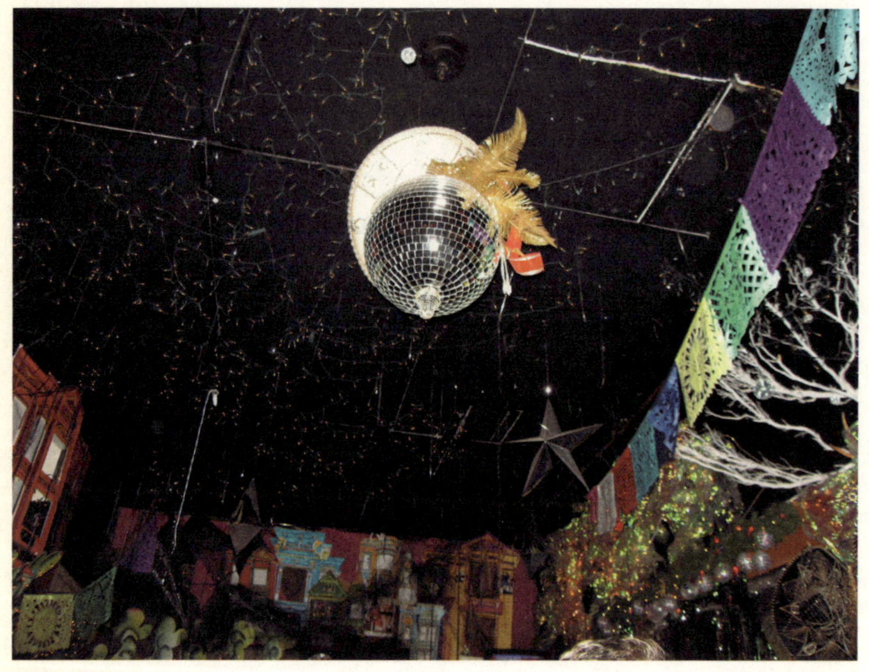

Roman Kurzmeyer
Wouldn't you say that Streuli's photographs show a self-directed perspective that can also be encountered in photography of other artists, for example in the work of Josef Albers from Mexico or Wols? In Albers, it is the interest in structures; Wols searches for the countenance of the real. I'm also thinking of the photographs that the art historian Aby Warburg brought home to the Old World from his 1896 trip to America. The pictures were taken during his stay among the Pueblos in Arizona. Among the Native Americans he encountered a strange visual practice that arrested him, perhaps in particular because it basically reminded him of his own. Warburg attempted to capture with his camera the influence of white civilization on the everyday life of the tribal culture, and was above all fascinated by the ritual dances of the Hopi and explored their symbolic dimension. Streuli is not collecting visual ideas for her painting in her photographs. I would rather argue the other way around: the photography leads out of the studio and documents the issues and components of her painting in the world. She rediscovers phenomena, situations, and processes outside the studio that she first got to know in the studio.

Fanni Fetzer
I share the sense that in her travel pictures Streuli is capturing in photography what she creates in her painting as a studio artist. Streuli once mentioned to me that she considers the New York photograph (see p. 276), for example, a particularly great picture, the kind that she herself would like to create. I take this to indicate she never tries to imitate a spray picture of this kind in the studio. On the contrary, on her travels she discovers images that she herself might well have created.

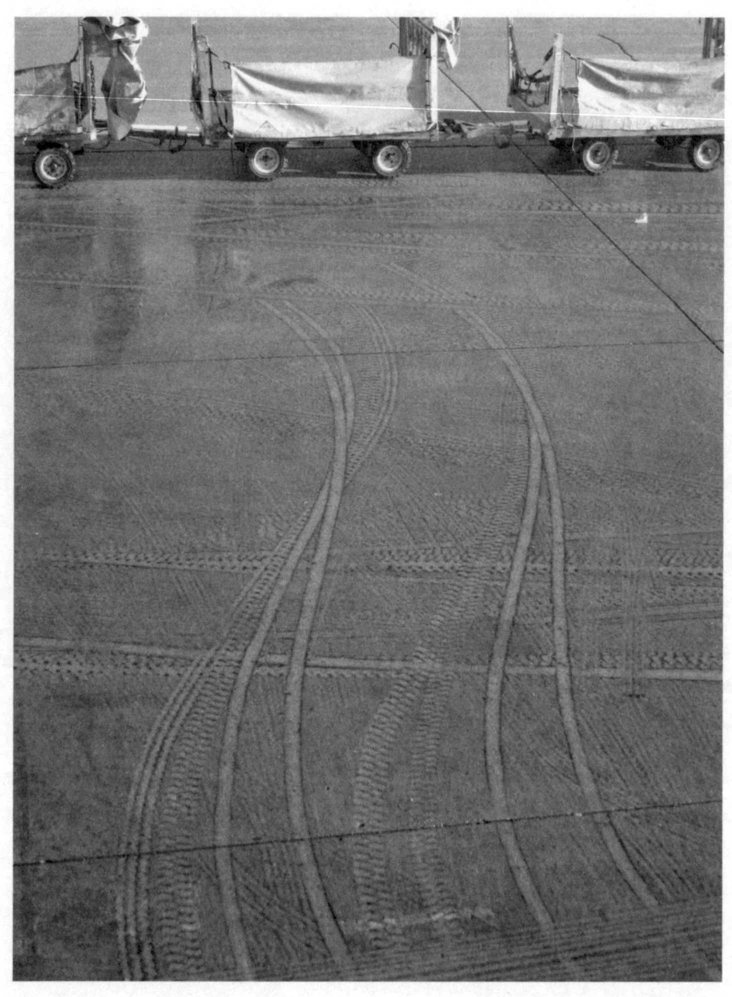

Roman Kurzmeyer
Yes, the picture taken on Metropolitan Avenue in Brooklyn of the cardboard used by a mechanic to work on is similar to the paintings. Streuli paints comparable forms, traces become figures, the cardboard in contrast remains an object without an art status, for the contours are nothing but unintentional traces of work. As a photograph in Streuli's œuvre, however, the meaning of the cardboard changes, and thus also its meaning; the traces appear as composition.

Susann Wintsch
Leaving the studio to find unfamiliar painting in spontaneous drawings on piles of soil or urban cement walls, Streuli contrasts such inscriptions with her own painting. I understand her as participating in the way not just people, but also machines shape the world, be it in Beirut, Kloten (see p. 272), or Waikiki (see p. 282). I was here, me too, me too! Each one of these interventions, even if they happen unintentionally, takes its place in the visible presence of prior hypotheses, immerses itself in it, and asserts its own trace, whether it reclaims an individual style, repeats a ritual sign, or sets an industrial mark. Modern cave painting, yes, cave painting.

Roman Kurzmeyer
Stone Age cave art, such as the negative impression of a hand, has not coincidentally been an issue since early modernism. Georges Didi-Huberman, who, like Max Raphael and Sigfried Giedion before him, occupies himself with these images, speaks of the handprint as the "touch of absence," and continues to ask whether these works of cave art are about the presence or representation of human hands. The hand was placed on the stone

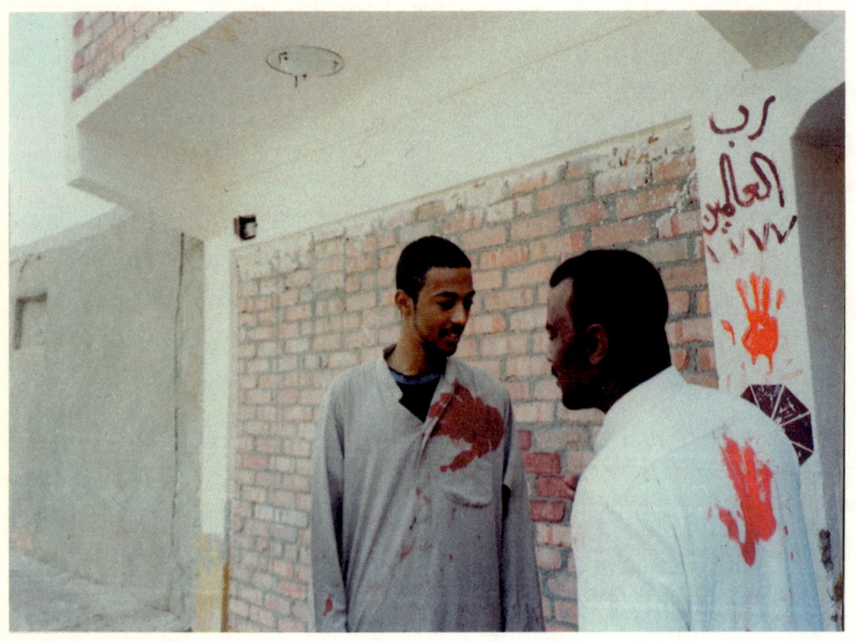
رب
العالمين

surface, and then colored powder was blown along its contours on the wall. Didi-Huberman interprets these hand representations as dialectical images that do not just present us with the touch become visible, but also with the absence of the person touching. This brings us back to Streuli's painting, where the relationship between presence and representation is also central. The cardboard from Brooklyn, in contrast, lacks this intentionality of being a picture, which first comes into play with the photograph of the cardboard.

Fanni Fetzer
I don't understand the cave painting metaphor. Streuli is not so much collecting human signatures, stamps, tags, or fingerprints, but rather evidence of her own working techniques. The photographs precisely enumerate Streuli's mode of working: cutting, doubling, prints, grooves, spray, stencil, neon, reflection are important in both her photography and her painting.

Susann Wintsch
Whether looking for the new and unused or for equivalences of one's own position in the rest of the world. Visual signs are very easy to exchange. Their meanings are perhaps not the same, for the exchange among the different cultures is strictly hierarchical. You'd only find that out by learning the language of the peripheral regions to be able to speak about it. Streuli's photographs present a great deal of "world," for they observe what the others outside are doing, where and how they set their signs. They could then be judged not only as signifiers of painting, but also as the documentation of a process of understanding the world. As Barnett Newman put it, the first human being was an artist, his or her language a

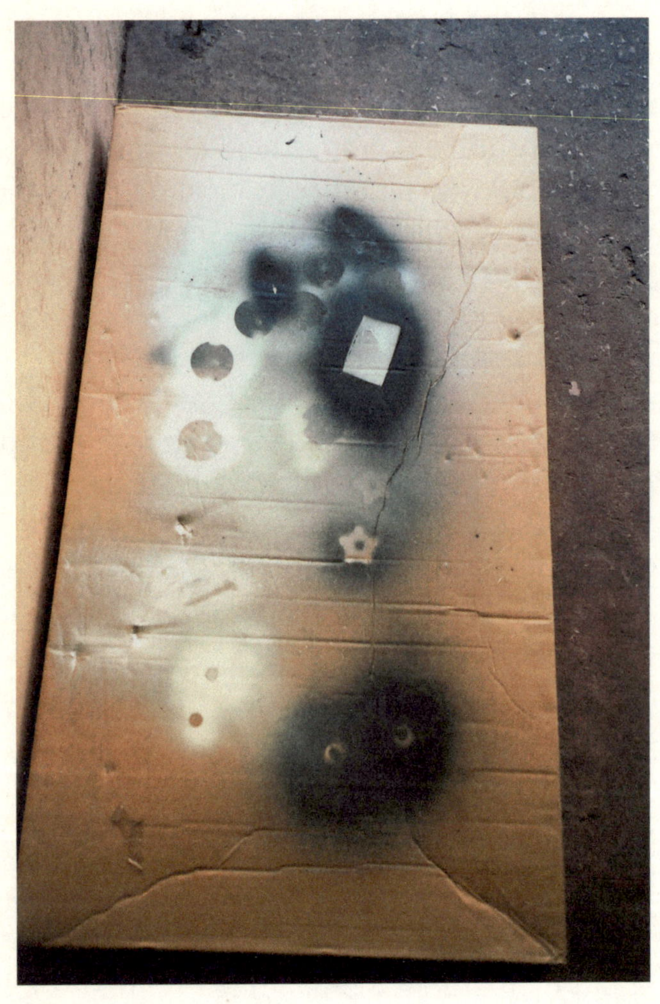

poetic scream with no claim to communication, for that scream first just breaks through the powerlessness in the face of the void (today, one would have to speak of an unbearable fullness). It is precisely those photographs that show people that attest to this mental intervention in the absent that Didi-Huberman was also addressing.

Roman Kurzmeyer

Yes, the photographs give the impression that Streuli was not primarily interested in the communicative function of these images; instead, she was trying to allow the forms to show themselves. There is a surplus of form. The photograph of the neon sign reading Eldorado (see p. 284) is just such a picture.

Fanni Fetzer

I like that formulation, "a surplus of form," and I find it interesting how the photographs of signs reading Eldorado (see p. 284) or Flower (see p. 278) make it easier for me to leave this surplus of form in Streuli's painting: why am I less subject to the need for interpretation when a huge photograph in neon blue promises me a flower that is so obviously not contained in this technical, cold typography?

Susann Wintsch

There are four pictures where the joy in nothing-but-form jumps right at me: Kloten, San Francisco, Hawaii, and Cairo (see pp. 272, 286, 280, 268). These are the least colorful pictures of the series. Here, the limited temporal duration of all action comes to light, it soon blurs, disintegrates, dissipates, or is bleached entirely. I'm touched by this sensibility for culture's fragility and transformation. Maybe the heterogeneous body of these travel pictures intends precisely that: they don't build bridges or try to grasp the specific characteristics of a foreign culture.

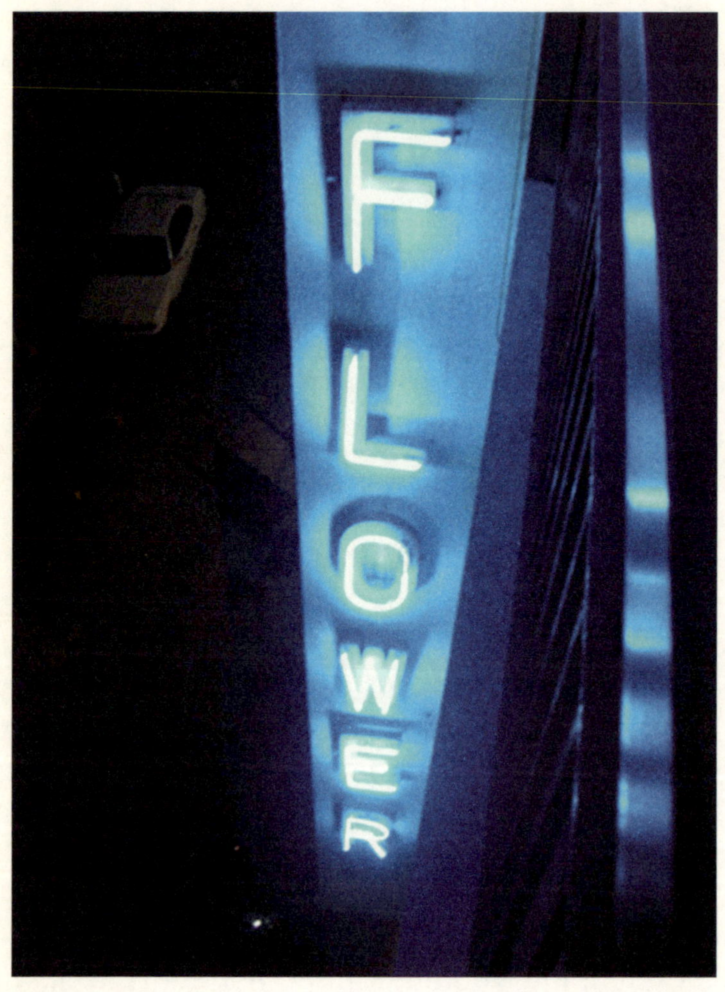
FLOWER

Indeed, they usually provide no insight at all about the precise location. They are basically fully decontextualized. Is this a radical, inwardly-turned reaction to the continuing failure of the West when it comes to observing other cultures?

Fanni Fetzer

The pictures you just mentioned are perhaps just the ones most obviously without context. For I think ultimately none of Streuli's travel photographs have a meaning in their location or time. Only the caption tells us where a photograph was taken or a picture was found; the images themselves betray precious little about that. If you ask whether this, let's call it void is a reaction to the Western observation of foreign cultures, aren't you assuming that we're talking about a consciously reflected strategy? That's not how I read these images. The term "travel photography" is perhaps misleading. While the photographs were taken while traveling, I'd doubt that they could not also have been created here, at home. When taking photographs, is Streuli not discovering things exotically alien in ourselves? In contrast to ethnology, which still often makes this mistake, the artist does not think she can actually capture the alien culture, know it, analyze it.

Categories like the alien and the familiar, the distant and the near I associate neither with Streuli's painting nor with her photography; a doily from her parent's house can find its way into her painting—as a stencil—just as easily as a piece of needlework from Cairo. I'd like to return once more to the fact that her photography strikes me, as someone viewing her painting, as a reading aid. That I can recognize in the photography a vocabulary, forms that also make it easier to decode the painting. Is that too banal or too subjective?

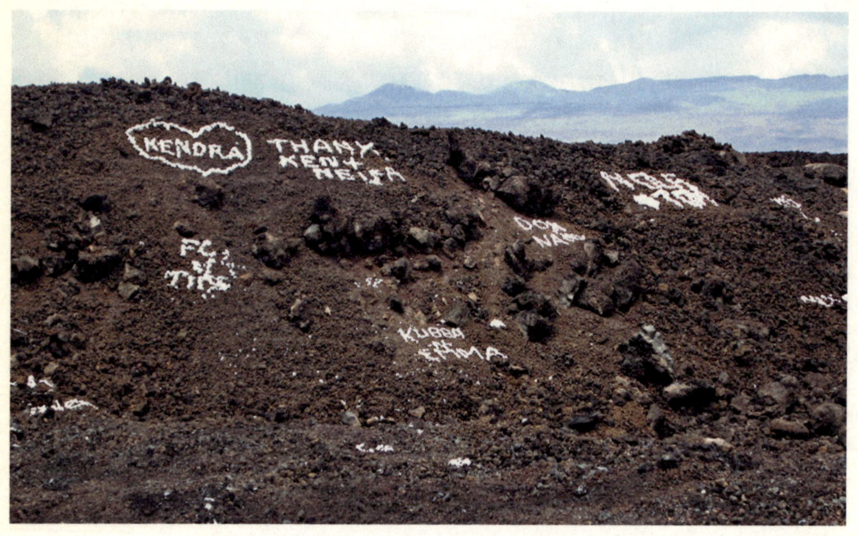
KENDRA

Roman Kurzmeyer
It is an instrumental way of seeing things, and to that extent relativizes the photographs as autonomous works. I also wouldn't call them travel photography. They are individual pictures taken on trips, and show this as well, but do not evoke travel itself. They attest to presence. They show how certain situations can seduce and captivate our gaze. Our perception is carefully guided. This concentration can be found in her painting as well. What I mean is that the photographs only open up the paintings to us in a very rudimentary sense. They are quite concrete and not fictional; to that extent they are perhaps programmatic works.

Susann Wintsch
I think the photographs without a context are particularly important, for they show the focal distance of the (photographic) gaze. As the titles show, they always refer to travel. But if they are not supposed to be anything but reading aids, I would be caught in the small world of a painting, it would mean consenting to an incestuous representation of the world. What would be the point of only looking for the foreign in the familiar? A purely formalistic interpretation of Streuli's images implies an apolitical and ultimately inhuman view of things. I would have to take Roman's worries about reduction yet a step further, for the photographs *have* to illustrate an autonomous aesthetic, for each image is explicitly searching for the other, even if on first glance it seems to reflect the familiar. The interesting thing is precisely that here a view of the other is being directed that in a very general way tells of the existential fragility of human traces, regardless of where they are.

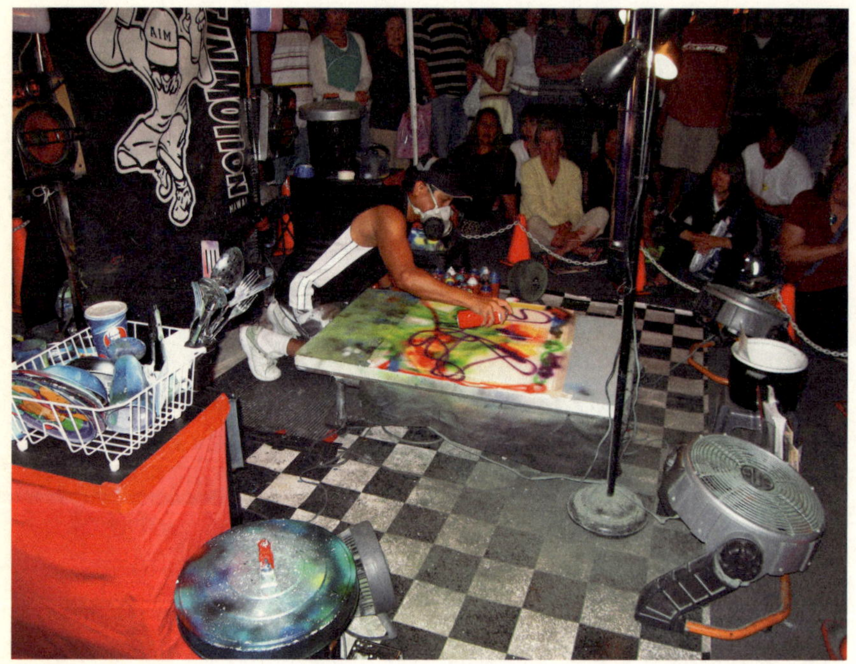
AIM

Fanni Fetzer
I don't really see the photographs as just evidence for a sensitive being human or participation in a fragmentary existence. And it's not so much the statement there that bothers me, but maybe the vocabulary. To me its sounds a bit too general, and perhaps too charged with pathos. I don't think it's incestuous or apolitical if the photographs report primarily of Streuli's view of reality and thus don't explore any other aspects of cultural critique. But now I'm coming to a point that we won't be able to solve in our conversation: I'd like to know what the artist herself has to say about her photography. The most impressive example of this kind that I know is Claude Simon, who collated a series of images from his archive to cover forty pages of a culture magazine, giving each image a caption. Since in his literary work, the description of images is a central issue, the photographs selected truly communicate his point of view due to the lines of text. But I like that: it is an invitation to get to know another person, and to not remain imprisoned in oneself as a beholder.

Roman Kurzmeyer
At least we know that Streuli never before published or exhibited her photography, and that it was her idea to contextualize the painting with these photographs. This self-image is at issue. One aspect of the artist's image of herself is that nature is of almost no importance. An exception is the photograph of Cairo after a sandstorm. But here as well, Streuli shows the city, and not the desert. They are cultural images. The specific thing here is the emphatic gaze on images that are reminiscent of art, and the compilation of individual, pictorial acts without any artistic intention. But what happens when we

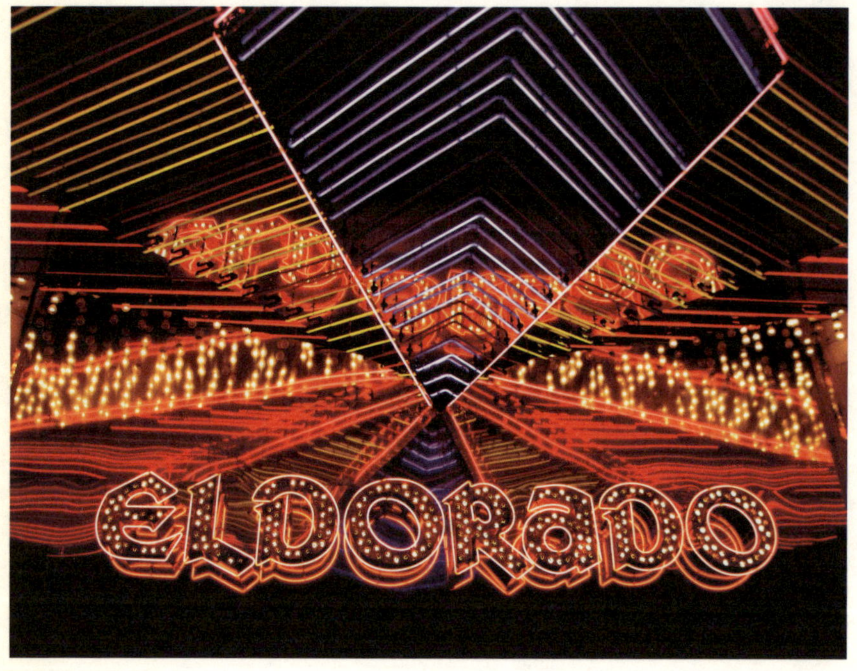
ELDORADO

get to the painting? What is Streuli's interest in the ornamental, the pattern, the imprint? Would it be wrong to say that Streuli here too is looking for the surprise evoked by the unexpected image, that an according number of steps take place intentionlessly and the density of the painted surfaces is the result of an unpredictable, albeit clearly structured process, where as I see it the development cannot be understood after the fact in looking at the individual picture?

Fanni Fetzer

I know from talking with the artist that her painting develops between intention and coincidence. A lot is planned, foreseen, arranged; but perhaps an equal amount she just allows to happen. Can it be that in her photography she is in a way directing our gaze towards this coincidental aspect of her work? That she discovers in reality what happened to her in the studio—and then takes a picture of it? As a beholder I can discover just as much in these photographs as the artist herself. In contrast to painting, where the artist knows more and can see more than the beholder.

Roman Kurzmeyer

But can the artist really see more? She knows more, of course, in particular she knows how the paintings were put together and went through each individual step. We need to envision this process: she cut stencils and stamps, dyed them, and transferred the representations by hand to the support. She applied them layer by layer, in so doing only in part covering layers of paint, again and again observing the work lying on the floor, and slowly generated a visual space that is quite a bit more complex and artificial that that of her photography. This is due to the

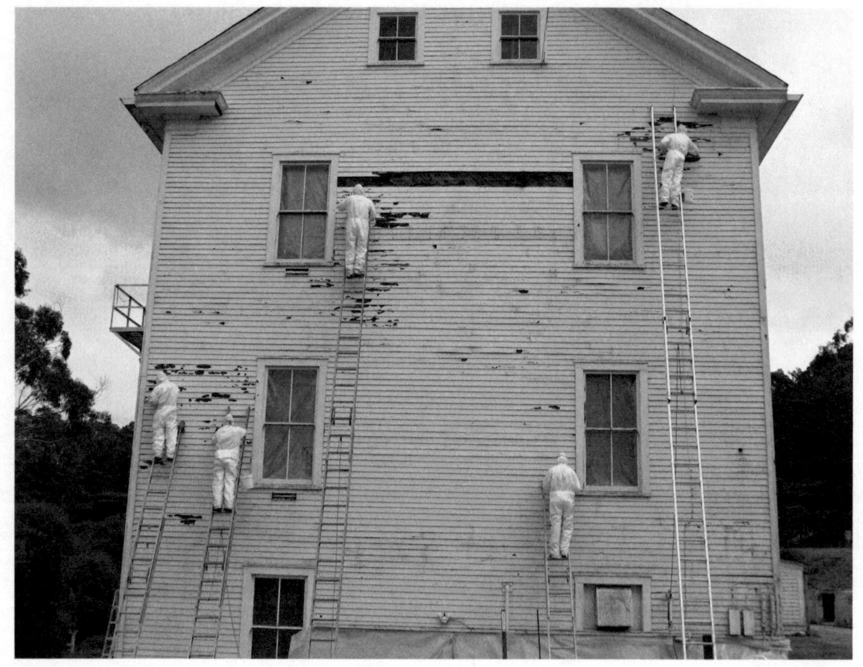

entirely different technique used here: her paintings are reminiscent of collages. When looking at the painting, the artist does not have the upper hand, for in contrast to the situative, pictorial photographs, that communicate a *single* perceived and reportable moment, the paintings tell of a great deal at the same time, and in different languages. The painting is like a resonance space of the technique that produced it. That's what interests me about it. To return once again to the relationship between photography and painting: wouldn't we have to ask whether Streuli approaches painting from photography, by using matrices, stencils, and printing blocks instead of painting with the brush?

Fanni Fetzer
The proximity to collage you mention is obvious. But I see photography as less important for her work than other techniques she uses in her painting. Are you proposing this simply because she rarely uses a brush for her paintings?

Roman Kurzmeyer
Niele Toroni works with the imprint of the brush. The brush is not just an instrument to represent a figure. It represents itself, depicts itself. When I ask whether Streuli brings painting in connection to photography, and I mention collage, then I am referring to the mimetic characteristics of her painting. What I see is perhaps fictional as an image. But in the modes of representation chosen by the artist, the real is highly present in her painting as well as in her photography.

Fanni Fetzer
Surprisingly, we can recognize in all her photographs what is depicted—the images ultimately retain their

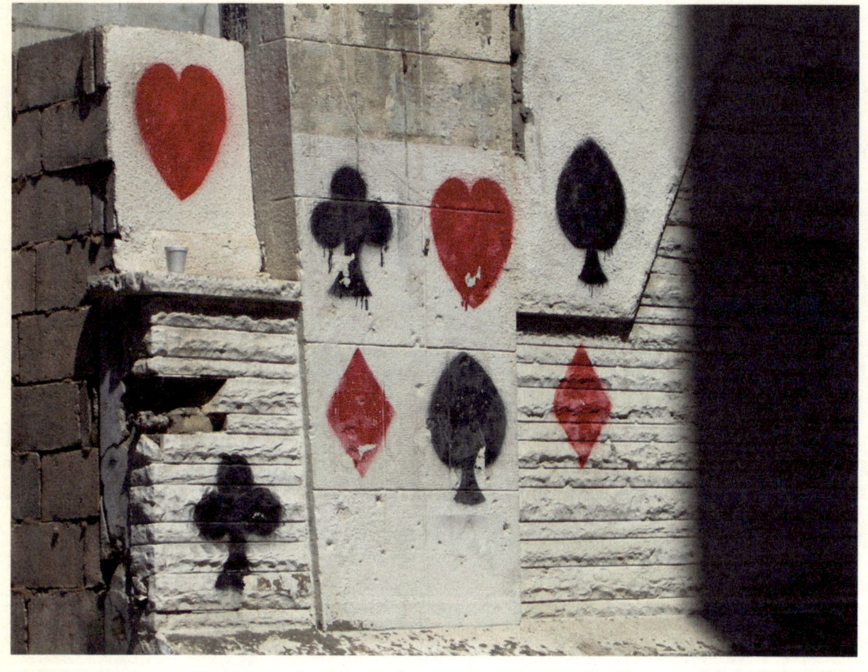

documentary character. All the same, I'd like to emphasize the complexity of her painting, and be more precise about something I said earlier: it the artist does not necessarily recognize more in her finished painting than the beholder, she does know how she made the image. In her photography, in contrast, she seems to have come to her subject just as freely, as suddenly as we have. The artist once told me that she often discovers her photographic subjects after developing the film. Out of all the photographs taken, a few stick out that seem to be more than just touristy. What then could the photographs be in relationship to painting? I see in the photographs that I share with the artist an experience of vision, and of course recall that when looking at her painting.

Susann Wintsch
Ornamentation in Streuli's painting creates an unbelievable density. Ornaments are lovely, but also oppressive. As soon as one enters this visual world, there is no escape from their beauty. It seems to be about this tension. The photographs are different; here the harmonies are constructed and taken apart, the compositional structures are coincidental, fragmentary, and fragile, most beautiful when they inscribe the first compositions in nothingness, as a metaphor for culture.

Roman Kurzmeyer
Metaphor for culture?

Susann Wintsch
If we don't assume that the photographs are reading aids, where all forms become ornament, if the piles of earth are simply raw piles of earth where humanity all the same has placed its ritual or sentimental compositions, it is as

if civilization were just being invented. The facade repair in San Francisco is also this kind of mental game, just as is the sandstorm in Cairo, even if these images argue from opposite sides: nature erodes, civilization as well, and ideally our brain as well. Robert Smithson spoke of the deposits of gritty reason, that is, the desire to subject everything to process, simply because that's nature's way. In Streuli's photography, the opposite is also explored, for example in Reno (see p. 284), which is paved entirely with ornamentation and rules. Comparing Reno and Hawaii (see p. 280) with one another is quite interesting. They are related, if we see the two as landscapes, and yet describe opposite poles, since they present a decadent fullness and an almost-nothingness in opposition to one another. Between the two lie all the gaps and fissures that Streuli observes in her surroundings that emerge in the unintentional nature of her photography and in the stylized composition of her painting.

2003
Ken Johnson
The New York Times

"[...] with playful freedom, Christine Streuli pours, smears, glazes and brushes, producing abstract paintings that are materially and optically captivating."

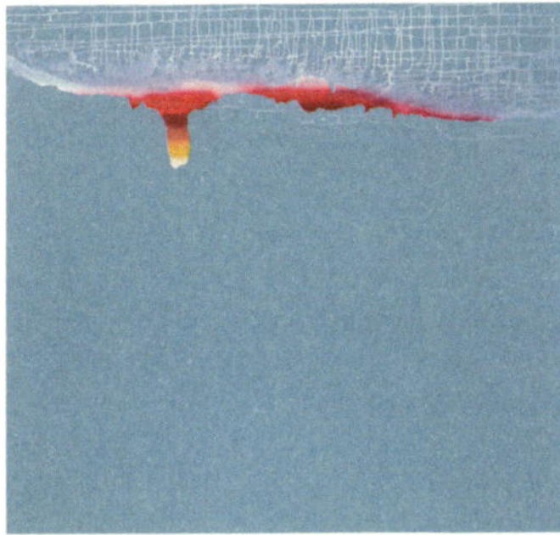

Delta, 2003

2003
Etienne Lullin
unpublished lecture

"The artist does not exclusively confine herself to the rectangular canvas in her method of working. At times, she goes beyond this limiting picture medium and applies paint, modeling clay, or adhesive film directly to the wall, thus addressing the spatial, site-specific situation and creating relations of tension. Often layered coats of paint can be discerned in her work, creating a spatiality and bearing witness to her profound understanding of space."

2003
Angelika Affentranger-Kirchrath
Neue Zürcher Zeitung

"The pictures of the young [...] Zurich-based artist Christine Streuli reveal a strong painterly impetus. Painting appears here as a joyous act. At the same time, nothing is left to chance, as can be deduced from her precise choice of titles. They neither offer explanations nor illustrate, but instead open up new modalities of vision and thought for the picture in question. Some works have something palimpsest-like about them. Areas painted two-dimensionally are partially covered by thick traces of varnish. Repeatedly, expanding grid and pixel fields can be seen, rendering the picture fields enigmatic."

2004
Beat Wismer
Cahier d'artiste

"The artist likes to draw, and through drawing moves ever closer—groping, questioning, experimenting—to the world outside and inside herself. It is a very open activity, without parameters and as yet hardly pictorial. Streuli's drawing is more of a process, open in all directions, of finding and assimilating images: the drawings, which also include numerous superimpositions on found visual material (pictures from newspapers etc.), are probably important for determining her own stock of images, but rarely become direct studies for paintings. Often they bear no title—by way of exception, one may be called 'my meager belongings'—whereas the painted pictures, whether small or large, rarely remain untitled: the artist's very deliberate choice of titles is a significant part of her work. These titles function neither as descriptions nor illustrations of the pictorial evidence; but they do succeed in putting a specific spin on the reading of the paintings."

2004
Bruno Steiger
Tages-Anzeiger

"It is precisely in her avoiding a personal, characteristic mode that stylistic features of Streuli's art can be made out. 'I aim for the opposite of recognizability,' the artist confirms; underlying this is the search for a style of painting that reestablishes its legitimacy with each individual picture, the 'search for valid images.'"

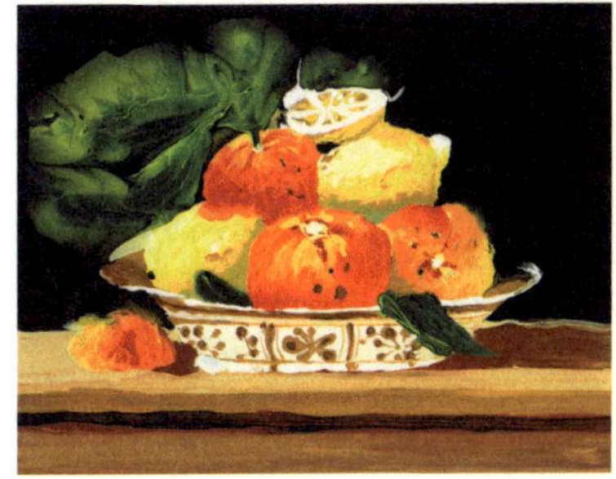

Zitrusfrüchte in Porzellanschale, 2004

2005
Thomas Kliemann
General-Anzeiger

"*Jackpot*, a picture that appears to incessantly hurl new elements from the background to the fore: bizarre ornaments, spheres, organic color structures. Such a disturbing and exciting 'painting as a latent place in which the images are suspended' (Beat Wismer) has never before been seen."

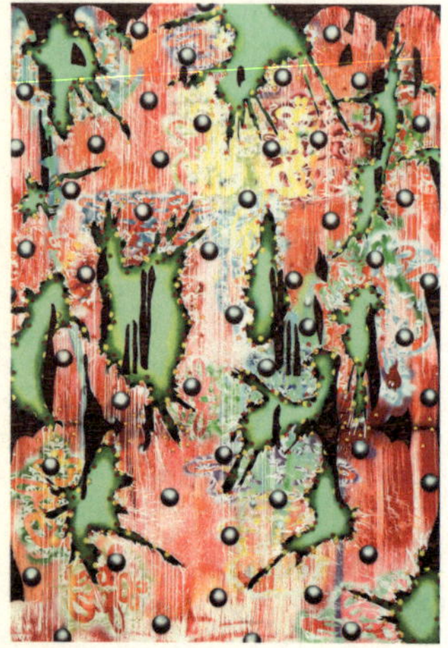

Jackpot, 2004

2005
Angelika Affentranger-Kirchrath
Neue Zürcher Zeitung

"In Streuli's works, the titles play a crucial role. As a name does for a child, the title makes the picture personally identifiable, it expands or specifies its content. [...] Streuli occasionally puts a painting she has begun aside to work on another one for a while. This readiness to distance herself creates room for conceptual decisions. Nevertheless, each work results from an own, specific impetus, it possesses its own validity, its own distinctive name."

2005
Dolores Denaro / Toni Stooss
Junge Schweizer Kunst

"Regarding the complicated discourse revolving around abstract painting, Christine Streuli [...] finds her own, characteristic position in painting between an *informel* style and pop culture in the contrastive and at once seamless connection between different painterly means of expression. The result is a blithely eventful pop loop shining in many colors on a toned gestural ground that reflects the history of the *informel*."

2005
Roman Kurzmeyer
Junge Schweizer Kunst

"By reproducing her brush strokes, paint drops, lines, or figures, instead of freshly applying them, Streuli arouses in the beholder a heightened attention for what is taking place in the painting and how. The individual picture reveals the way it was produced. The artist strengthens the autonomy of the painted picture and simultaneously refers to the artistic practice in the studio in each of her works."

2005
Anne-Ev Ustorf
Szene Hamburg

"Some artists can always be recognized by their artistic 'signature.' In the case of Christine Streuli, this would be difficult, because the Swiss artist, born in 1975, is entirely without inhibitions in regard to questions of style. Her large-format paintings are so varied that one often has the impression of looking at works created by different artists.. [...] Stays abroad appear to give the artist important stimuli. A stipend in Cairo resulted in large-format paintings with Oriental ornaments, a stay in New York led to a flood of strictly geometric patterns [...]. Even if it seems at first glance that Christine Streuli doesn't relate stories in her pictures and possibly chooses to avoid artistic determination through her great variety of styles, her patterns, structures and ornaments do impart to the viewer quite a bit about her influences and experiences."

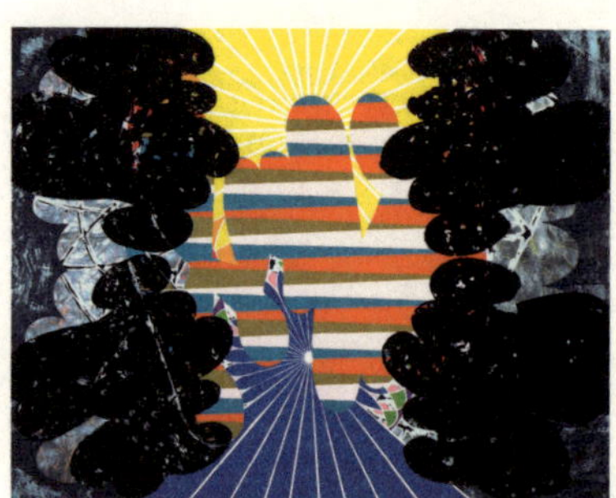

Radar, 2005

2005
Christine Streuli / Edgar Davidian
L'Orient-Le Jour

"'To start with, we need to clarify a misunderstanding that I am not an abstract painter,' she states, 'because eventually it is always a story about painting and not one of objects to be painted. As I work a lot with industrial varnish, my paintings are often 'glossy' and, as a consequence, everything is possible...' [...] And how does she define her painting? 'I do not permit myself to define a painter, but painting is a field of research... I look for different forms... how to transform these into something else by means of painting... It is like writing a poem or a letter; however I do this with colors. It is an exploration of materials, of colors. The ornamental or decorative aspect is not my objective. Above all, I am interested in displaying a picture as a painting. I am a painter and not a designer. I consider my works as a fantasy which says something. I do not like it that people see a specific thing in my work. I do not want them to have some kind of certainty in what they see, and would rather that they have an open door to numerous interpretations...'"

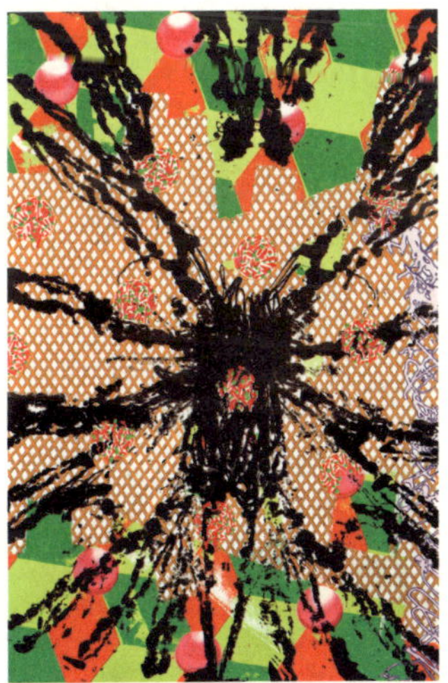

Humpty, 2005

2005
Dina Eppelbaum
Global City—Global Art?

"For Streuli, the appeal of painting lies in merging the creative processes that are applied unconventionally and in opposition to established practice. [...] It is not possible to classify Streuli's painting with any precision. Her pictures can evoke landscapes and urban environments as well as switching into an abstract idiom, or comprise both elements simultaneously."

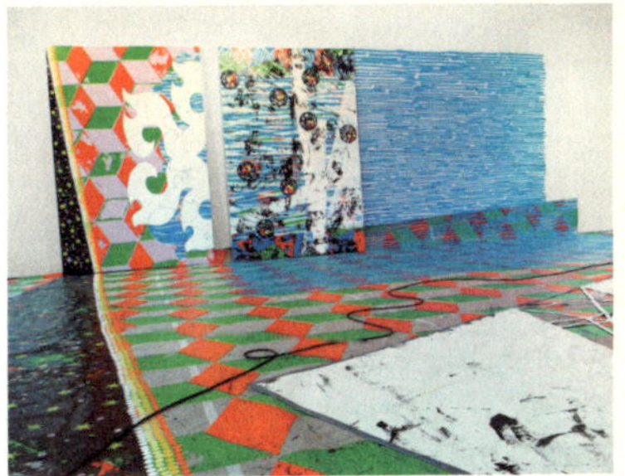

Ensemble Ensemble, 2005

2005
Beat Wismer
Dorothea von Stetten-Kunstpreis

"It only seems as if the artist applies the manual technique of painting without raising questions, in her 'search for the valid picture' (as the writer Bruno Steiger has aptly described Streuli's ambition); but anyone willing to attentively regard these paintings is indeed faced with fundamental questions of painting. Just like the artist, in front of and for each picture, evidently searches for a legitimization for its creation in painting and as painting." [ ] "Strikingly often, the figures in the pictures are arranged symmetrically: The blot or blob is often the picture's point of departure [...]. However, the originally accidental nature of the blot is strongly formalized: Streuli transfers such pictorial elements to templates, she saws the drawings out of wood with a fretsaw and uses this template to apply the figurations to the canvas. Or she works with found shapes and patterns out of which she makes templates and uses them as such. What takes place in the pictures is often developed by way of the detour of such self-produced aids that function as tools, so to say, to create her pictures: with these predetermined aids, she eludes the demands or temptations of free composition—something she mistrusts."

2005
Elio Schenini
Sentieri e avvistamenti

"The diatribe between abstraction and figuration, whose wake of polemics and counterpoints was etched on the entire twentieth century, in Christine Streuli's works seems a dusty matter without further reason to exist. In fact, the artist passes freely from replications of seventeenth century still lifes to reproductions of random areas of color on a canvas, similar to a Rorschach-test. And even the idea of style, which for so long represented the yardstick for measuring the worth of an artist, is continually contradicted by the artist, convinced that each painting is a visualization of a pictorial idea which calls for different solutions each time."

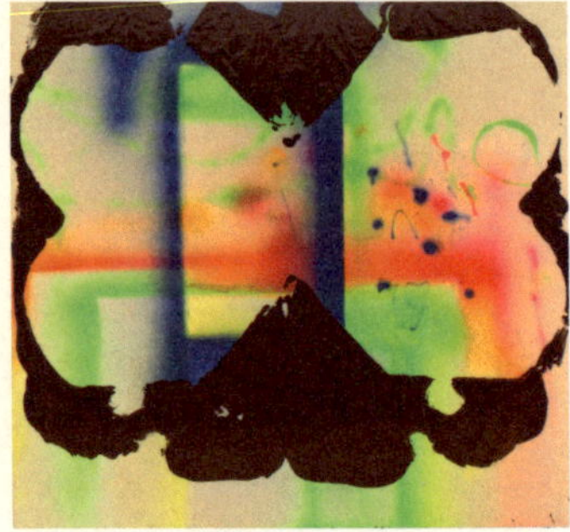

Faltblatt, 2005

2006
Bruno Steiger
Du

"In *Jackpot*, the dripping and hurling of action painting is at once carried to its extreme and broken through. In many different subtle masses of order, the artist would like to suggest that the whole thing is intentional and could not be at all different. She thus places 'contingency' in all meanings of the notion up for debate; in the end, chance as well as calculation prove to be uncontrollable variants of pictorial joy—not to say artistic pain. In the midst of the green blots occupying their space by bursting, the quietly vibrating grid of spheres attains a structuring function. In the dispersion of spheres, as arbitrary as it is balanced, this order is also to be seen as an extra, maybe even as a bluff. The truly stabilizing element of the arrangement consists in the discrete internal symmetries that can be discerned after looking at the picture for a while."

2006
Stefania Meazza
Segno

"Christine Streuli [...] who, using different pictorial techniques, especially acrylic and lacquer painting, is able to create pictorial compositions that reach to abstraction. Multiple levels and different *textures* merge, going from rhythmical and symmetrical shapes with an oriental touch, through paint running, reminding us of the *dripping* style, to virtual pixellated images. It is a new way of interpreting contemporary painting, where different ideas are put into practice with clear sensitivity and a post-modern feeling."

2006
Madeleine Schuppli
Bumblebee

"Symmetry is one of the compositional strategies that run through Streuli's works. Her paintings are closely related to one another; one work builds upon the next; an artistic experiment is given another chance in the next painting. In this way the artist explores the possibilities of mirroring, and each time the process ends differently. What is interesting here is that the symmetrical pictorial elements each contain reminiscences of various graphic and craft techniques which can be found in different cultures."

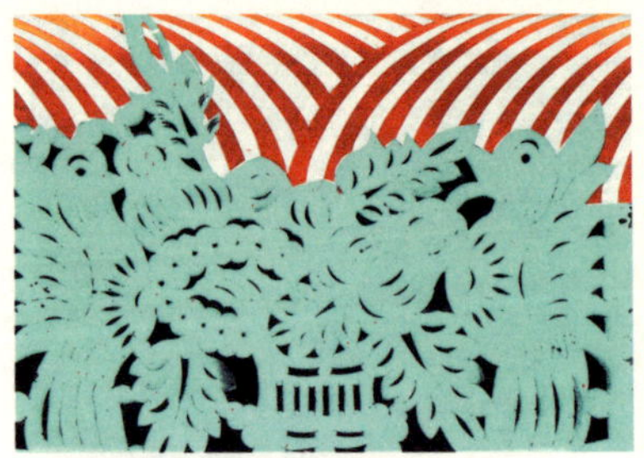

La Rondella, 2006

2006
Roman Kurzmeyer
Bumblebee

"Everything about Streuli's paintings can be perceived visually and yet they do not transfer themselves to the viewer as pictorial formulas but as vehicles for emotion. Together with their literary titles, temperature, speed and space are decisive factors in the quality of the aesthetic experience. Although, like many artists in post-war Western society since Rauschenberg, Streuli multiplies, staggers and mixes up the pictorial levels, her paintings contain no fragments of reality. Her work neither uses nor quotes silk-screens or photographs, although she also works with various graphic techniques in order to produce her pictures. But these works are based on elementary means of artistic portrayal such as lines, surfaces, dots, grids and ornaments, i.e., on non-representational shapes; shapes

Streuli does not, however actually use, but demonstrate in luscious, strong colors."

2006
Isabel Zürcher
Bumblebee

"Taking her inspiration from the iconography of Baroque still lifes or historical arabesques in graphics and architecture, Streuli avails herself of a vocabulary handed to her by tradition. And she is quite happy to re-orchestrate this vocabulary, preparing the insistent presence of the seventeenth-century still life objects in a new way, using the artificial colors of fresh paint, taking unabashed pleasure in the sensuality of flowing paint and getting lost in it. Her way of combining patterns and their reflections, ornamental details and their duplication echoes those of carpets and wallpaper or even the repeat pattern of printed fabrics." [...] "The outcome of Streuli's concentrated alertness is a body of work that leaves behind it not only the dogmatic differentiation between figuration and abstraction but also that polarity occasionally highlighted in current discourse between a self-referential artistic practice and one that relates to the social present. A connoisseur both of present-day tendencies and of the history of painting, she empathically corrects hastily formulated simplifications: 'The reason why contemporary painting interests me so very much is that for some years now people have been going in an unbelievably large number of different directions. I don't believe the idea that 'autonomous', 'self-referential' painting has got nothing to do with society and nothing to do with politics or interest in culture in a wider sense. Or vice versa, that figurative painting necessarily and automatically references the reality 'outside' the canvas. So actually, all that really interests me about this debate is a specific piece of work, of painting.'"

Further reading

Christine Streuli—Cahier d'artiste, with a text by Beat Wismer, Zurich: Pro Helvetia, 2004.

Yael Bartana, Christiane Baumgartner, Benjamin Bergmann, Christian Hahn, Christine Streuli. Dorothea von Stetten-Kunstpreis 2004, exhibition catalog, Bonn: Kunstmuseum Bonn, 2005.

Christine Streuli—Bumblebee, Nuremberg: Verlag für moderne Kunst Nürnberg, 2006.

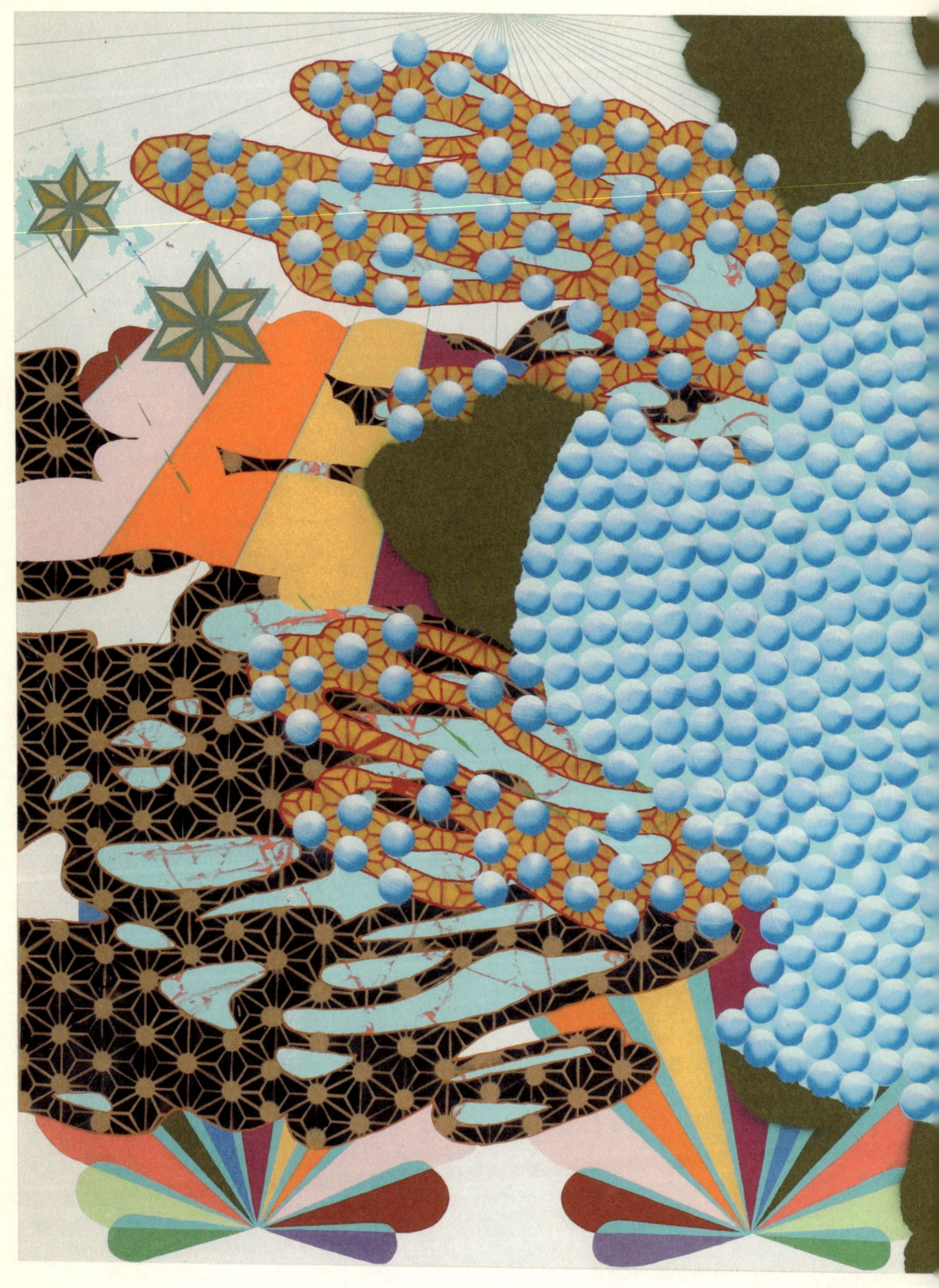

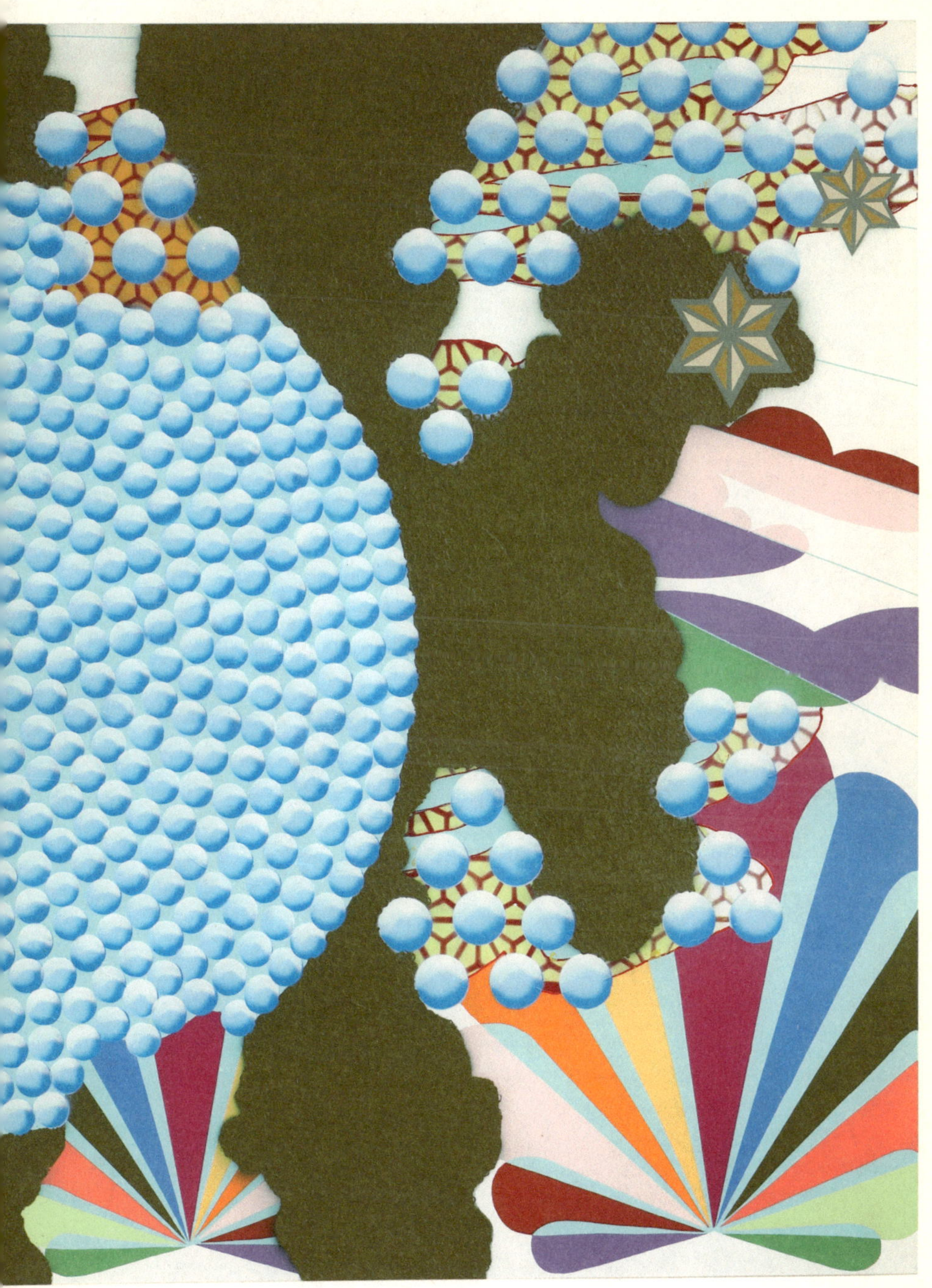

Closer, 2007
Acrylic and enamel on cotton
240×380 cm

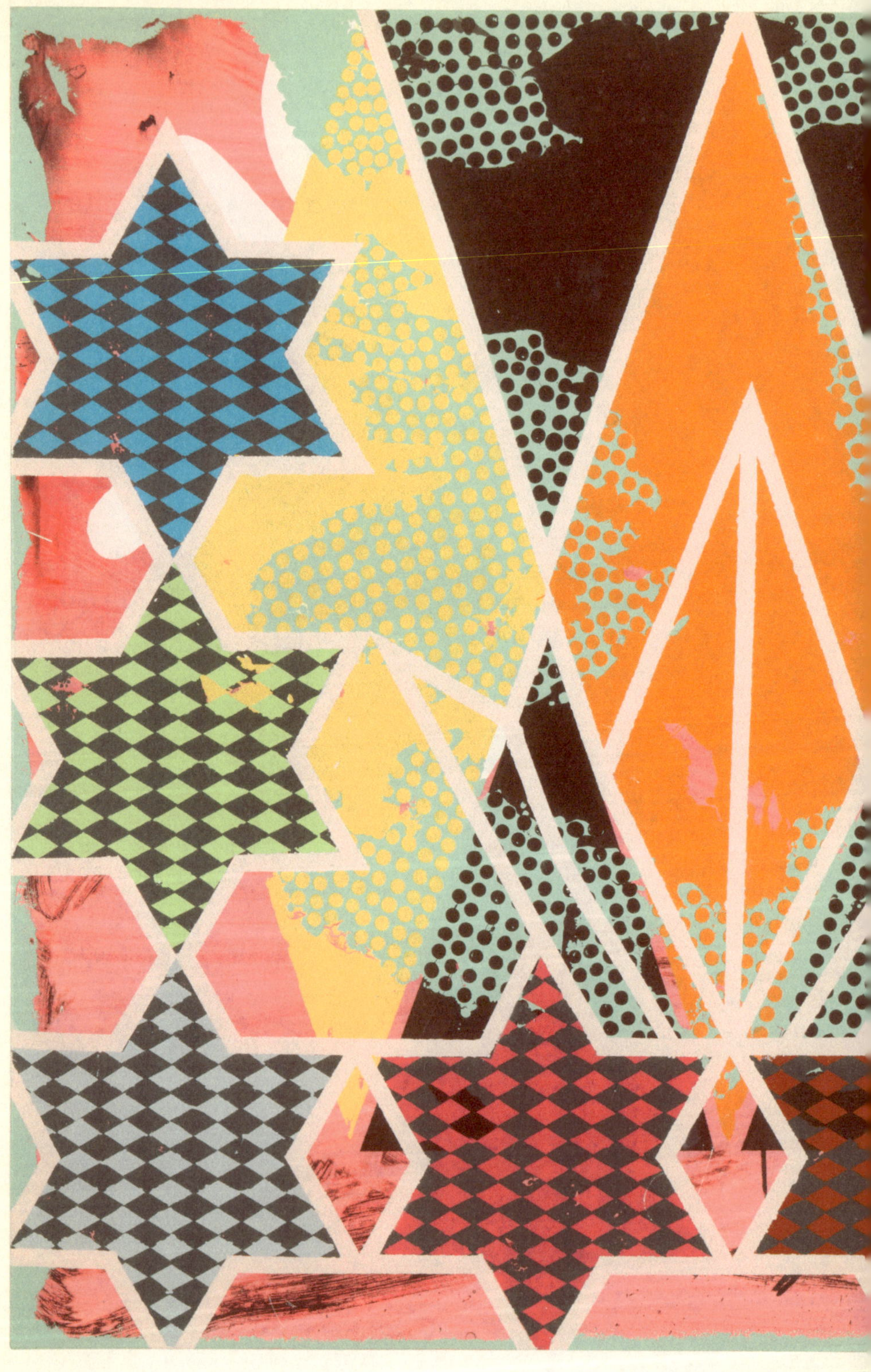

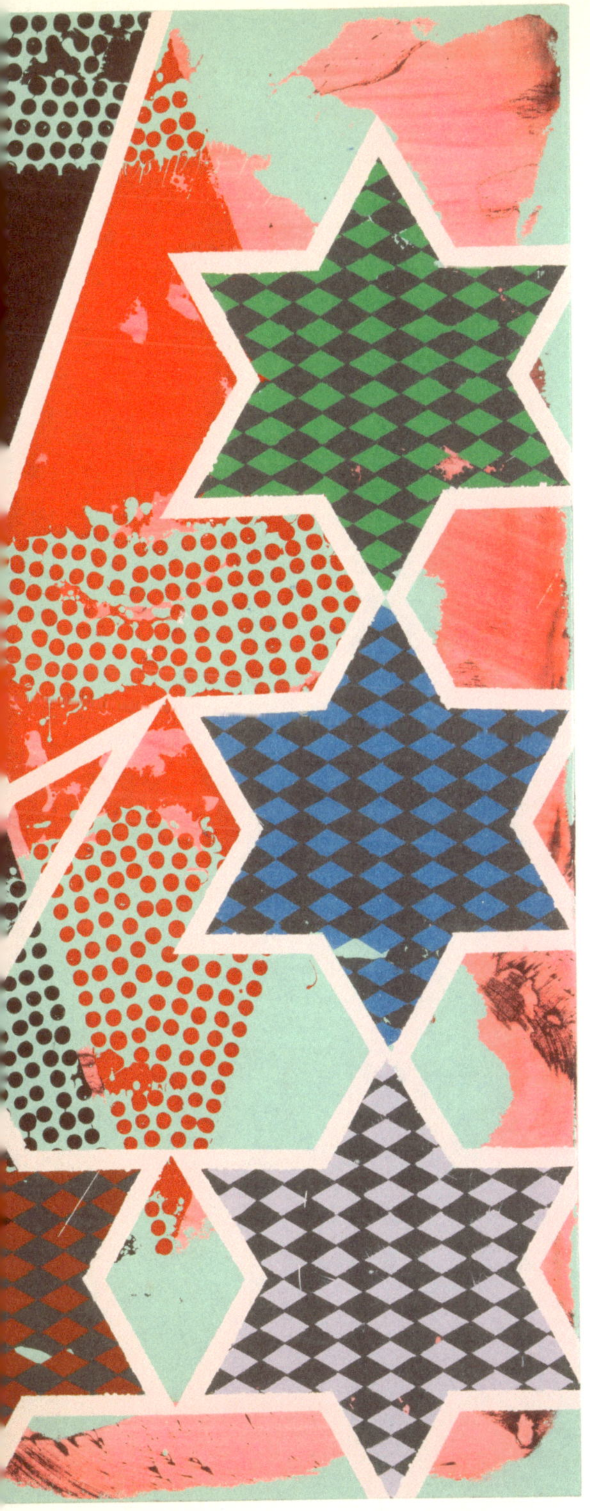

Krone, 2007
Acrylic and
enamel on cotton
120 × 140 cm

Spielhaus, 2007
Acrylic and
enamel on cotton
371×286 cm

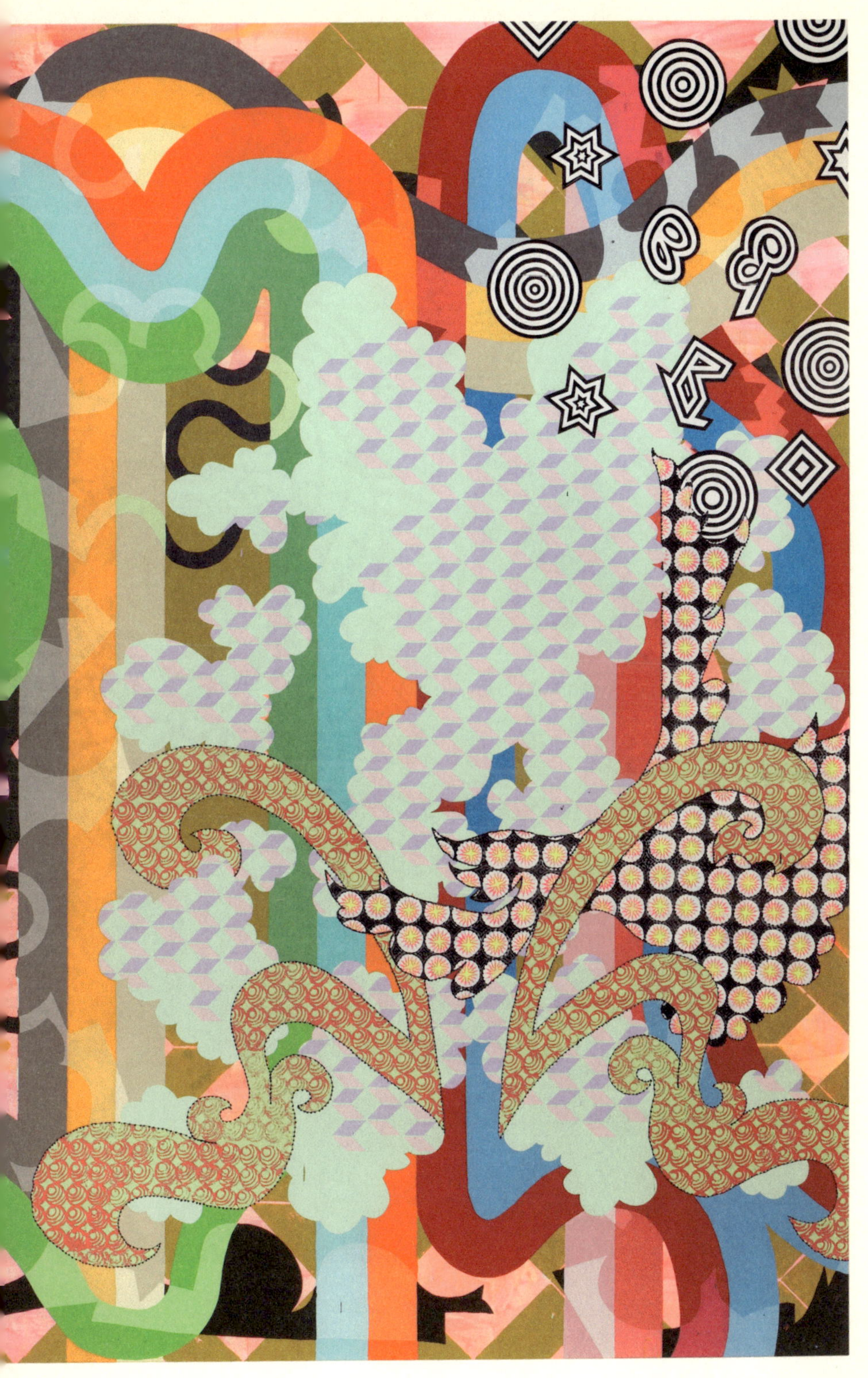

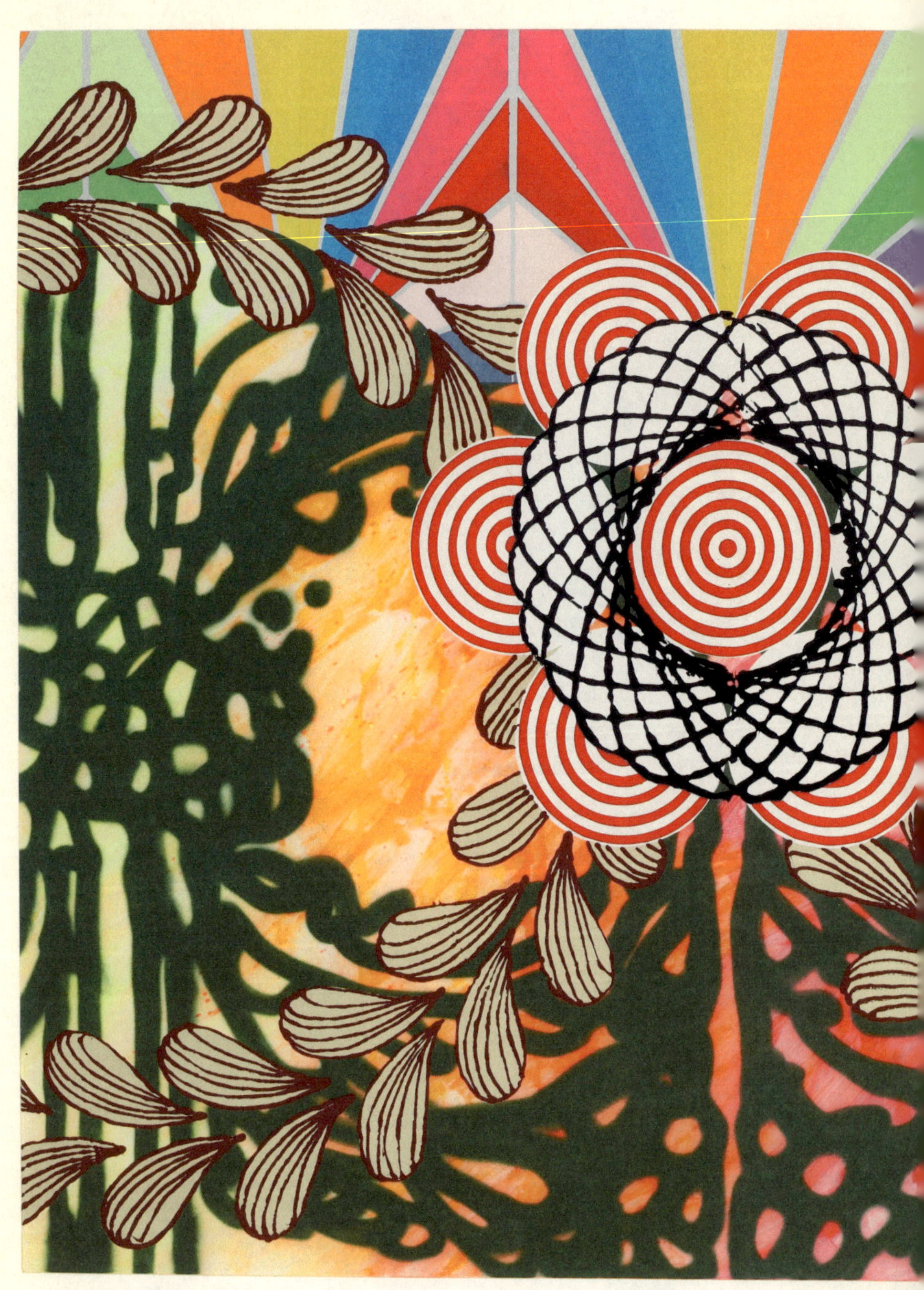

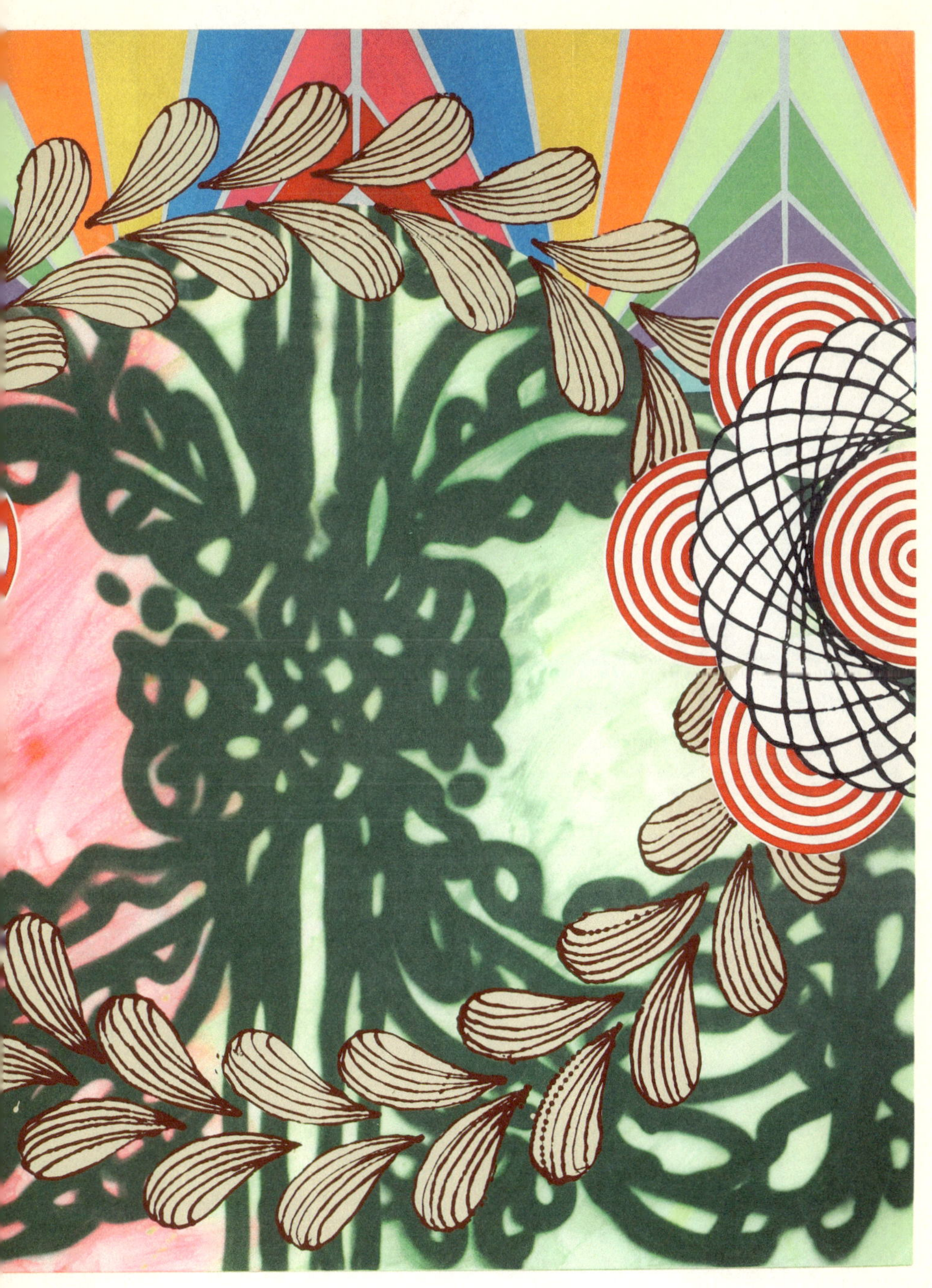

Neu_Rose, 2007
Acrylic and enamel on cotton
250×400 cm

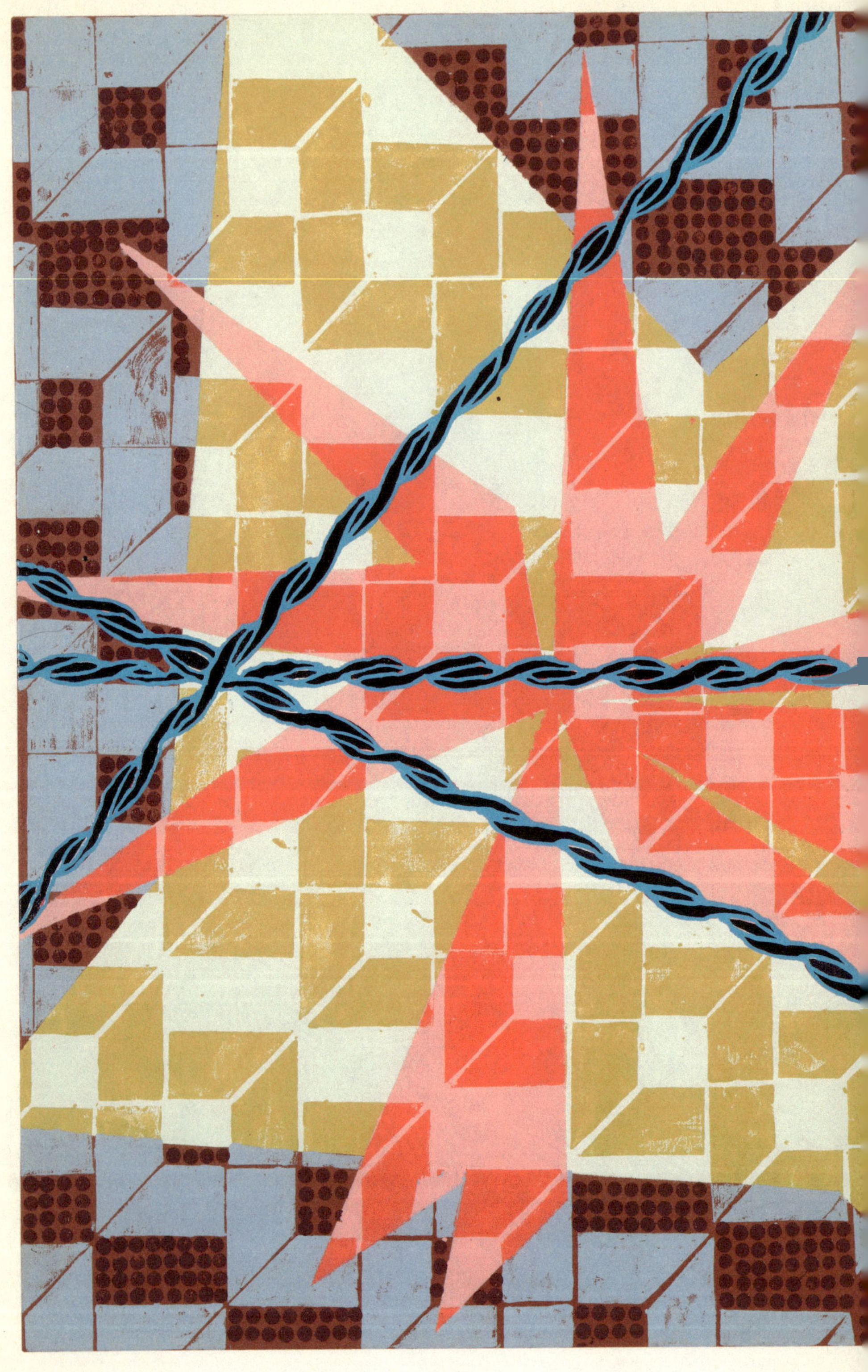

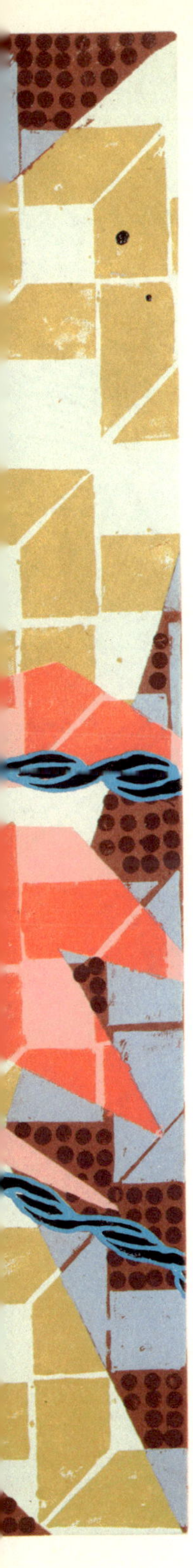

Strick, 2007
Acrylic and
enamel on cotton
140 × 120 cm

next page
Go North, Go South,
Go East, Go West, 2007
Acrylic and
enamel on cotton
286 × 371 cm

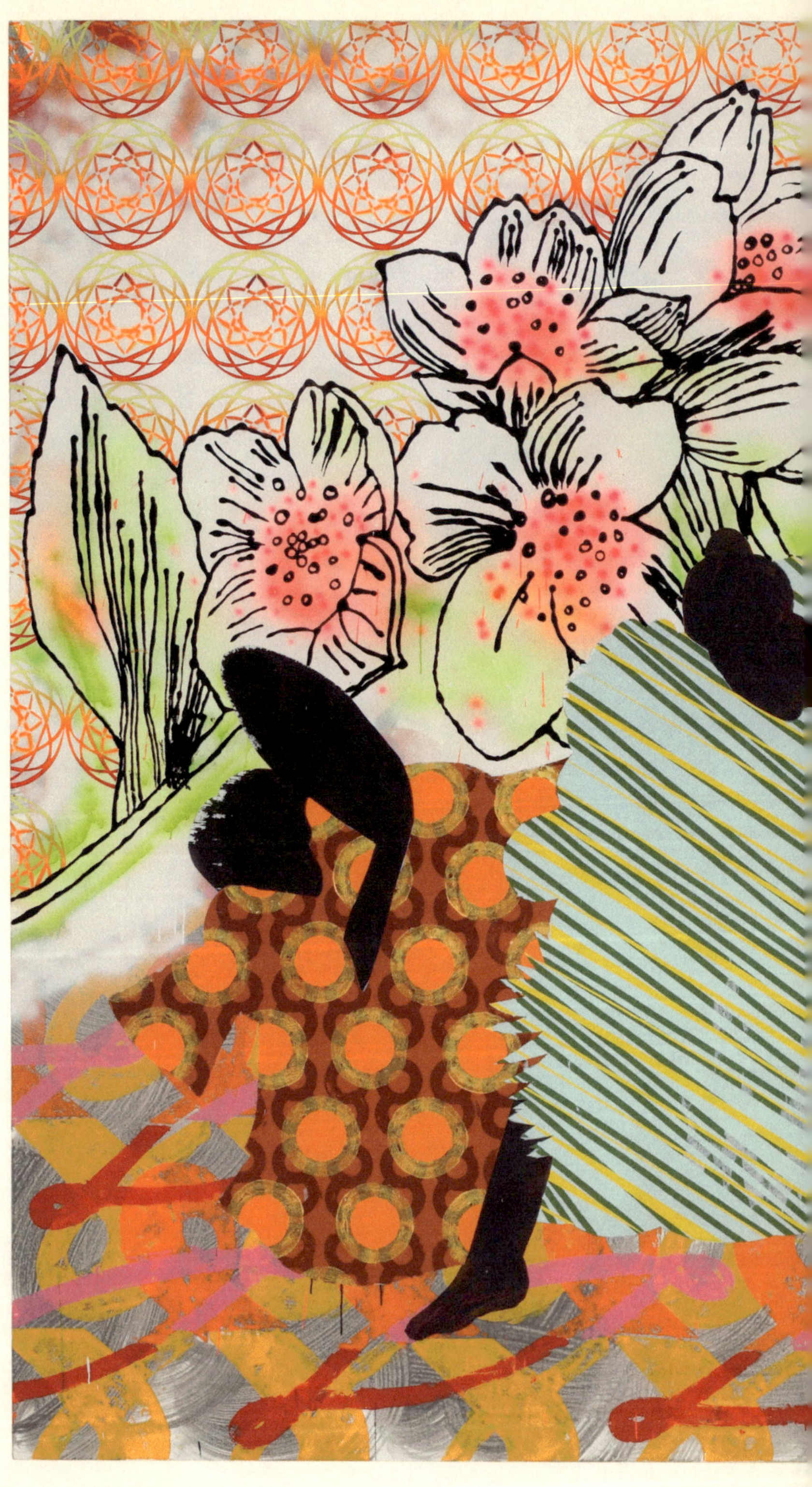

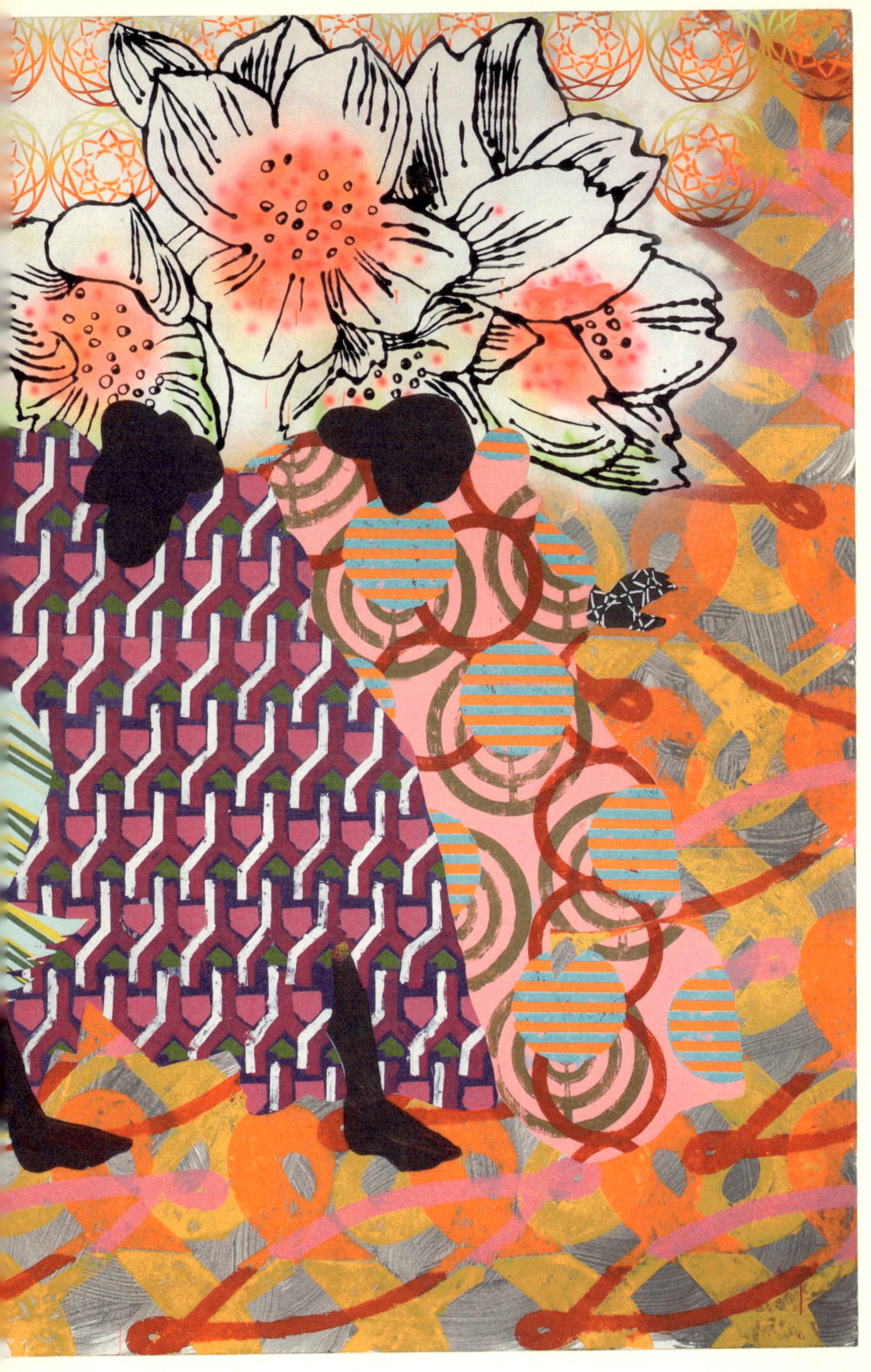

Vierzählig, 2007
Acrylic and
enamel on cotton
120 × 100 cm

next page
Z-Off, 2007
Acrylic and
enamel on cotton
286 × 371 cm

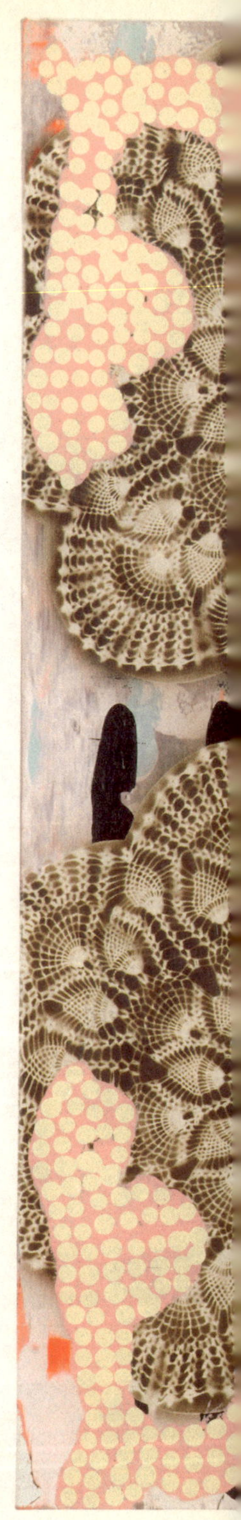

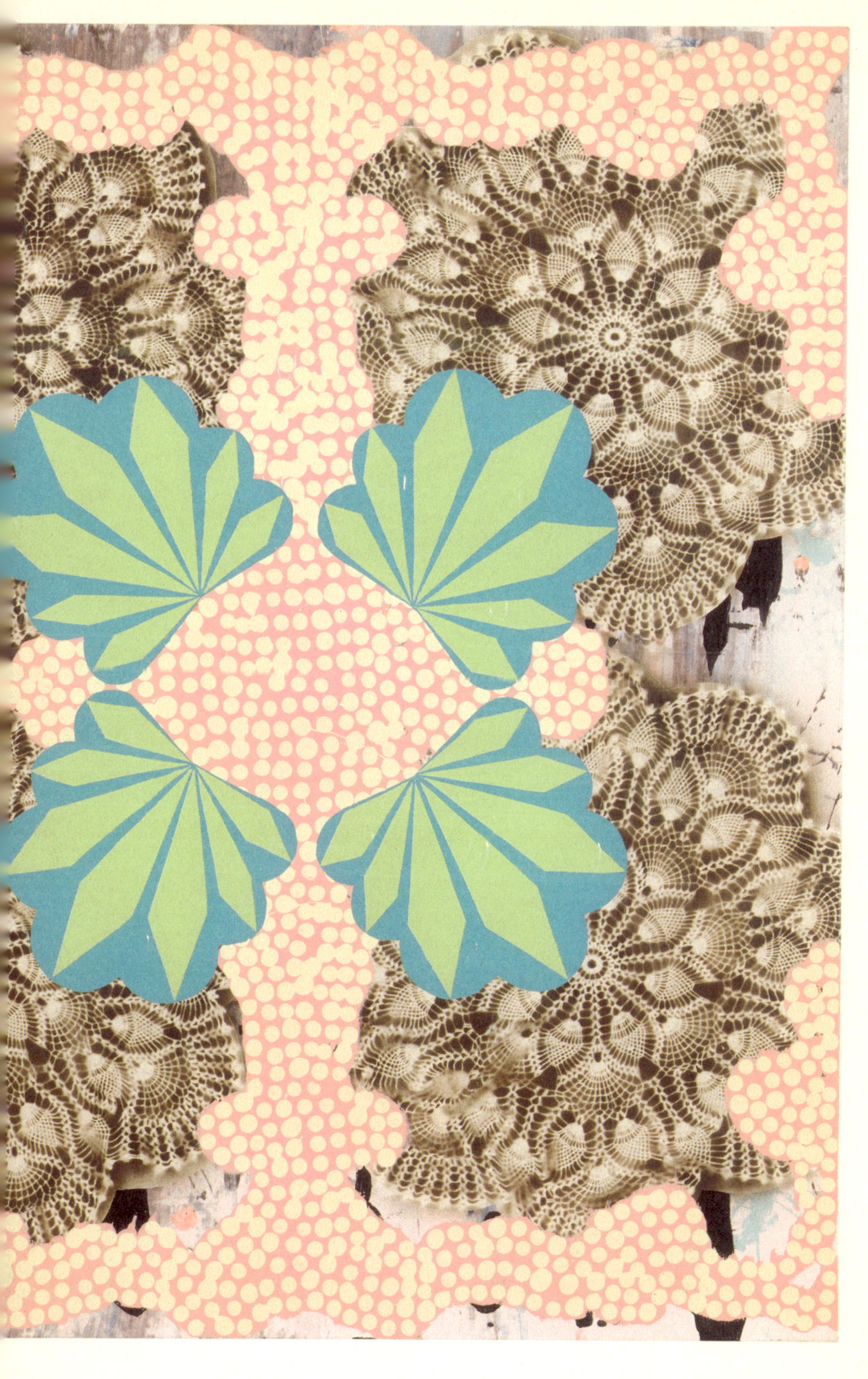

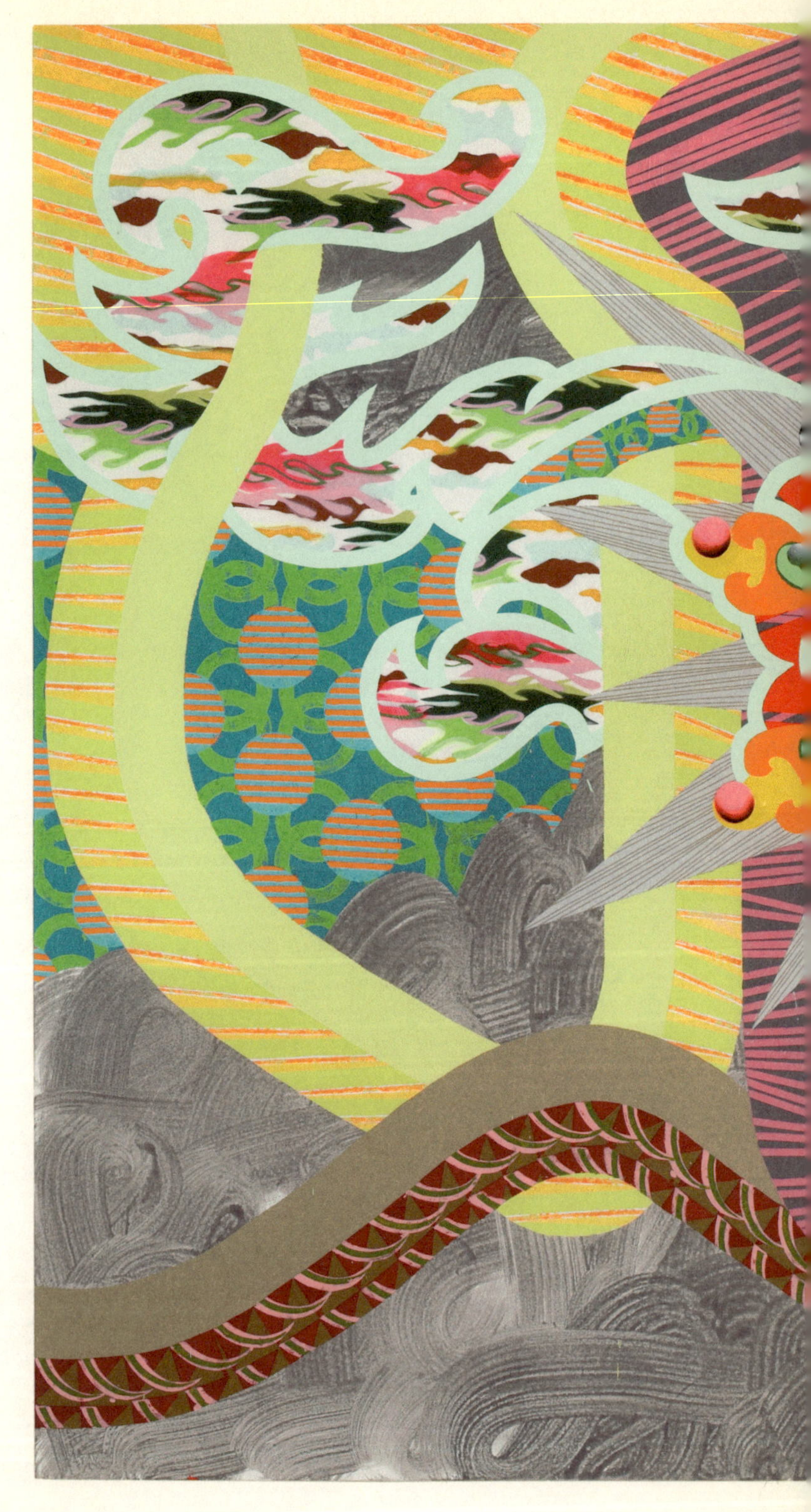

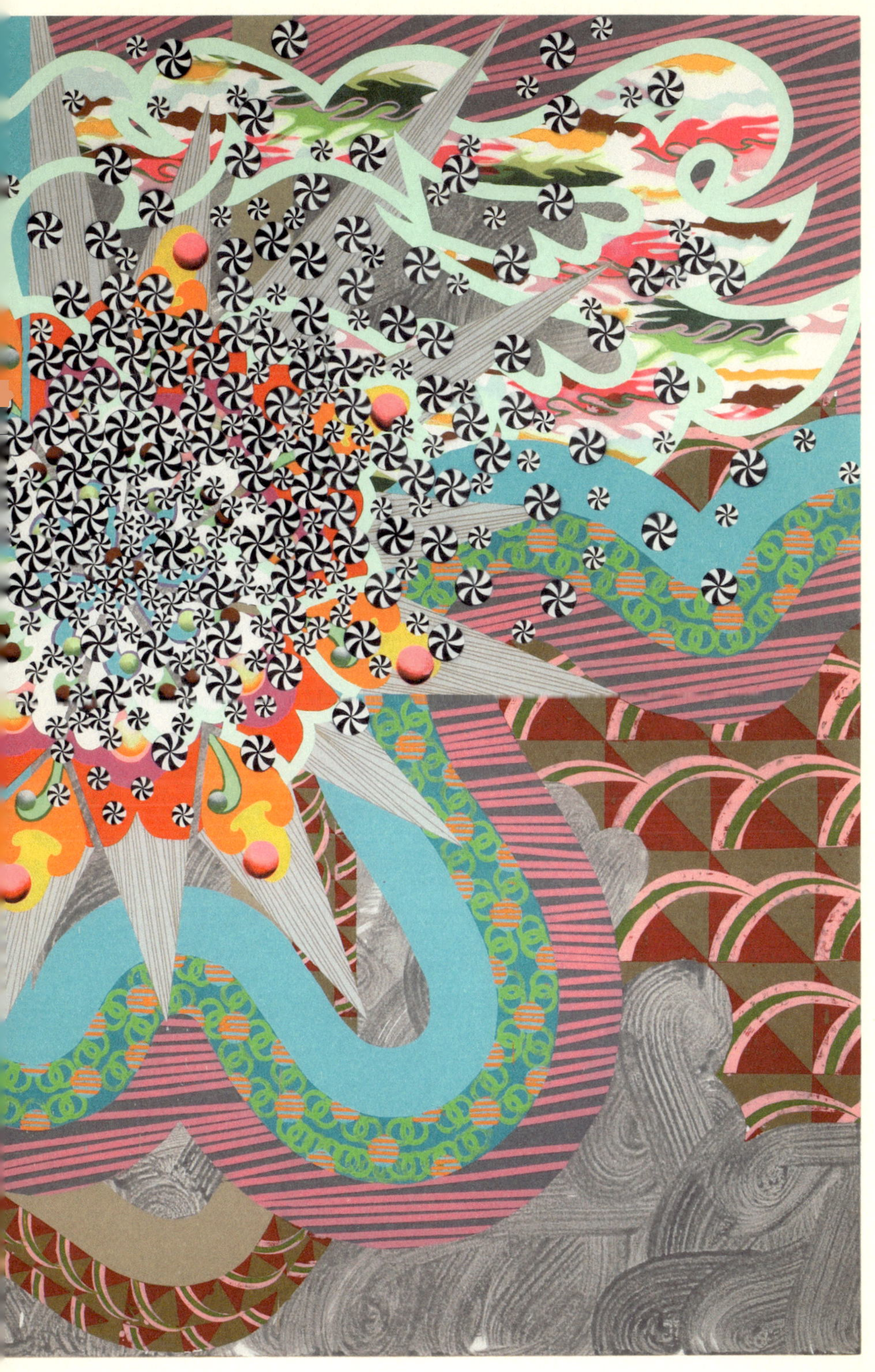

Urs Fischer (*1973) studied photography at the Hochschule für Gestaltung und Kunst in Zurich, visited De Ateliers in Amsterdam and was artist-in-residence at Delfina Studios in London. Solo exhibitions include Cockatoo Island, a Kaldor Art Project/Sydney Harbour Federation Trust, in Sydney in 2007, Paris 1919 at Rotterdam's Museum Boijmans van Beuningen and Mary Poppins at Blaffer Gallery in Houston in 2006, Jet Set Lady at Fondazione Nicola Trussardi in Milan in 2005, Urs Fischer—Espace 315 at Centre Pompidou, Paris and Kir Royal at Kunsthaus Zürich in 2004. Among others, he was awarded the Eidgenössisches Stipendium für freie Kunst by the Swiss Federal Office of Culture in 1995 and 1999 and the Kiefer-Hablitzel Stipendium in 1997. Urs Fischer lives and works in New York.

Yves Netzhammer (*1970) studied visual design at the Hochschule für Gestaltung und Kunst in Zurich. Solo exhibitions include an installation for the Karlskirche in Kassel (supporting program documenta 12, 2007), Endangered Amours at Museum Rietberg in Zurich in 2006, The Arrangement of two Opposites while their Maximum Contact is under Generation at Kunsthalle Bremen in 2005, The Surprising Displacement of the Predetermined Breaking Point of a Branch Grown under Optimal Conditions at Helmhaus Zurich and Das Gefühl präziser Haltlosigkeit beim Festhalten der Dinge at Krefelder Kunstmuseum/Kaiser Wilhelm Museum and Stiftung Wilhelm Lehmbruck Museum in Duisburg in 2003. Among others, he was awarded the Landis & Gyr-Grant for London in 2005, a studio scholarship from the city of Zurich for New York in 2001 and the Manor-Kunstpreis in 1999. Yves Netzhammer lives and works in Zurich.

Ugo Rondinone (*1964) studied at the Hochschule für Angewandte Kunst in Vienna. Solo exhibitions include Air Gets into Everything even Nothing/Get up Girl a Sun is Running the World, Creative Time, at New York's Ritz Carlton Plaza and Battery Park in 2007, Giorni Felici at Galleria Civica di Modena and Zero Built a Nest in My Navel at London's Whitechapel Gallery in 2006, Roundelay at Musée National d'Art Moderne/Centre Georges Pompidou in Paris in 2003, No How On at Kunsthalle Wien in 2002, So Much Water so Close to Home at New York's P.S.1 in 2000 and the 23rd São Paulo Biennale in 1996. He was artist-in-residence at P.S.1 in 1998/99. He was awarded the Eidgenössisches Stipendium für Freie Kunst by the Swiss Federal Office of Culture in 1991, 1994 and 1995. Ugo Rondinone lives and works in New York.

Christine Streuli (*1975) studied at the Hochschule für Gestaltung und Kunst in Zurich and at the Hochschule der Künste in Berlin. Solo exhibitions include Christine Streuli & Bruno Jakob at Kunsthaus Langenthal in 2007, Ensemble Ensemble at Kunstraum Kreuzlingen in 2005, Dorothea von Stetten-Kunstpreis at Kunstmuseum Bonn in 2004 and Something in Common at Massimo Audiello Gallery in New York in 2002. She was awarded a studio scholarship of the city of Zurich for San Francisco in 2005, the Swiss Art Award by the Swiss Federal Office of Culture in 2004, 2005 and 2006 and Pro Helvetia's Cahier d'artiste in 2003. She was artist-in-residence in Cairo in 2003 and took part in the International Studio and Curatorial Program in New York from 2001 to 2002. Christine Streuli lives and works in Zurich.

Bice Curiger (*1948) is a curator at the Kunsthaus Zürich, and editor-in-chief and cofounder of the art magazine *Parkett*. Since 2004, she has been editorial director of *Tate etc.* in London. During 2006 and 2007, she has spent a semester as Rudolf Arnheim Professor at Berlin's Humboldt-Universität. Recent exhibitions include The Expanded Eye and Peter Fischli/David Weiss: Fragen & Blumen, Kunsthaus Zürich.

Fanni Fetzer (*1974) is director at Kunsthaus Langenthal. After working from 1998 to 2004 as a member of the editorial team at the culture journal *Du*, she held a position from 2004 to 2006 at Kunstmuseum Thun, and is now curating a two-person exhibition with Christine Streuli and Bruno Jakob at Kunsthaus Langenthal. She writes on art and architecture, and also teaches at various art academies.

Gaby Hartel (*1961) is a cultural scientist and freelance writer. She recently curated Zwei mal zwei ist vier oder: Lust ist der einzige Schwindel, dem ich Dauer wünsche. Motive des Don Giovanni in der zeitgenössischen Videokunst, Kunsthalle Wien, (with Gerald Matt) in 2006 and the Internationales Festival für Radiokunst (with Frank Kaspar), Akademie der Künste, Berlin in April 2007. She is the editor of *The Eye of Prey. Samuel Becketts Film-und Fernsehkunst,* (with Michael Glasmeier), 2008.

Katarina Holländer (*1964) was born in Bratislava in the former Czechoslovakia and emigrated to Switzerland in 1968. She has worked as an editor and writer for various publications in Zurich and in Prague and in 2003 was awarded a prize for her writing by the Literaturhaus Zürich.

Jörg Kalt (*1967) is a screenwriter and film director, since 1991 he writes a column for the culture journal *Du*. He is currently working on his third feature film.

Friederike Kretzen (*1956) is a writer and has lived in Basel since 1983. Since 1993 she lectures at the Hochschule für Gestaltung und Kunst Zürich and the Hochschule für Gestaltung und Kunst Bern. Since 1996 she has been the Head of Creative Writing at the ETH Zurich. She has written numerous texts on art and is the author of two novelistic trilogies. Her most recent publication is *Weisses Album*, 2007.

Roman Kurzmeyer (*1961) is curator of Atelier Amden, an exhibition site showing contemporary art in Amden, Switzerland (www.xcult.org/amden). He teaches art theory at the Hochschule für Gestaltung und Kunst Basel and is curator at the Ricola Collection. He has written widely on various subjects, most recently *Kunst überfordern. Aldo Walker (1938–2000)*, 2006, and is the coeditor (with Tobia Bezzola) of *Harald Szeemann, With By Through Because Towards Despite: Catalogue of All Exhibitions 1957–2005*, 2007.

James Lord (*1922) is a writer based in Paris. His books include *A Giacometti Portrait*, first published in 1965, and *Giacometti: A Biography*, 1985. In addition he has published several volumes of autobiography and is working at present on a memoir of his experiences as an American soldier during World War II.

Roland Lüthi (*1961) is a specialist for old prints at Zurich's ETH-Library. He is currently working on projects that enable researching images in books published before 1900.

Ludger Schwarte (*1967) is an assistant professor at the Universität Basel, NCCR Iconic Criticism, and is coeditor of *Tiere: Eine andere Anthropologie*, 2004, and of *Cabinet, Laboratory, Theatre—Scenes of Knowledge in 17th Century*, 2005.

Marc Spiegler (*1968) is an international art world journalist, based in Zurich. He is cofounder of www.artworldsalon.com

Erik Steinbrecher (*1963) attended evening classes in art, completed his studies in architecture and lives in Berlin.

Klaus Theweleit (*1942) is a writer and professor for art and theory at the Akademie der Bildenden Künste in Karlsruhe and the Institute of Sociology at the Universität Freiburg. His work has focused on topics such as the theory of fascism, theory of violence, and popular culture. He is the author of several books, including most recently *Pocahontas in Wonderland: Shakespeare on Tour*, 1999 and *Friendly Fire: Deadline Texte*, 2005.

Philip Ursprung (*1963) is professor for modern and contemporary art at Universität Zürich. He is the author of *Grenzen der Kunst: Allan Kaprow und das Happening, Robert Smithson und die Land Art*, 2003, and editor of *Herzog & de Meuron: Natural History*, 2002.

Tan Wälchli (*1974) completed his doctorate in 2006 at the Universität Zürich on *Freud as Reader* and currently teaches at the Hochschule für Gestaltung und Kunst Zürich. He is conducting research in the field of design theory with Aude Lehmann under the label *Whyart. Whyart 3: Fashion* is scheduled for publication later this year.

Susann Wintsch (*1967) lives in Zurich, and is the editor of *Treibsand, a DVD-Magazine on Contemporary Art*; the most recent issue being *Analysing While Waiting (For Time To Pass): Contemporary Art in Tehran* (www.treibsand.ch). She is currently curating art projects for Zurich's new Letzigrund Stadium, and teaches art history at the Hochschule für Gestaltung und Kunst Zürich and F+F Schule für Kunst und Mediendesign.

Tim Zulauf (*1973) studied fine art at the Hochschule für Gestaltung und Kunst Zürich and works as a freelance author and theater director. He creates theater productions—several in close collaboration with Yves Netzhammer—with KMU Produktionen, a group of Zurich based theater and art practitioners. In 2007 he is working on a stage version of the film *Network* for the theater group 400ASA. Further projects can be found at www.zulauf.it

Image Credits

From Venice to Miami

Rote Socken in St. Petersburg, 2007.
© Erik Steinbrecher.—pp. 14–28

Turn Up the Volume

Gino n DJ, 2007.
Photographs by Urs Fischer.
© Urs Fischer.—pp. 48, 49, 50, 51, 56, 57, 59, 64, 65, 66, 67

Photograph by Eugene Tsaï.
© Eugene Tsaï.—p. 58

The Critics on Urs Fischer

Faules Fundament, 1998
Bricks, fruit, vegetables, mortar
Dimensions variable
© Urs Fischer. Courtesy Galerie Eva Presenhuber, Zurich.
Photo: Stefan Altenburger, Zurich.
—p. 72

Baum, 2002
Mixed media on wood
290×212×8.5 cm
© Urs Fischer. Private Collection, New York. Courtesy Galerie Eva Presenhuber, Zurich.
Photo: J. Littkemann, Berlin.
—p. 72

Kuckuck Backwards, 2004
Timber, aluminium, cement paint
162×200×64 cm
Installation view, Urs Fischer—Kir Royal, Kunsthaus Zürich, 2004.
© Urs Fischer. Kunsthaus Zürich. Courtesy Galerie Eva Presenhuber, Zurich.
Photo: Stefan Altenburger, Zurich.
—p. 73

Daylight Pillow, 2004
Aluminium, acrylic paint, light bulb
Ed. of 2+1 AP
125×140×94 cm
© Urs Fischer. Goetz Collection, Munich. The Dakis Joannou Collection, Athens. Tiqui Atencio Demirdjian Collection. Courtesy Galerie Eva Presenhuber, Zurich.
Photo: Stefan Altenburger, Zurich.
—p. 74

A Novel and It's Novelist, 2005
Aluminium, aludibond, gesso, acrylic paint, paint marker, varnish, latex paint, UV-inkjet print
208×273×6 cm
© Urs Fischer. Lindemann Collection, Miami Beach. Courtesy Galerie Eva Presenhuber, Zurich and Gavin Brown's enterprise, New York.
Photo: Stefan Altenburger, Zurich.
—p. 75

Office Theme/Addiction/Mhh Camera, 2006
Wood, aludibond, primer, oilpaint, acrylics, paper cement, cardboard, epoxy polymer, varnish, Epson ultrachrome inkjet print on canvas and Somerset velvet fine art paper
245.3×183×8.3 cm
© Urs Fischer. Collection François Pinault. Courtesy Galerie Eva Presenhuber, Zurich.
Photo: Stefan Altenburger, Zurich.
—p. 75

Addict, 2006
Epoxy glue, found furniture
155×72.5×73 cm
Installation view, Urs Fischer—Mary Poppins, Blaffer Gallery, the Art Museum of the University of Houston, 2006.
© Urs Fischer. Jumex Collection, Mexico. Courtesy Galerie Eva Presenhuber, Zurich and Gavin Brown's Enterprise, New York.
Photo: Rick Gardner, Houston.
—p. 76

Images—Urs Fischer

All photographs by Urs Fischer, 2007.
© Urs Fischer.—pp. 77–88

Art and Shock

Robert Crumb, Aline Kominsky, "Aline & Bobs spassige Spielchen," in Aline Kominsky-Crumb, Robert Crumb, *Schmutzige Wäsche Comics,* trans. Harry Rowohlt, German first edition, Zweitausendeins: Frankfurt am Main, 2002, p. 11. (Original title: The Complete Dirty Laundry, 1974.)
© 1974–2000 Robert Crumb, Aline Kominsky.
© 2002 Zweitausendeins.—p. 91

Jay Kinney, "Red Guard Romance," in *Young Lust,* no. 5, ed. Jay Kinney, Last Gasp: Berkeley CA, 1977.
© Jay Kinney.—p. 92

Kim Deitch, "Simian Sin," in *Young Lust,* no. 4, ed. Jay Kinney, Last Gasp: Berkeley CA, 1974.
© Kim Deitch.—p. 94

Trina Robbins, "Fox," 1972, in *U-Comix,* Sonderband Nr. 13, Bilder und Texte von Trina Robbins, Volksverlag: Linden, 1977, p. 39.
© Trina Robbins.—pp. 96, 103

Trina Robbins, "Rawhide Revenge," 1975, in *U-Comix,* Sonderband Nr. 13, Bilder und Texte von Trina Robbins, Volksverlag: Linden, 1977, p. 31.
© Trina Robbins.—p. 99

Bill Griffith, "Too Much Fun," in *Young Lust,* no. 5, ed. Jay Kinney, Last Gasp: Berkeley CA, 1977.
© Bill Griffith.—pp. 100–1

Rocky Trout, "The Fishy Facts of Life," in *Tits & Clits Comix,* Nanny Goat Productions/Last Gasp Publishing: Berkeley CA, 1980.
© Rocky Trout.—p. 102

Blalla W. Hallmann
Siehe! Siehe! Siehe!, 1990
Acrylic on glass, 120×100 cm
© Estate of Blalla W. Hallmann, Windsbach.—p. 104

Blalla W. Hallmann
Aus der Tiefe des Raumes, in der Stille der Nacht—Moonlight Serenade, 1991
Acrylic on canvas
150×100 cm
© Estate of Blalla W. Hallmann, Windsbach.—p. 106

Yves Netzhammer, videostills

Die begehbare Falle, 1999
Collaboration with Zuzana Ponicanova
Installation with monitor and objects
© Yves Netzhammer, Zuzana Ponicanova. Courtesy Galerie Anita Beckers, Frankfurt am Main.
—pp. 113, 119

Süsser Wind im Gesicht, 2004
Installation with projection, DVD Video/PAL
29 min. 14 sec.
© Yves Netzhammer. Courtesy Galerie Anita Beckers, Frankfurt am Main.—p. 114

Die ungenauen Körper, 2006
Video installation with 2 video works and 1 balloon,
DVD Video/PAL
13 min. 40 sec.
Balloon diameter: 180 cm
© Yves Netzhammer. Courtesy Galerie Anita Beckers, Frankfurt am Main.—p. 115

Die Zeit bis eine Form entsteht, addiert mit der Zeit, bis die Form zerstört ist, 2003
DVD Video/PAL
17 min. 50 sec., loop, sound
© Yves Netzhammer. Courtesy Galerie Anita Beckers, Frankfurt am Main.—p. 116

Image Credits

Die Anordnungsweise zweier Gegenteile bei der Erzeugung ihres Berührungsmaximums, 2005
Installation with projection on walldrawing and single channel projection, DVD Video/PAL
8 films between 2 min. 45 sec. und 7 min.
Feature film: 27 min. 37 sec.
© Yves Netzhammer. Courtesy Galerie Anita Beckers, Frankfurt am Main.—pp. 117, 128

Grosse Spiegel werden verloren: Informationen von Abwesenheit, damit Anwesenheit entstehen kann, 2000
Variable installation with monitors and video projector
18 min.
© Yves Netzhammer. Courtesy Galerie Anita Beckers, Frankfurt am Main.—pp. 118, 125, 126

Junge Äste ahmen alte Geweihe nach und alte Geweihe junge Äste, 1999
Installation with video projector, VHS and DVD Video/PAL
24 min. 30 sec.
Ed. of 5
© Yves Netzhammer. Courtesy Galerie Anita Beckers, Frankfurt am Main.—pp. 120–1

Wenn man etwas gegen seine Eigenschaften benützt, muss man dafür einen anderen Namen finden, 1997/99
DVD Video/PAL
42 min.
Ed. of 5
© Yves Netzhammer. Courtesy Galerie Anita Beckers, Frankfurt am Main.—pp. 122–3

Die umgekehrte Rüstung, 2002
Collaboration with Bjørn Melhus
DVD Video/PAL
23 min. 30 sec., loop
Figures: Yves Netzhammer, sound: Bjørn Melhus
Ed. of 5
© Yves Netzhammer, Bjørn Melhus. Courtesy Galerie Anita Beckers, Frankfurt am Main.—p. 124

Übungen machen Meister, die sich nicht an ihre Anfänge erinnern, 2000
Thematic work complex with 3 objects and 3 corresponding projections, DVD Video/PAL
Object 1 (horse): 3 min. 12 sec.
Object 2 (carousel): 6 min. 50 sec.
Object 3 (sleigh): 9 min.
© Yves Netzhammer. Courtesy Galerie Anita Beckers, Frankfurt am Main.—p. 127

The Critics on Yves Netzhammer

Übungen machen Meister, die sich nicht an ihre Anfänge erinnern, 2000
Thematic work complex with 3 objects and 3 corresponding projections
Object 1 (Horse)
Wood, cloth, wool
Ca. 150 × 220 × 220 cm
© Yves Netzhammer. Courtesy Galerie Anita Beckers, Frankfurt am Main.—p. 130

Videoskulptur, 2003
Installation with 4 films, 4 rear projections on canvas and 4 sculptures with integrated technics
Films between 3 and 7 min.
© Yves Netzhammer. Courtesy Galerie Anita Beckers, Frankfurt am Main.
Photo: Mancia/Bodmer, Zurich.—p. 131

Am Horizont können wir unsere Sinne ablesen, 2003
Installation with 2 synchronized projections, sound, DVD Video/PAL
5 min. 40 sec., loop
© Yves Netzhammer. Courtesy Galerie Anita Beckers, Frankfurt am Main.
Photo: Mancia/Bodmer, Zurich.—p. 132

Das Gefühl präziser Haltlosigkeit beim Festhalten der Dinge, 2003
Three-part installation with video projection
DVD Video/PAL
Ca. 20 min., loop
© Yves Netzhammer. Courtesy Galerie Anita Beckers, Frankfurt am Main.—p. 132

Süsser Wind im Gesicht, 2004
Installation with projection, DVD Video/PAL
29 min. 14 sec.
© Yves Netzhammer. Courtesy Galerie Anita Beckers, Frankfurt am Main.—p. 133

Die Anordnungsweise zweier Gegenteile bei der Erzeugung ihres Berührungsmaximums, 2005
Installation with projection on walldrawing and single channel projection, DVD Video/PAL
8 films between 2 min. 45 sec. and 7 min.
Feature film: 27 min. 37 sec.
© Yves Netzhammer. Courtesy Galerie Anita Beckers, Frankfurt am Main.—p. 133

Gefährdete Liebschaften, 2006
Four-part installation with sculptures and drawings
© Yves Netzhammer. Courtesy Galerie Anita Beckers, Frankfurt am Main.—p. 134

Drawings—Yves Netzhammer

All drawings by Yves Netzhammer, 2007.
© Yves Netzhammer.—pp. 135–47

Visual Essay by Roland Lüthi

1 Genesis Cap. VI. v.15. Arcae scenographia/I. Buch Moses Cap. VI. v.15. Perspectivische Vorstellung der Arch, in Johann Jakob Scheuchzer, *Kupfer-Bibel,* Augsburg and Ulm, 1731–1735, vol. 1, plate XXXIX.A preceding p. 53.
© ETH-Bibliothek Zürich, Sammlung Alte Drucke.—p. 150

2 Ursa Maior, in Johann Bayer, *Uranometria,* Augsburg, 1603, plate II.
© ETH-Bibliothek Zürich, Sammlung Alte Drucke.—p. 152

3 Vue d'une fosse aux ours au Jardin des Plantes, [Paris], d'après une photographie instantanée de M. Pierre Petit, in *La Nature: Revue des sciences et de leurs applications,* Paris, 10e année, 2e semestre, no. 479 (5. 8. 1882), p. 145.
© ETH-Bibliothek Zürich, Sammlung Alte Drucke.—p. 152

4 Fabrica machine volatilis, illustration for experiment XIV, in Johann Stephan Kestler, *Physiologia kircheriana experimentalis,* Amsterdam, 1680, p. 118.
© ETH-Bibliothek Zürich, Sammlung Alte Drucke.—p. 153

5 Monachus marinus. Ein Meermünch. Ein Münchsfisch, in Konrad Gessner, *Fischbuch,* Zürich, 1563, p. 105.
© ETH-Bibliothek Zürich, Sammlung Alte Drucke.—p. 153

6 Puer capite elephantino/ Infans cornutus ore patulo, illustrations for Liber V: Mirabilia, caput IV: De monstris humanis cum capite non humano, in Gaspar Schott, *Physica curiosa,* Würzburg, 1667, vol. 1, plate IX following p. 582, fig. VIII–IX.
© ETH-Bibliothek Zürich, Sammlung Alte Drucke.—p. 153

7 [Jakob] Degens Flugmaschine, in August Wilhelm Zachariä, *Die Elemente der Luftschwimmkunst,* Wittenberg, 1807, plate 1, fig. 1. © ETH-Bibliothek Zürich, Sammlung Alte Drucke.—p. 153

8 Painted engine cowling of a Loehle P-40 aircraft, Lakeland, Florida, ca. 1980s–1990s. © Tim Wright/Corbis.—p. 156

9 Le chien turc et gredin, in Georges-Louis Leclerc, comte de Buffon, *Histoire Naturelle,* Aux Deux-Ponts, 1786–1791, vol. 13, plate 26. © ETH-Bibliothek Zürich, Sammlung Alte Drucke.—p. 156

10 Le pithèque mâle et femelle, in Georges-Louis Leclerc, comte de Buffon, *Histoire Naturelle,* Aux Deux-Ponts, 1786–1791, vol. 13, plate 2. © ETH-Bibliothek Zürich, Sammlung Alte Drucke.—p. 156

11 Leo Wehrli, Model of Dimetrodon incisivus, [E.D.] Cope, Kammsaurier, compared to the size of a man, 1921. © Bildarchiv ETH-Bibliothek Zürich.—p. 156

12 Mandan chief, in Heinrich Rudolf Schinz, *Naturgeschichte und Abbildungen des Menschen der verschiedenen Rassen und Stämme,* Zurich, 1845, plate 38. © ETH-Bibliothek Zürich, Sammlung Alte Drucke.—p. 157

13 Hypolitus mâle, Herfe, Ilyrias et Manto, in Pieter Cramer, *Papillons exotiques,* Amsterdam, 1775, vol. 1, plate X. © ETH-Bibliothek Zürich, Sammlung Alte Drucke.—p. 157

14 Gustave Doré, Le petit Chaperon rouge au lit avec le loup, illustration for *Les contes de Perrault,* Paris, 1862, plate between p. XII and p. XIII. © Archivo Iconografico, S.A./Corbis.—p. 157

15 Friedrich Martin von Reibisch, untitled illustration of two knights at a tournament, in Franz Kottenkamp, *Der Rittersaal: Eine Geschichte des Ritterthums, seines Entstehens und Fortgangs, seiner Gebräuche und Sitten,* Stuttgart, 1842, plate 33. © Stapleton Collection/Corbis. —p. 158

16 View of the cabinet of curiosities of Ferrante Imperato, [Naples, 1599], in *Historia naturale di Ferrante Imperato Napolitano,* Venice, 1672, plate preceding book 1. © Enzo & Paolo Ragazzini/Corbis. —p. 158

17 Le doubler, in François Robichon de La Guerinière, *Manuel de cavalerie,* The Hague, 1742, plate 3, [fig. 2]. © ETH-Bibliothek Zürich, Sammlung Alte Drucke.—p. 159

18 Erlegung eines grossen Alligators, in Franz Keller-Leuzinger, *Vom Amazonas und Madeira,* Stuttgart, 1874, plate preceding p. 67. © ETH-Bibliothek Zürich, Sammlung Alte Drucke.—p. 159

19 Expérience exécutée au laboratoire de la Sorbonne sur la force musculaire de la mâchoire d'un crocodile, in *La Nature: Revue des sciences et de leurs applications,* Paris, 10e année, 1er semestre, no. 450 (14.1.1882), p. 97. © ETH-Bibliothek Zürich, Sammlung Alte Drucke.—p. 159

20 William Heath, Grimaldi and the Nondescript in the pantomime *The Red Dwarf:* The Clown kills the Pantaloon and afterwards dresses him in the skin of a lion, the head of an ass, eagles wings, cats feet & a fishes tail, Bertram W. Mills Collection, ca. 1810s–1820s. © Hulton-Deutsch Collection/ Corbis.—p. 159

21 Postcard of children posing for a photograph, ca. 1910. © Lake County Museum, Wauconda, Illinois/Corbis.—p. 162

22 Disposition [d'un] aquarium marin pour l'étude de la locomotion dans l'eau, in Etienne-Jules Marey, *Le Mouvement,* Paris, 1894, p. 210, fig. 156. © ETH-Bibliothek Zürich, Sammlung Alte Drucke.—p. 162

23 Manège pour la détermination graphique des mouvements de l'aile: pigeon attelé au manège et muni de tambours à transmission rectangulaire conjugués, in Etienne-Jules Marey, *Physiologie du mouvement,* Paris, 1890, p. 110, fig. 54. © ETH-Bibliothek Zürich, Sammlung Alte Drucke.—p. 162

24 Adventure with curl-crested toucans, in Henry Walter Bates, *The Naturalist on the River Amazonas,* London, 1863, vol. 1, frontispiece. © ETH-Bibliothek Zürich, Sammlung Alte Drucke.—p. 162

25 Manège pour la détermination graphique des mouvements de l'aile: disposition d'ensemble, in Etienne-Jules Marey, *Physiologie du mouvement,* Paris, 1890, p. 110, fig. 55. © ETH-Bibliothek Zürich, Sammlung Alte Drucke.—p. 162

26 Piquets avec une corde pour faire pâturer les chevaux et muselière pour contenir les bestiaux, in Charles Lasteyrie du Saillant, *Collection de machines,* Paris, 1820–1821, vol. 1, animals, plate III, fig. 1–3. © ETH-Bibliothek Zürich, Sammlung Alte Drucke.—p. 163

27 Poulailler ambulant, in Charles Lasteyrie du Saillant, *Collection de machines,* Paris, 1820–1821, vol. 1, poultry, plate II, fig. 2. © ETH-Bibliothek Zürich, Sammlung Alte Drucke.—p. 166

28 Niche à chien, in Charles Lasteyrie du Saillant, *Collection de machines,* Paris, 1820–1821, vol. 2, animals, plate I, fig. 5. © ETH-Bibliothek Zürich, Sammlung Alte Drucke.—p. 166

29 Du galvanisme appliqué à la tête d'un boeuf récemment assommé, [illustration of] experiments XL-VIII–LII, LVII–LX, in Giovanni Aldini, *Essai théorique et expérimental sur le Galvanisme,* Paris, 1804, plate 2, fig. 1–6. © ETH-Bibliothek Zürich, Sammlung Alte Drucke.—p. 166

30 Collier à piquant, in Charles Lasteyrie du Saillant, *Collection de machines,* Paris, 1820–1821, vol. 2, animals, plate IV, fig. 6. © ETH-Bibliothek Zürich, Sammlung Alte Drucke.—p. 166

31 Nid pour les canards en forme de poire, in Charles Lasteyrie du Saillant, *Collection de machines,* Paris, 1820–1821, vol. 1, poultry, plate II, fig. 4. © ETH-Bibliothek Zürich, Sammlung Alte Drucke.—p. 166

32 Pare-vue, in Charles Lasteyrie du Saillant, *Collection de machines,* Paris 1820–1821, vol. 2, animals, plate IV, fig. 3. © ETH-Bibliothek Zürich, Sammlung Alte Drucke.—p. 167

Image Credits

33 Oeuillère, in Charles Lasteyrie du Saillant, *Collection de machines,* Paris, 1820–1821, vol. 2, animals, plate IV, fig. 4.
© ETH-Bibliothek Zürich, Sammlung Alte Drucke.—p. 167

34 Abri pour donner du sel aux bestiaux, in Charles Lasteyrie du Saillant, *Collection de machines,* Paris, 1820–1821, vol. 2, animals, plate I, fig. 4.
© ETH-Bibliothek Zürich, Sammlung Alte Drucke.—p. 167

35 J.J. Grandville, Pierre Jules Stahl, *Vie privée et publique des animaux,* Paris, 1868, [vignette on the] frontispiece.
© ETH-Bibliothek Zürich, Sammlung Alte Drucke.—p. 168

36 J.J. Grandville, Se regardant dans la glace, il se trouve joli garçon, [untitled] illustration for "Les contradictions d'une levrette," in J.J. Grandville, Pierre Jules Stahl, *Vie privée et publique des animaux,* Paris, 1868, p. 294.
© ETH-Bibliothek Zürich, Sammlung Alte Drucke.—p. 168

37 Restauration du squelette de Gastornis Edwardsii, oiseau éocène de 3 mètres de hauteur, in *La Nature: Revue des sciences et de leurs applications,* Paris, 10e année, 1er semestre, no. 466 (6. 5. 1882), p. 353, fig. 1.
© ETH-Bibliothek Zürich, Sammlung Alte Drucke.—p. 168

38 Willhelm Busch, "Fräulein Ammer kos't allhier mit Schnick, dem allerliebsten Tier," illustration for "Die Strafe der Faulheit," in Otto und Hermann Nöldeke, *Wilhelm Busch-Buch,* Leipzig, 1930, p. 193.—p. 168

39 Wilhelm Busch, "Sie füttert ihn, so viel er mag, mit Zuckerbrot den ganzen Tag," illustration for "Die Strafe der Faulheit," in Otto und Hermann Nöldeke, *Wilhelm Busch-Buch,* Leipzig, 1930, p. 193.—p. 168

40 Le mulet Rigolo, in *La Nature: Revue des sciences et de leurs applications,* Paris, 10e année, 1er semestre, no. 448 (31. 12. 1881), p. 75, fig. 4.
© ETH-Bibliothek Zürich, Sammlung Alte Drucke.—p. 168

41 Mouvement des pattes d'une crevette, in Etienne-Jules Marey, *Le Mouvement,* Paris, 1894, p. 222, fig. 165.
© ETH-Bibliothek Zürich, Sammlung Alte Drucke.—p. 168

42 J.J. Grandville, [untitled] illustration for "Les contradictions d'une levrette," in J.J. Grandville, Pierre Jules Stahl, *Vie privée et publique des animaux,* Paris, 1868, p. 299.
© ETH-Bibliothek Zürich, Sammlung Alte Drucke.—p. 169

Where Do We Go from Here?

Allen Ruppersberg, Cover (detail), *The Secret of Life and Death,* volume I 1969–1984, exhibition catalog, The Museum of Contemporary Art, Los Angeles, ed. Julia Brown, Black Sparrow Press: Santa Barbara, 1985.
© Artist and The Museum of Contemporary Art, Los Angeles.
—p. 172

The Critics on Ugo Rondinone

Heyday, 1995
Polyester, cotton, hair, wooden floor, wooden wall, paint, perspex
Dimensions variable
Ed. of 2+1 AP
© Ugo Rondinone. Courtesy Galerie Eva Presenhuber, Zurich.—p. 216

Guided by Voices, 1999
Neon, perspex, transluscent film, aluminium
330×785×10 cm
Ed. of 2+1 AP
Installation view, Guided by Voices, Kunsthaus Glarus, Glarus, 1999.
© Ugo Rondinone. Courtesy Galerie Eva Presenhuber, Zurich.—p. 216

If there Were anywhere but Desert. Tuesday, 2002
Fibreglass, paint, clothing
51×167×118 cm
© Ugo Rondinone. Private Collection, France. Courtesy Galerie Eva Presenhuber, Zurich. Matthew Marks Gallery, New York.—p. 217

No How On, 2002
46 pillars, mirror, paint, 6 dvds, speakers, sound
Modular system
Ed. of 3
Installation view, No How On, Kunsthalle Wien, Vienna, 2002.
© Ugo Rondinone. Courtesy Galerie Eva Presenhuber, Zurich.—p. 218

Roundelay, 2003
Outside part: 3 plaster walls
550×1200×1200 cm
Inside part: 6 walls of wood, jute and felt, light bulb, 6 dvds, 6 projections, 18 speakers, sound
500×1000×1000 cm
Ed. of 3+1 AP
Installation view, Roundelay, Centre Georges Pompidou, Paris, 2003.
© Ugo Rondinone. Courtesy Galerie Eva Presenhuber, Zurich.—p. 218

When the Water Went South for the Winter it Carried Us down like Storm Driven Gulls, 2003
Out of Reach until it's Magic We Are Crossing our Own Stony Ocean, 2003
Across Dark Stream of Shooting Stars, 2003
We Sail into Pleasure and Unload our Spacious Soul, 2003
Everything Gets Lighter Everyone Is Light, 2003
Semi-transparent, cast resin
300×240×240 cm;
307×277×247 cm;
300×240×240 cm;
280×280×160 cm;
294×223×248 cm
Installation view, Zero Built a Nest in My Navel, Whitechapel Gallery, London, 2006.
© Ugo Rondinone. Courtesy Galerie Eva Presenhuber, Zurich.—p. 219

Sunrise. August, 2004
Sunrise. September, 2004
Sunrise. October, 2004
Cast aluminium
Between 100×72×32 cm and 115×60×37 cm
Ed. of 1+1 AP
Installation view, Sunsetsunrise, Sommer Contemporary Art, Tel Aviv, 2004.
© Ugo Rondinone. Private Collections, Europe. Courtesy Galerie Eva Presenhuber, Zurich. Sommer Contemporary Art, Tel Aviv.—p. 219

Images—Ugo Rondinone

Moonrise. West. December, 2004
© Ugo Rondinone. Private Collections, USA/Europe. Courtesy Galerie Eva Presenhuber, Zurich. Matthew Marks Gallery, New York.
—p. 221

Lessness, 2003
Installation view, Lessness, Galerie Almine Rech, Paris, 2003
© Ugo Rondinone. Private Collection, France. Courtesy Galerie Eva Presenhuber, Zurich.
—pp. 222–3

Image Credits

Lowland Lullaby, 2002
© Ugo Rondinone. Courtesy Galerie Eva Presenhuber, Zurich.
—pp. 224–5

Dreiundzwanzigsteraprilzweitausend-undnull, 2000
© Ugo Rondinone. Private Collection, Germany.
Courtesy Galerie Eva Presenhuber, Zurich.—pp. 226–7

Siebenundzwanzigsterjunizwei-tausendundzwei, 2002
If there Were anywhere but Desert. Tuesday, 2002
Installation view, No How On, Kunsthalle Wien, Vienna, 2002
© Ugo Rondinone. Private Collection, France. Courtesy Galerie Eva Presenhuber, Zurich. Matthew Marks Gallery, New York.—pp. 228–9

All those Doors, 2003
Installation view, Long Nights Short Years, Centre d'Art Contemporain Le Consortium, Dijon, 2004
© Ugo Rondinone. Courtesy Galerie Eva Presenhuber, Zurich. Matthew Marks Gallery, New York.—pp. 230–1

The Third Hour of the Poem, 2005
© Ugo Rondinone. Private Collection, France. Courtesy Galerie Eva Presenhuber, Zurich.—p. 232

Visual Essay by Roland Lüthi

1 [Untitled illustration], in William Derham, *The artificial clock-maker*, London, 1734, frontispiece.
© ETH-Bibliothek Zürich, Sammlung Alte Drucke.—p. 236

2 Modo di componer' l'horolog[io] con l'aria o con vento, in Domenico Martinelli, *Horologi elementari*, Venice, 1669, Terza parte: Dell'aria, chapter II, p. 141, fig. XV.
© ETH-Bibliothek Zürich, Sammlung Alte Drucke.—p. 236

3 Astrolabe du XVIe siècle, in Pierre Dubois, *Histoire de l'horlogerie*, Paris, 1849, plate between pp. 24 and 25, [fig. 2].
© ETH-Bibliothek Zürich, Sammlung Alte Drucke.—p. 236

4 Pendule astronomique à équation, in Pierre Dubois, *Histoire de l'horlogerie*, Paris, 1849, p. 203, fig. 4–5.
© ETH-Bibliothek Zürich, Sammlung Alte Drucke.—p. 237

5 Jeu du carillon de l'horloge de Liège, in Pierre Dubois, *Histoire de l'horlogerie*, Paris, 1849, p. 94.
© ETH-Bibliothek Zürich, Sammlung Alte Drucke.—p. 238

6 Schwarzwälder Kuckucksuhr, sogenanntes Jagdstück, ca. 1900, Deutsches Uhrenmuseum Furtwangen.
© Deutsches Uhrenmuseum, Furtwangen/Wikimedia Commons.
—p. 238

7 Schwarzwälder Kuckucksuhr, souvenir purchase, 2004.
© Erik Pawassar/zefa/Corbis.
—p. 238

8 Horloge de Lyon [Cathédrale de Saint Jean], in Pierre Dubois, *Histoire de l'horlogerie*, Paris, 1849, plate between pp. 92 and 93.
© ETH-Bibliothek Zürich, Sammlung Alte Drucke.—p. 239

9 Horloge à poids dite de Henri VIII, XVIe siècle, appartenant à S.M. la Reine d'Angleterre, in Pierre Dubois, *Histoire de l'horlogerie*, Paris, 1849, frontispiece.
© ETH-Bibliothek Zürich, Sammlung Alte Drucke.—p. 239

10 De modi del biligare le campane grandi, che facilmente tirate per sonare si movino, in Vanoccio Biringuccio, *De la pirotechnia*, Venice, 1559, Libro sesto, chapter XIIII, p. 100.
© ETH-Bibliothek Zürich, Sammlung Alte Drucke.—p. 239

11 Clepsydre à tambour d'après le père Alexandre, in Pierre Dubois, *Histoire de l'horlogerie*, Paris, 1849, p. 61.
© ETH-Bibliothek Zürich, Sammlung Alte Drucke.—p. 243

12 Memento mori watch given by Mary Queen of Scots to Mary Setoun, her maid of honour [XVIth century], in *The Illustrated London News*, 22.9.1849.
© Corbis.—p. 244

13 Montre du XVIIe siècle appartenant à M. Jacquart, in Pierre Dubois, *Histoire de l'horlogerie*, Paris, 1849, plate following p. 100, fig. 1.
© ETH-Bibliothek Zürich, Sammlung Alte Drucke.—p. 244

14 Montre du XVIIe siècle appartenant à l'auteur, in Pierre Dubois, *Histoire de l'horlogerie*, Paris, 1849, plate following p. 100, fig. 2.
© ETH-Bibliothek Zürich, Sammlung Alte Drucke.—p. 244

15 Pendule à quarts et répétition ordinaire, in Pierre Dubois, *Histoire de l'horlogerie*, Paris, 1849, p. 114, fig. 6; p. 112, fig. 1; p. 112, fig. 2.
© ETH-Bibliothek Zürich, Sammlung Alte Drucke.—p. 246

16 Machine planétaire, composée par A[ntide] Janvier, in Pierre Dubois, *Histoire de l'horlogerie*, Paris, 1849, plate between pp. 182 and 183.
© ETH-Bibliothek Zürich, Sammlung Alte Drucke.—pp. 248–9

17 Horloge à verge, in Pierre Dubois, *Histoire de l'horlogerie*, Paris, 1849, p. 131, [fig. 3].
© ETH-Bibliothek Zürich, Sammlung Alte Drucke.—p. 252

18 Echappement impraticable, in Pierre Dubois, *Histoire de l'horlogerie*, Paris, 1849, p. 131, [fig. 1].
© ETH-Bibliothek Zürich, Sammlung Alte Drucke.—p. 252

19 Horloge dont le balancier est mû par l'effet d'un encliquetage, in Pierre Dubois, *Histoire de l'horlogerie*, Paris, 1849, p. 130, [fig. 1].
© ETH-Bibliothek Zürich, Sammlung Alte Drucke.—p. 252

20 Horloge à poids et pendule sans échappement, vue de profil, in Pierre Dubois, *Histoire de l'horlogerie*, Paris, 1849, p. 130, [fig. 4].
© ETH-Bibliothek Zürich, Sammlung Alte Drucke.—p. 252

21 Mostra simile a quelle che si vedono nelle facciate delle chiese e delle torri, in Domenico Martinelli, *Horologi elementari*, Venice, 1669, Prima parte: Dell'acqua, chapter XII, p. 53, fig. IV.
© ETH-Bibliothek Zürich, Sammlung Alte Drucke.—p. 253

22 Compositione d'un horologio fatto alla similitudine di quello che si vede nella famosissima piazza di Venetia con i Mori che battono l'hore e i Rè Magi che trapassando salutano la Beatissima Vergine, in Domenico Martinelli, *Horologi elementari*, Venice, 1669, Prima parte: Dell'acqua, chapter XIV, p. 105, fig. XII.
© ETH-Bibliothek Zürich, Sammlung Alte Drucke.—p. 253

Image Credits

23 Cadrature de répétition à tout ou rien, in Jean André Lepaute, *Traité d'horlogerie*, Paris, 1767, plate V.
© ETH-Bibliothek Zürich, Sammlung Alte Drucke.—p. 253

24 Cadrature de pendule à répétition, in Jean André Lepaute, *Traité d'horlogerie*, Paris, 1767, plate IV.
© ETH-Bibliothek Zürich, Sammlung Alte Drucke.—p. 253

25 Pendule à quarts et répétition ordinaire, in Pierre Dubois, *Histoire de l'horlogerie*, Paris, 1849, p. 113, fig. 5.
© ETH-Bibliothek Zürich, Sammlung Alte Drucke.—p. 254

26 Modo di far il vaso di moto misto, che servirà per mostrar' e battere l'hore, in Domenico Martinelli, *Horologi elementari*, Venice, 1669, Prima parte: Dell'acqua, chapter IV, p. 41, fig. I.
© ETH-Bibliothek Zürich, Sammlung Alte Drucke.—p. 256

27 [Construction d'un cadran solaire]: proposition IX: tailler les corps réguliers en pierre ou en autre matière solide, in Pierre de Sainte Marie Magdeleine, *Traité d'horlogiographie*, Paris, 1641, planche 57, p. 235.
© ETH-Bibliothek Zürich, Sammlung Alte Drucke.—p. 258

28 Mostra senza ruote con il suo contrapeso, in Domenico Martinelli, *Horologi elementari*, Venice, 1669, Prima parte: Dell'acqua, chapter VI, p. 49, fig. III.
© ETH-Bibliothek Zürich, Sammlung Alte Drucke.—p. 258

29 Modo di aggiunger' [ai] horologii la campana per il battere dell'hore e per lo svegliarino, in Domenico Martinelli, *Horologi elementari*, Venice, 1669, Prima parte: Dell'acqua, chapter X, p. 72, fig. VII.
© ETH-Bibliothek Zürich, Sammlung Alte Drucke.—p. 258

30 Horologio che mostra e batte l'hore con un vaso solo, in Domenico Martinelli, *Horologi elementari*, Venice, 1669, Prima parte: Dell'acqua, chapter XII, p. 93, fig. X.
© ETH-Bibliothek Zürich, Sammlung Alte Drucke.—p. 259

A Surplus of Form

All photographs by Christine Streuli, 2001–2006.
© Christine Streuli.—pp. 268–88

The Critics on Christine Streuli

Delta, 2003
Acrylic and enamel on cotton
174×188 cm
© Christine Streuli.
Ricola Collection.
Photo: Heinrich Helfenstein, Zurich.—p. 291

Zitrusfrüchte in Porzellanschale, 2004
Enamel on aluminium
25×33 cm
© Christine Streuli. Kunsthaus Zürich, Vereinigung Zürcher Kunstfreunde, Gruppe Junge Kunst.
Photo: Heinrich Helfenstein, Zurich.—p. 291

Jackpot, 2004
Acrylic and enamel on cotton
360×255 cm
© Christine Streuli.
Private collection, Zurich.
Photo: Wolfgang Burat, Cologne.—p. 292

Radar, 2005
Enamel on cotton, 190×240 cm
© Christine Streuli.
Courtesy Sfeir-Semler Gallery, Hamburg.
Photo: Wolfgang Burat, Cologne.—p. 292

Humpty, 2005
Acrylic and enamel on cotton
300×200 cm
© Christine Streuli.
Steinrich-Sultier Collection.
Photo: Andreas Ilg, Zurich.—p. 293

Ensemble Ensemble, 2005
Installation view, Ensemble Ensemble, Kunstraum Kreuzlingen, 2005.
© Christine Streuli.
Photo: Peter Moser-Kamm, Kreuzlingen.—p. 293

Faltblatt, 2005
Acrylic and enamel on wood
55×60 cm
© Christine Streuli. Private collection.
Photo: David Aebi, Zurich.—p. 294

La Rondella, 2006
Acrylic and enamel on wood
23×34 cm
© Christine Streuli. Courtesy Monica De Cardenas Gallery, Milan.
Photo: Annalisa Guidetti/Giovanni Ricci, Milan.—p. 294

Paintings—Christine Streuli

Closer, 2007
© Christine Streuli. Courtesy Mark Müller Gallery, Zurich. Sfeir-Semler Gallery, Hamburg. Monica De Cardenas Gallery, Milan.
Photo: David Aebi, Burgdorf.
—pp. 296–7

Krone, 2007
© Christine Streuli. Courtesy Sfeir-Semler Gallery, Hamburg.
Photo: Andreas Ilg, Zurich.
—pp. 298–9

Spielhaus, 2007
© Christine Streuli. Courtesy Mark Müller Gallery, Zurich. Sfeir-Semler Gallery, Hamburg. Monica De Cardenas Gallery, Milan.
Photo: David Aebi, Burgdorf.
—pp. 300–1

Neu_Rose, 2007
© Christine Streuli. Courtesy Mark Müller Gallery, Zurich. Sfeir-Semler Gallery, Hamburg. Monica De Cardenas Gallery, Milan.
Photo: David Aebi, Burgdorf.
—pp. 302–3

Strick, 2007
© Christine Streuli.
Courtesy of the artist.
Photo: Andreas Ilg, Zurich.
—pp. 304–5

Go North, Go South, Go East, Go West, 2007
© Christine Streuli. Courtesy Mark Müller Gallery, Zurich. Sfeir-Semler Gallery, Hamburg. Monica De Cardenas Gallery, Milan.
Photo: David Aebi, Burgdorf.
—pp. 306–7

Vierzählig, 2007
© Christine Streuli. Courtesy Mark Müller Gallery, Zurich.
Photo: Andreas Ilg, Zurich.
—pp. 308–9

Z-Off, 2007
© Christine Streuli. Courtesy Mark Müller Gallery, Zurich. Sfeir-Semler Gallery, Hamburg. Monica De Cardenas Gallery, Milan.
Photo: David Aebi, Burgdorf.
—pp. 310–11

322 Text Credits

The Critics on Urs Fischer

pp. 72–6
(Texts compiled and edited by Anna Lehninger)

Paul Ardenne, "Urs Fischer," in *Art Press*, issue no. 301, Mai 2004, pp. 82–3

Kirsty Bell, "Urs Fischer," in *Frieze*, issue 67, May 2002, p. 103

Daniel Binswanger, "Langeweile beim Nasenbohren," in *Weltwoche*, no. 12, March 2004, p. 9

Giovanni Carmine, "Urs Fischer—Personal Weather," in *Flash Art*, January-February 2004, p. 84

Alison Gingeras, "Openings. Urs Fischer," in *Artforum International*, May 2003, p. 158

Alison Gingeras, "a little bit of ash on my lap. Image Selection, Urs Fischer," in *Urs Fischer—Espace 315*, livre numéro 2, exhibition catalog, Centre Pompidou, Paris, ed. Françoise Bertaux, Paris: Éditions du Centre Pompidou, 2004, p. 42

Jörg Heiser, "Of Cats and Chairs," in *Urs Fischer—Kir Royal*, exhibition catalog, Kunsthaus Zürich, Zurich: JRP|Ringier, 2004, p. 52

Anna Helwing, "Fundament-gefummel: 'Stormy weather' von Urs Fischer," in *Das Kunst-Bulletin*, no. 3, March 1999, p. 21

Sue Hubbard, "Things are not what they seem," in *The Independent*, January 10, 2005, p.12

Nicola Kuhn, "Ich beiß' auf deine Witze," in *Der Tagesspiegel*, June 2, 2005

Tom Morton, "Roll With It," in *Frieze*, issue 86, October 2004, p. 140

Beatrix Ruf, "Urs Fischer—Time Waste," in *Urs Fischer—Time Waste. Radio-Cookie und kaum Zeit, kaum Rat*, exhibition catalog, Kunsthaus Glarus, Glarus: Edition Unikate, 2000, p. 5

Beatrix Ruf, "'Wanted to turn the music on but it was already playing'," in *Parkett*, no. 72, 2004, p. 79

Beatrix Ruf, "Urs Fischer—Private Politics," in *The Vincent van Gogh Biennial Award for Contemporary Art in Europe 2006*, exhibition catalog, Stedelijk Museum Amsterdam, Rotterdam: Veenman Publishers, 2006, p. 15

Claudia Schmuckli, "Just Push Play," in *Urs Fischer—Mary Poppins*, exhibition catalog, Blaffer Gallery, the Art Museum of the University of Houston, Texas, 2006, p. 36

Nicolas Siepen, "Nichts für Bing Crosby," in *Frankfurter Allgemeine Zeitung*, no. 29, February 4, 2002, p. 6

Roberta Smith, "The Listings," in *The New York Times*, February 25, 2005

Claudia Spinelli, "Urs Fischer in der Galerie Walcheturm," in *Das Kunst-Bulletin*, no. 4, April 1996, p. 40

Claudia Spinelli, "Leicht, nicht seicht," in *Weltwoche*, no. 29, July 2004, p. 83

Brigitte Ulmer, "Der Kunstrebell," in *Bolero Men*, March 3,2004, p. 15

Mirjam Varadinis, "Sweet Failure-Art: Raw or Cooked?," in *Urs Fischer—Kir Royal*, exhibition catalog, Kunsthaus Zürich, Zurich: JRP|Ringier, 2004, p. 143

Stefan Zweifel, "Im Universal-schaum," in *Frankfurter Allgemeine Zeitung*, July 23, 2004, p. 36

The Critics on Yves Netzhammer

pp. 130–4
(Texts compiled and edited by Anna Lehninger)

Angelika Affentranger-Kirchrath, "Bruchstellen. Yves Netzhammer im Helmhaus Zürich," in *Neue Zürcher Zeitung*, no. 29, February 5, 2003, p. 42

Barbara Basting, "Pygmalion am Computer," in *Tages-Anzeiger*, January 25, 2003, p. 50

Beate Ermacora, "Schnittstellen," in *Yves Netzhammer. Das Gefühl präziser Haltlosigkeit beim Fest-halten der Dinge,* exhibition catalog, Krefelder Kunstmuseen/ Kaiser Wilhelm Museum, Stiftung Wilhelm Lehmbruck Museum, Duisburg, Bielefeld: Kerber Verlag, 2003, p. 15

Wulf Herzogenrath, "Satire und tiefere Bedeutung," in *Kunstzeitung*, no. 56, April 2001, p. 17

Silke Hohmann, "Die Melancholie des Pixelmenschen," in *Frankfurter Rundschau*, April 16, 2003

Andreas Jürgensen/Simon Maurer/ Tim Zulauf, "Chain of Actions," in *Yves Netzhammer—The Surprising Displacement of the Predetermined Breaking Point of a Branch Grown under Optimal Conditions*, exhibition catalog, Helmhaus Zürich, Zurich, in collaboration with Institut für moderne Kunst Nürnberg, Nuremberg: Verlag für moderne Kunst Nürnberg, 2003

Gisela Kuoni, "Yves Netzhammer im Museum Chasa Jaura," in *Das Kunst-Bulletin*, no. 10, 2004, p. 50

Frank Laukötter, "Testing Actions in Images," in *Yves Netzhammer—The Arrangement of two Opposites while their Maximum Contact is under Generation,* exhibition catalog, Kunsthalle Bremen, eds. Wulf Herzogenrath and Frank Laukötter, Nuremberg: Verlag für moderne Kunst Nürnberg, 2005, p. 33

Gerhard Mack, "Bilder der Verun-sicherung," in *NZZ am Sonntag*, January 19, 2003, p. 47

Claudine Metzger, "Yves Netz-hammer," in *Sturzenegger-Stiftung. Jahresbericht Erwerbungen 2004*, Schaffhausen: Sturzenegger-Stiftung, 2005, p. 138

Text Credits

Catherine Riva, "Le monde selon Netzhammer," in *Le Matin*, February 23, 2003

Nils Röller, "Elektronische Blindheit," in *ZappingZone*, ed. Gerhard Johann Lischka, Berne-Zurich: Benteli Verlag, 2007, pp. 178–9

Anna Schindler, "Vom Puppenhaus ins Sterbezimmer," in *Kunstzeitung*, no. 80, 2003, p. 16

Peter P. Schneider, "Sprachbildspeicher. Sexualität, Fruchtbarkeit und Liebe in Zeiten des Computers," in *Züritipp. Tagesanzeiger*, January 17–23, 2003, p. 62

Claudia Spinelli, "So cool, dass das Herz klopft," in *Weltwoche*, no. 5, March 2003, p. 92

Markus Stegmann, "Erschrecke die Schnecke nicht," in *Wenn man etwas gegen seine Eigenschaften benützt, muss man dafür einen anderen Namen finden. Manor-Kunstpreis Schaffhausen*, exhibition catalog, Museum zu Allerheiligen, Kunstverein Schaffhausen, Schaffhausen: Museum zu Allerheiligen, Kunstverein Schaffhausen, 1998

Heidrun Wirth, "Vom Schwimmen im Niemandsland," in *Kölnische Rundschau*, November 6, 2003, p. 22

Stefan Zucker, "Gelatinekarten und Ananasblüten," in *Tages-Anzeiger*, October 10, 2001

Tim Zulauf, "Unfassbare Abnutzungen. Überlegungen zum Materialitätsbegriff von Yves Netzhammer," unpublished lecture, April 12, 2006

The Critics on Ugo Rondinone

pp. 216–20
(Texts compiled and edited by Anna Lehninger)

Markus Boden, "Ugo Rondinone," in *Artinvestor*, no. 2, 2003, p. 60

Meghan Dailey, "Ugo Rondinone. Matthew Marks Gallery/Swiss Institute," in *Artforum International*, XL, no. 10, Summer 2002, p. 175

Catherine Francblin, "Artiste du mois: Ugo Rondinone," in *Beaux Arts Magazine*, no. 201, February 2001, p. 31

Alison Gingeras, "Being a Box Man—Ugo Rondinone's Existential Quest," in *Ugo Rondinone—Zero Built a Nest in My Navel*, exhibition catalog, Whitechapel Gallery, London, Zurich: JRP|Ringier, 2005, p. 279

Gaby Hartel, "Is Gravity still what It Was? Embarking on a Voyage into the Inner Self," in *Ugo Rondinone—No How On*, exhibition catalog, Kunsthalle Wien, Vienna, ed. Gerald Matt, Kunsthalle Wien, 2002

Gaby Hartel, "Ugo Rondinone—Roundelay," in *Roundelay*, exhibition catalog, Centre Pompidou, Paris: Centre Pompidou, 2003, p. 9

Martin Herbert, "Ugo Rondinone. Whitechapel Art Gallery," London, in *Artforum International*, XLIV, no. 7, March 2006, p. 289

Laura Hoptman, "Love Invents Us Life—And then what Do We Do?," in *Ugo Rondinone—No How On*, exhibition catalog, Kunsthalle Wien, Vienna, ed. Gerald Matt, Kunsthalle Wien, 2002

Andreas Jürgensen, "Ugo Rondinone. Coming up for Air," in *175 Jahre Württembergischer Kunstverein*, exhibition catalog, Stuttgart, 2002, p. 68

Kathrin Luz, "Schöne Hüllen, leere Körper, traurige Blicke," in *Frame*, no. 01, January-February 2000, p. 46

Eva Marz, "Der Künstler wohnt hier nicht mehr," in *Süddeutsche Zeitung*, no. 151, July 3, 2002, p. 15

Stéphanie Moisdon, "Ugo Rondinone: On Butterfly Wings," in *FROG*, no. 4, Autumn-Winter 2006, p. 80

N.N., "Rondinone, Ugo," in *Benezit. Dictionary of Artists*, vol. 11, Paris: Éditions Gründ, 2006, p. 1329.

Niru S. Ratnam, "Just a phase I'm going through," in *The Face*, vol. 3, no. 48, January 2001, p. 92

Philippe Régnier, "Seductions in the Plural," in *Ugo Rondinone—Where Do We Go from Here?*, exhibition catalog, 23rd Biennale of São Paulo, ed. Pierre-André Lienhard, Baden: Lars Müller Publishers, 1996

David Thorp, "Artist in the Landscape," in *Ugo Rondinone—Zero Built a Nest in My Navel*, exhibition catalog, Whitechapel Gallery, London, Zurich: JRP|Ringier, 2005, pp. 275–6

Pádraig Timoney, "Ugo Rondinone," in *Contemporary*, issue 46, December 2002, pp. 44–7

Cristina Travaglini, "Ugo Rondinone," in *Mousse*, September 2006, p. 12

Éric Troncy, "Ugo Rondinone" in *What Is Art (Today)? Qu'est-ce que l'art (aujour'hui)?*, ed. Fabrice Bousteau, Paris: Beaux Arts Magazine, 2002, p. 202

Philip Ursprung, "Ugo Rondinone," in *Biografisches Lexikon der Schweizer Kunst*, vol. 2 (L–Z), ed. Swiss Insitute for Art Research, Zurich: Verlag Neue Zürcher Zeitung, 1998, p. 890

Linda Yablonsky, "Ugo Rondinone," in *Art+Auction*, October 2004, p. 46

Text Credits

The Critics on Christine Streuli

pp. 291–5
(Texts compiled and edited by Anna Lehninger)

Angelika Affentranger-Kirchrath, "Identität und Fremdsein," in *Neue Zürcher Zeitung*, November 5, 2003

Angelika Affentranger-Kirchrath, "Farb-Universen. Jessica Stockholder, Katharina Grosse und Christine Streuli bei Mark Müller," in *Neue Zürcher Zeitung*, March 30, 2005

Edgar Davidian, "Christine Streuli: 'La peinture est un champ de recherche...'," in *L'Orient-Le Jour*, September 20, 2005, p. 6

Dolores Denaro/Toni Stooss, "Christine Streuli," in *Unter 30 III. Junge Schweizer Kunst*, exhibition catalog, CentrePasquArt, Biel: CentrePasquArt, 2005, p. 3

Dina Eppelbaum, "Christine Streuli," in *Global City—Global Art? Contemporary Zurich Art at the Steinfels Office Building*, ed. Hans-Jörg Heusser, Zurich: Zurich Cantonal Bank, 2005, pp. 74–5

Ken Johnson, "Something in Common," in *The New York Times*, January 18, 2003

Thomas Kliemann, "Mit der Achterbahn in die Zukunft," in *General-Anzeiger*, January 20, 2005

Roman Kurzmeyer, "Christine Streuli," in *Unter 30 III. Junge Schweizer Kunst*, exhibition catalog, CentrePasquArt, Biel: CentrePasquArt, 2005, p. 29

Roman Kurzmeyer, "Poetic reflexion," in *Christine Streuli—Bumblebee*, Nuremberg: Verlag für moderne Kunst Nürnberg, 2006

Etienne Lullin, "Christine Streuli," *Ehinger & Armand von Ernst Kunstpreis*, unpublished lecture, May 27, 2003

Stefania Meazza, "Alex Katz—Christine Streuli," in *Segno*, no. 206, January-February, 2006, p. 75

Elio Schenini, "Christine Streuli," in *Sentieri e avvistamenti. Giovane arte contemporanea in Svizzera. Una selezione dai Cahiers d'artistes della Fondazione svizzera per la cultura Pro Helvetia*, exhibition catalog, Centro d'Arte Moderna e Contemporanea, ed. Bettina Della Casa, La Spezia: CAMeC, 2005, p. 58

Madeleine Schuppli, "Symmetries," in *Christine Streuli—Bumblebee*, Nuremberg: Verlag für moderne Kunst Nürnberg, 2006

Bruno Steiger, "Auf der Suche nach dem gültigen Bild," in *Tages-Anzeiger*, July 24, 2004, p. 43

Bruno Steiger, "Ein Bild wie Weihnachten in Las Vegas: Christine Streulis Jackpot," in *Du. Zeitschrift für Kultur*, no. 5, 2006, p. 21

Anne-Ev Ustorf, "Ich ist viele. Christine Streuli spielt mit Oberflächen und Texturen," in *Szene Hamburg*, September 2005, p. 52

Beat Wismer, *Christine Streuli—Cahier d'artiste*, Zurich: Pro Helvetia, 2004, p. 33

Beat Wismer, "Die Schatten des Hintergrundes, oder: Malerei als latenter Ort, in dem die Bilder aufgehoben sind. Zur Malerei von Christine Streuli," in *Yael Bartana, Christiane Baumgartner, Benjamin Bergmann, Christian Hahn, Christine Streuli. Dorothea von Stetten-Kunstpreis 2004*, exhibition catalog, Bonn: Kunstmuseum Bonn, 2005, p. 95

Isabel Zürcher, "Who is afraid of painting?," in *Christine Streuli—Bumblebee*, Nuremberg: Verlag für moderne Kunst Nürnberg, 2006

Colophon

This book is published by the Swiss Federal Office of Culture on the occasion of the Swiss participation at the 52nd Venice Biennale 2007 with the artists Yves Netzhammer and Christine Streuli at the Swiss pavilion, Urs Fischer and Ugo Rondinone at the church of San Stae.

Exhibition
June 10–November 21, 2007

Commissioners
Urs Staub, Andreas Münch

The following members of the Federal Art Commission selcted in 2006 the four artists to represent Switzerland:
Stefan Banz, Mariapia Borgnini, Jacqueline Burckhardt, Silvie Defraoui, Peter Hubacher, Simon Lamunière, Hans Rudolf Reust, Hinrich Sachs, Sarah Zürcher

Editor
Daniel Kurjaković

Editorial assistant
Anna Lehninger

Publishers
Swiss Federal Office of Culture, Berne, and JRP|Ringier, Zurich

Art direction and design
Aude Lehmann, Lex Trüb

Authors
Vanessa Beecroft, Ralf Beil, Davide Croff, Bice Curiger, Fanni Fetzer, Ingvild Goetz, Eva González-Sancho, Ulrike Groos, Paul Groot, Marina Gržinić, Gaby Hartel, Jörg Heiser, Katarina Holländer, Claudia Jolles, Jörg Kalt, Kasper König, Friederike Kretzen, Roman Kurzmeyer, Elisabeth Lebovici, Michael Lingner, James Lord, Roland Lüthi, Michael Lüthy, Ken Lum, Oliver Marchart, Rita McBride, Heike Munder, Marie Muracciole, Hans Ulrich Obrist, Sandi Paučić, Stella Rollig, Nicolaus Schafhausen, Christoph Schenker, Katharina Schlieben, Peter J. Schneemann/Nicola Müllerschön, Ludger Schwarte, Dieter Schwarz, Marketta Seppälä, Marc Spiegler, Erik Steinbrecher, Barbara Steiner, Robert Storr, Klaus Theweleit, Birgid Uccia, Philip Ursprung, Gianfranco Verna, Anton Vidokle, Tan Wälchli, Florian Waldvogel, Susann Wintsch, Rein Wolfs, Tirdad Zolghadr, Tim Zulauf

Translations
Brian Currid (Critics, Editorial note, Fetzer/Kurzmeyor/Wintsch, Fischer, Flusser, Hartel, Kafka, Preface, Schwarte, Survey, Theweleit, Ursprung, Weiss), Wilhelm Werthern (Curiger, Schwarte, Ursprung), Karl Hoffmann (Critics, Wälchli), Bruce Lawder (Holländer, Kalt, Kretzen), Michael Eldred (Survey), Sebastian Lohse (Survey), Almag Institut (Critics)

English editing and proof reading
Barnaby Drabble

Basic research and translations
Astrid Näff (visual essays
Roland Lüthi)

Transcriptions
Anna Lehninger (Curiger, Fischer, Schwarte), Angelo Romano (Curiger, Schwarte)

Editorial office assistance
Gabriel Katzenstein

Printing
Vögeli Druckzentrum, Langnau CH

Binding
Schlatter AG, Liebefeld

Paper
Munken Print Cream 18 90 g/m², Munken Print White 15 300 g/m²

Typefaces
Bau Regular, Bau Italic
Arnhem Regular, Arnhem Italic

Acknowledgments
Estate of Blalla W. Hallmann, ETH-Bibliothek Zürich/Sammlung Alte Drucke, ETH-Bibliothek Zürich/Bildarchiv, Galerie Anita Beckers, Monica De Cardenas Gallery, Galerie Mark Müller, Galerie Sfeir-Semler, Galerie Eva Presenhuber

Distributed by
JRP|Ringier
Letzigraben 134
CH-8047 Zurich
T +41 (0) 43 311 27 50
F +41 (0) 43 311 27 51
www.jrp-ringier.com
info@jrp-ringier.com

ISBN 978-3-905770-70-4

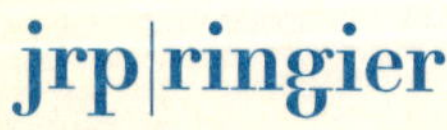

JRP|Ringier books and DVDs are available internationally at selected bookstores and from the following distribution partners:

Switzerland
Buch 2000, AVA Verlagsauslieferung AG, Centralweg 16, CH-8910 Affoltern a.A., buch2000@ava.ch, www.ava.ch

Germany and Austria
Vice Versa Vertrieb, Immanuelkirchstrasse 12, D-10405 Berlin, info@vice-versa-vertrieb.de, www.vice-versa-vertrieb.de

France
Les Presses du réel, 16 rue Quentin, F-21000 Dijon, info@lespressesdureel.com, www.lespressesdureel.com

UK
Cornerhouse Publications, 70 Oxford Street, UK-Manchester M1 5NH, publications@cornerhouse.org, www.cornerhouse.org/books

USA
D.A.P./Distributed Art Publishers, 155 Sixth Avenue, 2nd Floor, USA-New York, NY 10013, dap@dapinc.com, www.artbook.com

Other countries
IDEA Books, Nieuwe Herengracht 11, NL-1011 RK Amsterdam, idea@ideabooks.nl, www.ideabooks.nl

For a list of our partner bookshops or for any general questions, please contact JRP|Ringier directly at info@jrp-ringier.com, or visit our homepage www.jrp-ringier.com for further information about our program.

Schweizerische Eidgenossenschaft
Confédération suisse
Confederazione Svizzera
Confederaziun svizra

Swiss Confederation

Federal Department of Home Affairs FDHA
Federal Office of Culture FOC

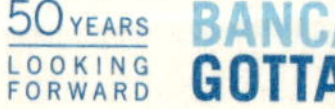